# A SHORT HISTORY
# OF WORLD WAR I

# A SHORT HISTORY OF WORLD WAR I

## by JAMES L. STOKESBURY

William Morrow and Company, Inc.
New York   1981

**Library of Congress Cataloging in Publication Data**

Stokesbury, James L
   A short history of World War I.

   Bibliography: p.
   Includes index.
   1. European War, 1914-1918.  I. Title.
D521.S85   1981       940.3      80-22206
ISBN 0-688-00128-9
ISBN 0-688-00129-7 (pbk.)

Printed in the United States of America

3  4  5  6  7  8  9  10

*For Nana, nicest of grandmothers,*
*and the best of friends as well*

# Acknowledgments

This book was completed during a sabbatical leave from university duties, and it is a pleasure for me to be able thus publicly to thank the Board of Governors of Acadia University for the granting of that year's leave. My thanks go as well to the Acadia University Library and the Cambridge Military Library, Halifax, and to my colleagues in the Department of History at Acadia. Particular mention is due to Drs. A. H. MacLean of Acadia, T. V. Tuleja of St. Peter's College, Martin Blumenson of Washington, and Theodore Ropp of Duke University, and to Ann Elmo of New York, all of whom have encouraged and supported me for many years, and to whom I owe the most profound gratitude. It has been a pleasure to collaborate with Mr. Robert Bender of William Morrow and Company. Thanks are due to Mr. David Green of Acadia, for family anecdotes of World War I soldiers, and once again I thank Miss Debbie Bradley for her skill and patience at typing. None of the above, of course, bear any responsibility for mistakes of fact or interpretation. A word of praise must be added for Kevin, Bria, and Mike for being so tolerant of a father who is all too often mentally revisiting the battlefields of some distant war, and as always the deepest thanks go to Liz.

# Contents

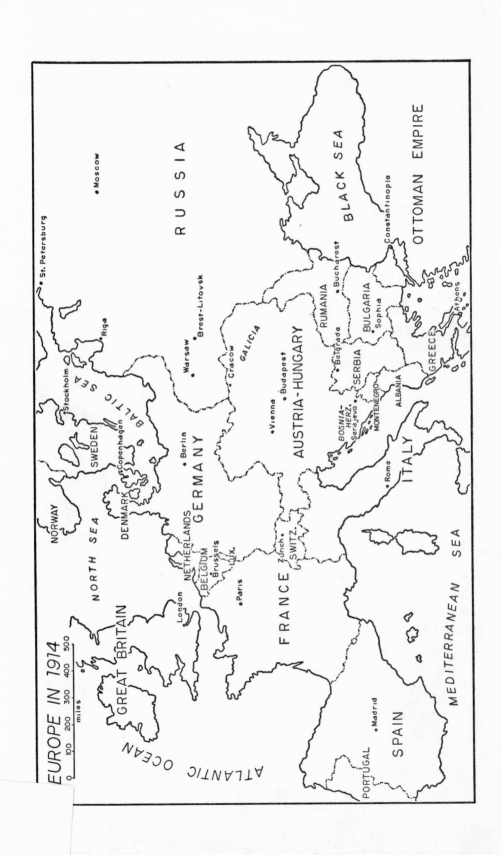

EUROPE IN 1914

# 1. The Long Fuse

THE SUMMER OF 1914 was the fairest in living memory. Grass had never been greener, nor skies bluer. Europe lay rich and ripening under the warming sun, and from the Ural Mountains to the wave-beaten west of Ireland the cows fattened, the newborn animals played in the rich fields, and lovers strolled in the country lanes. Cities, filled with the noise of horse-drawn wagons, street-cars, and increasing numbers of automobiles, appeared to be busy, happy places; couples thronged the sidewalk cafes, enjoying life in this best of all possible worlds. So beautiful was that summer that those who survived it invested it with a golden haze; it assumed a retrospective poignancy, as if before it, all had been beautiful, and after it, nothing ever was again. It became the summer that the world ended, and it was somehow fitting that it should therefore be the most glorious summer ever.

Such a vision was the trick of selective memory. The weather was indeed fine, but thinking men and women were aware that Europe lived on a powder keg, and had for years. A series of profound social changes had led to dangerous imbalances in politics, and these in turn led to one crisis after another. It was in that memorable summer that the states of Europe finally used up their maneuvering room, and the resulting explosion brought their complacent society tumbling down around them.

The most profound of all the changes arose from the population explosion which had begun in Europe in the late eighteenth century, ushered in by new developments in agriculture and more especially in medicine. This rapid growth derived less from the increase in the birth rate than from the decline in the death rate, so that more people reached maturity and were able to produce children. At the beginning of the nineteenth century the population of Europe was roughly 50 million; by 1820 it was about

11

100 million, and by 1870 it had reached the 200-million mark. By 1914 it had topped 300 million. In terms of the classical theories of Thomas Malthus, the multipliers began to take effect about mid-century, and thinking people questioned seriously how long the trend could continue unchecked.

The increase in numbers was necessarily coupled with an increase in the production of goods and services. The Industrial Revolution, first in Great Britain and then, after the Napoleonic wars, on the Continent, had made Europe the workshop of the world. Even with huge numbers of working people in essentially nonproductive jobs such as domestic service, the increase in European production was greater than the increase in its population. This had all sorts of ramifications and side effects—for example, it started Karl Marx thinking about a materialistic heaven on earth, and why it was denied to most people. But broadly speaking, these developments meant increased amenities for larger numbers or alternatively increased frustration for those who believed they were one way or another kept from receiving their fair share. In spite of progressive social legislation, too many people still led lives of drudgery in mines, factories, or sweatshops.

As they usually do in human affairs, the frustrations loomed larger than the satisfactions, and it was these, in part, that gave rise to an increasing number of new doctrines which gained currency in the later part of the century. Socialists and Communists vied with each other in the stridency of their demands, Anarchists made a party out of their belief that there should be no parties, and Nihilists made a creed out of believing in nothing. The tolerant eighteenth- and early nineteenth-century attitudes of a benign and disinterested liberalism were discarded, the rationalism of Locke and Descartes gave way to the dark uncertainties of Nietzsche and Freud.

The greatest of all the new "isms" was nationalism. Among the upper classes, and particularly among the royalty and nobility of Europe, those vestigial remnants of the past, cosmopolitan attitudes were still preserved. But for the middle and lower classes, increasingly dominant in the age of expanding mass education and ever-wider franchises, the country was all. The days of the eighteenth century, when a person's loyalty lay to class or locality, had been trampled underfoot by the armies of the French Revolution, and their grave scattered with flowers by the Romanticists. "This is my own, my native land!" was the cry of millions; all

good stemmed from The Nation, and schoolmasters who would
never be required to do it quoted admiringly to boys who would
the old Latin tag, "It is sweet and fitting to die for one's country."
The Nation became personified in the political cartoons of the
day: John Bull of England, Marianne for France, the Kaiser or
the Tsar themselves for Germany and Russia. Italy, Spain, and
the Balkan States were usually drawn half-size. The pressure to
belong was so strong that vigorous campaigns were launched
against minorities; the Poles in the Russian Empire, always rebel-
lious subjects of the Tsar, were made to conform to Russian ideas;
there was widespread anti-Semitism in central Europe. The English
thought themselves above this sort of thing but still taught only
English in Welsh schools.

These nations had all become intensely egocentric—so intense
was nationalism that the states or powers were inevitably spoken
of as if they were individual persons—because a sense of national
self-satisfaction was achieved only at the expense of another nation.
A nation got territory by taking it away from someone else, which
is one explanation for the solidification of the state system, or the
rush to parcel out the non-European world, the imperialism that
was so notable a feature of the last quarter of the nineteenth
century. A nation grew by asserting its right to do so. Darwin had
said the fittest survived, and the Social Darwinists completed the
circle. The best way to demonstrate fitness to survive was to dominate one's fellows; the European powers joined in a game of
"beggar my neighbor," the result of which was simply to prove they
were fit to play the game in the first place.

A natural son of nationalism was therefore born, called militarism. Manly virtues were obviously in for an era that admired
Rudyard Kipling's poetry, and what truer test of manliness than
war? War was highly attractive to the generation before 1914,
partly because it had fought so few of them, and those it had fought
had not been very bloody. There had not been a major European
war since 1815. There had been several between major powers.
France and Great Britain had fought Russia in the fifties, not very
effectively; France had fought Austria in 1859, but Emperor Napoleon III had been so dismayed by the sight of blood that he had
quickly called it off, a humanitarian decision for which he is regarded disparagingly by admirers of his uncle, who indeed had no
such reservations. Germany had taken on Austria, but that had
lasted only a few short weeks, and then in 1870 Germany had top-

pled France in one of the great upsets of the century—in fact, of modern history. All these wars had either been short, or in the case of colonial ones, far away, and they were correspondingly attractive. In the first decade of this century, soldiers still dressed in colorful uniforms, and war appeared a useful shortcut to diplomacy, a handy problem-solving device.

Two things changed that. One was technology, the second was the growth of an interlocking system of alliance.

The technological advances that changed the nature of war at the end of the nineteenth century had not been fully absorbed by the soldiers who waged it, or by the theorists who told them how to do it. New methods of transport and communication, new ways of preserving and handling food, all the developments of the Industrial Revolution that were to have a profound effect on the conduct of war, were often not directly related to it. The most outstanding example of that is probably the development of a device to control cattle in the western plains of the United States, barbed wire. Its inventors never imagined its military potential, but by World War I it had become one of two or three main factors of the soldier's life—or death. In the war, British soldiers produced their own parody of the music hall songs: "I know where your sweetheart is—'e's 'angin' on the frontline wire!"

Other items, even specifically military developments, were incompletely understood. The machine gun had been perfected in the years before the turn of the century. One writer hailed it as a marked improvement, pointing out that it would enable Europeans to civilize and Christianize the backward races of the world more quickly. Western European observers, however, had curious blind spots. Every major state in Europe sent officers to watch the fighting in the Russo-Japanese War. The tactics of the war were a remarkable foretaste of what was to come, with trench warfare, sieges, and incredibly bloody attacks against field fortifications. The observers watched Russians and Japanese being mowed down in swathes by machine-gun fire and returned home to write: The machine gun is a vastly overrated weapon; it appears highly doubtful that it would be effective against trained European soldiery. Apparently they did not consider Japanese, or even Russians, to be in that supposedly elite category.

There had been still more startling developments in artillery, with ranges and firepower greatly increased. Battlefield distances necessarily opened out, and battles became even more difficult to control than they had been in the past. As tactical communications had not kept pace with gunnery development, all the generals could do was set a plan in motion, then sit back and hope it worked. Usually it did not.

Soldiers and military theorists had given a great deal of thought to the problems of modern war. They were not, as is the popular opinion, stupid, uncaring Colonel Blimps. But their experiences and their own preconceptions led them in disastrous directions. The wars of the mid-nineteenth century had been short, and they had been won by the state that got the most men in the field the earliest; theorists concluded that mobilization of a vast number of men was of primary importance. If they could get more men in the field faster than their adversary, they would have the initiative. The enemy would become progressively more disorganized and would end, in a short time, by conforming to the dominant will, which was what Clausewitz said was the aim of warfare. So the theorists opted for conscription of masses of men, and for rapid mobilization plans to utilize them. As the American Civil War general Nathan Bedford Forrest was reputed to have said of his way of waging war, "I gits there fustest with the mostest"; European theorists, in innumerable volumes of jargon, raised that basic principle to an esoteric dogma.

Regrettably, there were points they missed. They did not realize that artillery, machine guns, and barbed wire had given temporary battlefield dominance to the defensive. They believed firmly in the principle that it was the offensive that won wars, and beyond that, that it was spirit, élan, ésprit, that made the offensive dominant. The French were the worst in this respect. Falling behind Germany in all the major measures of modern power, they came to rely more and more on the overriding importance of offensive spirit. Their theorists proved to their own satisfaction that French dash would always win against German method; eventually, they sacrificed a generation on the altars of that belief.

The thinkers also forgot some of the nonmilitary changes in attitude. Everyone believed wars would be short, because they would entail one massive, exhausting effort. No country could for long sustain that effort. They forgot the passions unleashed by nationalism and underestimated the extent to which people would sacrifice their whole being for their countries.

Here and there a few men saw where the trends of war were

leading. The most important of them was a man named Ivan Bloch. Having made a fortune as a railroad magnate, he turned his attention to the study of war and wrote a massive seven-volume work entitled *The Future of War in Its Economic and Political Relations: Is War Now Impossible?* He proved that it was; he showed that modern weapons would lead to siege warfare on an immense scale, in which the spade would be as important as the gun. Stalemate would result, and the belligerents, unable to sustain the fantastic economic drain, would be forced to sue for a compromise peace. Few people read his work; Bloch was a Polish-Russian Jew, he had never been a soldier, and therefore he could know little about the subject of war.

In France there was a man named Henri Philippe Pétain, who was the stormy petrel of French military theory; to all the highflown ideas about French spirit he replied with a dour "Fire kills." As a result he had made enemies. Early in his career a commanding officer had written on his fitness report, "If this man rises above the rank of major it will be a disaster for France." He had made it to colonel, but on the eve of war he was about to retire, a cynical failure whose ideas were rejected by his fellows.

By 1914 the generals were ready for the great war that they had known was coming for a long time. They had their mass armies made up of conscripts and reserves, they had their mobilization tables and their war plans, and they had their firm ideas of how the war would be fought, and how they would win it—and they were all wrong.

The vast, cumbrous alliance system changed the situation as much as the evolving technology did. In 1870–71, in the Franco-Prussian War, the great German Chancellor Otto von Bismarck completed the work of German unification, and brought the separate German states together under the leadership of Prussia. When the German Empire was proclaimed in the Hall of Mirrors at Versailles, it meant the end of French domination of Europe, a domination that had lasted since 1648.

Bismarck did not expect the French to like the new order of things, and he was right. Throughout the next several years he managed to keep France isolated; he secured an alliance with Austria, whom Germany had also recently defeated, and with Russia, who hated Austria. For more than a decade Bismarck successfully juggled Germany, Russia, and Austria in the Three Emperors'

League. This left France no major power with whom to ally on the Continent, so Germany was safe from French revenge.

The problem for Bismarck was that Austrian and Russian ambitions, especially in the Balkan Peninsula, were essentially incompatible. Gradually, he tied Germany closer to Austria than to Russia. In 1882 he signed the Dual Alliance with her, which was shortly joined by Italy to make the Triple Alliance. However, it was not until after the accession of Kaiser Wilhelm II in 1888 and the dismissal of Bismarck that Russia was allowed to go by default.

As soon as Russia was cast loose, the French began to court her. French banks arranged loans to build Russian railroads, and there were state visits back and forth. It was all rather amusing to European diplomats, for the Tsar of Russia was still the most autocratic of rulers, and the French were still regarded as wild and unstable republicans. But suddenly here was the Tsar listening to bands playing the "Marseillaise," and the President of the Republic standing at attention for "God Save the Tsar." Wilhelm threw the Russians aside in 1890, and by 1893 they were virtually allied with France. Bismarck's *ménage à trois* had been an unnatural one, to say the least, but it was more likely to preserve peace than the new alliances, which saw the major powers ranged into two potentially hostile camps.

Great Britain remained a free-floating variable. The British did not wish to be permanently allied with anyone, adhering strictly to Palmerston's candid, "Britain has no eternal friends or enemies; Britain has only eternal interests." But as the new century opened, it became more and more difficult to sustain what her newspaper editors called "splendid isolation." The world was moving too fast for that, and recent events such as the South African War, when the entire non-British world had cheered for the Boer republics, had shown her just how lonely and un-splendid isolation could be. By 1900 the British were shopping for friends.

They would have liked an alliance with the Americans, but the Yankees were shy, still remembering George Washington's advice to remain free of entangling alliances, and highly conscious of the important Irish vote in domestic politics. Failing that, the British would have been happy with closer relations with the now-emergent white dominions of their great empire. Regrettably, just because these dominions *were* emergent, they had no desire to tie themselves once again to mother's apron. Though they did far more than their share when the time came, they would not make any specific advance commitments. Still looking for an ally external to Europe, the British eventually settled on the Japanese, and in 1902 the Anglo-Japanese Naval Alliance was signed. Useful, but not especially germane to the problems of the Continent.

Finally, then, it came down to an alliance with a power in Europe itself. The norm was for Britain to ally with the second or third state of Europe against the first. The second or third state had always been one of the German ones, and Kaiser Wilhelm being Victoria's grandson, Edward VII's nephew, the British would have liked an alliance with Germany.

What the Germans could have had for the asking, they preferred to get by bullying. Wilhelm was a highly unstable ruler, who still ran his country in an erratic fashion. Faced with his outbursts and foolishness, the British drifted away from Germany and into the arms of France. The underlying logic of the situation, that France was now the second power and Germany the true threat to the European balance, largely escaped the British, so in a rather bemused way they gradually discovered that it was France and not Germany with whom they now had a community of interests.

Not only did they slowly reach accommodation with France, but under her good offices, they even found themselves becoming friendly toward Russia, whom they had cordially disliked for generations. A main theme of British nineteenth-century diplomacy had been to prevent Russian encroachment on the Dardanelles, Afghanistan, and India, and in the Far East. But by 1907—such was the pressure of European events—Britain, France, and Russia were for practical purposes allied against Germany, Austria, and Italy. The sides were drawn for a major war.

What the alliance system really did, of course, was not so much protect its members as guarantee that if there were a flareup involving two of the major powers, there would probably be a general war rather than a local one. That conclusion became more obvious as the prewar scene lurched from crisis to crisis, until all the options except war were used up.

The series of crises that led to war derived from conflicting ambitions and aspirations among the major powers. None of them wished to fight a general European war, but all of them had their own policies and their own hopes, either for aggrandizement, or else simply to retain the position of preeminence they already enjoyed. The successive crises served to solidify the alliance system and also led the military leaders of the respective countries to make and then to refine their war plans. Under the circumstances, it was highly likely that someday, somewhere, some crisis would end in an explosion.

For a generation there had been several trouble spots in the world, where the imperial ambitions of the powers cut across each other. But by a decade before the war, attention had centered on two of them, the Balkans and North Africa, and all four crises that are of direct importance to the developing situation were centered in these two bothersome areas.

In 1905 the French were pursuing an expansionist policy in Morocco, attempting to add this independent, feudal enclave to their growing north and west African empire. The Germans decided to protest this, not because the area was so vital in itself to their interests, but because they believed that in this way they could break the recently established Anglo-French entente. In March of 1905 the Kaiser visited Tangier, pranced about on a white charger —which incidentally he did not enjoy, not being an exceptional horseman—and assured the Sultan of Morocco of his friendship should it ever be needed.

The effect of this First Moroccan Crisis, as it became known, was exactly the opposite of what the German Foreign Office had hoped. Instead of being pushed farther apart, the British and French joined closer together. The British, who consistently refused to formalize their "understanding" with France, proposed "full and confidential discussion . . . in anticipation of any complications." In the inevitable conference which met at Algeciras to discuss the matter, only Austria sided with Germany, even her ally Italy aligning with the Anglo-French, and the Germans went home very displeased. The French and British military and naval staffs began "conversations," and Germany's position had definitely slipped a notch.

The second major blow-up came in the Balkans. Here the situation was so involved as to make the affairs of North Africa look like child's play. The complications arose out of the decline of the Ottoman Empire, known these many years past as "the sick man of Europe." As Turkish power receded in the Balkan Peninsula, a multisided wrangle developed to see what would replace it. The indigenous Christian Balkan peoples wished to be independent and to go their separate ways.

Regrettably, they all hated each other, Serbs disliking Bulgarians, Bulgarians despising Greeks, Greeks distrusting Albanians, and so on around the circle. As these peoples were Orthodox Christians, Russia had declared herself to be their protector, a pose which neatly dovetailed with the ancient Russian ambition to get to the Mediterranean. The most distressing complication, however, was that supplied by the Dual Monarchy, the Austro-Hungarian Empire. This ancient dynastic creation, the most august in Europe, ruled over by the House of Hapsburg, was an anomaly in the twentieth century, for it was built not on the principle of nationality but on the principle of personal dynastic rule. The Emperor Franz Josef, who had been on the throne ever since 1848, ruled over a polyglot creation in which even the dominant peoples, Austrians and Hungarians, were minorities among the assorted Slavic groups: Poles, Czechs, Slovaks, Slovenes, Croats, and Serbs. Austria was opposed to Russian intervention in the Balkans, and she was further opposed to independence for the Balkan States, because independence for them meant agitation within her empire: The various subject minorities longed to gain their freedom from Austro-Hungarian dominance and to be united with their brethren across the frontiers. The Balkans was truly the powder keg of Europe.

In 1908 Austria proclaimed the annexation of the provinces of Bosnia and Herzegovina, which she had occupied militarily ever since 1878. The provinces were largely Serbian in population, however, and the announcement of the annexation caused a roar of outrage in neighboring Serbia, which had always looked on Bosnia and Herzegovina as an eventual legacy. Serbia was essentially a client state of Russia, and though the Russian Foreign Minister had secretly agreed in advance to the Austrian move in return for concessions, the Russians now decided they must protest. When they did, the Germans stepped forward, and the Kaiser announced that he was loyally supporting his ally, and anyone who went to war with Austria would have to fight Germany as well. The Russians, who were definitely not ready for war, especially with Germany, quickly backed down, and the Kaiser, who had a knack for phrases that came home to haunt him, was delighted with diplomacy that consisted of shaking "the mailed fist."

Once it was over, the Bosnia-Herzegovinan affair seemed like much ado about nothing, but it had a terrible sequel. The two provinces remained a troublesome area for Austria. Their chief city was Serajevo, and Serbian nationalists were highly active there. The

Kaiser, though resentful of not having been consulted in advance by Austria, had tied his country even more closely to her, the weakest major power in Europe. And the Russians, worst of all, decided that their aims in the Balkans would not stand another such humiliation. Rather than back down again, they would fight.

The penultimate straw came in 1911, when there was a second Moroccan crisis. Once again the French were pushing their claims, and once again the Germans decided to take official exception to it. This time they sent a gunboat to the port of Agadir. For a while the matter hung fire, but then it was the British who stepped forward. They did not of course speak in terms of "mailed fists," but David Lloyd George, a politician hitherto thought to be both pacifist and mildly pro-German, made an outspoken speech at the Mansion House in which he clearly stated that Germany's behavior was intolerable. Coming from such a person, the speech showed the Germans that Britain was solidly against them, and they backed off once more. And again the British and French concerted their plans, agreed to naval spheres of responsibility in the Mediterranean, and further agreed that Britain would commit troops to the Continent to fight alongside the French armies when war should come.

For the next three years diplomats hesitated to take drastic steps. There were minor disturbances, including two small wars among the lesser Balkan States. But the major powers remained aloof. The lines were drawn, everyone knew that one more fatal move might carry them into a general war, and everyone drew back from taking it. One more crisis would destroy the fragile equilibrium of European statecraft, and having so cavalierly dealt with that equilibrium in the immediate past, the politicians now walked softly. They recognized that they were approaching a point beyond which none of them could see.

# 2. The Explosion

FRANZ JOSEF I, Emperor of Austria and King of Hungary, was eighty-four in 1914. He had occupied a throne since his eighteenth birthday, and though the ruling philosophy of his House, as expressed by its greatest minister, Prince Metternich, had been, "Govern and change nothing," he had nonetheless presided over a great many changes in his time. He did not think all of them were for the better, and he was now a tired old man whose only god was duty and whose only aim was the preservation of his dynasty. Far more than Louis XV, he was entitled to say, "After me the deluge."

He had already seen many tragedies. In 1898 his wife, Elizabeth of Bavaria, was stabbed to death in Geneva by an Anarchist. Far more crucial, as far as the dynasty was concerned, had been the suicide of his only son in 1889. In a scandal that shook the empire the Archduke Rudolf killed his seventeen-year-old mistress and himself at Mayerling. There were no more males in the immediate line. The legacy of empire fell on the shoulders of Rudolf's cousin, Francis Ferdinand.

Rudolf had been mildly brilliant, an erratic comet blazing in the monarchical heavens, which may be why he committed suicide, as his father would give him no part in government. Francis Ferdinand was a dull stick, but he was far more stubborn than his cousin. Denied a role in the running of the empire, he developed a life of his own. He became the supporter of minority aspirations, a policy that made him cordially hated by the bureaucracy and the upper echelons of the Hapsburg state. He went his own way in other matters, too: He married beneath him. The lady indeed had a title; she was Countess Sophie Chotek von Chotkowa und Wognin. That might have been thought sufficiently noble even for a Hapsburg, but it was not. When Francis Ferdinand overrode all the obstacles put in his way and married the woman in spite of them, she was constantly humiliated at the imperial court. Nonetheless, it was a great marriage and a far greater love than that of poor adolescent Rudolf and his teen-age sweetheart.

This was the Francis Ferdinand, champion of the minorities, and this his morganatic wife, who decided to visit Bosnia-Herzegovina in the summer of 1914. The Archduke was Inspector-General of the Armed Forces, and he proposed to review the troops on summer maneuvers and then with his wife tour the provincial capital, Serajevo. It was very ordinary summertime activity.

There was a warning beforehand that an assassination attempt might be made. It was completely ignored by the authorities; there were always warnings of such plots, for assassination was one of the hazards of the monarchical trade. The provincial governor was quite confident that his virtually nonexistent security measures were sufficient. And in fact, before the official visit, the Archduke and his wife had slipped into town quite unannounced and wandered around the bazaar, surrounded by an admiring crowd, and shopped for antiques.

But this time the warning was in earnest. A Serbian terrorist organization named the Black Hand had trained a group of operatives, teenagers most of them, and infiltrated them into Bosnia with orders to kill. The degree of complicity of the Serbian government has been argued for years. It seems that the government officially knew nothing about it, but unofficially knew that something was in the wind. The warning to the Austrian government had been delivered by the Serbian Ambassador in Vienna, but his personal unpopularity accounted for some of the skepticism with which it was received. The truth was that Serbia was regarded as an international pest, her present King, Peter Karageorgevich, had come to his own throne by murder and assassination, and the whole country was a snakepit of intrigue. No one would believe that the government was innocent of the plot, if it was. It hardly improved the case for Serbia that the leader of the Black Hand was Colonel Dragutin Dimitrijevic, who was also the head of Serbian military intelligence.

On the morning of June 28 Francis Ferdinand and his wife paid their official visit to Serajevo. As they proceeded through the town in an open car, the first of the Black Hands threw a bomb at them. Their chauffeur saw it coming and stepped on the gas. Sophie, on the near side, ducked, Francis Ferdinand deflected it with his arm, and it bounced off the back of the car, to explode behind them, wrecking the next car and wounding several aides and onlookers.

The bomb-thrower, nineteen-year-old Nedjelko Cabrinovic, swallowed a cyanide pill and jumped into the nearby river. Neither the pill nor the river worked, and he was hauled out and nearly lynched. Francis Ferdinand, conscious of his less than overwhelming popularity in the empire, commented sourly that Austria would probably give him the Medal of Merit, and the procession continued on to the town hall, where the guests listened to a flustered mayor give a speech of welcome. Between Cabrinovic and the town hall, they passed four other would-be assassins, including young Gavrilo Princip, all of whom funked the task.

After the speech, the royal party decided to visit the hospital and see how the wounded were doing. They started off again. The chauffeur, unaware of the change in plan, took a wrong turn. An aide ordered him to stop the car to turn around, right in front of Gavrilo Princip, who, quite by chance, had drifted into a perfect position.

Princip stepped up to the running board and fired two shots. Members of the procession heard the noise and crowded around, the police seized Princip immediately and hustled him off before he could swallow his cyanide pill, and no one was sure what had happened exactly. The car went into reverse, with Francis Ferdinand and Sophie sitting there calmly.

Then the Archduke opened his mouth and a gout of blood spilled over his tunic. He turned to his wife, begged her not to die, and collapsed. He had been shot in the neck. She was hit in the lower stomach and bleeding internally; she was already dead. Within minutes, so was he.

The store in front of which all this happened is now the Princip Museum, and on the sidewalk are two footprints in the cement to commemorate where the hero of his country stood. He died in prison during the war, of tuberculosis, having indeed set in train events that were to achieve a greater Serbia.

For some time paralysis gripped the empire. The truth was that many Austrians thought they were better off without Francis Ferdinand, and his remains and those of his wife were hastily and gracelessly buried in the hope that if they were out of sight they would be out of mind. Once that was taken care of, the only real leadership, and it was negative, was exercised by the Chief of the Austrian General Staff, General Franz Conrad von Hötzendorf. Conrad was sure that Russia would not intervene in this affair, and while the Austrians sent a police commissioner down to Serajevo to carry out an investigation, Conrad began his work. He wanted war with Serbia, and he was going to get it.

It is one of the ironies of history that states in trouble almost always think they can extricate themselves by creating more trouble. If they are having difficulty balancing their budgets, they think that a war, which is always expensive, will solve the problem. If they are on the verge of collapse from internal discontent, they think that war will unite the masses behind their leaders. If they are threatened on their frontiers, they convince themselves that war will remove that threat. Austria was all of these, and to Conrad von Hötzendorf the answer was a good war, a national purgative that would solve Austria's problems in one swift, surgical operation.

Conrad of course planned a short war. Russia would not fight; surely no one else would go to war on behalf of a ragtag little state that was hardly respectable. It seemed to him that this was Austria's last chance to assert her importance in European affairs and to reverse once and for all the disastrous slide toward destruction that had characterized imperial policy in late years.

With the aged Emperor steeped in fatalism, Conrad succeeded in carrying the government with him. The investigation in Serajevo, though it could not come up with the precise connection, had unearthed enough to reveal that Serbia was involved somehow. Through early July the Cabinet came around; they decided they must wait a while, until the harvest was in, but by late July they were ready. On the 20th they produced an ultimatum. At that moment, however, the President and the Premier of France were on a state visit to Russia. The Austrians decided to wait until the visit was over; it would give the French and Russians less chance to concert their measures. So on July 23 the response to the assassination was at last made public: It was a forty-eight-hour ultimatum to Serbia.

The Serbian reaction was fundamentally unimportant; Austria's note had been designed to make acceptance impossible. The Austrian ministers had concocted a series of demands which would have practically destroyed Serbian sovereignty, if Serbia gave in to them. In fact, Serbia did agree to almost everything; the only points at which she stuck were those demanding the right of Austrian officials to conduct a semi-judicial investigation on Serbian territory. Upon receipt of Serbia's reply, the Austrian Ambassador at Belgrade immediately shut up shop and left the country. Serbia had ordered mobilization even before replying to the note. As soon as the response to the ultimatum reached Vienna, Conrad insisted upon the mobilization of eight army corps, half the imperial army. In both Belgrade and Vienna there was a feeling that at last the fatuities of diplomacy were over, and men were now masters of their fate.

They could hardly have been more mistaken. What happened in Austria and Serbia mattered far less than what had already happened in Berlin, and was about to happen in St. Petersburg.

It had been of vital importance to the Austrian government to know that they would not stand alone, if it became necessary to fight. They had to reassure themselves that Germany would back them up, as she had in 1908. On July 5, therefore, the Austrian Ambassador had approached the Germans and been given an interview with the Kaiser. Wilhelm did not want to be too closely involved before the fact, though he was willing to be so after it. He therefore received a pretty clear intimation of what Austria was up to and gave it his blessing; this was the Kaiser's "blank check"; having told Austria he would stand by her in any circumstances, the Kaiser then casually informed his senior Foreign Office and military men of what he had done and went off on his yacht, the *Hohenzollern,* for a short summer cruise.

Just as the Serajevo crisis was seen as Austria's last chance to assert her primacy in the Balkans, Wilhelm saw it as Germany's last chance to preserve a worthwhile alliance. Austria was her only real friend, and if Austria were not self-assertive, she would not be worth much. The Kaiser thought he was strengthening his alliance and his ally; he was also, of course, still fascinated by the practice of bully-boy diplomacy. What he was in fact doing was giving over his responsibilities to the Austrian government. The strongest of the great powers thus made itself a negligible factor in European diplomacy at a crucial moment; the Kaiser had foolishly put Germany in the Austrian pocket.

Even this need not have been fatal. The really fatal mistake was Austria's assumption that for her alone did Serajevo represent a last chance at great-power status. What really turned it into a war was the fact that Russia felt the same way.

As soon as the ultimatum was delivered to Serbia, the Russians were informed of it. Their Cabinet decided on the 24th that as a line of policy, they must not allow Serbia to be attacked and absorbed by Austria. The next day the Austrian government assured the Russians that it would not annex Serbian territory; ironically, the Hungarian leader in the imperial Cabinet had agreed to the ultimatum and war only on that express condition, as he did not want to see any accession of population to the Slavic minorities within the empire. That assurance was still not enough. The Russians could not stand another 1908, and they decided upon a forward military posture. They issued preliminary mobilization orders and decided to go to war if Austria actually attacked Serbia. That decision was reached on the 25th, the same day the French government assured Russia of its support, and the Serbs replied to the ultimatum. The shadows were lengthening.

On the 26th, the British became involved. The Foreign Secretary, Sir Edward Grey, proposed a general conference to deal with Balkan matters. This had worked in 1912 during the Balkan wars, but it seemed old hat now. France and Russia both agreed, the former with alacrity, the latter with little relish. Austria said no; she would not submit a matter of national honor to international discussion. Well, if it were a matter of national honor . . . Sonorous phrases such as that always meant trouble. Germany backed Austria.

Now the terrible, tangled logic of dual ententes and alliances began to unfold. The crisis gained momentum, and men such as the Kaiser and the Tsar, who had not tried to stop it when it could be stopped, found themselves unable to do so when they wanted to.

On the 27th the French issued standby mobilization orders. That day the Royal Navy returned to harbor from its summer maneuvers; the program this year had been, luckily, a practice mobilization. Now, with the ships back in port, the reserves were retained at their stations and not allowed to disband. Sir Edward Grey promised Russia full diplomatic support from Britain; he had made his bid with his plan for a conference. Rebuffed, he now let events take their course.

Austria declared war on Serbia on July 28. Though they bombarded Belgrade the next day—it was right across the frontier— the Austrians were nowhere near war readiness and would not be until the end of the second week of August. They jumped the gun because they feared something would come of all the talk. Even their staunchest friend, the Kaiser, on seeing Serbia's reply, had remarked that it really removed all cause for war. But Austria wanted her punitive war, and by declaring it prematurely, she ensured she was not going to be talked out of it. Upon the news of the bombardment reaching the capitals of the world, the Germans urged Austria to occupy Belgrade and then begin talks once more. Sir Edward Grey urged the same thing. St. Petersburg remained ominously silent; the Russo-Austrian talks were broken off. If Austria wanted a war, she should have it—but not just with Serbia.

Councils were divided in Berlin. The Chief of the General Staff, Helmuth von Moltke, wanted to mobilize. The Chancellor, Bethmann-Hollweg, and the Kaiser were trying to backpedal as fast as they could. They urged Vienna to talk to the Russians again, and they also began to worry seriously about the western powers. Bethmann offered Britain a guarantee that Germany would, after she had won the war, retain neither French nor Belgian territory, if Britain remained neutral. His point gave away the entire German war plan, but it did him no good; the British rejected any commitment.

If confusion reigned in Berlin, it was compounded in St. Petersburg. The Tsar was under heavy pressure from his military men and Foreign Minister Sazonov to order a general mobilization. With Belgrade being shelled, he agreed. Then a telegram arrived from the Kaiser, pleading restraint and telling what pressure the Germans were putting on the Austrians to back off. The Tsar withdrew the mobilization order. Next the Rusians decided upon partial mobilization, against Austria but not Germany.

On the 30th the Tsar changed his mind yet again. By now the Russian generals were becoming frantic in the face of his vacillation. Their war plans had been carefully constructed over years, but they were like machines so finely tuned that one false touch in the start-up sequence would throw them out of order. After years of careful planning, they were not ready for a real crisis and the hesitancies and uncertainties that were its inevitable accompaniment. Once more the Tsar caved in before their anguished importunities and ordered a general mobilization.

That did the trick. There was now the certainty of a general war —in eastern Europe. On the 31st Germany responded to Russia's mobilization order with a twelve-hour ultimatum. At the same time the German Ambassador in Paris formally asked the French government what their attitude would be in a Russo-German war. The British government requested a statement from Berlin that the neutrality of Belgium, guaranteed in the Treaty of 1839, would be respected. The Germans curtly refused. At five that afternoon Austria decreed a general mobilization; by now few people cared what Austria decreed.

France replied to the German question on the next day, August 1. As a reply it was not very helpful: The government would be guided by France's own best interests. A more revealing response came in mid-afternoon; at 3:55 general mobilization was ordered, and throughout the Republic the gendarmes went out with their posters and their hammers and tacks, and all over the country they put up the papers with the crossed tricolors at the head of them, requiring reserves and conscripts to report to their depots. A mere five minutes later the same scene was reenacted in Germany, as she also issued war orders. At the same time she promised Britain that she would not attack France if Britain stood neutral. Three hours later, her ultimatum to Russia having expired, she issued a formal declaration of war.

The British government still did not know what to do. It had no formal alliance with France, but it did have a military commitment greater than the politicians fully realized. After a good deal of argument, the Cabinet agreed to offer France assurances that Britain would protect her coast. This was on the 2nd. By then the German troops were moving into Luxembourg, and the German Ambassador to Belgium was demanding free passage for German troops through the little country. Belgium refused. The next day Germany declared war on France. And on the 4th, using the violation of Belgian neutrality as an excuse to honor its *de facto* alliance with France, Britain declared war on Germany. Germany responded with a declaration of war on Belgium. It was not until the 6th that Austria finally got around to declaring war on Russia.

The issue of war in eastern or central Europe was decided as soon as Russia determined to back Serbia. It was compounded by Germany's uncritical support of Austria and the feeling of the German generals that they were better off fighting Russia now than later. But the extension of the war to western Europe was rather a different matter. Though the interlocking alliance system made that extension likely, it did not make it certain. The blame for that could be laid less at the door of the politicians than at the door of the soldiers. Politically, the demands by Germany on Belgium and France were laughable. Their necessity was military, for the Germans in the years before the war had knowingly locked themselves into a war plan that required them to fight France and Russia simultaneously. Whom the gods would destroy, they first drive mad. . . .

The German war plan was the most important of all the plans of all the belligerents. It was what ultimately turned a European war into a world war. The others, even the French, may be dismissed summarily.

The Austro-Hungarian General Staff had two war plans; one was predicated upon a war with Serbia, the other on a war with Serbia backed by Russia. In the face of a rapidly shifting crisis, the soldiers ended up putting both of them into operation, and units on the Russian frontier marched two thirds of the way across the empire, heading for Serbia, and then turned around and marched back again to their original positions so they could fight the Russians. Even without the intervention of an active enemy, the Austrians did their best to wear out their armies as soon as possible.

Russia also had two war plans. The Russian-occupied territory of Poland jutted into the eastern face of the German Empire, a great salient with East Prussia to the north of it and Austro-Hungarian Galicia to the south. One Russian plan was therefore in response to a German offensive against them, in which case the Russians would fall back out of Poland to a line running roughly north-south across the base of the salient, and here they would hold until ready to assume the offensive. However, if the Germans put their main offensive strength in the West, then the Russians would attack out of Poland, into Prussia from the south and east, and possibly into Galicia from the north and east.

The French situation was slightly more complicated, for in the years before the war, France had gone through a series of military policy upheavals. Doctrinally committed to the theory of the all-out offensive, they had adopted in 1911 an idea designated Plan XVI; this called for a major concentration of troops in eastern France and a straightforward drive into the lost provinces of Alsace-Lorraine, German-held since the Franco-Prussian War, but never forgotten. Shortly after the adoption of this plan, however, a new commander-in-chief of the French Army, General Victor Michel, correctly decided that the German offensive would come through Belgium. The Vosges Mountains in eastern France were difficult country in which to operate; they are not high mountains, but they are rough, tumbled country with few communications facilities. Michel therefore suggested changing the French plan and came up with the idea that the French should attack northeast through Belgium, that is, that the French should violate Belgian neutrality and meet the anticipated German thrust head on. The government's response to this useful proposal by its commander-in-chief was to fire him.

Michel was replaced by General Joseph Joffre, and Joffre produced Plan XVII, which was a modified Plan XVI. It called for an immediate two-pronged invasion of Alsace-Lorraine. In deference to his predecessor's view, however, Joffre planned to retain two armies in reserve on his left flank, to watch southern Belgium. Joffre, shortly to become the saviour of his country, was a large bear of a man, whose greatest qualities were patience and a complete refusal to be panicked. He was not a man of enormous intellect, and in his reading of the situation as war neared, though he made several correct assessments, he made several more mistaken ones. He guessed, correctly, that Italy would remain neutral when war broke out, and that France had little to fear on that score. However, he thought the Russian operations would have more effect on events than they did, and he also thought the British would be more help to him than they were. His greatest error was in thinking the Germans had far fewer troops than they were actually able to mobilize.

The British plan had little effect on the whole matter. In 1911 they had been caught badly short by the Second Moroccan Crisis, when their service chiefs revealed that they had not concerted their ideas at all. Their generals were preparing to go to France, but their admirals were not preparing to take them there. In the three years since then they had done rather better. Now they were ready to send a British Expeditionary Force to France; however, it was to be small, only a matter of four divisions of infantry plus cavalry and artillery, roughly 100,000 men. That was a drop in the bucket against 2 million Germans or substantially more than a million Frenchmen. The initial importance of the British lay less in their numbers than in the commitment they implied. When asked the absolute minimum number of troops with which France would be content, the politician Georges Clemenceau had replied, "One, and we shall take good care to get him killed." Beyond getting to France, the British planned little more than to fall in on the French left flank and conform to their presumed advance.

Count Alfred von Schlieffen had been Chief of the German General Staff from 1891 to 1906 when he retired. The great plan named after him was formulated in its essentials by 1895; after that it was simply a matter of refinement, or, in the case of Schlieffen's successor, tampering. Working in the early nineties, when the Kaiser's diplomacy was allowing Russia to slide into an alliance with France, Schlieffen concluded that in the event of a general European war, Germany was likely to have to fight France and Russia at the same time. For central-European Germany, the problem of the two-front war, with all that entails in logistics, communications, allocation of forces, has always been a military nightmare.

Schlieffen's answer to the problem was nothing if not audacious. He calculated, correctly, that the Germans were the fastest mobilizers in Europe. The French were the second-fastest; the Russians the slowest. On the basis of that he thought Germany could defeat France in six to eight weeks and then defeat Russia. He would not really fight a two-front war, but rather two single-front wars, the first of which would be over before the second really began. This was obviously a tall order, but its feasibility was borne out by the European experience of short wars through the last half-century.

To defeat France in such a short time still called for daring of a high degree. Schlieffen correctly assumed that the French, in the event of war, would launch an offensive into Alsace-Lorraine. Given their penchant for the offensive, it was the only thing they could do. He himself would put minimal holding forces on the German border and let them retire before the French pressure. For while the French moved eastward, they would actually be trapping themselves and doing the Germans' work for them. The main German attack would come through Holland and Belgium, swinging west to the Channel coast, and then crashing south beyond Paris, where there would be no troops at all. The Germans would swing around to the east, taking Paris as they passed it, and then would press the French up against the German holding operation in Alsace-Lorraine. It was a vast single-wing envelopment, played out over the entirety of western Europe, and the result would be to put the French armies in a German bag within six weeks. If it worked, it would even be more a matter of marching than of fighting, for the Germans would cut across the French lines of communications as they moved east from Paris, and the French armies would wither on the vine.

Violating Dutch and Belgian neutrality did not bother Schlieffen unduly; the Low Countries were the classic invasion route from the North German plain into France, and the discomfiture of the inhabitants of the area had been a feature of European wars and politics for centuries.

Having defeated the French, the Germans would then rapidly move their armies by train across Germany—not for nothing did they have the best railway system on the Continent—and meet and defeat the Russians, who by this time would still just be getting organized.

Schlieffen devoted his life to his plan, and some of his phrases summed it up: "Let the right-flank grenadier brush the Channel with his sleeve." His dying words were, "Keep the right wing strong."

Unfortunately for Schlieffen his successor did not heed his advice. Helmuth von Moltke was the nephew of the great Field Marshal Helmuth von Moltke who had directed the Wars of German Unification and been the military counterpart of Bismarck. When made Chief of the German General Staff in 1906 he had doubted his fitness for the job and had confessed to a friend that "I lack the capacity for risking all on a single throw." This was a remarkably prescient self-assessment, and that particular capacity was exactly what the Schleiffen Plan required of the leader who was to put it in action. Every great leader, especially in war, has to have the element of the gambler in him, and Moltke lacked it. He was willing to take the greatest gamble of all, war, but he wanted a sure thing when he did so. He tried to hedge his bets.

Where Schlieffen had insisted the strength of the right wing was everything, Moltke weakened that very wing. He reallocated troops so the holding operation on his left was stronger, the maneuvering wing on his right weaker. He also decided not to violate Dutch neutrality, but to squeeze his communications south of the bottom of Holland and go only through Belgian territory.

The Schlieffen Plan, or the modified version of it, was predicated on the likelihood of a two-front war. After nearly twenty years of playing with it and refining it, the German Army had come to accept it as the be-all and end-all of strategy. By 1914 it was the only way they could see to fight their war. Their war

turned the possibility of a two-front war into the
ne; they had developed a self-fulfilling prophecy.
mpletely neglected the probability that the violation
Countries would bring Britain into the war, though
cursory study of history would have shown them that
had gone to war for that very reason for at least two cen-
The Germans thought the Schlieffen Plan guaranteed them
ry within three or four months. What it really guaranteed was
if for some reason they did not win within that time, they
ould ultimately lose the war.

So as August opened they all marched off to the great adventure.
Crowds in the cities sang "God Save the King" or the "Marseillaise" or "Deutschland über Alles" and so forth. Reserves hurried
to their depots, volunteers rushed to the recruiting stations to get
in before the fun was over. Bands played, girls threw flowers,
soldiers in new kit chalked slogans on railway cars and grinned
self-consciously at photographers. In all the explanatory or self-
justificatory writing during and after the war, great efforts were
made to explain how the horror came about. All the diplomats
and soldiers took care to explain that the big mistake had been
made by someone else. Such exculpatory writing was done when
men realized what a terrible thing war was, and what a monster
they had unleashed. But in 1914 young Rupert Brooke was writing
his war sonnets, "Now God be thanked, Who has matched us
with His hour. . . ." The real truth that had to be explained away
was that people wanted war. Canadians, South Africans, and
Australians rushed to join up. Hundreds of young Americans
slipped over the border to Canadian recruiting stations. It was
going to be jolly good fun, and for a few shining moments, the
future belonged to long lean ships in the North Sea and all the
beautiful young men tramping along the hot dusty roads of Europe.
It was great to be alive.

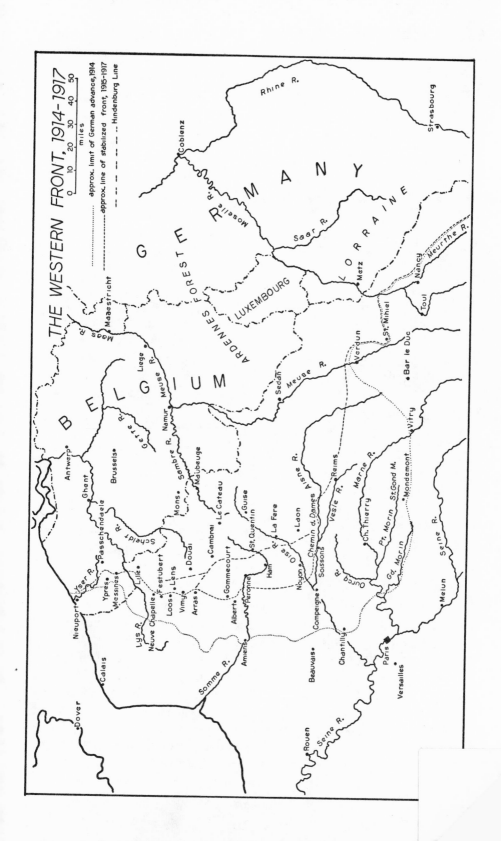

THE WESTERN FRONT, 1914–1917

miles
0   10   20   30   40   50

............ approx. limit of German advance, 1914
_____ approx. line of stabilized front, 1915–1917
– – – – – Hindenburg Line

# 3. The Opening Battles in the West

To THE HISTORIAN analyzing a campaign, events unfold with a certain preordained majesty. Even to the general in command of a battle, there is a certain apparent development. He issues his orders, his staff prepares papers and passes them on to subordinate authorities, and things happen. Pins are moved on a map, reports come in and are digested, more pins are moved, and a discernible sequence takes shape.

From the level of the field commander on down, say from the division, brigade, and battalion level, it looks a little different. Here the sequence is less visible, and the machine moves by fits and starts. The presumably ordered whole cannot be grasped, and the horizon closes in. A unit receives its orders, it moves in a given direction, it bumps into another unit trying to use the same road to move in a different direction. Poor staff work there. Every staff has movement tables that tell how long it takes a unit of a given size to get from point A to point B, how long it takes a battalion to pass a crossroad; so many men carrying so many pounds can march so fast and so far in a given time. But try to do this with two million men at once, as the Germans were doing, or one and a third million, as the French were, and things go wrong. Orders are missed, units cannot be found, reserves cannot catch up with their battalions, tired soldiers straggle and find wine cellars, colonels go off for too good a lunch, staff officers who should be watching their organization tables think instead of their mistresses, scouts report enemies where there are none, and miss seeing enemies where there are. The "fog of war," which is really no more than the imperfections of humanity trying to work out plans that take no account of imperfection, settles over the countryside. In

36

the midst of that fog are three million men, wearing several different uniforms. Eventually, they blunder into one another and start killing one another. The orderly pins on the map at headquarters translate in reality into little bunches of men—tired, sweaty, thirsty, above all scared—wondering where they are and shooting at other men equally tired, bewildered, and scared.

The historian can say that the opening of the campaign in the West resolved into three series of several smallish battles. The first series consisted of the Germans forcing their passage through Belgium. The second was the "battles of the frontiers," which comprised the encounters in Lorraine, the Ardennes, at the Sambre, and the battle of Mons. The final series was the Allied retreat, which saw the two battles of Le Cateau and Guise. Taken all together, these fights set the stage for the climactic battle of the Marne. In reality, they were far less orderly than such a sequential presentation would suggest.

Though the German government had requested free passage through Belgium, they did not expect to get it. Belgium as a state was a political convenience, arising out of the fact that neither the Dutch, the French, nor the British were happy to have any one power controlling Antwerp and the mouth of the Scheldt; as the old saying has it, "Antwerp is a pistol pointing at the heart of England." Belgium had become an independent country in the 1830's, its neutrality guaranteed by all the powers in 1839. This treaty was the "scrap of paper" over which the Kaiser said the British were going to war.

Even though Belgium was officially declared to be "perpetually neutral," King Albert of the Belgians had a respectable little army —about the same size as the British Expeditionary Force, in fact —and the country was ready to defend its position. The key to that position was the great fortress complex of Liége. By the accidents of history, there is a small piece of Holland, known as the Maastricht appendix, the province of Limbourg, which runs thirty-odd miles south up the Maas River from Holland proper. This appendix is the portion of Dutch territory whose violation Schlieffen had originally proposed. South of it is a thirty-five-mile gap, Belgian territory, to the northern edge of the Ardennes Forest. It was through this gap that Moltke intended to pour the three German armies of the right wing, the business end of the Schlieffen Plan. To do it, the Germans had to force their way past Liége.

King Albert could read a map as well as the Germans could, and he was a man of considerable presence. His country's strict interpretation of its neutrality had prevented any military agreements with France or anyone else, but the Belgians were prepared to fight. The city of Liége was ringed by twelve independent fortresses in a circle of just over ten miles' diameter. Liége was advertised as one of the strongest positions in Europe, which it probably was.

As did everyone else, Albert expected the German advance to be slower than it proved to be. His war plan was to concentrate his field army forward on the west bank of the Meuse—which is the Belgian and French name for the Dutch Maas River—with its left anchored on Liége and its right upriver on Namur. This would either hold the Germans up completely, or, more likely and perhaps more desirably, keep them away from most of Belgium and channel them off to the southwest, toward France, which was where they were going anyway.

Unhappily, Albert's reach exceeded his grasp. The call-up of the Belgian trained reserves so disordered the regular army that it was unable to assume its battle stations before the German flood hit. Albert got one infantry division into Liége to reinforce General Gérard Leman, the fortress commander, and then withdrew with the rest of his troops behind the Gette, twenty-five miles northwest, to put his army together. Leman was ordered to hold on to the end.

The Germans had long considered the problem presented by Liége; it was a textbook matter, and they had spent a great deal of time on it. The difficulty was that they could bypass the city, with the 1st Army to the north of it, and the 3rd Army to the south of it, but they could not secure their vital communications lines until it was taken by the 2nd Army in the middle. To do this they created a special assault force, what would today be designated a task force, whose sole mission was the destruction of the Liége fortresses. This trained group, in existence for years, had long been stationed right up against the border. It was going to take the Germans two weeks to have their mobilization complete to the last shell for the last gun. In that two weeks, the special assault force had to take Liége and clear the road to France.

Germany declared war on Belgium on August 4, but the cavalry patrols of the Liége force had already crossed the frontier the day before. The whole force was over the border simultaneously with the declaration of war, and on the 5th Liége was summoned to surrender. When General Leman refused, the Germans immediately opened their attack.

Their plan was to penetrate between the forts, take the city itself, and then reduce the forts one by one. Meanwhile, a wide-flung cavalry screen would fend off possible reinforcement. The first attack broke down with heavy losses; Leman threw up rough field fortifications in the gaps between the forts, and the German dead piled up against them. On the 6th Leman sent away his infantry; he saw he would soon be cut off and decided to fight on as long as he could with his fortress troops.

A second attack came that night, and again it made little headway. Some of the leading assault units were near collapse when the 2nd Army's Chief of Staff, General Erich Ludendorff, came up and rallied them and got the attack going again. The end result of the struggle was that the Germans broke into the city, through the fortress line, and Ludendorff bluffed the Belgians in the city itself into surrendering.

The forts still commanded the city, but the Germans had completed the first phase of their plan. They were now able to get up their heavy guns, including the largest made to that time, 420 mm. monsters especially constructed with Liége in mind. The Belgian forts had been designed to withstand 210 mm. fire, for when they were built, no one thought a fortress would ever have to face anything heavier than that. Now the Germans methodically went about their reduction of the fortresses one by one. It took them until August 12 just to get their monster howitzers up and in position, but after that it was only a case of battering the works down around the heads of their dazed and weary defenders. The last two of them surrendered on August 16. The Germans meanwhile had completed their mobilization by the 14th. The stubbornness of the Belgians held them up two more days until Liége was finished, but by the 16th, the road to France was open; the field-gray tide was ready to roll.

Unlike the Schlieffen Plan, which was highly detailed, the French Plan XVII was more a statement of general intent. It called for the concentration forward of all the French armies, and then for them to move to the attack as they were fully mobilized. The French offensive therefore caused a flare of encounter battles to run from the Vosges all the way up to the Belgian border, until all along the line the armies were grappling together.

The fastest off the mark were the French 1st and 2nd armies, under Generals Dubail and Castelnau. They jumped off toward the northeast on the morning of August 14, broke across the frontier against slight resistance, and made good progress into Lorraine. The French were elated; their offensive doctrine was working to perfection, and they were moving into what every man of them regarded as their own provinces, stolen by the Germans forty years before. The first war issue of the Paris weekly *L'Illustration* featured a romantic drawing of a handsome French subaltern, sword dangling from his wrist, sweeping into his arms a fainting young maiden labeled Lorraine, both of them standing over a broken frontier-barrier post. At General Headquarters Joffre ignored the early hints that large numbers of Germans were massing north of the Ardennes; he remained wedded to his conviction that they did not have enough troops to concentrate that far north.

What the French hit in Lorraine was the German 6th and 7th armies, both for operational purposes under the command of Crown Prince Rupprecht of Bavaria. Rupprecht was largely a figurehead; something has to be done with Crown Princes, and they tend as a group to like to command armies. The real power in 6th Army was General Kraft von Dellmensingen, Rupprecht's Chief of Staff. A very able soldier, Dellmensingen was letting the French come on in accord with the Schlieffen Plan but also planning a counterstroke when they should be fully committed, which was not in the plan.

On the 20th, after six days of slow withdrawal, the Germans judged the battle was ripe. They had already taken a heavy toll of attackers, for the French were advancing as if at Waterloo. Their battalions would form up in the open, officers out in front with white gloves, swords unsheathed. The French looked gallant and beautiful in their dark-blue overcoats and red trousers and kepis. There had been an attempt before the war to put them in more somber uniforms that might provide a modicum of camouflage, but it had been squelched. Debate had even reached the Chamber of Deputies, where the cry of the opposition, "*Le kepi rouge, c'est la France!*" ("The red kepi *is* France!") had carried the day. The red trousers and kepis showed brightly against the August colors, the long wicked bayonets, nicknamed "Rosalie" by the infantry, glittered in the sun, and the French would sweep forward in long lines in perfect order.

The German machine guns would open up and slaughter them.

When the Germans counterattacked on the 20th, therefore, they hit an enemy already weakened by his own successes and the losses sustained in gaining them. Fierce fighting blew up all along the line of contact; the French were weaker in machine guns than the Germans, but they had a beautiful little gun howitzer, the famous "French 75," and time after time the gunners dancing around their pieces would shoot the heart out of German attacks. Still, by the end of a long day, the French were fought out. That night, after dark, they started back the way they had come. The Germans took up the chase and pressed hard. The French 1st Army, on the southern edge of the battle, fell back in good order, but 2nd Army nearly collapsed under the main German blow. Had it not been for one corps of it, the "Iron Corps" commanded by General Ferdinand Foch, it might have fallen apart altogether. By August 22 the French were back on the heights along the Meurthe River, just barely in front of Nancy.

The German plan was more dislocated by success in the Battle of Lorraine than the French was by failure. For Rupprecht now wanted to keep going. He bullied Moltke, who lacked the personal power to say no to him, into moving six temporary corps south. These corps were slated for support of the right-wing encirclement. Now they became a further subtraction from that crucial wing and a reinforcement where they were not really needed. Rupprecht wanted to convert Schlieffen's single-wing movement into a double-wing envelopment, a super-sized model of Hannibal's immortal victory at Cannae played out over the whole map of France. The trick could not be done. The French on the defensive proved as strong as the Germans had, and the Lorraine battle burned down from mutual exhaustion.

While this was going on, the French 3rd, 4th, and 5th armies were intended to advance into and through the Ardennes. The Ardennes was bad country to maneuver in, but Joffre was sure he could get his three armies through and into open country beyond before they made contact with the Germans. General Ruffey's 3rd and Langle's 4th began their move as ordered. On the northern flank of this, however, General Lanrezac at 5th Army balked. He was hearing more and more about Germans north of the forest, and he pestered Joffre with his complaints. Joffre still clung to a belief that the Germans did not have enough strength to move west of the Meuse River, but finally, in deference to Lanrezac, he allowed him to shift northward toward Namur, into the angle formed by the Sambre and Meuse rivers.

Joffre was wrong about getting clear of the forest, too. Ruffey and Langle met the German 5th and 4th armies, under the Crown Prince of Prussia and General Albrecht. These two armies were in effect the hinge of the Schlieffen Plan, and they had regulated their advance in conformity with the swing of the three armies farther north. On August 22, in the middle of the forest, the two German armies met the two French armies, and again there was fierce fighting around the little forest hamlets, and along the glades and lanes of the woods. As in Lorraine, the French had the worst of it and fell back badly battered. The Germans estimated that they had wiped out both armies—they were quite mistaken—and pressed on. Actually, the French were still full of fight, though by now Joffre was ruthlessly weeding out officers from the rank of colonel on up. A host of over-age or underaggressive commanders suddenly and peremptorily found themselves relieved of command. Ruffey was soon replaced by General Sarrail, but he was only the most visible of many changes.

With Lorraine and the Ardennes battles both going against them, the French were in trouble. How big that trouble was they were about to discover. As he moved up toward Namur, Lanrezac was putting 5th Army neatly in a salient. Two of the three German armies of the maneuvering wing were headed straight for him, for now the Schlieffen Plan was fully under way. The German 3rd Army under General Hausen was marching south of Liége and headed for Lanrezac's right flank; General Bülow's 2nd Army was now past Liége and moving toward Lanrezac's front and left flank. Somewhat isolated over to the French left, the British had gotten organized and were moving up to contact. No one in France as yet knew that the German 1st Army under General Kluck was rushing down on them.

Lanrezac and Bülow met along the Sambre on the 21st. The Germans came on hard, and the French lost the bridgeheads and then the line of the river. Lanrezac pulled out a corps under General Franchet d'Esperey—"Desperate Franky," the British called him—and sent it west to come in on Bülow's open flank. He also asked the British to turn to their right and hit that flank as well. Just as he was getting ready for this counterstroke, Hausen showed up to the east, and the French right flank was in serious trouble.

D'Esperey countermarched his corps and shored up the defense at the other end of the line in a splendid effort. On the night of the 23rd Lanrezac made the painful decision to retreat, and it was as well he did; the next morning Bülow and Hausen hit hard, but hit air. The French were gone.

That left only the British, over on the open flank. The dispatch of the British Expeditionary Force to France had gone without a hitch. The whole consisted of a cavalry division and two infantry corps, the Ist under General Douglas Haig and the IInd under Horace Smith-Dorrien. The whole B. E. F. was commanded by General Sir John French, an energetic, politically acute little man who liked his allies but was excessively conscious that this small force was all Britain had to fight with.

The B. E. F. concentrated at Le Cateau and moved up to take station alongside Lanrezac. Lanrezac and Sir John French had already met, and the French general had treated his British ally with a mixture of hauteur and contempt that Frenchmen often adopt when they believe themselves firmly in the ascendant. The B. E. F.'s leader was a genuine francophile, however, and at this stage he was determined to help out to the limit of his resources. On the 22nd the British advance reached Mons, just over the Belgian frontier, and took up a defensive position along the straight line of the Mons-Condé canal, Haig on the right, Smith-Dorrien in the town and strung out along the canal to the west. Their right flank was covered by their cavalry, and it in turn linked up with French General Sordet's cavalry corps of 5th Army, just about exhausted from its tussles with the Germans. The British were not impressed with the weary French and the way they mishandled their all-but-broken-down mounts.

Meanwhile, General Kluck had been roaring through Belgium. The Belgian field army had withdrawn toward the northwest, eventually ending up around Antwerp, where the British sent over a naval and Royal Marine force to help them out. Kluck was forced to drop off a corps to cover them, though this job was supposed to have been done by one of the units Moltke sent off south. Kluck, a first-class, hard-driving soldier, was further handicapped by being put under Bülow's operational control, as Moltke himself found his communications inadequate for handling all three of his wheeling armies together. This was unfortunate; if any one commander should have dictated the direction of the wheel, better it had been Kluck on the flank than Bülow in the middle. It was further unfortunate in that Kluck was a good soldier, while Bülow was but a mediocre one. As Bülow concentrated against Lanrezac, he ordered Kluck to turn from southwest to south. The result was that, instead of dashing past the B. E. F. on their open flank and catching them disastrously, Kluck hit them head on at Mons on the morning of the 23rd.

When his advance first made contact, Kluck did not even know the British were in France yet, such was the tremendous fog of war in these opening weeks. The Kaiser, in another one of his unfortunate phrases, had dismissed the British as "a contemptible little army." Now Kluck's people were to find out if the Supreme War Lord knew what he was talking about. Indeed, it was an army from the past, in many ways. It consisted of long-service volunteer soldiers—no conscripts here. It had learned hard lessons in South Africa about marksmanship, so though it was short on machine guns and artillery support, every soldier in the B. E. F. was a trained shot. As the Germans developed their attack, they came on in heavy masses of field gray. Time and again the British shot the heart out of their attacks, until the German forward officers reported that *all* the British were using machine guns, and the dead and wounded piled up around the canal crossings and in the streets of Mons.

Neither French, who was away when the battle began, nor Kluck exercised any control over it. On the British side it was entirely Smith-Dorrien's battle, Haig being left alone east of the town. The Germans just kept on coming, and eventually, as there were a lot more of them than British, they got over the canal and into the town. Levered out, Smith-Dorrien fell his troops back in good order and took up another position about two or three miles to the south. The British decided they would hang on here, but at nightfall word came in from Lanrezac: He was falling back, and the B. E. F. must conform. The great retreat had begun.

For the British, the Retreat from Mons passed into legend. Something in the British character has a penchant for hanging in there when things look bleakest, and many of their most stirring stories are built around retreats, on Corunna in 1809, from Kabul in 1842, from Mons in 1914, and to Dunkirk in 1940. A great number of people who lived through World War I firmly believed in the Angel of Mons or the Archers of Agincourt. In the first story, as Smith-Dorrien's IInd Corps lay exhausted on their arms the night after battle, an angel on a white horse, armed with a flaming sword, appeared in the sky and rode threateningly against the German Army, preventing it from advancing. In the second, a party of British troops during the retreat found themselves cut off on the battlefield of Agincourt. The next morning, as they stealthily began to move out, they discovered the surrounding Germans all dead, each killed by a longbow's arrow. One thing was certain, and that was that as the B. E. F. took up its retreat, it needed all the help it could get.

Both Joffre and von Moltke came to the rescue. Joffre now realized that the entire French view of the war was wrong; his offensives had been halted all along the line, and the enemy had developed overwhelming strength in an area where they were thought not to have anything substantial. But the French troops were being pressed back on their own communications, they had the interior lines, and as long as Joffre remained calm and in control of himself, France might yet escape disaster. This he managed to do. His emotional thermometer hovered around zero at the most exciting of times; he continued to dine well, to have an afternoon nap and a good sleep at night. He strolled about the grounds of his headquarters at Vitry le François, and he began reordering his world. Without undue haste, he took troops out of the line in the south and east and slipped them northwest. As the British retreated, a provisional corps, reserves in their thirties and forties, showed up on their hitherto open left flank. Joffre calmly laid out the lines of retreat for the northern Allied forces, back to the line of the Somme River-Verdun. He beefed up the strength of the "entrenched camp" around Paris, using the Paris garrison commander, old General Gallieni, as the nucleus of that particular body. The French had already had 300,000 casualties, most of them in their ill-conceived offensives; they were tired, and they were hurt, but they were not yet beaten.

Moltke, on the other hand, was rapidly going to pieces. He was way back at Coblenz, 110 miles from his nearest troops, and a good 175 from the vital right wing where Kluck was still chasing the B. E. F. southward. A view based on caricatures of national stereotypes would have put Joffre in command of the Germans and Moltke in command of the French, for at the former's headquarters all was calm and serene, while at Moltke's, everyone from assorted visiting royalty on down was infected with the jitters. Moltke ate little and slept less. His nervousness infected his staff. Though he could not stand the heat, he was still in the kitchen.

Moltke's greatest problem was that he was increasingly operating in the dark. Hs communications facilities were swamped by messages, and the messages themselves were almost invariably inaccurate. For all their training and their professional expertise, this was the first war the Germans had been in since 1870; intelligence assessments and evaluations were wildly off the mark. The Germans scored tactical successes all along the line, but they believed they had already won the war in the West. Thus, Moltke allowed himself to be bullied into transferring corps to the south for the new offensive there planned by Rupprecht. When panicky news came in from the eastern front, where the Russians seemed to be doing better than they were supposed to be doing, Moltke sent off two more corps to East Prussia—and again he took them from his right wing. So with detachments one way and another, he had reduced his critical mass by more than one quarter. In the first ten days of fighting, the German Army had been weakened more by Moltke than it had by the French.

Little of this slippage was apparent to the hard-pressed French and British troops plodding along the roads back into France from the Belgian frontier. The retreat had begun on the 24th. As the British moved south, Sir John French momentarily considered shutting himself and his army up in the fortress of Maubeuge. Fortunately, he decided against it and went on past the Forest of Mormal. On the night of the 25th, the B. E. F. adopted a defensive line around Le Cateau, with Haig's still nearly untouched Ist Corps on the right, and Smith-Dorrien's tired IInd Corps on the left. French issued orders to continue the retreat the next day. Haig's people moved out on schedule. Smith-Dorrien, however, did not get the order until after midnight. He informed French that his troops were exhausted, and that if he were to break contact with the Germans, he would have to put them on the road right away. He did not think it could be done and preferred to fight a battle in the morning, give the Germans a bloody nose, and then scoot off while they recovered.

To this, French simply returned a noncommittal reply and then drove off with the Ist Corps, leaving the hard-used IInd Corps to its own devices. Daybreak saw IInd Corps on its own.

Kluck attacked as soon as his troops came up, and by mid-morning the situation for the British was getting tricky. Both Smith-Dorrien's flanks were open, and the Germans were gradually lapping around them. The Tommies held hard in the center, but soon after noon the right flank began to cave in, losing most of its artillery, and being pushed back into a hairpin bend. Then the left started to cave, too. At this point the British were saved temporarily by the arrival on their left of Sordet's French cavalry. Though the newcomers were in condition to accomplish little, the Germans had to stop to figure out what on earth they were and where they had come from. Cavalry usually presaged infantry, and the Germans had no desire to be caught in flank as they were catching the British in flank. By the time they put all the pieces together the day was gone.

That night Smith-Dorrien successfully pulled back and got away clean. The Germans, obsessed by the idea that the British had come from the Channel ports and would be heading back toward them, kept wanting to slide westward, while the British were going more nearly south, back through St. Quentin. So Smith-Dorrien inflicted his bloody nose, but it cost him one fifth of his effectives to do it. His casualties were about 7,800 out of 40,000 engaged.

Le Cateau was the biggest British battle since Waterloo, and though Smith-Dorrien had done what he hoped to do, it was still a defeat; the British had not only lost many men, but they had also lost nearly forty guns. Every soldier knows that battles, even victorious ones, cost casualties, but to lose guns is a sure sign that the enemy has won and dominates the battlefield.

Therefore, when the reports of Le Cateau reached Joffre, he began to think that the British were on their last legs—a point with which Sir John French was quite in agreement. Joffre decided he must relieve the pressure on his ally and so he ordered Lanrezac to attack westward and hit the flank of Kluck's 1st Army, slowing him down and giving the British a breather. The problem with that was that Lanrezac was in poor shape himself, almost as hard pressed by Bülow as the B. E. F. was by Kluck. He did not care much for his allies, and thought they ought to be able to look after themselves; after all, they had already siphoned off his cavalry someplace over to the west. What more could they want? Grumbling all the way, Lanrezac prepared to do as he was told.

He had his army about half-shifted to face west on the morning of August 29 when Bülow hit his right. Just over the Oise River, around Guise, the French stood and slugged it out with two of Bülow's three corps, including the Prussian Guards. Both sides took heavy punishment, but by mid-afternoon the German weight was beginning to tell, and in desperation, Lanrezac ordered his reserve, Franchet d'Esperey, to counterattack. For once the French took time to prepare a coordinated, planned attack, and at sundown they crashed into the Prussians and drove them back to the river bank. It took Bülow a day and a half to get over the startling discovery that his enemies were still alive and well, and by the time he did, they and the B. E. F. had both pulled out again.

The news of Guise did not reach Moltke for two days, until August 31. When it did, it was reported as an overwhelming victory, even though it had not appeared as such to the men who fought it. The report confirmed Moltke in his view that the French were all but finished, and hoping only to hold on until something in Russia happened to rescue them. Moltke therefore issued what were basically pursuit orders, telling his three right-wing armies to keep moving so the French would not have time to rally. He ignored reports of French troops massing around Paris. He ordered Kluck to swing as wide as possible, to break up any potential French concentration on the open flank, but he also ordered Kluck to keep in continuous contact with Bülow, and Bülow with Hausen, and so on right back to the pivot of the wheel. This left Kluck up in the air. Either he could swing wide and do as he was supposed to—and be all by himself—or he could cut in and maintain contact, also as he was supposed to, and have a secure left flank. As he had already brushed off the rudimentary French forces, those over-age reserves off to the west, and as he knew nothing of the troops near Paris, he decided logically to pull in and stick close to Bülow. On August 31, Kluck changed the axis of his advance from southwest to south-southeast. It would carry him east of Paris, heading for the Marne River.

# 4. The Marne and the Race to the Sea

As AUGUST TURNED the corner into September, northern France was filled with the sounds of battle. Long columns of blue-coated infantry marched north to war, or south away from it. The countryside was littered with debris, the extra equipment that tired men cast off so they might march farther or faster, broken-down horses, abandoned wagons. Except where the opposing sides had actually clashed and where the dead still lay in the open, looking strangely two-dimensional as they flattened into the growing grass, there was little war damage. The weather stayed good, and only around a few towns was there much evidence of shelling. In Paris the headlines were ominous, as the place names reported in the communiqués crept closer and closer to the capital. Old men muttered that it looked like 1870 all over again. In some of the government offices they started burning files, and the occasional whiff of smoke hung over the city.

But it was not 1870. There was no Emperor to accuse, and no one yet lost confidence in the army. Every day the trains from the south and east brought more soldiers into the stations, and the columns with the long rifles and the bright bayonets tramped steadily through the streets, across the city and out on the northeast side. There was less band music, and fewer flowers thrown, but there was a more businesslike look about the whole thing. The casualty lists were already appalling, the war was becoming real, and the holiday atmosphere seemed out of place now, so far had people's attitudes changed within a fortnight.

Old Papa Joffre—he was only in his early sixties, but his grandfatherly attitude earned him a fond nickname from his troops—was still hard at work. As the Germans spread over the map in late August, he responded by forming two new armies, shuffling units about to put them where most needed. He activated the 6th Army, under General Maunoury, around Paris; this was to be the operational arm of the entrenched camp commanded by Gallieni. Behind the hard-pressed 5th and 4th armies he built up the 9th. Command of that went to Foch, he of the "Iron Corps" in the Battle of Lorraine. Foch was practically the high priest of the doctrine of the offensive, and he was now going to get his chance. Joffre was developing a pretty clear picture of what was happening. When Kluck made his all-important turn to the south, east of Paris, the allies picked it up by aerial reconnaissance, the first intervention in history of what was to become a significant new aspect of warfare. On the basis of this newly gained intelligence, Joffre decided that when the Germans swung in enough, he would pull a Schlieffen Plan in reverse: His new armies would attack back up and across the German line of communication, and the biter would be bitten.

The British were out of it for the moment. Sir John French was badly shaken by Mons and Le Cateau. Even though his little army, the "Old Contemptibles" as they proudly called themselves, had acquitted itself well on the field, it had still been pushed back, it was still retreating, and it still had heavy casualties. French, like everyone else, had little idea of the realities of European war. His last battle service had been in South Africa, where fighting had been bitter enough, but casualties relatively few. But unlike everyone else, French knew his army was all Britain had. His instructions had been contradictory: to cooperate with his ally, but to preserve his army. The French had already lost more than three times the fighting strength of the entire B. E. F. By the first of September, Sir John French was a badly shaken man, and to French requests for help he replied that his force was no longer battleworthy; he intended to retreat south of the Seine.

Events were already outpacing Joffre's plan for a flanking counteroffensive. Kluck was still driving on, flanking Lanrezac's 5th Army and forcing it to continue withdrawing. Bülow was still pushing it straight back. There was a widening gap between the continuous French line that ended with Lanrezac, and the garrison of Paris and 6th Army. Lanrezac himself was tired and worn out, steeped in pessimism. On the 3rd, Joffre showed up at his headquarters, listened to his tale of woe, and sacked him. Franchet d'Esperey took over. Joffre needed fighters, and Desperate Franky, as d'Esperey was called, could be counted on for that; happily he also got on well with the British, which Lanrezac had not done.

The British remained a problem. At the start of the war the Prime Minister, Mr. Herbert Asquith, who was the most unwarlike of men, had appointed Lord Kitchener as Secretary of State for War. Kitchener's was a name that conjured up visions of imperial battles and the thin red line for Englishmen, and his presence gave the government a badly needed boost in its military appearance. On September 1 he had shown up in Paris, met French, and after listening to a lengthy and vehement presentation of the B. E. F.'s difficulties, had taken him into a private room for some home truths. It would be interesting to know what was said, for Kitchener was never a man to mince words. In spite of that, Sir John French was still hemming and hawing on the 4th when Joffre issued the orders for what was to be the battle of the Marne.

Therefore, a tired Joffre went to visit French on the 5th. They met in Melun, thirty miles south of Paris. The French commander put his case slowly and patiently, as would a parent trying to deal in the midst of a family crisis with a fractious child. He said he was about to fight the battle that would save France or lose the war, that he was going to commit his entire army, to the last company; he had already issued an order of the day stating that there was to be no more retreat; the Germans must be stopped, or the French Army must die in its tracks. He could not believe the British would refuse to help at this supreme moment, and he ended by telling French that "the honor of England is at stake." The chastened French replied that he would do what he could and invited Joffre and his party to tea.

On the other side of the hill, the Germans were having their problems, too, the chief among them being that their commander did not know what was happening. Moltke, completely in the dark, though he had now moved his headquarters forward to Luxembourg, was obsessed by the feeling that his battle was running away with him. He was correct. His left was quiet; in the center Rupprecht was still trying to push the French off the heights along the Meurthe, and up past that the Crown Prince of Prussia was having his troubles where the enemy were clinging around Verdun. Albrecht's 4th Army was doing well, getting down past Verdun, but beyond him it was very difficult to see exactly what was going on. Perhaps things were proceeding well, but Moltke could not be sure. Hausen was advancing around Reims and beginning to meet some of Foch's new 9th Army. Bülow was still pushing toward the Marne, but where was Kluck? Unsure of this last, Moltke ordered Kluck to advance in echelon behind Bülow, supporting his advance and covering his flank and rear.

This was awkward for Kluck, because in fact he was two days out in front of Bülow, still bulldozing everything ahead of him, crossing the Oise and the Ourcq and heading toward Château-Thierry on the Marne. When Moltke's order belatedly reached him, he concluded that the best way to support and protect Bülow was simply to keep on going. Dropping another corps, the IVth Reserve under General Gronau, to fend off any sortie from Paris, he kept on south. By the evening of September 5, Bülow's 2nd Army had come up and faced Foch's 9th across the St. Gond Marshes, which provide the headwaters of the Petit Morin, a tributary of the Marne. The main body of Kluck's 1st Army was on Bülow's right and slightly ahead still, facing d'Esperey's 5th Army across the Grand Morin. There was then a gap of fifteen miles back to the northwest, where Gronau's IVth Reserve Corps, still north of the river, faced west against the threat of troops from Paris. The stage was set for the Battle of the Marne.

On the morning of September 5 Moltke was sufficiently alarmed by the news of troops massing in Paris to order a whole change of direction. This was the definitive termination of the Schlieffen Plan. He directed Kluck and Bülow to stop their advance south, and instead to face west, prepared to fight a defensive battle. Kluck, receiving this order, but still not told of events in Paris that necessitated it, thought Moltke had finally lost his wits completely. He ordered a continuation of the southern advance. Nevertheless, just to be on the safe side, he sent orders back to Gronau to hold up his march and face to the west.

Gronau could hardly do anything else. His troops were now crossing the Ourcq, a tributary stream that flows into the Marne from the north. It runs through the plateau of Brie, fairly rough country with abrupt little cuttings caused by streams. As Gronau advanced, his cavalry screen on the right flank kept bringing in alarming news of French cavalry and, even more ominous, of long columns of French infantry on the march. The French horsemen were Sordet's cavalry corps, down now to a few exhausted squadrons, and they were not strong enough to cover their infantry's advance from German eyes. When Kluck's stop order arrived shortly before midday, Gronau was happy to comply, and he threw his corps into a defensive line along several little ridges.

In the afternoon the French came up, and their advance guards developed Gronau's line. There was a series of sharp flaring encounters, and the French were forced to go to ground. Gronau correctly realized that he was facing only the advance of what had to be a major force, and he informed Kluck that he was in trouble. Kluck all this long day was forcing the pace on toward and across the Marne, over the Petit Morin and the Grand Morin. In the evening a liaison officer from Moltke's headquarters, Colonel Hentsch, reached him. The German staff system seldom employed such officers, so when it did, it meant something serious was in the air. Hentsch finally explained to Kluck the intelligence assessments the General Staff had made of what was happening in Paris, and a reluctant Kluck was forced to acknowledge that all did not look as good as he had supposed. In the midst of this a report asking for reinforcements came in from Gronau. Kluck still did not wish to be convinced but finally ordered one of his corps to countermarch and shore up Gronau. That was the first retrograde movement of the German Army, and the tired soldiers saddled up and went back the way they had come.

The troops Gronau's Germans met on the 5th were the first of Maunoury's advance, coming out of Paris to take the enemy in flank and rear. They did not know the Germans were as close as they were, and the fighting around the Ourcq was a pure encounter battle. The French attack was slated for the next day, the 6th, and when they jumped off that morning, they were in for a hard fight. Gronau had been reinforced, had fallen back and dug in during the night, and was ready for them. In a savage battle all day the Germans were slowly but not significantly pushed back. Yet this affair was changing the whole picture of the campaign, for by the 7th, virtually the whole of Kluck's 1st Army was countermarching, sucked into the maelstrom on the Ourcq. Kluck gave up contact with Bülow and left only a thin cavalry screen and a weak infantry rear guard to hold his former front. By the evening of the 6th, a thirty-mile-wide gap was opening up in the German advance.

On that same day, both d'Esperey's 5th Army and the B. E. F. advanced. The British were so far to the south that they had merely a day of marching, without making any contact with the enemy. The French left met two of Kluck's corps, which hit them hard and held them on the Grand Morin before breaking contact and going back north. Their right came up against Bülow's men, trying to obey the new order to face west, on the Petit Morin, and the two fought each other to a halt. Meanwhile, Bülow's left was in trouble; Foch, though ordered to stand on the defensive, had attacked north of the St. Gond Marshes. The Germans threw his troops back handily, inflicting heavy casualties, but just the simple fact that the French were still attacking scared Bülow. He interpreted it as new strength rather than what it was, Foch's blind adherence to the offensive in spite of reality.

For the next two days the issue hung in the balance. On the Ourcq there was savage fighting all day Monday, the 7th. As they came out of Paris, Maunoury flung each of his divisions into the attack. Kluck threw his troops in with equal fervor as they completed their countermarch from the Marne. The dead piled up in the little villages, and the French put in attack after attack. Many of them were reservists, tired and confused, but they fought on all through the day. At one point in the afternoon, a German counterattack caught the 63rd Reserve Division just past the crest of an attack and broke it. The Germans swept forward; at the last minute Colonel Robert Nivelle, an artilleryman, limbered up his 75s and advanced into the fleeing infantry. Mere yards from the oncoming gray-coats, he swung his guns around, unlimbered, and opened shrapnel fire. This halted the German push, and the French rallied.

A steady stream of wounded men and broken units flowed back down the road to Paris, accompanied by cries for support from Maunoury. His left flank was wide open, he was heavily outnumbered, time was against him. In Paris, old General Gallieni decided he must get help out to the battlefield in a hurry. A division from 3rd Army, way over past Verdun, had just detrained. On Gallieni's order, the Paris gendarmes flagged down taxis and sent them to the railway stations and the squares where the troops were mustering. Two full regiments were packed in the cabs, and off they went in convoys, up the road to battle. It was not much—postwar legend would have it that every soldier in France traveled in every taxi in Paris—but it caught the popular imagination, and it worked. Sixth Army held on, and by the end of the day had absorbed all of Kluck's forces.

That same day the British were still advancing into the void; they made no contact. To their right 5th Army too moved slowly and cautiously; Bülow was pulling back his exposed right wing, and there was little fighting on that front. But Foch's 9th Army was in serious trouble, battered all day by Bülow's left wing and increasingly, as the long day went on, by the right wing of Hausen's 3rd Army.

This lasted all the next day, too. At three on the morning of the 8th, Hausen's men hit Foch's right and drove it back three miles. All day Foch's weary men stood up to German advances. Foch dashed from headquarters to headquarters, meeting all pleas with one response: Attack! If troops were exhausted, attack; if casualties were insupportable, attack; if ammunition was gone, attack with the bayonet. The attacks got thinner and thinner, but they kept on; Moroccans, Senegalese, reservists, regulars, boys in their first battle, and old men who could remember 1870. By the end of the day French attacks were hardly recognizable as such, just a shuffling line of tired dirty men, barely able to hold their long rifles at high port as they staggered forward.

That day on Foch's left 5th Army could not cross the Petit Morin. The British were held up by German cavalry and still did not reach the Marne. Up on the Ourcq, Kluck and Maunoury's battle was burning down for lack of fuel. But after dark, once again taking time to prepare an attack as he had at Guise, Franchet d'Esperey launched a night drive that levered Bülow's right flank off the Petit Morin. In despair, Bülow pulled back his right, opening the gap with Kluck just a little bit farther.

Von Moltke had done nothing all this time. He issued no orders, and his field generals hardly bothered to inform him what was happening. Gradually, he became aware that there was a large gap between Bülow and Kluck, but he still could not figure out the position exactly. Finally, he sent Colonel Hentsch on another tour of the front, with verbal orders that apparently permitted Hentsch to authorize a general withdrawal if a local one were already in progress. No one to this day knows exactly what Hentsch was empowered to do. Hentsch found things going satisfactorily as far as Hausen, whose army was preparing for its climactic struggle against Foch. But at 2nd Army, Bülow was finished. The night attack against him had finally broken his will, and he was preparing orders for a general retreat of his whole army. Hentsch agreed with this estimation and went off to inform Kluck it was time to quit. Early on the 9th Bülow began his march north.

Kluck still wanted to fight, however. He was ready to develop

Maunoury's open northern flank when the B. E. F. got across the Marne and in turn flanked him. That finally convinced him, too, that it was time to go.

Hausen and Foch were the last to give it up. There the German drive reached its high water mark. They had driven the Moroccans out of the Château de Mondemont, on Mount Aout, a little hill south of the St. Gond Marshes. The French spent the whole day of the 9th trying to get it back, officers still in white gloves leading suicidal charges against the German machine gunners, bugles blowing, swords and bayonets and rifle butts like something out of Napoleon's day. Eventually, the French battered the Germans out of the château with howitzers, which was what they should have done in the first place. When day broke over the battlefield on the 10th, it was quiet at last; the Germans were slogging north-ward, back the way they had come. The Battle of the Marne was over.

Whether or not the Schlieffen Plan could have worked is one of those questions that have tantalized military historians ever since the event. On the face of it the answer appears to be a qualified no, and some commentators have maintained that it was little short of ludicrous to expect that several million men could be moved around Europe successfully in the space of a few short weeks; on that level, something was bound to break down, and the plan was doomed from the start. A more technical response is to say that it was impossible for the Germans to expect they could march faster over hostile country with a disrupted communi-cations network than the French could transfer their forces by train over a still functioning system. In that view, the German attack was a sort of blitzkrieg without the blitz. It is true that Schlieffen never got as many men as his original plan was predi-cated on, but it is equally possible that more men would just have clogged the works even more, creating a sort of rolling snowball that self-destructs by falling apart faster as it rolls and gets bigger.

Yet another view is that the plan might have worked had Moltke not tampered with its dispositions at the start and made a series of progressive mistakes as he went along. He changed the ratio between his wings, and virtually every move he made during the campaign served to aggravate that imbalance. It thus becomes possible to argue that the difference between winning and losing was the difference between Joffre and Moltke. Joffre kept his head, won his battle, and saved his country from crushing defeat. Moltke lost his head, his battle, and quite possibly the war. He also lost his job. On September 14 he was relieved of command.

Finally, on a larger view, it is perhaps legitimate to ask if Europe would not have been better off had the Schlieffen Plan worked. During the war the Germans came to be seen by the Allies as fiends incarnate, the Hun who raped nuns and bayoneted babies, but that view of them was a creation of the war itself. It is true that even their early demands for peace terms were exaggerated, but would a German hegemony of Europe have been any worse than the subsequent course of the war, with its millions of deaths, its influenza epidemic, its Bolshevik Revolution? Is it too imaginative to say that if the Schlieffen Plan had worked, Adolf Hitler might have remained a private in the Linz Regiment and Joseph Stalin a Georgian peasant? The Battle of the Marne was the end of the Schlieffen Plan, the end of the era of short wars, and the end of the old Europe as well.

None of this was apparent to the generals frantically planning their next move, and certainly not to the tired thousands who now took up their retreat or their pursuit toward the Belgian border. For half a million men—German, Belgian, British, and above all French—the war was over, as they lay in agony in rough hospitals, already overflowing, or as their bodies bloated and decomposed on the banks of the Ourcq or in the St. Gond Marshes. For the rest of Europe, the war went on.

The denouement of the Schlieffen Plan was a series of battles miscalled "the race to the sea." It started at and after the Marne and ended at the seacoast with the advent of winter weather in mid-November. The series was miscalled because no one wanted particularly to reach the seacoast; what both sides wanted was to get around the enemy's northern flank and break once more into open country for maneuvering.

As the Germans disengaged on the Marne they fell back to an east-west line running from Noyon to Verdun, generally along the heights just past the Aisne River. The western end of this line was along a feature known as the Chemin des Dames. They took up their position here on September 14, and for the next three days the Allies, especially the British, battered against them. On the 18th this First Battle of the Aisne ran down. The German field fortifications, machine guns, and supporting artillery proved a combination impossible to break. This was the begining of trench warfare and a ghastly preview of what lay ahead. Joffre, taking heavy losses for little result, decided to sideslip the Germans where their flank ended in air at Noyon, and thus the race to outflank was on.

The next leap took the combatants north across the Oise into Picardy. Here in the fourth week of September they clashed again, from Noyon north to the Somme River. The new Chief of the German General Staff, Erich von Falkenhayn, managed to shift his armies north just as the French and British were doing, and neither side could gain an advantage. By September 26 they had dug their trench lines as far as the Somme.

From the end of September through the first ten days of October they fought the First Battle of Artois, from the Somme up to the Belgian border. This was ground later to be occupied by the B. E. F., and the names here became horribly familiar as the war went on: Albert, Arras, Vimy, Loos, Festubert, Neuve Chapelle. The Germans reached the frontier by the 10th, fought out again.

Falkenhayn was meanwhile cleaning up his back areas. The French fortress of Maubeuge, which Sir John French had momentarily considered as a bolt-hole, fell on September 8. It took another month to lever King Albert of the Belgians and his little army out of Antwerp. He and his British reinforcements from the Royal Naval Division finally abandoned the city and made their way westward to the seacoast, and Antwerp surrendered on October 9. The Belgians fell in with the general Allied line where the little River Yser runs in to the sea at Nieuport, and the line was complete from the Swiss border to the Channel coast.

Neither side was ready to admit the possibility of stalemate yet, and there were frantic efforts to break through and restore mobility before winter weather hardened the defense systems. In mid-October Falkenhayn hit the British and Belgians along the Lys and nearly broke through their trench crust. The British hung on, but the Belgians on their left managed to survive only by letting the seawater in and flooding the last ten miles of their line up to the coast. An Allied counterattack suffered huge casualties and gained nothing. Falkenhayn had one last try in the north, around Ypres. He attacked at the end of October and kept on until November 11, at one point being stopped literally by the last Allied reserves and the advent of winter. This month of frightful butchery in Flanders—the old medieval name for the territory from the

Scheldt River to the Channel now came back into general usage—went down as the First Battle of Ypres.

All along the line, as the movement toward the coast was being fought out, men struggled to escape the suffocating, congealing growth of field fortifications. The Germans attacked around Verdun in September and got nothing for their pains except a small bothersome salient east of the city at St. Mihiel, a point they would hold for four years until the New World came to redress the balance of the old. They then attacked farther south in the Vosges and achieved nothing. Finally, in mid-December, Joffre ordered a general attack; it collapsed after four days. Nothing daunted, he opened a more specific one in Champagne. That went on into the new year, and again there was nothing to show for it but pitiful bundles of dead men and overcrowded hospitals.

Ivan Bloch had been right; the spade had become as important a weapon of war as the rifle, and everywhere along the line now, men were digging for their lives. A static front was rapidly developing, much to the disgust of generals who liked their troops to keep active. As the Germans were on foreign territory, they had been able to be choosier about their positions; they were not as fussy about giving up a few yards of someone else's sacred soil, not if it meant better observation and firing positions. Everywhere they held the high ground. It was up to the Allies to lever them off of it, and the onus of attacking therefore rested with the French and British.

Unless, of course, something happened in the East to upset this horrible equilibrium. Perhaps the Russian Steamroller might come to the rescue.

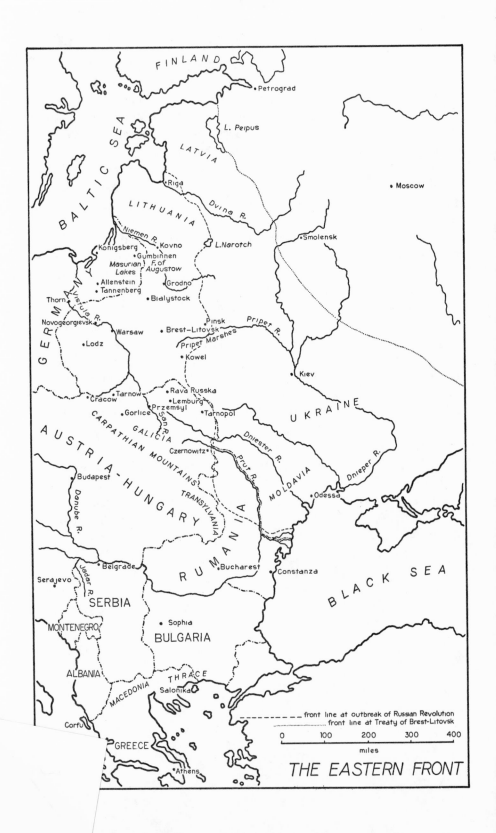

THE EASTERN FRONT

# 5. The War in the East

FROM THE SWISS BORDER to the North Sea was a matter of some 300 miles. From the eastern end of East Prussia, around the Polish salient and down to the point where the borders of Austria-Hungary and Russia met neutral Rumania, was a straggling line substantially more than 1,000 miles long. At the opening of the war, therefore, the Eastern Front was a good four times as long as the Western Front. From the German concentration area to Paris was roughly 200 miles, but from East Prussia to St. Petersburg was twice that far, and even from Warsaw to Vienna was 300. Historians, as do soldiers, neglect geography at their peril, and these simple distances explain a great deal of what happened and what did not happen on the Eastern Front in 1914.

The Schlieffen Plan had dictated that the German effort in the East would be initially defensive, secondary to the war-winning campaign in the West. The Russians were not disposed to go along with the Germans' view of priorities, and they were prepared to take the offensive at the outset of war, though their preparations, as did everyone else's, proved unrealistic when exposed to the hard light of twentieth-century warfare. The clash that developed in East Prussia completely dwarfed the Austrian invasion of Serbia which was ostensibly what the war was all about.

As a people, the Russians responded enthusiastically to the declaration of war. In 1914, Russia was a troubled but awakening giant; for the last twenty years she had been going through the trauma of an industrial revolution, and just as that process had brought immense suffering and dislocation to western Europe a century before, it had done the same to Russia now. Hundreds of thousands of people were jammed into industrial slums, there were new classes of rich and poor, there was great intellectual ferment as the political development of the country lagged behind economic and social change. Russia remained dogged by her historic problems of political authority, of land distribution, of westernization versus conservatism. The near revolution of 1905 had brought change more to the form than to the substance of her governing institutions. The Romanov, as was the Hapsburg, dynasty was a holdover from the feudal past and could be seen, depending on the vantage point of the viewer, as either the epitome of all that was backward and reactionary in Russia, or as the last bastion of stability against the forces of anarchy. Leon Trotsky, one of the few genuine revolutionary geniuses, maintained that Russia was actually on the verge of revolution in 1914 and that only the patriotic outburst that accompanied the declaration of war saved the regime for a few more years. That probably overstated the case. There were certainly deep currents of dissatisfaction in Russian life, but it took the hammer-blows of two and a half years of war to bring them into the open.

In the period before the war, the Russians had made serious efforts to modernize and build up their armed forces. They had taken a humiliating beating in the Russo-Japanese War in 1904–5, when they had never really had a chance to develop their strength. They had still not been ready to stand up to Austria and Germany at the time of the Bosnia-Herzegovinian crisis of 1908, but they had been making steady progress since then. Indeed, their development was one of the factors that made the German General Staff desire war in 1914, before Russian preparations advanced any further. For the Germans, 1914 was almost preemptive war.

Unhappily for Russia, the development of the army was partially crippled by divisions within it as to the directions to be taken. There were rivalries between aristocratic and lower-class officers, between infantry, cavalry, and artillery, between General Staff adherents and field command positions, and especially between personal cliques, the most important of them centering around General V. A. Sukhomlinov, the leading military politician, and his many adversaries. These quarrels and divisions caused an impressive army of 1,300,000 trained men and 5 million reserves to limp into battle in August of 1914.

All three powers, Germany, Austria-Hungary, and Russia, had paid serious attention to the problem presented by the Polish salient. The Germans had fortified towns around the southeastern shoulder of East Prussia, but the area was weakly garrisoned by the 8th Army, with its field commander authorized to fall back west of the Vistula, abandoning all of East Prussia if absolutely necessary. To the south of the salient, the Austrians crammed four armies forward into Galicia, but they had still extensively fortified the northern slopes of the Carpathian Mountains, their natural defensive barrier.

The Russians had been even more cautious. They refused to station troops west of the Vistula for fear of their being cut off by a combined enemy attack across the base of the salient. They built up a great base around Warsaw, and they fortified eastern Polish centers near the frontiers. To prevent a rapid German advance into Poland they deliberately adopted a different railroad gauge from that used by the Germans. This would hamper German utilization of the Russian railroad system in the event of invasion; unfortunately, it would also prevent Russian use of the German railroad system in the event of a Russian invasion of Prussia. Doubly unfortunate, because it was the Russians who chose to advance.

The decision had been made as early as 1910. At that time the Russians had correctly decided the Germans would attack France first when war began, that France would appeal for help, and that Russia must be prepared to give it. From those sensible premises they rapidly went astray. Their initial proposal called for an all-out offensive into East Prussia as the only possible way to relieve the French. To develop the strength for that, however, they would have to downgrade both their fortresses and their armies guarding the Austro-Hungarian frontier. This prospect opened the door for vicious faction-fighting within the army, and the end result was that the fortress advocates, united with those who feared the chimera of an Austro-Hungarian attack, carried the day. Immense sums continued to be put into fortresses and fortress artillery, the main bulk of the field army was concentrated on the Galician frontier—and then the Russians planned a major attack into East Prussia to relieve the French anyway. By 1912 they had already set the stage for their own disaster.

The operation order for the invasion of East Prussia called for a converging drive by two separate forces. General Paul Rennenkampf's 1st Army was to drive west from its concentration areas on the Niemen River, north of Grodno. Meanwhile, General Samsonov's 2nd Army, mobilizing around Bialystok, was to move westward, then wheel north and drive into East Prussia from the south. Hopefully, these two converging armies would catch the German defenders in a vise between them and clear East Prussia.

Their mobilization went remarkably well. Supplies were lavish, with plenty of guns and shells, sufficient transport, and the initial stages of the movement going like clockwork. The Russians were well prepared for the war they expected to fight, and on August 17, slightly prematurely according to their schedules, but with all ostensibly in order, Rennenkampf crossed the frontier.

The fact that an army could mobilize did not necessarily mean it could move or that it could fight or that its generals knew how to handle it in action. Once on the road, the Russians ran into difficulties. The East Prussian-Polish frontier crossed a wilderness of forests, bogs, and lakes. Roads were few, deliberately undeveloped by the Russians as a defensive measure, and now hampering them in their advance. Lateral communications between the two armies were practically nonexistent, but that mattered little as the two commanders did not like each other anyway. Samsonov was a Sukhomlinovite, and Rennenkampf an anti-Sukhomlinovite; their respective Chiefs of Staff were just the opposite. None of the four bothered to inform the others of what they were about, and, disdaining any effective cavalry screens or reconnaissance, both armies pushed blindly into the void.

On the other side General Max von Prittwitz, commander of the German 8th Army, had drawn up his four corps in a long line covering the lakes and forests across the frontier. His left rested on Gumbinnen, his right on Allenstein, a distance of about eighty-five miles. He was outnumbered, but in the Russians' blundering advance he saw opportunities. The Russians were chattering over their radios, and the Germans were able to intercept and decode situation reports and orders from higher commands. Some Russian messages were even uncoded, because the recipients lacked codebooks for deciphering. Von Prittwitz judged that it was safe to leave one corps facing the slower 2nd Army, while he concentrated three against 1st Army.

His plan was nearly upset by a corps commander, General von François, who thrust his left flank corps boldly forward to bash the first Russians over the border. This was bad, for von Prittwitz' timing depended upon the Russians coming to him, not on his having to go in search of them. Happily for the Germans, Rennenkampf ignored this bloody nose and pushed on, still with no cavalry out in front nor with any idea of what amount of enemy he faced. On the night of the 19th–20th he sent out a plain-language stop order to his scattered forces. A reluctant von Prittwitz decided his time was running out and therefore advanced to attack him around Gumbinnen on the 20th.

The resultant battle was a costly draw. On their left, the Germans achieved surprise when they hit the Russians at four in the morning and made some ground. But on the right and in the center, troops arrived worn out from an all-night march and attacked dug-in Russians in full daylight. They took a severe battering and made no progress. After being deluged with artillery, they were pushed back in a disorderly retreat—a plain rout in some units —and by the end of the day, von Prittwitz' whole strategic plan for East Prussia was falling apart. To cap his difficulties, word reached him that Samsonov's army was now advancing and seriously threatening his line back to the Vistula.

The German commander's response to all this was to panic. He shut himself up in his office, got on the phone to von Moltke in Coblenz, and told him his tale of woe: a battle lost, a corps routed, his communications threatened. He wanted to retreat immediately behind the Vistula and abandon all of East Prussia; unless reinforced he could not even guarantee to hold on there. Von Moltke responded quickly; he fired von Prittwitz.

As his replacement the Germans called out of retirement a general named Paul von Hindenburg; to give the sixty-seven-year-old man some help, they appointed to the Chief of Staff position the hero of Liége, General Ludendorff. This launched on their careers the duo that came to personify Germany's war effort—and that led her to her ultimate defeat. Von Moltke also dispatched east troops from his apparently successful right wing.

While Hindenburg and Ludendorff were meeting and traveling eastward, headquarters in East Prussia was working out its own salvation. Von Prittwitz' operations officer, Colonel Max Hoffman, had convinced the defeated commander and his Chief of Staff that it was impossible to pull back to the Vistula, because Samsonov was already eighty miles nearer to it than the Germans were. The only remedy was to proceed as originally planned, move the beaten units from Gumbinnen back to the southwest, and hit Samsonov with everything they had. Hoffman issued the orders; Hindenburg and Ludendorff, already thinking on the same lines, reached Army Headquarters just in time to agree to what was in train—and to take the credit for it.

The Russian 2nd Army, meanwhile, was making its way through that tangle of lakes and forests on the frontier. Again there was no cavalry screen, and the Russian radios broadcast orders in clear, which the Germans gratefully received. By August 24, when one of the Russian corps ran into the lonely German right-wing corps left behind to guard Allenstein, the Germans had a better picture of Russian dispositions than the Russians themselves did. After a sharp little corps-sized battle, Samsonov sent out orders for the whole army to stand fast and rest, and presumably give him time to find out where he was, on the 25th. The same day, Rennenkampf equally obligingly announced that he was making but a short advance, so the Germans knew they had plenty of time to deal with the southern threat. While the Russians dithered, the German soldiers hurriedly tramped back to the southwest. Garrison troops from as far away as the Vistula and the fortress of Konigsberg arrived by rail, and the Germans converged, in a long noose, around the bewildered 2nd Army. Bumping into flanking units and cavalry, they began driving them in. Samsonov was making desperate efforts to find out what was happening and to keep control of his units, but he was hampered by the poor Russian communications, as well as by the inability of his staff officers and some of his fellow commanders to overcome their personal animosities even when faced with disaster. Indeed, on the eve of the Battle of Tannenberg, most of them did not know they were faced with disaster; they thought things were going fairly well.

General von François, the corps commander who had upset the Gumbinnen plan, attacked the Russian left flank on the 27th. He had brought his troops down by rail, they had been reinforced with artillery from the fortress of Thorn, and they opened their attack with an overwhelming deluge of shells that blasted the Russians out of their hastily dug trenches. The Russian infantry broke and fled for the rear, even before the German barrage lifted. Samsonov's left flank was therefore wide open.

Meanwhile, over on his right, the same sort of thing had befallen his other flanking corps. It too had been defeated, and it too had retreated precipitately back across the frontier. News of these disasters was slow getting to Army Headquarters, with the unfortunate result that Samsonov was still ordering an advance by his center when both his flanks had collapsed and disappeared.

The three corps of the Russian center hit the German XX Corps, and hit it hard, around Tannenberg. The Germans replied with a spirited counterattack, but still had heavy going against the Russian weight. Ludendorff therefore directed von François to swing north and lift some of the pressure off the German center, but von François, who must have been a somewhat difficult subordinate, completely disregarded his orders and continued pushing east. He ended up with his corps strung out in a line that was both long and weak, but that blocked the escape route of Samsonov's center. By the evening of the 29th the three Russian corps, roughly 150,000 men, were well and truly trapped.

The rest of the battle was a straightforward slaughter. Samsonov directed his army to break out, but could exercise no real control. Inside a steadily shrinking pocket, Russian regiments and squadrons staggered this way and that, blasted by artillery, raked by machine guns, trying vainly to escape or to fight their way through the German grip. The ten-mile-wide trap east of Tannenberg was turned into a vast abattoir of dead and dying horses and men. Soldiers cowered under the shellfire or shot themselves or vainly dashed against the German positions. Some of the German soldiers themselves went mad as the slaughter continued, field pieces firing over open sights into the seething masses of Russians.

By the time it was over, 125,000 men were killed, wounded, or captured. Samsonov was never found and was reported to have committed suicide. The Russian people were plunged into despair, and the Germans elated beyond measure. Five hundred years earlier, in 1410, the Poles had virtually wiped out the Teutonic Knights on that same battlefield. Now German papers crowed that at last they were revenged. A sober mind might ask what hope there was for Europe if blood memories lasted that long, but for the Germans, good news was still coming; now Hindenburg and Ludendorff turned back to deal with Rennenkampf.

Having done absolutely nothing either to cooperate with Samsonov, or to save him from disaster, Rennenkampf took up his advance once again. As soon, however, as he received word of his colleague's defeat, he threw his army into what was supposed to be a defensive posture. He strung out all five of his corps in a long line, holding only a weak two divisions in reserve. His position looked like that of the general who had shown Napoleon a plan whereby all the French troops were neatly lined up on the frontier, on which Napoleon commented, "It's beautiful; what do you want to do—prevent smuggling?"

After discovering where the enemy was, Hindenburg and Ludendorff decided they would launch a double attack; they had now been reinforced from the west, though they had wired that there was no need, so there were plenty of troops for them to employ. Four corps would pin the main Russian position in the north, while two would break through the thin Russian line in the south, around the Masurian Lakes. After breaking the Russians, these corps would wheel north across the line of retreat, and it would be Tannenberg all over again. The German commanders were under heavy pressure to let Rennenkampf go and move south on Warsaw as a means of relieving the Austro-Hungarians, but they decided to finish with the bird in the hand first.

The battle opened on September 8. The German advance in the south hit the Russian line and made little progress, though it did succeed in attracting Rennenkampf's weak reserve. On the 9th the pinning attack in the north was stopped cold, but that day von François' infantry, after marching nearly eighty miles in four days, crashed through the southern end of the Russian position. Rennenkampf, seriously alarmed at last, issued orders for a general retreat.

All the corps in line were now faced with a desperate scramble to get away over the poor frontier roads. Long columns of tired soldiers shuffled on; they started in the early predawn hours of the 10th, marched into the rising sun and all through the day and on into darkness again. The roads were littered with abandoned wagons, broken-down horses, and footsore stragglers, but march discipline remained remarkably good, and the army, disheartened though it was, did not fall apart.

In this desperate situation they were saved less by their own marching than by Rennenkampf's determination. Finally acting like a general, he sent two of his divisions in a sacrificial spoiling attack right at the German center. Charging into the German XX Corps, they drove it back in disarray, leaving both its flanking units exposed. This fierce struggle in his center caused Ludendorff to hesitate at the vital moment; he had seen how bravely the Russians fought at Tannenberg, launching suicidal attacks when a western army would have recognized defeat. Now he called in his pursuit, and the death of those two brave divisions allowed 1st

Army to get away. The Battle of the Masurian Lakes was not another Tannenberg after all.

It was still bad enough; in five days Rennenkampf had managed to lose another 125,000 Russian soldiers, immense amounts of stores, guns, and transport, and Russia's reputation as a great military power. The forces of the Tsar had been in East Prussia for exactly four weeks, and they had lost more than a quarter of a million men and had their military organization, at least in that area, disrupted for the foreseeable future. Western liaison officers, unaware that their own casualties—and generalship—were equally as bad, wrote home that little dependence could henceforth be put on Russia.

What happened in East Prussia stole the headlines from the other battles on the eastern front, but in fact the war raged all through central Europe, and there were even more massive battles to the south while Tannenberg and the Masurian Lakes were being fought, and on into the winter.

Western Poland was left largely alone, as the Russians had wisely refused to concentrate that far forward into the salient. Activity here was confined largely to a bit of frontier raiding. South of the Pripet Marshes, however, the Russians had concentrated four armies, the Southwest Army Group commanded by General Ivanov. Opposite them in Galicia the Austrians had also concentrated four armies; actually, they had but three and a half, for the 2nd Army was busy countermarching while its leaders tried to decide if they were to fight Serbs or Russians.

General Ivanov had chosen to attack into eastern Galicia, and had massed his two strongest armies for that task. General Conrad von Hötzendorf, however, had decided to attack out of western Galicia. Therefore, the stronger Austrian forces met the weaker Russian forces, and vice versa. Conrad, in truth, did not particularly want to attack at all, but he did so largely under German pressure. Retreating before the Russian advance in East Prussia, wanting time to finish off France, as they expected to do shortly, the Germans asked the Austrians to conform to their vision and timing of the war, and a somewhat reluctant Conrad agreed to do so. It is one of the many ironies of World War I that Austria and Russia, both the weaker powers in their respective alliances, constantly overexerted themselves at the behest of their stronger allies.

Upon doing so they invariably ran into trouble, from which they had to be rescued. This made their allies regard them as all the more weak and undependable and as needing direction. That direction always entailed further sacrifice and further subordination. It created a vicious circle, and eventually both states cracked under the strain of it.

As neither side used its cavalry properly for reconnaissance, the initial contact took the form of a series of blundering encounter battles. The Austrian advance on the left hit the Russians on August 23. The Russians, outnumbered three to one, were pushed steadily back; as he had no idea this was the main advance, Ivanov chose to resolve his problem by relieving his army commander, which did little to offset the numerical disparity. The Austrians kept on advancing.

Conrad, who thought he was handily beating the main Russian concentration, compounded his error by pulling troops from his right to sustain his successful left. It was a terrible shock to him, then, when on the 26th the main Russian advance hit his weakened right. The two armies were now in a position of pushing each other around in a circle. Confusion increased. In the center the Austrians nearly won an encirclement victory over General Plehve, who refused to recognize he was in a battle, but they pulled back just in time to avoid complete triumph, scared of their open flanks. On their right they lost the fortress of Lemberg and began calling for German help. By the first of September, both armies were trying to envelop each other and changing plans in the midst of their operations. The result of this was that a forty-mile gap opened up in front of the central Russian Army, Plehve's, and more by good luck than good management, he advanced into it. He ended up taking the eastern Austrian armies in flank and rear around Rava Russka. Conrad ordered a general retreat which got totally out of hand, and before the Austrian units could be pulled together again, they had fallen back a full hundred miles, into the foothills of the Carpathians, and lost more than 350,000 troops. Their losses were especially heavy in Germanic, as opposed to Slavic, units, and Conrad began crying for support from his ally.

The Germans, however, had just had their own disaster on the Marne, and the new Chief of the General Staff, von Falkenhayn, had no troops to spare from the West. He ordered Hindenburg and Ludendorff to form a new army, the 9th, and send it south to help out the Austrians. It eventually fell in on their left, around Cracow, and by the end of September, both sides were ready to try again, for the French were also demanding further efforts from the Russians.

French pleas led to a general readjustment of the Russian front. The Russians had decided anyway that they had done as much as they could in the Carpathians for the immediate future, and they therefore began shifting their armies northward for a drive out of the Polish salient and into Silesia, the industrial heart of Prussia proper. In the midst of this shift, they were forestalled by an Austro-German, mostly German, offensive up out of western Galicia, aimed eventually at Warsaw. The month of October was taken up with this drive, which Hindenburg saw less as a war-winner than as a temporary move to disconcert Russian preparations. He realized that he had only some eighteen divisions against sixty-odd of the Russians, and it was a measure of his expectations that his advancing troops were ordered to prepare roads and bridges for demolition when they should be forced to retreat.

Nonetheless, the Germans still got nearly to Warsaw before the Russians pulled themselves together in the middle of the month and started driving them back. By the end of October the lines were roughly back where they had started from, and the Russians were still planning their drive into Silesia.

Hindenburg and Ludendorff knew all about this; they could hardly be unaware of it, as the Russians had not yet overcome their tendency to chat in clear on the radio. Elevated now to command the entire Eastern Front, and not just East Prussia and detachments, the Hindenburg-Ludendorff team planned yet another spoiling advance, this time from the northern shoulder of the salient, parallel to and just west of the Vistula. They beat the Russians to the draw by three days, for their offensive jumped off on November 11, the Russian Silesian one on the 14th.

The German drive hit Rennenkampf and his 1st Army; as he had in the past, he had his corps scattered all over the map, and the Germans handily defeated them in detail. It took the Russian high command, the Stavka, three days to find out what was happening to their general, which explains why their own drive went off on schedule: They did not even know they were in difficulties. As their 2nd and 5th armies pushed west in a leisurely fashion, their 1st on the north was falling apart, and the entire right flank of their attack was wide open. Not until the 16th did they tumble to what was happening.

When they did, though, they moved fast. Both 2nd and 5th armies were ordered to countermarch and to shore up their comrades. By then the Germans were hoping to encircle what was left of 1st Army around Lodz. They nearly made it, but some units of 5th Army, marching more than seventy miles in forty-eight hours—anyone who thinks that is not an accomplishment ought to try it—came up just in time, and though the Russians were badly battered, they were not destroyed.

It was the end of the Silesian offensive, however. The Russian armies fell back on Warsaw, and the Germans occupied all of western Poland. Though no one could know it at the time, the opening of that Silesian offensive marked the farthest west Russian armies would get in this war. Not for thirty years would they exceed that, and when they did, it would not be for the greater glory of the Tsar.

There was one last gasp on into the winter. The new Chief of the General Staff, von Falkenhayn, was a convinced Westerner, but the prestige of Hindenburg and Ludendorff was such that they extracted permission for a last try to win the war quickly in the East. There was to be a joint offensive, Austrians out of Galicia, and Germans out of East Prussia, with reinforcements from the Western Front. The date was set for mid-February.

The Austrian contribution was a disaster. Uninspired, even by— or perhaps because of—the presence of German troops, the Austrians advanced with no enthusiasm whatever, and after taking their losses, gave it up as a bad job. Their fortress of Przemysl, cut off and surrounded way back in September, now surrendered, giving up 100,000 men and 1,000 guns, so the net result of the great offensive in the south was defeat and despair.

In the north the Germans did slightly better. They drove the Russians back from the East Prussian frontier and inflicted heavy casualties on their 10th Army. One corps was surrounded in the Forest of Augustow, but the rest of the army got away. The Russians still fought as doggedly, even heroically, as they had before, and in spite of shortages of guns and ammunition now beginning to show up among the combat units, they still put up a stiff fight. This Winter Battle of Masuria was fought in the midst of the worst possible weather, blizzards and intense cold, and some German units lost a third of their strength to frostbite. When both sides gave over, exhausted, late in February, the Germans had inflicted another 200,000 casualties. But they had not won their war.

A microcosm of the great battles in the north was fought out between Austria and Serbia, who waged virtually their own private war during the opening stages of the larger conflict they had unleashed. The Serbs had a small, tough army of about 200,000 men under Field Marshal Radomir Putnik. The Austrians started out with perhaps 300,000 in two armies, 5th and 6th, under the supreme command of General Oscar Potiorek. The disparity in numbers was offset by the fact that the Serbs had three unfordable rivers guarding their frontier, and their country itself was barely passable to a modern army. It was equally offset by the fact that Putnik was an extremely able soldier, his army battle-tested in the Balkan wars, while Potiorek was simply another also-ran.

Therefore, when the Austrians launched their invasion of Serbia on August 12, the Serbs fell back slowly before it. Only 5th Army made any real progress, and as soon as it was far enough out on a limb, Putnik dealt it a sharp rap at the Jadar River, and within ten days, the Austrians were back over the frontier on their own territory, sadder but wiser than they had been before.

Two weeks later Putnik decided on his own invasion and moved across into Bosnia, hoping to inspire a revolt among the Slavs in these always fractious areas. He had little luck and had to scuttle back into his own hills when the Austrians launched their second invasion of Serbia on September 8.

Once more Putnik's little army fought a ferocious series of battles. The fact that the numbers here were smaller than in the other theaters of war did not mean the battles were any less vicious—in fact the contrary was often the case, as Slav and Magyar and Teuton slugged it out with a sort of primitive tribal ferocity. This time the Serbs were slightly less successful, and when both sides had fought to exhaustion, the Austrians still held toeholds on the enemy side of the frontier rivers.

Putnik concluded that his position was pretty vulnerable, especially to a flanking drive from the north, so when Potiorek opened his third invasion, in the first week of November, the Serbs slowly fell back. The poor terrain and the bitter weather—snow in the higher passes—were doing the Serbs' work for them. Putnik gave up his capital, Belgrade, without a fight, then, after a month of letting the Austrians drag themselves into the interior, he struck.

There was no real plan, just a straightforward push by thousands of fighting-mad Serbs. The Austrians tumbled back down the rough hills and mountains a great deal faster than they had climbed them, and in mid-December Belgrade was freed again, and the third invasion of Serbia was over. The Austrians decided to give it up for the winter, having lost just about half of the 450,000 men they had put all told into the effort. The Serbs had lost just under half of the 400,000 they had eventually mobilized, but they were happy to give over, too; a typhus epidemic was adding to their troubles.

So the winter rains and snows came on. The ground dissolved into mud and then froze. The weather covered the mounds of decomposing flesh and rotting clothing that had once been men, mounds that lay scattered thinly here, piled thickly there, on the plains of northern France, in the valleys of the Vosges, around the bogs and lakes of East Prussia, and along the slopes of the Carpathians. The war was to have been over in six or eight weeks, perhaps three months at the outside, and for substantially more than a million men, it was. They had gone forth in the pride of manhood and youth, and they had fought, and died, as animals. And now the survivors lived as animals, huddling in burrows in the ground, digging like moles. So far had their search for glory brought them.

# 6. The War at Sea

IF EVENTS ON LAND, with their indecisive ferocity, confounded the prophets, so too did the war at sea. Here imaginative theorists had developed a carefully constructed scenario of the course of the war. Once again they were mistaken. The most inventive writer of futuristic fiction before the war could not have sold a plot in which he accurately predicted that when war broke out, very little would happen at all.

Naval games had been one of the parlor preoccupations of the Edwardian era. The British believed they had the greatest navy in the world and had always had it and would always have it. After a struggle that lasted two and a half centuries, Britannia had ruled the waves triumphantly, so triumphantly that for three generations after Trafalgar in 1805 there had not even been a serious contender for her place. To nineteenth-century Englishmen this seemed no more than the proper order of things, and they took it as a matter of course that this happy state should prevail forever.

The truth was less palatable than reality, for in fact the British had coasted on their laurels for a century and had grown complacent and careless in their dominance. The late nineteenth-century Royal Navy was a comfortable club ruled over by a group of old fuddy-duddies who thought God had ordained what their grandfathers had fought to achieve. There were on record captains who threw overboard their annual allotment of practice shells rather than have the powder smoke dull their paint- and brass-work.

In the later part of the century this complacency was challenged, both internally and externally. A group of younger officers within the navy began a virtual revolution in gunnery, propulsion, and signaling techniques. The navy was so massive, so cumbersome, so tradition-bound an organization that the change could not occur at the center; it was rather like the Copernican Revolution, attacking established authority on the periphery of its system and then gradually working its way to the middle. The change finally reached the heart of the navy with the advent of Admiral Sir John Fisher as First Sea Lord, and though Fisher was only the most famous of many reformers, his was the name the public associated with the new navy, and his the creation that typified it, the dreadnought-type battleship.

The *Dreadnought* was launched in 1906 and was to the public a major revolution in naval development, the first all-big-gun battleship. That the British introduced such a ship was more a tribute to their building capacity and Fisher's drive than to their inventiveness, for the idea had been in the air for several years and really went back to an Italian designer, Vittorio Cuniberti. The claim that the British, by introducing the new type, had therefore willfully sacrificed their great lead in the older type of battleship was quite mistaken.

With the advent of the dreadnought the world had a new currency in which to count naval power. Setting aside the whole complex problem of naval strength and what was necessary for it, the newspapers of the world simply counted dreadnoughts. A naval fever gripped the industrialized world, and the naval building race became a major feature of prewar tension. It reached the dizzying heights of mobs in London chanting, "We want eight, and we won't wait!" and the great naval reviews of the day were viewed as an expensive form of sporting event, in which one side's dreadnoughts were toted up against another side's, to the delight of Sunday supplement readers. By 1914, the Royal Navy had twenty to Germany's thirteen, and the lesser powers had smaller numbers, so that different situations could be created by predicating different likely or unlikely combinations.

Against the British, it was the Germans who counted most, for in the nineties Germany had replaced France in naval affairs as well as others. Until the eighties, the French were still perceived as the major threat. Their sailors and theoreticians had, as always, grappled with the problem of how to defeat Great Britain when they did not possess the brute strength to do so. They had come up with an old idea dressed in new clothes. Led by the Minister of Marine, Admiral Aube, French sailors produced the *Jeune École* ("Young School") of thought. It was obvious to them that Great Britain was increasingly dependent on imports, both of food and raw materials, for her survival, let alone her predominance. Therefore, the French concluded that commerce warfare, which they had practiced for centuries, unsuccessfully, could now bring Britain to sue for peace. The Mistress of the Seas was herself subject to strangulation.

The tragedy of French naval history had always been that with excellent material, her navy had pursued a faulty doctrine; now, ironically, with an excellent doctrine, France, and the rest of the world as well, went off on what was arguably a faulty material tack. By the early twentieth century, inventors were producing the commerce raider *par excellence*, the submarine. No one initially saw it as that, however; the early submarine ideas were concentrated on using it as an adjunct to battle fleets, and hardly anyone before 1914 thought man would be so inhuman as to use a submarine against merchant ships. Instead, the naval world followed the teachings of American Admiral A. T. Mahan, that the battle fleet was the be-all and end-all of naval warfare and that commerce warfare could never win against a fleet possessing major battleship strength. As this was what the British had believed all along, they happily accepted Mahan's ideas; and so, perhaps unfortunately for themselves, did the Germans.

It was the Germans who now presented the external challenge to the Royal Navy's complacent supremacy. And as the new Royal Navy was considered the child of Fisher, so the new German Navy was the child of one man, Admiral Alfred von Tirpitz. Before his day, the navy had been little more than an adjunct to the German coast artillery. It was Tirpitz who gained the Kaiser's ear, and in the nineties he and his master embarked on a building program the end-product of which could be aimed only at the Royal Navy.

The British, who were usually well disposed toward Germany, never understood why the strongest land power in the world, one to whom a navy was and could only be of peripheral importance, insisted on building up major naval strength. In fact, few people ever since have understood it, for the German Navy was based on intangibles, and on long-standing feelings of inferiority. The Germans wanted a navy not because they needed one, but simply because they *wanted* one. Any arguments based on reason paled before that irrational fact. So they built a navy, and of course, being Germans, they built an excellent one. Their ships were marginally better than the British equivalents, for they did not have the world-wide problems and commitments the British had.

Lacking a far-flung empire and trade responsibilities, they were able to build a battle fleet simply to meet the Royal Navy in the North Sea. Not designed for exceptionally long periods on foreign stations, their ships could feature better compartmentalization and therefore better damage control than the British. The growing High Seas Fleet soon became the major bugbear of the Royal Navy.

Though the British were annoyed by these developments, they were certainly not intimidated. They tried to reach accommodation with the Germans, but the Germans refused to accept the validity of British claims about the vital nature of sea power for Britain and its secondary nature for Germany. So the British matched and outmatched the Germans; if Germany wanted a naval race, she should have it. Fisher muttered to King Edward about the desirability of a "Copenhagen" against the Germans, referring to the time during the Napoleonic wars when Britain had launched surprise attacks against the neutral Danish fleet to prevent its coming under hostile control. But in the end, the British just settled down to outbuild the Germans and to wait until they came to their senses; they never did.

When war broke, then, both sides possessed major battle fleets concentrated in the North Sea, and both expected immediate action. Sailors and the public alike anticipated a sudden clash of arms, a sort of super-Trafalgar, one glorious climactic burst of fire. And of course when the smoke cleared, there would be the Royal Navy, ruling the seas as always, and the world would continue on its ordered course.

Since the outnumbered Germans pretty well shared this vision and since they had a sensible desire not to figure in it in their expected role, they simply refused to come out. The great clash did not occur. A generation brought up on the glories of Trafalgar forgot that that one stupendous day had been preceded by more than a decade of hard grinding work. And was followed by almost another decade's work.

It was to be nearly two years before the great fleets met in battle, and in all those months, both sides groped for each other. There was some fighting and a great deal of dogged routine effort, but except for a few flareups, little of it made headlines. As far as the Royal Navy was concerned, the headlines were bad as often as they were good.

To put it in some kind of order, which the events themselves really denied, there were three types of actions. First was a series of clashes as the British dealt with various German units either at large when the war began, or subsequently sent out through the blockade to function as commerce raiders. Second was the preliminary sparring between light and medium units in the North Sea, which was eventually to lead to the main battle-fleet action. Third was the process by which the submarine gradually intruded on the consciousness of both British and Germans, growing for the former from nuisance to major menace. The first of these series was pretty well played out in 1914–15, the second through 1916, and the third lasted through the whole war.

With the enemy units at large on war's outbreak the British first found themselves engaged in the Mediterranean. In this sea so vital to their imperial interests, they had made an agreement with the French. The latter, who were transferring troops from their North African Empire to metropolitan France, were to dominate the western Mediterranean; the British, from bases at Malta, Cyprus, and Alexandria, were to look after the eastern end.

The Central Powers had substantial numbers of ships in the inland sea. Austria-Hungary held six battleships and several cruisers at her base at Pola on the Adriatic, but they were not of too much concern; geography told heavily against the Austrians when it came to naval power. Also at the Austrian port were the German battle cruiser *Goeben* and the light cruiser *Breslau*. Against these the British had a battle-cruiser squadron of three ships, plus four armored cruisers, an aging intermediate type of vessel that died out during World War I, four light cruisers, and four destroyers. The British immediately set out to trap the Germans.

British commanders assessed correctly that the Germans would try to interfere with the French crossing of the western Mediterranean. German Admiral Souchon successfully got out of the Adriatic trap just as war was declared and headed west before the British could cut him off. He threw some shells into a couple of Algerian ports, with little result, topped up his bunkers with coal at Messina in Sicily, and took off again. He evaded the armored cruisers patrolling the mouth of the Adriatic in wait for him and steamed east, at one point exchanging long-range and ineffectual salvos with the shadowing *Gloucester*.

The British had missed one vital piece in the puzzle. Both they and Souchon believed the Germans were trapped, but they assumed the enemy could only attempt an attack on the French or scoot back into the Adriatic. Unaware that Turkey had signed a secret alliance with Germany even before war began, they discounted the possibility that Souchon would head for what they thought was neutral Constantinople. This was exactly where he did go, and on August 10, the two ships steamed into the Dardanelles and slowly up the Sea of Marmora to Constantinople, where they were greeted deliriously by the Turks. The British were immensely chagrined, they court-martialled their Mediterranean commanders, who were acquitted—the failure had been basically one of diplomatic intelligence—and two days later the German government announced the "sale" of the two ships to the Turks. Even this was another slap in the face, for the Turks had contracted to have battleships built in British yards, and these were taken over by the Royal Navy at the opening of the war, against vigorous Turkish protests. Within three months, the *Goeben* was leading Turkish attacks on Russian bases in the Black Sea, bringing Turkey overtly into the war.

If the *Goeben* affair was humiliating, the next clash was disastrous. A substantial German squadron under Admiral Graf von Spee was at large in the Pacific. Based at Tsingtao, on the China coast, where Germany had acquired a concession in the nineties, the squadron was at Ponape in the Carolines on a training cruise when war was declared. They were thus advantageously distant both from the British at Hong Kong and the Australians at Sydney, as well as from the Japanese, who insisted on coming into the war on Britain's side for reasons of their own. Admiral von Spee decided his best bet was to sail for the west coast of South America, where he would get a friendly welcome in Chile, and where he ought to find numbers of British shipping to harass. He detached the light cruiser *Emden* on a raid into the Indian Ocean and took his little fleet eastward.

While the Germans made a pleasant cruise across the southeastern Pacific to Valparaiso, picking up a couple of west coast cruisers on the way, numerous British merchant ships cleared the South American coast, getting safely through the Panama Canal or around the Straits of Magellan. The British Admiralty had stationed a smallish squadron off Pernambuco in Brazil under Admiral Christopher Craddock. They instructed him that as his force was enlarged, he should extend his patrol area south to the

Plate Estuary, and then when he felt strong enough, around to the Chilean coast.

In this game of hide and seek the advantages were all with the Germans: to protect their commerce, the British had to be everywhere; to attack it, the Germans had only to be in one place at one time. Late in October, Craddock moved south with a small force built around the old predreadnought battleship *Canopus.* She was so slow and weak that he eventually left her behind to catch up as she might, and when he moved into the Pacific, his squadron consisted of two armored cruisers, *Good Hope* and *Monmouth*, the light cruiser *Glasgow*, and the armed merchant ship *Otranto*. With this weak, ill-assorted force he met von Spee off Coronel on November 1.

The Germans had everything in their favor. Their two armored cruisers, *Scharnhorst* and *Gneisenau*, were the best in the fleet, and their three other cruisers were modern units. They had better fire-control systems than their adversary, and the circumstances of their meeting silhouetted the British against the afterglow of the sun, leaving the Germans hidden in the evening haze of the Chilean coast. Craddock might conceivably have run for it. Instead, at 6:18 in the evening, he sent his last signal, "I am going to attack the enemy now."

Though the gunnery duel lasted for more than an hour, there was never the slightest question of the outcome. The entire German squadron suffered only six hits and two men wounded. The British flagship, *Good Hope*, took more than thirty hits herself. She blew up and sank at eight o'clock. The Germans ran down the crippled *Monmouth* and finished her off an hour later. *Glasgow* and *Otranto* slipped away into the darkness.

The waves had hardly closed over the two British ships before the storm of their sinking hit the Admiralty. There was bitter criticism in the press, by no means ill-informed, of the Admiralty's measures and of the amateurish meddling of the political First Lord of the Admiralty, Winston Churchill, in the deployment of the navy. Something had to be done, and fast. While the Germans went north to celebrate their victory at Valparaiso, the Royal Navy sent a major force dashing south to the Falkland Islands. By December 7 Admiral Sir Doveton Sturdee had concentrated there with two battle cruisers, *Invincible* and *Inflexible*, and three more armored cruisers, as well as several lesser vessels.

Sturdee's task was still a needle-in-a-haystack affair, and it was whispered in the corridors of the Admiralty that he had been given the command because Fisher, the First Sea Lord, did not like him. Not that Fisher wanted him to fail; however, if by chance he did, the ax might as well fall on someone Fisher would just as soon be rid of. But von Spee conveniently put his head in the noose. The Germans showed up at the Falklands less than twenty-four hours after Sturdee's arrival. Had they borne right in, they might have caught the British coaling and in complete disarray; instead they turned and began to run for it.

The British were slow clearing the harbor, but this time nature was on their side. It was a fine day with unlimited visibility, the British had the advantage in both speed and gunpower, and they now did to von Spee what he had done to Craddock. Of eight German ships, only two escaped, a coal collier to be interned in Argentina, and the small cruiser *Dresden*, to be run down and blown up off Chile three months later. The German tap had been answered with a hammer blow.

There were assorted other taps, all annoying, but all eventually futile. The *Emden*, detached from von Spee's squadron, cruised successfully in the Indian Ocean for two months; she sank a Russian cruiser and a French destroyer, as well as 70,000 tons of British shipping. She also performed a couple of shore bombardments, including, interestingly enough, one on the Indian coast at Madras as an incentive to the Indians to rid themselves of the British. But in the second week of November she was caught by the Australian cruiser *Sydney*, which stood off at long range and pounded her to death. The *Karlsruhe* raided profitably in mid-Atlantic until an internal accidental explosion sank her, and various other raiders also achieved some embarrassment of the British. Yet by the end of 1914, virtually all of them were hunted or already caught. The vast complex of ships, bases, and signaling stations that made up the Royal Navy showed its true value, and by 1915 British commerce was proceeding almost as if it were peacetime. The submarine was yet to come, but the surface threat, outside the North Sea, was practically mastered. Britannia still ruled the waves.

While all these affairs took place on the oceans, the main fleets on either side of the North Sea continued to sniff at each other like two suspicious and potentially angry dogs, neither of whom quite dared try conclusions with the other. The British definitely had the edge in numbers, as well as an overwhelmingly favorable geographical position. Under the overall command of Admiral Sir John Jellicoe, a cautious but canny and thorough professional, the Grand Fleet had its main units concentrated north of Scotland in Scapa Flow, a barren, windswept anchorage in the Orkney Islands. A small portion of it was at Cromarty Firth in northern Scotland, and the battle cruisers were at Rosyth, a bit farther down the coast. Light units were guarding the Channel from Harwich, just above the mouth of the Thames. All in all, the fleet was stationed in a long arc across the line of German advance.

The Germans, on the other hand, possessed but a short North Sea coastline, and their possibilities were very limited. Their main fleet base was in Jade Bay, at Wilhelmshaven, just west of the mouth of the Weser River. To watch the British bases, German patrols had to cover an arc 600 miles long; the British had less than a hundred miles to keep under observation.

Both sides adopted a wait-and-see strategy. The British knew they were essentially dominant, and that all they had to do was preserve the status quo to stay that way. If this seems to lack the Nelson spirit, it must be said in Jellicoe's defense that he had more to lose than to gain by any ill-advised action. Britain was more dependent on her navy than Germany was on hers, and Jellicoe, in Churchill's often-quoted remark, really was "the only man who could lose the war in an afternoon." What the press and public eventually forgot was that the converse was not true, and he was not the only man who could *win* the war in an afternoon. Right from the start, Jellicoe announced he intended to play a careful game. He assumed that if the German High Seas Fleet came out, it would do so only if it thought it had a good chance to trick or trap him, by drawing him into a mine or torpedo ambush which would reduce his numbers and give the Germans a fair shot at him. So he declined to be drawn.

The Germans for their part displayed precisely the attitudes inferior but aspiring naval powers have always displayed. Having built a powerful and impressive fleet, they then were scared to use it for its designed purpose: to fight. The sailors and officers were madly anxious to come to grips with the British, as indeed the British were to meet them. But the higher commanders, and most particularly of all the Kaiser, dared not risk the ships on which they had lavished so much time, money, and affection.

Their beautiful battleships were toys too expensive to play with. At the beginning, of course, the sailors were totally subordinated to the army's view of how the war would go, and it seemed senseless to risk destruction of the fleet in a war that was scheduled to be won in six weeks anyway.

So the Germans did little to interfere with the passage of the British Expeditionary Force to France. A German minelayer, the *Königen Louise*, was caught and sunk, though not before she had sown mines that sank a British cruiser in return. Then each side settled down to a wary patrolling routine, hoping to steal a march on the other.

The Germans quickly established a standard pattern. Before dark every day they sent a destroyer force out from Jade Bay to the area just west of the island of Heligoland, which controlled the approaches to their base. The destroyers were accompanied out by a supporting force of cruisers, which then went back home. At daylight the cruisers came out again and took the destroyers back in with them.

British submarines on the prowl in Heligoland Bight soon picked up this pattern and reported it back to Harwich, where their light forces were concentrated. The submarine force commander, Commodore Roger Keyes, got together with the cruiser force commander, Commodore Tyrwhitt, and together they sold the Admiralty the idea of trapping the Germans.

The ensuing Battle of Heligoland Bight, fought on the morning of August 28, was a minor triumph that might very well have been a disaster. The British sent out a decoy force to draw the Germans westward, plus a trapping force to cut them off. Then, unknown to both of these, the Admiralty sent out two further forces of progressively heavier units in support. Meanwhile, the Germans, picking up an unusual amount of radio traffic on their listening devices, decided the British were up to something and chose to trap the trappers in their turn. So they sent out extra forces as well. When they all came together around Heligoland at first light and shortly thereafter, there was a very considerable mixup. The British, with much the heavier metal, succeeded in sinking a German destroyer and three light cruisers in return for very slight damage to their own ships. However, several British ships very nearly fired at other British ships, and in one case a British cruiser tried hard to ram one of her own submarines. Churchill called it a "brilliant and timely episode" in which the

British enjoyed very good luck. They certainly had good luck, and it was timely; at the end of August, 1914, Allied newspapers were desperate for any positive news. But the action was far less than brilliant, and it was painfully obvious to the commanders on the spot that the Admiralty's meddling and trifling and sending units to sea without telling friendly vessels they were likely to meet had led to very real embarrassment. It was early days yet.

The overall effect, however, was very salutary for the Royal Navy: It gave the Kaiser cold feet. He was extremely distressed at the losses and issued strict orders that the High Seas Fleet was to undertake virtually no action at all without his express permission. As that permission was to be granted only if the sailors could guarantee an absolutely sure thing, and as there are few of those in war, Heligoland Bight may be said to have been a major setback for the Germans. Seldom could such minimal losses have been so damaging to a force.

The sparring continued. German battle cruisers threw some shells at the Yorkshire coast in December, and the British battle-cruiser force, under its energetic admiral, David Beatty, made another sweep into Heligoland Bight on January 19, 1915. This made the Germans decide on a trap of their own.

The High Seas Fleet commander, Admiral von Ingenohl, ordered Admiral Hipper to sea with his battle cruisers on January 23. They were to sweep out to the Dogger Bank in the middle of the North Sea, hoping to catch British light units by surprise. Hipper went out with three battle cruisers, *Seydlitz, Moltke*, and *Derf-flinger*, and the armored cruiser *Blücher*, as well as a variety of smaller supporting units.

Once more the British were ahead of him. Some months earlier the German cruiser *Magdeburg* had sunk in the Baltic. Russian divers had recovered her code books and had passed them on to the Admiralty. For the entire war, the British read the German radio traffic almost as if it were their own. Fifteen minutes after Hipper cleared Jade Bay, Beatty left Rosyth with five battle cruisers: *Lion, Tiger, Princess Royal, New Zealand,* and *In-domitable*. They were to meet various supporting and light units east of the Dogger Bank at daylight on the 24th.

Everyone showed up right on schedule, the British meeting just before seven and the Germans arriving as arranged—though not by them—a few minutes later. When his lookouts spotted the tripod masts of British heavy units over the horizon, Hipper discovered pressing business elsewhere and took off for the southeast, old *Blücher* struggling gamely to keep up in the rear.

Beatty settled in to a stern chase, with his ships in line off the Germans' starboard quarter. He had a slight edge in speed and gunpower, if a bit thinner armor, and it looked as if the Germans had a long day ahead of them. Then things began to go wrong.

The British opened fire as they came within range and started to haul up on the Germans. *Blücher* was soon hard hit, and Beatty shifted fire up the line to bring the more forward Germans under his guns. But the British ships got mixed up in their fire distribution, some counting targets from the front of the German line, some from the rear. *Seydlitz* was badly hit and saved from complete destruction only by the timely and sacrificial flooding of her after magazines. But all the Germans concentrated their fire on Beatty's flagship, *Lion*, and she was soon in trouble. A hit on her forward "A" turret went right through and put it out of action. Several more hits holed her on the exposed port side, and by midmorning she was listing and slowed to fifteen knots. She fell out of line, hoisting flag signals to the rest of her squadron to continue the action. Some of these were not seen in the battle smoke, and some were misinterpreted, so that, instead of closing with the fleeing and battered German battle cruisers, the entire remainder of the British heavy units swung off and pounded the already dying *Blücher* to death. As the overwhelmed armored cruiser rolled over and sank, the rest of the Germans escaped into the afternoon. Beatty was furious; he should have had all four; instead he got one, and that the weakest of the lot.

The Dogger Bank action was the first real fight between major units of the war. It was thoroughly analyzed by both sides, as neither was satisfied with its performance. The British made strenuous efforts to improve their tactical signaling and command procedures; they neglected the material side of the matter. The hits on *Lion* had shown that most battle damage was going to occur to horizontal surfaces, for the range of the fighting meant hits by plunging shells. The Germans improved their horizontal armor and their damage-control handling; the British did not. It was also obvious that there were deficiencies in British shells; they tended to break up on impact, rather than penetrating through the enemy's armor plating as they were supposed to do before exploding. Here again the British failed to correct deficiencies, and these were shortcomings that were going to cost the Royal Navy dearly at some point in the future.

Nevertheless, the British had again emerged ahead on points, and as before, the greatest effect of the battle was on the German naval commanders. Admiral von Ingenohl lost his job for having been too daring, an assessment by the Kaiser with which more junior officers would hardly agree. The new commander, Admiral von Pohl, was ordered not to risk his ships. By early 1915 the British appeared to dominate the North Sea as they did the rest of the world's oceans. Only the telltale track of the submarine periscope rippled the calm waters of their situation.

Conventional naval officers did not know what to make of the submarine. As did nearly all new weapons systems, it attracted a small band of prophets and devotees, who believed it was the answer to everything, and repelled a much larger number of people, who insisted long after they were proven wrong that it was worthless. The earliest submarines were far more dangerous to their own crews than to anyone else, but by 1914, they had become usable weapons. The chief problem was that no one knew exactly what to do with them.

In the first decade of the century, there had been conferences on the laws and usages of war, and the participants had agreed that the submarine would be used only in a way that made it effectively worthless anyway. Submarines could be employed freely against enemy warships, for warships and men in uniform were legitimate targets. As a commerce raider, however, the sub was supposed to take all the precautions a normal warship would; before sinking a merchantman it must stop it, search it and examine its cargo manifest to make sure it was carrying war matériel, give the crew and passengers time to abandon ship, and make provisions for the safety of everyone. This was such a tall order for a tiny, vulnerable submarine that it practically meant no commerce warfare. That, in turn, made little difference, as most theorists did not see it fulfilling that role anyway.

When war began Germany possessed eighteen submarines active in the North Sea. They were small, cruised at only five knots, and carried four torpedo tubes and several mines. Though both the torpedo and the mine were recognized as dangerous weapons, naval writers paid more attention to the torpedo boat and the torpedo-boat destroyer as delivery systems than to the submarine.

On September 5 the submarine U-21 sank the scout cruiser *Pathfinder* in the Firth of Forth. Less than three weeks later the submarine gave real proof of what it could do. Three British armored cruisers, *Aboukir, Hogue*, and *Cressy*, were on patrol off the Dutch coast in an area known as the Broad Fourteens. The cruisers had been refitted from the Reserve Fleet and were manned with both reserve and new-intake men, as well as a contingent of naval cadets. They were following a regular, conventional patrol pattern when sighted by U-9. The German fired and hit *Aboukir*, whereupon both *Hogue* and *Cressy* stopped to help her. Neither of the latter two seems to have given much thought to the possibility of a submarine attack; their captains thought *Aboukir* had either hit a mine or perhaps had had an internal explosion in one of her elderly boilers. Presented with such a sitting target, U-9 promptly sank *Hogue* and *Cressy*, too. There was very considerable loss of life and vehement criticism of the Admiralty by the pundits for putting such vulnerable ships in a dangerous spot. The British quickly discovered that the submarine was going to be more trouble than they had thought and began some serious experimentation on anti-submarine devices.

Meanwhile, something like a submarine panic swept the Grand Fleet, and lookouts everywhere sighted submarines with alarming regularity. Four more warships were actually sunk before the end of the year, and at one point the main battle-fleet was so windy that it was withdrawn from the North Sea, first to the west coast of Scotland, and then over to Lough Swilly in Northern Ireland, while the submarine defenses of Scapa Flow were strengthened. Even this withdrawal was costly, for one of the newer battleships, *Audacious*, hit a mine off the Irish coast—the mine had been laid by the auxiliary cruiser *Berlin*, not by submarine—and blew up and sank while the British were trying to tow her to port. That was on October 27, so as early in the war as that the German submarines were making their presence felt and were even influencing the strategic dispositions of the Grand Fleet. Obviously, as a new weapon the submarine was a comer.

It was not yet a commerce raider. By the end of 1914 the Germans were still not interfering with merchant commerce. The British, however, had immediately proclaimed the Central Powers to be under blockade and were already searching and seizing ships bound for Germany. Naval blockade was a noose providing for slow strangulation of an enemy, and the British planned to tighten that noose just as much as they possibly could. The Germans, with their own commerce raiders swept from the seas, would soon be looking for ways to weaken British trade in return. The way this war was shaping up, no one who possessed a workable weapon was likely to refrain long from employing it.

# 7. The Western Front, 1915

SIX TO EIGHT WEEKS of war had come and gone and had stretched to more than twenty, and still there was no decision, and not likely to be one for the foreseeable future. All of the prognosticators had been proven false. The one who had come closest to reality, Ivan Bloch, had been mistaken when he said that the interlocked world economy would prevent a long war. It was true that governments, had they had to spend only what they possessed, would already be feeling the pinch of near-bankruptcy. However, the tremendous burst of patriotism and nationalistic fervor that had greeted the war had also unlocked the springs of credit. Government bond issues were subscribed and oversubscribed within hours of their offering, and, contrary to Bloch's ideas, the world did not dissolve in financial panic. Instead, there was an incredible surge of business and investment prosperity. For everyone from prostitutes to munitions manufacturers to retirees with pension funds to invest, the war was a source of potential profit. In spite of the stupefying casualty lists, by the start of 1915 the iron had not yet sunk into Europe's heart.

With the preconceptions shown to be false, reassessment was now necessary. What kind of war was this, and how was it to be waged and won? After Joffre's first Champagne offensive the Western Front had temporarily quieted. The Eastern Front was still ablaze but obviously not in a decisive way. Both sides had to stop and ponder. Faced with a new equilibrium, a new stalemate, what were they to do?

Von Clausewitz, sitting scribbling notes in his study at the War Academy, had written that war was but an extension of politics, politics, if you like, carried from the plane of talk to the plane of action. The state chose to achieve certain aims, and having made its choice, it then pursued them. If it could attain its ends by diplomacy, so much the better, for that was usually cheaper, and as a process was less susceptible to loss of control than war. But if the desired ends could not be achieved by diplomacy, then the state moved to employ force: It went to war. In spite of having served through the Napoleonic wars, Clausewitz saw nothing immoral—or indeed moral—about this: This was simply reality.

It was certainly the reality of the early twentieth century. Europe had been poised on a knife-edge equilibrium, divided into hostile camps each of which feared and distrusted the other. Eventually, the tension had become too great, the forces of disequilibrium had overpowered those of equilibrium, and Europe had gone to war in the confident expectation that resort to this new level of activity would resolve the perceived difficulties.

Clausewitz, however, had dimly seen—he died before he fully worked out the nuances, which is why his work is so difficult to read—that war tends to get out of control. He had written that once war was joined, "Each of the adversaries forces the hand of the other, and a reciprocal action results which in theory can have no limit."

Here lay the fly in the ointment of the Clausewitzian world. The theoretically limitless adversarial response had always before been limited by extremely practical circumstances. The states of the preindustrial, prepopular-government world had never managed to engage in "total" war. They had never been able to raise the money for it, they had never been able to conscript sufficient numbers of their subjects or citizens to wage it, they had never been able to produce enough surplus from a subsistence economy to generate immense amounts of war matériel. The religious fervor of the early seventeenth century had died out and was not replaced by an equally deadly devotion to an ideal until the rise of nationalism. But now, a mere eighty years after Clausewitz had written, the European world possessed all the necessary ingredients to carry its wars to totality. The theoretically limitless reciprocal action could be pursued much farther than it ever had been in the past. Governments could generate credit, factories could spew out guns, planes, and endless ammunition supplies, and men could be induced to die for slogans in greater numbers than ever before. And at the start of 1915, they still stood in the shallows of the water; no one knew yet just how far war could or would go. While the generals and leaders groped for some way out of their difficulties and adjusted to new realities, the war took on a life of its own.

Spring of 1915 brought both a quickening sense of great events and a growing feeling of frustration. The fighting had assumed a static pattern of deadlock, and in this year leaders had to attempt some alternative to the stalemate along the trenches. They explored all sorts of expedients to break the equilibrium: diplomatic, in the search for new allies capable of tipping the balance; strategic, in an effort to open up new fronts of action that might exert definitive leverage on the main fronts of the war; technological, as each side sought to develop new gadgets and weapons to give them an edge in the fighting.

For both Germans and British, there was disagreement among the higher leaders as to how the war should be handled. In Germany the new Chief of the General Staff, General von Falkenhayn, was convinced that the war could be won for Germany only in the West; he saw that it had now become a war of attrition, in which victory was to be achieved only by wearing down the enemy to a point of exhaustion. He wanted to do this to France and Britain. It was obvious that the German forces were qualitatively superior to the Russians, and that the Russians were therefore vulnerable. But the great distances of the Eastern Front gave the Russians room to retreat almost indefinitely, and von Falkenhayn therefore believed an attrition victory could not be obtained in the East. He wished to fight in the West. He and his views, however, were both overshadowed by the increasing influence of the victorious pair from the Eastern Front, Hindenburg and Ludendorff. Having made their mark in the East, they continued to believe and to assert with all the strength of their formidable reputations that they could win the war in their theater if permitted to do so. After acrimonious discussion, the German higher commanders finally agreed on a defensive posture in the West, while they tried to win the war against Russia.

The British had the same sort of problem, for they too developed at an early stage differences of view between "Westerners" and "Easterners." In 1915 the former were led by Sir John French, who as commander of the B. E. F. naturally believed that the war would be lost or won in France and that everything Britain could give should go into the Western Front, and Lord Kitchener, the Secretary of State for War, who was in the process of building up a massive volunteer army to fight in France. The term "Easterner" was something of a misnomer for the opposition to this group in the War Cabinet, for they did not particularly want to fight in the East *per se;* rather they wanted to fight anywhere but on the Western Front, and especially anywhere that British sea power and what they saw as England's traditional mobility and amphibious capability might be brought to bear. Why, they asked, fight the war in accordance with the German view of how it ought to be done? Why not use their advantages rather than beat their heads against the Germans' strong defenses? The leaders of this view were Sir John Fisher and, even more, Winston Churchill, the First Lord of the Admiralty, the most warlike of the civilian members of the government.

For the moment the point was academic, as the British were still building their armies and, until they were built, had to conform largely to the view of the war held by their allies, the French. And of course in France there was no such divided counsel. The French knew who the enemy was, where he was, and how he had to be fought. There was no other place for them than the Western Front. The Hun must be driven from the sacred soil of France. While the Germans concentrated on the East, and the British built their armies, 1915 was to be France's year—and a bitter, bloody one it was.

Joffre's attacks in the center of the front, which made up the First Battle of Champagne, collapsed and burnt themselves out by early March of 1915. While these were progressing to their expected and unhappy conclusion, the French leader planned a further offensive up in Artois. This was to be a corollary to Champagne, and he intended to seize the commanding height of the Douai Plain, a feature called Vimy Ridge; taking this would allow him to hit through to the German rail and road network that supported all the northern part of their front. To free troops for the task, he asked the British to extend their front and provide support for the attack.

Sir John French could not do it. The British were rapidly building up—they went from ten to thirty-seven divisions in 1915 —but they had not gone far by March, and many of the troops they did produce were siphoned off to the Mediterranean. Unable

to take over part of the French front as Joffre requested, the
B. E. F. commander decided to do even better: He would attack
the Germans on his own.

This he did at Neuve Chapelle on March 10, entrusting the
assault to General Douglas Haig's troops, which had now become
1st British Army. Haig had planned and prepared well. He unleashed the first really massive artillery barrage of the war, and,
pitting four divisions against one German, the British swept
forward and punched a sizable dent in the enemy line. They took
the village of Neuve Chapelle on the first day and looked by the
next morning as if they might break into the clear. However, they
lost their momentum while von Falkenhayn quickly rushed up
reserves, and the position stabilized by March 13. Haig had pushed
a salient a mile and a quarter wide and a thousand yards deep
into the German line at a cost of about 13,000 casualties; the
British thought they had done very well for themselves and believed that with a little better coordination and a little more refinement, they might well break through completely the next
time.

Before Joffre could reshuffle all his troops and launch his Vimy
Ridge drive, von Falkenhayn jumped off with an attack of his
own. Though committed to a western defensive, he had no intention of leaving the initiative wholly to the enemy. He designed
a limited operation around Ypres to straighten out his line, to
cover the fact that he was pulling units out and sending them
east, and to spoil the French preparations. This Second Battle of
Ypres began on April 22.

The fighting in late 1914 had left the Allies in possession of
a salient in front of the town of Ypres, about five miles deep and
six or seven across at its base. This ragged line was held by two
French divisions on the northern face and by General Smith-
Dorrien's 2nd British Army from there south, five divisions strong
in the salient. Against these von Falkenhayn massed eleven divisions. He also brought into play a new weapon, so Second Ypres
represented one of the early attempts to achieve surprise by technological innovation.

In the middle of the nineteenth century a mildly eccentric
British admiral, Lord Cochrane, had suggested that Britain might
attain permanent supremacy by the employment of a new weapon.
Two or three times committees of the Admiralty examined the
proposal and came to the conclusion that it was so hideous that

its use was quite unthinkable; any power that used poison gas would inevitably be branded as beyond the pale of civilization for all time and Cochrane's idea was quietly buried. Since that time, chemistry and warfare had both made rapid progress. Now, early in 1915, Allied intelligence heard rumors that the Germans might conceivably be going to use gas. Not knowing exactly what to do about it, the Allied commanders decided to do nothing.

They were little more lax in this than were the Germans, for though von Falkenhayn had agreed to give it a try, he did not think it would work. The technicians advising him thought Ypres was the best place for an experiment, having the optimum combination of trench lines, terrain features, and potential winds. But having prepared for the attack with gas, von Falkenhayn was so certain of its failure that he provided no reserves to exploit any breakthrough.

The Germans opened a short but intense bombardment on the afternoon of the 22nd, directed against the French troops, a division of Algerians and one of Territorials, reserves from the oldest classes. In the midst of the bombardment a yellowish-green cloud began rolling over the ground toward the French lines. It was chlorine gas, which attacks the lungs and respiratory system, destroying the mucous membranes of the air passages. As the cloud hit the Algerians' line they broke for the rear; the panic and the gas spread to the Territorials, and they too joined in with their fleeing comrades. Suddenly, there was a hole four miles wide in the Allied line. The Germans pushed boldly forward into this, until they met their own gas—and the Canadians.

The British flank, where it joined the French, was held by the 1st Canadian Division, some units of which had been in the line for little more than a month. Now, with their flank completely enveloped, choking and spitting, the Canadians held on grimly and threw back wave after wave of Germans. Whether possessed by the courage of innocence, or simply too ignorant of war to know when to run away, they fought and died in the midst of the swirling yellow fog. Many of those who survived the battle spent the rest of their lives in agony in veterans' hospitals, but for those crucial hours they provided a rock past which the German tide could not flow. By next morning the Allies had rushed up reinforcements and strung weak lines of troops across the gap.

General Foch, who was commanding the Northern Army Group, ordered an immediate counterattack. The French did nothing; they were still trying to collect their broken divisions. Smith-Dorrien, implying that Foch's orders were nonsense, which they were, proposed instead to retire back to a line just in front of Ypres. Sir John French was so angered by this sensible suggestion that he immediately sacked Smith-Dorrien and replaced him with Sir Herbert Plumer—who then retired to a line just in front of Ypres.

The battle went on into May, with both sides slugging it out, but the Germans never recovered their initial advantage. On May 24 they tried another even bigger gas attack, but the British held fast, though again with terrible casualties, and the next day the Germans gave up. They had flattened out the Ypres salient, though the Allies still held a gentle curve before the town. Von Falkenhayn suffered about 35,000 casualties, and the British and French nearly twice that. Such a casualty ratio was an impressive display of offensive skill; it would have been even more favorable for them had von Falkenhayn put any faith in his new weapon. As it was, he had forfeited a major potential advantage, especially since the prevailing winds over most of the front generally blew toward the German and away from the Allied lines. This was far from the last time that the value of a new invention was sacrificed because those who employed it did not really believe in it.

Von Falkenhayn's spoiling attack had taken much of the strength out of Joffre's Artois offensive, drawing off seven of the divisions slated for that operation, but it had not stopped it. Joffre was determined to get Vimy Ridge, and his attack opened in early May. With nine divisions up and nine in reserve, the French jumped off on the 9th after five days of heavy artillery preparation. These were first-class troops, the center corps of the assault commanded by Henri Philippe Pétain, now a general, and they made good progress. They drove the Germans back two and a half miles and fought their way up the western slopes of Vimy Ridge. At one point they reached the crest, then, as was now becoming the pattern, they were pushed off. The Germans could bring reserves forward faster over their undamaged communications system than the French could get theirs up through the morass of the battlefield. With the possibility of a breakthrough gone, the battle degenerated into a simple killing match, and finally both parties subsided after a week. There was a further flareup in June, but Vimy Ridge was securely German, and the French had lost another 100,000 men confirming that dismal fact.

The British supported this French effort with an attack to the north on the Aubers Ridge. They were, however, feeling the effects of ammunition shortages, their factories still not being fully geared for war, and the attack collapsed ignominiously. Then, responding to Joffre's pleas for further support, the B. E. F. attacked again at Festubert in mid-May. They gained three quarters of a mile and lost heavily doing so. When the British after Festubert asked for more troops from the Dominions, the Canadian Minister of Militia, Sir Sam Hughes, responded that for British tactics cattle would be more suitable than men.

The spring was now gone, and so was the Allies' offensive capacity. They were fought to a standstill. Sadly, Joffre decided he was not going to drive the Germans out of France this season. But he would try again in the fall. The Western Front quieted momentarily as the new troops trained for the slaughter, and the ammunition dumps began to grow once again.

Papa Joffre hoped to renew his offensive as quickly as possible, but the Allied buildup was hampered by severe shortages, especially of artillery shells. Nineteen fifteen was the year of "the shell crisis"; commanders complained that they never had enough artillery to support their operations; the British were particularly short, and their troops were forced to ration ammunition, so that the British batteries, only half as numerous as the French, were able to employ but limited quantities of shells. The home government got around this by appointing the energetic but obnoxious David Lloyd George as Minister of Munitions, and he gave the munitions industry such a thorough shake-up that eventually it was producing all that even the soldiers could demand. Surpluses were not available in 1915, however, and the British would have liked to wait until the next spring for the big offensive. Joffre insisted instead that it come as soon as possible, and the French were ready by September. The British reluctantly but loyally agreed to conform.

Joffre's plan was not very imaginative, but then, there was little that imagination could do with the Western Front. One flank rested securely on Switzerland, and the other on the Flanders seacoast. There was thus no chance of outflanking, at least as far as France itself was concerned. To maneuver around a flank one must first break through the line at some point and thus create the flank to begin with. So the attackers were once again reduced to a straight frontal attack. The only chance for surprise was in the matter of where that frontal attack might come.

Here again choices were limited. The terrain was too poor for any major attack southeast of Verdun; the French had indeed tried to pinch out the St. Mihiel salient in April and had been badly beaten up for their pains. From Verdun the line ran roughly west to Compiegne, then roughly north to Flanders and the coast. Joffre wanted to hit some place where a breakthrough would be to some advantage, where he would get to a communications nexus, and not just push the Germans farther back and then have to do it all over again. So he decided on a repeat performance of early 1915; he would again launch his main attack in Champagne, between Reims and Verdun. Then a subsidiary northern attack would try once more to take Vimy Ridge, while the British just to the left of that took Loos. It was the spring plan all over again, with minor juggling, but there seemed little else to do.

This, regrettably, was as patently obvious to the Germans as it was to the French. A military operation is like a large geometric theorem, and given the same known elements, commanders will pretty well come up with the same solutions. Von Falkenhayn and Joffre, faced with the same problem, though they were on opposite sides, reached essentially the same conclusion. The German chief called back four divisions from Russia and began to dig.

The magnitude of French preparations would have given the game away, even if von Falkenhayn had not been able to figure it out logically. For new roads had to be built, new ammunition dumps created, new assembly areas staked out for the assaulting troops. German patrols, aerial reconnaissance, and spies picked up the plan, and by the time Joffre was ready, so was von Falkenhayn. He developed a new defensive wrinkle, so Second Champagne marked another stage in the evolution of the art, just as Second Ypres did. Behind his first defensive line von Falkenhayn constructed a second one, thus initiating the concept of defense in depth. Now, if the French managed to break through the first line, they would simply come up against the second one. As Napoleon said, the art of war is very simple; everything is in the practice.

Joffre slated two of his best army commanders for the offensive, Pétain and de Langle de Cary. He massed more than thirty divisions on a fifteen-mile front, facing about twelve German, and he prepared down to the last detail. Cavalry stood waiting in reserve, ready to dash through the broken line and exploit a victory; buses were brought up to carry the reserve infantry through into open country. When the assault opened on September 25, the French were determined it was going to be a war winner.

Three days later it was all over. After heavy artillery preparation, the infantry had dashed boldly forward. Sweeping past the German defenders of the first line, they had broken triumphantly through a relatively thin frontline crust. At one point the German local commander was on the verge of giving up and ordering a full-scale retreat, but von Falkenhayn, hustling back from the East, arrived just in time to restore his confidence. At the same time, when the French had outrun their own artillery and were in the open, tangled up from getting through the German line, they ran headlong into the second line, well dug in, completely untouched by artillery and with its own artillery firing in support, free of French counterbattery fire. The great offensive stopped as if pole-axed, and Joffre, displaying far more wisdom than some of his colleagues, had sense enough to know when to stop.

But then, of course, the Germans counterattacked. They wished badly to recover the useless territory the French had taken, and so the battle seesawed on for another month, and it was the first week of November before the front finally quieted down. The French proclaimed a victory, and perhaps it was; they had taken about 20,000 German prisoners, almost all of them in the first three days, and well over a hundred guns. They had also inflicted 75,000 casualties on the Germans. It cost them 145,000 of their own, a high price to pay for a few square kilometers of valueless ground.

In the north the Allies did not even enjoy the illusory satisfaction of claiming a victory. In the Third Battle of Artois the French had another crack at Vimy Ridge. Again they tried as gallantly and bravely as flesh and blood could do; again they reached the crest of that blood-soaked ridge, and again the Germans came back as doggedly as before and drove them off. All through October the men in field gray and in the new French uniforms of the famous "horizon blue" grappled with one another, and when they finally fell back exhausted it was as it had been before. The Germans still held the ridge, and it was just that much more thickly strewn with bodies.

Even at that, what happened to the French paled before what happened to the British north of them. Sir John French had not wanted to attack when he did or where he did around Loos, which was a chopped-up coal field, but in both he had been overruled by Kitchener's loyal support of Joffre's plan. Haig's 1st Army attacked with six divisions, three of them regulars of the Old Contemptibles, one a Territorial division, made up of reserves, and the last two volunteer divisions of the "new army," men who had answered Kitchener's famous "I want you!" poster. Now they found out what Kitchener wanted them for.

In their assault, which coincided with that of the French to the south, the British employed poison gas themselves for the first time. It helped gain some initial successes, though in places it blew back and hampered their own advance. In the first day they got through the first German line and by nightfall were halfway to the second one. The followup force arrived exhausted and all mixed up during the night, thoroughly confused and marched practically off their feet.

When the British renewed their drive they came up against the second German line, just as the French had done. They could see no way to solve their problem except to fix bayonets, clamber out of their scratched-out trenches, form lines in open or extended order, and plod grimly forward.

The Germans in the second line could hardly believe their eyes, and memoir-writers recorded their shock at seeing these British troops come on as if it were a year earlier. For the German machine gunners, it was a pure slaughter, and they traversed up and down the rows, knocking the soldiers over as if they were ducks in a shooting gallery. In vain the British struggled to get forward, and in the few cases where they got that far, to break the enemy wire, but inevitably, they had too much and finally broke. It was one of the few occasions of the war when the Germans finally just gave up killing and let the vanquished flee to the rear, and the battle went down in German history as the *lechenfeld von Loos*, the "corpsefield of Loos."

Sir John French was finished, replaced as commander of the B. E. F. by the 1st Army commander, Douglas Haig, whose troops had just been slaughtered on the corpsefield. Haig had all the right connections, moneyed family, a tour as aide de camp to the King, a brilliant record, and he looked as good as—or at least no worse than—anyone else.

He was to have some time to get his feet under him anyway, for the weather had now broken, and the fighting on the Western Front was over for 1915. The butcher's bill had been enough for one year. The British losses had been about 279,000, and Loos had seen the end of the old British Expeditionary Force. There were few of them left now; they lay around Mons and Ypres and Festubert and Loos, and the old regular army was gone forever. Its survivors busied themselves training replacements and volunteers, for great things were expected in the spring.

The Germans too had suffered, though nothing like the casualty ratio of the British. Their losses for the year on the Western Front were tallied at 612,000; more than another half a million gone, still they held northeastern France, with no sign yet of being driven back whence they had come. Indeed, since Hindenburg and Ludendorff had not managed to win the war in the East in spite of all their promises, von Falkenhayn was now preparing to win it in the West.

He might well succeed, for the French were the most battered of all. The unceasing battles, the mindless dedication to the offensive, always the offensive, had cost them the frightful toll of 1,292,000 casualties in 1915 alone. It was an open question just how much more of that France could stand.

And yet there was no slacking. Through 1915 new countries had been sucked into the war, new theaters and fronts opened up, new possibilities explored. The war was becoming Leviathan, all-consuming; a juggernaut, crushing everything in its path. In 1915, the events on the Western Front had been but one disaster of many.

# 8. Widening the War: Turkey, Italy, and the United States

IT IS A RARE PEOPLE—or state—who, caught in a bad war, can have either sufficient sense or sufficient control over events to get out of it. Wars are meant to be won, and governments do not readily confess to mistakes, especially after they have killed several million of their citizens in the making of them. As soon as it became apparent to the belligerents that they were not going to achieve victory by late 1914, they began a frantic search for some magic ingredient that would solve their problem. To many of the leaders of France, Britain, Russia, Germany, and Austria, one obvious answer was to widen the war.

The widening process had already begun with the entrance of Turkey soon after the beginning of hostilities. By the turn of the year only the United States and Italy, of all the states that might be considered great powers, still held aloof, and Italy soon joined the war. The Americans were seen by Europeans as a rather peculiar breed, and in fact they needed special handling for most of the war before they finally consented to join actively in it.

The problem of Turkey, or the Ottoman Empire as it was then, was a major bone of contention for the European powers. The empire had for one thing been in decline since at least 1683, when the last great Turkish invasion of Europe swept up through the Balkans and the Danube Valley as far as Vienna. Since those glorious and gory days the Turks had slowly receded to the southeast. The Austrians and the Russians had taken successive chunks out of the empire, like sharks gnawing at the carcass of a dying whale, and through the nineteenth century the peoples of the Balkans had broken away as well and formed their own independent or semi-autonomous states; Serbia, then Greece, then Bulgaria and Rumania. By the end of the century Russian armies had marched to within smelling distance of the Golden Horn, and the Ottoman Sultans were kept on their thrones less by their own efforts than by the reluctance of the western powers to see Russians in the Mediterranean.

In return for this support, the western powers had demanded their own pound of flesh. Calling themselves the empire's friends, they had stripped her of her outlying possessions every time they demonstrated that friendship. In 1878, for example, Britain and France supported Turkey at the Berlin Conference. In return France took Tunisia away from her, and Britain took the island of Cyprus. Four years later the British were at it again and took over the control of Egypt.

One positive result of this gradual shearing off of the imperial territory was that it forced some Turks finally to restorative measures of their own. These were constantly hindered by Sultan Abdul Hamid II, but the cup ran over in 1908, and a group of mostly western-educated radicals calling themselves the Young Turk movement seized power. They reestablished the constitution Abdul Hamid had granted in a weak moment, set up a parliament, and as all good radicals do, immediately fell to quarreling among themselves. The next year the Sultan supported a counterrevolution, and when it fizzled, out he went, to be replaced by his inept brother, Mohammed V.

The real leadership of Turkey was now exercised by the Young Turks, but they remained hopelessly divided, especially on the issue of whether or not liberal principles ought to be extended beyond the Turks themselves and to the subject empire. One branch of the revolutionaries wished to grant freedom to the subordinate groups still under Ottoman control, another believed fiercely that freedom for Turks did not entail freedom for minorities.

The minorities had their own views on this, and in the years after 1908 there was ferment all around the empire. Restlessness in Christian Armenia resulted in the massacre of large numbers of Armenians by the Moslem Turks; indeed, the Armenians were one of the most-often massacred groups in history. The Albanians rose up in 1910, there was constant guerrilla warfare between the Turkish overlords and the Arabs in the Arabian Peninsula, and in 1911 Italy went to war with Turkey. Thwarted by the French grab of Tunisia of 1882, Italy now took over Libya as a consolation prize. Next the Balkan wars threw the shrinking empire into a ferment through 1912 and 1913.

Meanwhile, the great powers kept a watchful eye on all this traditional Levantine mayhem. The Austrians picked up bits and pieces where they could—hence the Bosnian-Herzegovinian crisis of 1908; Russia regarded the Serbs as her particular clients and cast covetous eyes toward the Dardanelles. Britain and France remained suspicious of Russian intentions, even after they became ostensible friends. Germany, initially under the cunning hand of Bismarck, played the "honest broker," assuring the Turks that she wanted nothing but friendship from them, a policy that paid handsome dividends. The Turks gave the Germans important economic concessions, and Germany embarked on the dream of the "Berlin-to-Baghdad railway." Perhaps even more important, German officers re-formed and revitalized the Turkish Army, so that by 1913, though no one in the West knew it, the Turks were leaning heavily to the German side.

The key element in this was the emergence of a politician named Enver Pasha; in 1913 he carried out a coup d'etat that left him and two colleagues in control of the country for the foreseeable future. Enver was markedly pro-German, so much so that late in the year he appointed the German general Liman von Sanders as virtual commander-in-chief of the Turkish Army.

The British still hoped they might preserve their officially friendly standing with the Turks, as it was now a long time since Britain had taken any of Turkey's territory away from her, but Enver was firmly committed to his German friends. In the midst of the Serajevo crisis he offered Germany a Turkish alliance directed against Russia. The Germans were delighted and wasted no time accepting. The offer was made on July 27, and the treaty signed on August 2. Few people knew of it, least of all the British, and they still thought Turkey was neutral until the *Goeben-Breslau* chase left them sadly disabused. The Germans had been marginally better friends than the British, and the Russians had certainly been far worse enemies than the Austrians, so Turkey slipped more or less naturally into the Central Powers' orbit. Late in October the Turks' ships bombarded Russian Black Sea ports, and in early November the appropriate declarations of war were exchanged. Britain immediately proclaimed the formal annexation of both Cyprus and Egypt, and at the turn of the year the Turks began their land war by a campaign in the Caucasus Mountains, directed as much against the Armenians as against the Russians.

* * *

Italy was accounted the weakest of the great powers, though in 1911 her population was only fractionally smaller than that of France. The existence of 35 million Italians counted less than the fact that the country was poor, lacking most of the basic resources of a modern industrial state, and still somewhat fragile politically, having been united for only half a century. Her attempts to achieve equality with the other states of Europe had been constantly prevented by one circumstance or another. The Hapsburg Empire still held substantial numbers of ethnic Italians in the north and around the head of the Adriatic, an area referred to by Italian patriots as *Italia irredenta*, "unredeemed Italy." The Italian hope of African empire had been upstaged by France's seizure of Tunisia in spite of the many Italians already living there and by defeat in Ethiopia, and the takeover of Libya had not provided an adequate compensation for previous humiliations. All these failures and shortcomings had resulted in a national history of frustration and thwarted ambition.

The Tunisian imbroglio had led Italy into alliance with Germany and Austria-Hungary, even though the latter was less popular with the Italians than France was. This Triple Alliance of 1882, as were all the treaties of the time, was a defensive one, and when war broke out, Italy stood on the letter of her agreement. As Germany and Austria-Hungary, by presenting ultimata, were legally and technically the aggressors, Italy was not obliged to enter the war on their side. She announced her neutrality.

Then, though the government had refused to enter the war, it demanded that Italy should still profit from the fighting. If Austria improved her position in the Balkans, Italy was entitled to compensation for that, even though she had done nothing to achieve it. And Italy had a clear idea of what she wanted: the Trentino, a salient of Austrian-held territory for which the Irredentists had been clamoring these forty years past. In November, when Baron Sonnino became Italian Foreign Minister, the claims increased in stridency.

This presented the Germans with a problem. They admitted there was some justice in the Italian claims, based both on ethnic lines and on specific articles in the Triple Alliance treaty. However, it was the Austrians and not the Germans who would have to pay the price of such justice, and the Austrians adamantly refused to do so; they had gone to war to keep their empire from falling apart, and they saw no reason to contradict that by giving away parts of it. Eventually, German representations prevailed, and the Hapsburg government allowed that yes it would cede the Trentino, but only after the war was won.

That was in March of 1915, but by then such a grudging concession was no longer sufficient. The Italians had upped their demands, and they wanted the South Tyrol immediately; a free state —that is, one dominated by them—around Trieste; and assorted islands that would give Italy both a stranglehold on the Adriatic and access to the hinterland of the Balkans. Not until May did the Germans badger the Austrians into granting these concessions as well, and by then it was too late; the Italians had taken their shopping list and gone elsewhere.

Buying Italian friendship was much easier for Britain and France than it was for Germany and Austria. Such a purchase required the latter two to surrender their own territory, held for generations. But Britain and France could offer the Italians large amounts of other peoples' territory; as it cost them nothing, they were willing to promise much. While Baron Sonnino was auctioning his support to Germany, the Italian Prime Minister, Antonio Salandra, was seeing what the Allies would pay. They bid not only everything and more that the Italians wanted from the Hapsburgs, but they also held out enticing views of imperial spoils. Italy's colonial territories of Libya, Eritrea, and Somaliland would be enlarged if Britain and France's empires were—and who could doubt that they would be?—and in the highly likely event that Turkey were partitioned, Italy was to get a whole Turkish province, that of Adalia. The Russians, still looking out for the interests of the Serbs, objected to giving Italy the entire Dalmatian coast of the Adriatic, but that was Russia's problem and Serbia's hard luck; Serbia was already in and need not be considered unduly. It was Italy that had to be wooed.

Some of the provisions of the Secret Treaty of London, signed on April 26, while Italy was still negotiating with the other side, were ironic to the point of absurdity. Italy was to get part of the war indemnity at the end of the war, she was to pressure the Pope not to initiate peace moves, and she was to commence hostilities within a month. The Allies promised to give Italy war loans, and strangest of all, to protect her from attack by Austria, though one might legitimately ask why a power who needed to be protected was such a desirable catch as an ally.

The country itself was in turmoil, with all sorts of groups vociferously championing one course of action or another. Some wanted Italy to remain neutral, some wanted to intervene on the side of the Allies, a smaller group perhaps wanted to join the Central Powers. Both Allies and Central Powers were busily supporting newspapers to propagandize their own point of view; the Allies, for example, subsidized a Socialist paper, *Avanti*, edited by a man named Benito Mussolini. So confused was the situation that Salandra resigned at one point; King Victor Emmanuel III refused his resignation, and he returned to power and took Italy into the war on May 23, 1915.

It was not all simply a land grab; there were historical claims to some of the territory Italy wanted, and Italians believed just as firmly as other Europeans that they had a role to play in what was then widely regarded as Europe's "civilizing mission." Yet Salandra's war cry of *Sacro egoismo*, "sacred egoism," was one that rang strange on the world's ears, and on Italy's, too, as soon as her sons found out what war was really like.

The new ally was poorly prepared for war. Her commander, General Luigi Cadorna, had about 875,000 troops in thirty-some divisions, far more than the Austrians could dispose on his immediate front. But he was short of artillery, transport, and all the ancillary services that keep an army functioning. The Austrians, already on a war footing and at the moment doing well in the East, were readily able to reinforce against him.

Even worse was the geographic and strategic situation, for it would have been difficult to devise a harder military problem than that faced by the Italians. The Italo-Austrian frontier, running about 275 miles from the Swiss border to the Adriatic Sea just west of Trieste, was in the shape of a rough S laid on its side. The western curve of the S extended down into Italy and was the Trentino; the eastern curve bulged up into Austria and put the Italians into a large salient. Virtually the entire frontier ran through mountains, and everywhere the Austrians held the higher ground. The Italians must fight east, north, and west with their communications threatened from the Trentino, and almost nowhere could they strike at a decisive target. The only slight possibility of gain lay at the very eastern end of the line, in the area between the Judrio and the Isonzo rivers. Here a drive of less than ten miles might gain the Austrian town of Gorizia. Such a drive was about all Cadorna could see to do; unhappily for the Italians, the Austrians knew that very well.

In spite of the difficulties of his situation, Cadorna loyally attacked on the day of Italy's declaration of war. His enemies elected to hold fast while they remained preoccupied with events on the Eastern Front, but they had about fourteen divisions to pit against the Italians, and the Germans, though not yet officially at war with Italy, sent down mountain units to help hold the Trentino.

Cadorna's 1st Army hit this salient from its southern face, and his 4th from the southeast. Their only possible line of advance was to clear the passes through the river valleys, the Adige Valley to the south and the Brenta on the southeast. Both routes led to Trent, and on from there to Bolzano. When the attacks opened, the Austrians fell back from the frontiers to a shortened line of fortified positions, and there they sat; nothing further the Italians could do served to dislodge them.

The Italian main attack was over in the east, toward the Isonzo River and Gorizia. Here again the Austrians gave up a little territory; before the drives of the 2nd and 3rd armies they surrendered the line of the Judrio River, which was not really defensible, and fell back to the Isonzo, which was.

The Austrian commander on the Isonzo front was a Hapsburg Archduke, Eugene. Accepting the deficiencies of his manpower, but believing correctly that that was more than compensated for by the strengths of geography, he committed his forces simply to holding their positions. In a small way, the situation was analogous to that on the Western Front: the onus of attack was on the Allies, and their enemies possessed the more favorable lines. But where heights in France were measured in tens of meters, in Italy and Austria they were measured in hundreds; the commanding hills east of the Isonzo towered more than 600 meters above the floor of the valley. Cadorna told his troops to drive over them.

Of course it could not be done, but Italian soldiers, in the name of *sacro egoismo*, tried as bravely as anyone could possibly have asked. On June 23 Cadorna launched the First Battle of the Isonzo; it collapsed with no appreciable gain by the end of the first week of July. Ten days later he began the Second Battle of the Isonzo, only to give it up with no gain on August 3.

By the time the weary soldiers recovered their breath and rebuilt their supplies and shattered formations, ten weeks had slipped by. Then, under the pressure of the coming autumn rains, cold at

Alpine heights and temperatures, they opened the Third Battle of the Isonzo in mid-October. It lasted until early November: no gain. Finally, desperate to break through before winter stopped them completely, from November 10 the Italians fought the Fourth Battle of the Isonzo. It ended on December 2, a happier day for the Austrians than it had been 110 years ago, for it was the anniversary of Napoleon's great victory at Austerlitz over them and the Russians.

Now the snows came on and covered the pitiful remnants of men and the debris of battle. Huddled in the cold, in holes and trenches scraped out of the living mountain rock, the men of both armies settled down to the grim task of surviving the winter, until spring, until they should be ready to fight all over again. For gains that were imperceptible, Cadorna had suffered 66,000 killed, 190,000 wounded, and more than 22,000 captured. He had, however, inflicted 165,000 casualties on the defenders, and for what it was worth, opened another front, like another bleeding sore, in the body of the Hapsburg Empire.

Neither the entry of Turkey on the Central Powers' side nor the entry of Italy on the Allies' had provided sufficient weight to tip the balance of war. The deadly equilibrium continued, yet politicians and military leaders still cherished the delusion that some small accession of strength to their own side would give them enough of an edge to win the war. Both sides pursued their attempts to win allies with unflagging vigor, casting promises before the uncommitted in the hope that they would return benefits. They courted Bulgaria, Rumania, Greece, Portugal, and dissident groups within each other's empires. But most of all they courted the last great neutral, the storehouse of money, supplies, and fresh manpower. Most of all they courted the United States.

When war broke out, President Woodrow Wilson was in the middle of his first term of office. He immediately declared American neutrality, and though he and other Americans were dismayed by the violence of the conflict and especially by the outrage to Belgium, he cautioned his country to be "impartial in thought as well as in action." The President himself was far more interested in domestic affairs than in foreign, and what little interest Americans had in matters beyond their own borders had recently been directed toward Latin America. If this were just another of Europe's endless progression of internecine squabbles, better leave them to it.

For Americans, times were good. The country was feeling the impulse to greatness. In fifty years the population had just about doubled, and there were 100 million Americans in 1914, surpassed among the nations only by Russia, India, and China. The United States produced more steel than her two nearest competitors, Germany and Britain, combined. In twenty years the exports of manufactures had increased more than 500 percent. The country built 1,700,000 automobiles in 1914. She was well on the way to replacing Britain as the "workshop of the world," and the future looked bright indeed. The war was a nuisance, and it was someone else's nuisance at that.

This initial attitude of lofty indifference soon ran into trouble. The vast majority of Americans came from Europe, and many of them had come fairly recently. Fifteen million Americans had been born in Europe, and the parents of many more than that were foreign born, too. Inevitably, they soon took sides. Generally, they sympathized with the Allies; the fact that English was the common language was of immeasurable value to Great Britain, and of course there were ties of sentiment with France that went back to the American Revolution. On the other hand, German immigrants were the largest single non-English-speaking group at the time; they were particularly strong in the Midwest, and they naturally supported the German view of events. Gradually, however, under the impact of German policies and British capitalization on them, opinion began to veer more and more strongly toward the Allies.

From the early stages of the war British propaganda was directed toward showing that the Germans were "the Hun," and that the British and the French were the defenders of the values of western civilization and of democracy as well. The autocracy of the Russian regime was played down, that of the Kaiser played up. German brutality was trumpeted to the skies, and in truth there was brutality to point up: The Germans had burnt the heart of medieval Louvain in Belgium, because they claimed Belgian civilians had sniped at them; they tried and shot the British nurse Edith Cavell, who had helped prisoners escape from behind German lines. Because the Germans did what they did, it was the more readily believed that they also did what the British and French said they did, and thus the Allied view of the war gained further acceptance in the United States.

More subtle, but probably more important in the long run, was

the effect of the war on the American business and financial community. As the only one of the big three industrial nations to be
neutral, the United States was soon flooded with orders for war
matériels, and since in the twentieth century almost every item
was war matériel, the entire economy felt a surge of prosperity.
Orders poured in from France, Britain, and Russia. There were
also orders from Germany and Austria-Hungary, but the Central
Powers were soon being squeezed out by the general Allied control
of the sea lanes. Preserving strict neutrality, the United States announced that anyone was free to buy, yet the British Empire disposed of more than 20 million tons of merchant shipping to
Germany's 5.5 million. It was not long before American business
and American buyers of war bonds came to have a vested interest
in an Allied victory. If Britain and France collapsed, a lot of
Americans were going to find themselves bankrupt.

In the last general European conflict, the Napoleonic wars, the
greatest issue between the belligerents and the major neutral state
was maritime rights. In Napoleon's day, the Americans had had a
near war with France and a real one with Britain over their claim
that a neutral ought to be able to go where he pleased and do as
he wanted. The same problem had arisen during the American
Civil War, with the Union this time playing the role of infringer
of neutral rights, and the British the defender of them. Now the
same thing happened all over again. Americans insisted they should
be free to trade with whomever they pleased, but both the Germans
and the British objected to this. At first, American antagonism
was directed chiefly against Great Britain, and she lost considerable
initial sympathy by her narrow interpretation of neutral rights.
Relying on the long-range impact of their sea power, the British
introduced several policies objected to by the Americans.

The problem of a naval blockade is that it is a relatively slow
weapon, and to be effective, it must be made as comprehensive as
possible. British attempts to make it so were regarded as highly
arbitrary and quite possibly illegal by the United States. First the
British declared the Central Powers, essentially Germany, to be
under blockade. The chief effect of this initially was a dramatic
increase in goods flowing to the neutral Scandinavian States, where
they were then being transshipped to Germany. The British responded by declaring an extension of their blockade from belligerents themselves to countries known to be trading with the enemy.
They next moved to a major lengthening of the contraband list, so

that items never before regarded as such were now listed as materials of war, and their import into a blockaded nation prohibited. To back up their position they began ordering neutral ships into Allied ports for search and verification of their papers. What really incensed Americans was the British practice of blacklisting any American firms known to be trading with the enemy and attempting to get their contracts broken or to shut down their suppliers. American business saw this as an intolerable infringement on its right to run its own affairs and to make profits and became highly indignant.

At the behest of its citizens, the American government continually protested these inroads on its freedom, but it did so in a curiously half-hearted way. Wilson when talking with the British Ambassador made it perfectly clear that he was speaking for the record, and that the British government need not take his complaints seriously. There was, finally, one convincing reply the British could make to any neutral anger: Whatever we may be doing, at least we are not killing anyone.

For by now the Germans were, and that eventually made all the difference. With the High Seas Fleet shut up in the North Sea and the surface raiders swept from the oceans, the Germans fell back on the submarine as the primary weapon for commerce warfare. Here again, as on land, there was an ascending scale of inhumanity. The submarine was deadly, but it was small and vulnerable; it could provide none of the courtesies and safeguards demanded by international law or the usage of the sea. The British could do little against the new weapon. They thought it was impossible to convoy ships, though they had done so in their great wars in the past. The submarines ranged at will, and the British employed feeble measures against them. They introduced decoy ships, with hidden armaments, so that when the Germans surfaced to sink a helpless merchantman, they would suddenly be attacked by heavy concealed guns. The British began arming merchant ships generally; neither the guns nor the gunners were very effective, but even if they forced the subs to remain submerged and use torpedoes instead of gunfire, that meant the submarine ran out of torpedoes faster and had to go back to base sooner.

Since the Germans risked their lives and their ships to make a surface sinking, or even to warn a merchantman, they soon stopped doing it. They began sinking without warning. They declared the waters around the United Kingdom to be a war zone and announced that any vessels found in them would be sunk on sight. When the American government responded forcefully, the Germans could not help but observe that Americans were applying a double standard: They *meant* their protests to Germany, they did *not* mean their protests to Britain. Germans were accused of killing Americans but to the Germans it was American shells that were being sold to Britain to kill Germans. So the circular argument raged across the Atlantic.

It reached a crescendo in May of 1915. On the 7th of that month the great Cunard liner *Lusitania* was sunk by a U-boat off the coast of Ireland. Of the 1,198 people who were killed, 128 were Americans. The United States went into a frenzy; argument swept back and forth for months. The British capitalized on what they termed a barbaric outrage pure and simple and insisted that the *Lusitania* had been perfectly innocent. Wilson threatened war, and the Germans backed off, promising not to sink passenger ships and to warn other ships before sinking them.

The doubts lingered. Pages were missing from the *Lusitania*'s cargo manifest, and the Admiralty's role in the dispositions that led to her sinking—the lack of escorts at crucial points of her voyage, for example—was highly questionable. The First Lord, Churchill, had openly speculated on the beneficial propaganda effect England would gain if a great liner carrying neutrals were sunk by a German U-boat. The ship was in fact an armed merchant cruiser, and she carried both war matériel and military personnel, facts of which Wilson was well aware but of which he chose to be officially ignorant. His Secretary of State, William Jennings Bryan, resigned rather than support Wilson's strong note to the German government. But Wilson still protested, and the Germans backed down.

For the moment, that was as far as matters went. The Americans would protest, they would not fight; there was such a thing, Wilson said, as being too proud to fight. Increasingly, he saw himself and his country as the only possible instrument of mediation. Meanwhile, the Allies bought their sustenance at the cornucopia of American industry, hoping eventually to bring the United States in. The Germans, resigned to diplomatic second place, wished only to keep her out. The equilibrium, the status quo, and the agony continued.

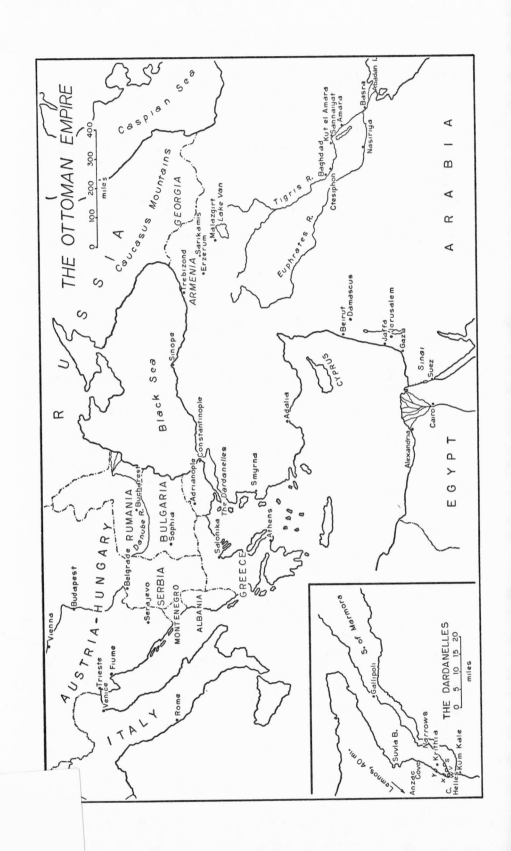

THE OTTOMAN EMPIRE

miles
0   100   200   300   400

Caspian Sea

RUSSIA

Caucasus Mountains

GEORGIA

ARMENIA
Trebizond
Erzerum • Sarikamis
• Malazgirt
• Lake Van

Tigris R.
Baghdad
Kut el Amara
Ctesiphon • Sannaiyat
• Amara
Basra
• Abadan I.

Euphrates R.
• Nasiriya

ARABIA

Black Sea

Sinope

Constantinople
Adrianople
The Dardanelles
Smyrna

• Adalia

CYPRUS

Beirut •
• Damascus

Jaffa •
• Jerusalem
Gaza •

Sinai
Suez •

Cairo •

Alexandria •

EGYPT

AUSTRIA-HUNGARY

Vienna •
Budapest •

Belgrade •
Danube R. • Bucharest
RUMANIA

Sarajevo •
SERBIA
BULGARIA
• Sophia

MONTENEGRO
ALBANIA

Salonika •

GREECE
Athens •

Trieste •
Venice • Fiume

• Rome

ITALY

THE DARDANELLES

S. of Marmora

Gallipoli •

miles
0  5  10  15  20

Suvla B.

Narrows
• Krithia
Anzac Cove
C. x Y.
Helles Kum Kale

Lemnos 40 mi.

# 9. The Dardanelles

THERE MUST STILL, the leaders thought, be some way to avoid the frightful ongoing slaughter of the Western Front. The year 1915 was one of experiment: gas and defense in depth in France, the extension of the war to Italy and the eastern Mediterranean, acceleration of the submarine war. None of these resolved the problem, and in Britain and Germany the chief military and political minds grappled with the elusive formula that would bring victory. The Germans, dominated by Hindenburg and Ludendorff, sought their decisive encounter on the Eastern Front. The British opponents of the Western Front mentality found support from Russia.

When Turkey launched her ill-fated campaign in the Caucasus Mountains at the turn of the year, the Russians believed they were in real trouble. They were not at all certain that they could sustain yet another major front, and therefore they pleaded with their western allies to create some kind of diversion. The request arrived just in time to put new hope into those who desired a more imaginative waging of the war, and especially to give ammunition to the already formidable persuasive talents of Churchill. Armed with this, he set out to convince the British government of the feasibility of a new scheme: forcing the Dardanelles and knocking Turkey out of the war.

Churchill's was a mind made of quicksilver. In a War Cabinet notable chiefly for the lack of military skill or ardor of its members, he stood out like the proverbial sore thumb. At the very start of the war he had gone traipsing off to Antwerp with the Royal Marines, determined to see some of the action as the British hoped in vain to hold a substantial piece of Belgian territory. Failing in that, he constantly tried to get the government to do something, anything, that would end the impasse in France. The First Sea

Lord, the equally formidable Admiral Sir John Fisher, supported and seconded him; at one point Fisher was full of ideas for a major fleet sortie into the Baltic to attack Germany from the Pomeranian coast, an idea which fortunately sank of its own weight.

Churchill and Fisher were opposed by the forceful Lord Kitchener, the Secretary of State for War, whose prestige was even greater than theirs. Kitchener invariably supported the French view of how the war should be fought, since their view conformed with both his own and that of his commanders in the field. When the Cabinet sitting in London could hear the mutter of the guns across the Channel, it was difficult for them to think of other places.

Yet the British had already taken desultory action against the Turks. When Turkish troops temporarily threatened the Suez Canal, they had reinforced the garrison of Egypt. An expedition from India had landed at the head of the Persian Gulf in November of 1914, and it was inching its way toward Baghdad. They had also, in the same month, thrown some naval shells at the defenses of the Dardanelles. When the Russian request arrived, therefore, it was less a complete bolt from the blue than it was an added argument to support ideas already germinating in the War Council.

Regrettably, British thinking about the Turks was colored by ignorance and heightened by optimism. Churchill's ideas were usually basically sound, but throughout his career he had a tendency to get carried away by the possibilities he saw in them. Now he predicted that Turkey would collapse with the slightest of pushes, and that if she did so, the entire edifice of the Central Powers might well come down with her. It would be possible to ship great amounts of supplies through to Russia, a point which neglected the fact that both Britain and France were in the midst of their own shell-shortage crises. It was also highly likely, thought Churchill, that the entire Balkan Peninsula would immediately come over to the Allied side; this would completely compromise Austria-Hungary, and on and on, in a sort of vintage domino theory.

In the War Council, Kitchener threw cold water on the scheme, saying that the army had no resources whatever to devote to Turkey at this time. The new divisions were still training, and the French, as always, were clamoring for British support, while Joffre got ready for his spring offensives. Churchill, with a mildly enthusiastic Fisher trailing in his wake, offered to do the job with the navy alone, and since the navy had cleared most of the German raiders off the seas and needed some useful work to do, the thing was agreed. Just what in fact *was* agreed remained something of a problem, for the minute of the War Council stated that there should be "a naval expedition in February to bombard and take the Gallipoli Peninsula with Constantinople as its objective." The ambiguity inherent in this minute derived from the incomplete understanding by virtually everyone of just what they were trying to do, coupled with their optimistic predictions of how readily Turkey would fold up. It was confidently expected that the mere arrival of a British fleet would cause a popular uprising and the fall of the pro-German government of Turkey.

By late January the Royal Navy was gathering ships to make its effort. The commander, Admiral S. H. Carden, intended to proceed calmly and systematically; there was no point in a mad dash up the Dardenelles that might leave him stranded even if he were successful. He intended rather to bombard and destroy the Turkish shore batteries as he went and sweep up their mines, so that when he arrived in the Sea of Marmora and off Constantinople, he would have behind him a secure line of communication back to the open sea.

While Carden was making his preparations, the War Council in London was having second thoughts in both directions. Sir John Fisher began to think the Dardanelles operation was undesirable after all but remained officially silent about it. The rest of the leaders became increasingly intoxicated with the ripe fruits about to fall into their hands and decided they had better provide some troops, not to fight their way into Turkey, but to garrison it after it had fallen to them.

Nor were the Turks entirely unaware of what was going on. Since his appointment as commander of their army late in 1913, the German general Liman von Sanders had thoroughly reworked and revitalized the army that had done so poorly in the Balkan wars. The casual British bombardment in November, 1914, had confirmed the Turks in their expectation of a more serious attack sometime in the future, and they had done their best to prepare new gun positions and to build up their defenses. When Carden anchored his force at the Greek harbor of Mudros on the island of Lemnos, a mere forty miles from the Dardanelles, the Turks knew what was coming as well as he did.

\* \* \*

No one on the Allied side expected serious opposition. The Anglo-French naval squadron consisted of a dozen predreadnought battleships, and subsequently the brand-new superdreadnought *Queen Elizabeth* and other new ships were added to it. With knowledge of what the big German guns had done to Liége before them, the Allied commanders believed that they would quickly smother Turkish guns in old forts or scanty earthworks. They neglected the fact that plunging howitzer fire has a far different effect from that of flat-trajectory naval gunfire; most of their ships lacked the newer types of sights and gunnery-control mechanisms, but again no one thought such refinements necessary for this corner of the war.

The first step in Carden's plan for navigating the straits was to destroy the forts guarding the entrance at Cape Helles on the Gallipoli Peninsula and Kum Kale on the Asiatic shore. After that there was a straight run of about twelve miles, which offered good hidden positions for small forts or for field artillery batteries. The channel here was from two to four miles wide. Next was a sharp left turn, four miles long, known as the Narrows, where the shores were only a mile apart, and where the current ran at five knots. Finally, there was an easy twenty-mile run to the town of Gallipoli and the Sea of Marmora itself. Getting to and past the Narrows was the hard part. The Turks had covered the way with twenty forts, with field artillery batteries, and with belts of mines sown across the stream.

The British admiral decided he was ready to open his attack on February 19, an auspicious date, as it was the anniversary of the British forcing of the straits in 1807. Early in the morning some of the older battleships moved in; sailing back and forth at a calm pace, they began a leisurely shelling of the four entrance-forts, two on each shore. The battleships kept at long range; the shells burst about the forts; nothing happened. The Turks did not open fire in return. After a while the sailors decided they would have better luck if they anchored, so they did and kept on shooting. Still no reply; were the forts empty? Had the Turks already fled? At mid-afternoon the ships weighed anchor and closed the range to three miles. The leisurely cannonade kept on. Finally, just before five, when the British were convinced they were either firing at nothing or had long ago completely wrecked the forts, the Turks opened fire in return. Forty-five minutes later the Allied squadron withdrew.

It was hardly a satisfactory beginning. To make it worse, the weather turned bad on the morning of the 20th, so it was not until the 25th that the ships came back. This time, with better positioning so they could spot one another's fall of shot and signal corrections, the heavy guns silenced the four outer forts in two days. Landing parties of marines and sailors went ashore and blew them up, and the fleet was into the straits.

Carden now reported that he needed fourteen days more of good weather to clear the passage. However, the weather remained changeable, and he also found that the farther he got into the straits, the harder the Turks fought back. Their field artillery was a particular nuisance. A battery would gallop up, unlimber, throw a few shells at the big ships from close range, limber up, and take off before the British or French could register on them. It was all very annoying. On March 4 when marines landed to blow up some silent forts the Turks drove them back to their boats handily.

Nor did the minesweeping go well. This branch of naval warfare was in its infancy, and to sweep mines the British impressed fishing trawlers and their crews. Towing long cables between them, ships were supposed to snag the mines' cables, bring them to the surface, and then destroy them with small arms fire. The trawler-sweepers were handicapped by the fact that their speed was barely higher than that of the current coming out of the straits, and the crews, never under fire before, were reluctant to take many risks. Churchill at home grumbled, "How could they be driven off by fire that caused no casualties?" and ordered Carden to press on.

The pounding of the forts was still going on, at some points with the battleships firing from west of the peninsula, across it, to hit forts on the eastern side. This was practically useless; as there was no way to spot fall of shot, it was impossible to correct the targeting, and the navy was increasingly frustrated. On the Western Front they were now using aircraft for artillery spotting, but at the Dardanelles this was difficult. All the navy had available were seaplanes, and they were so underpowered that often they were unable to get off the water; their engines could not develop enough speed to break the surface tension on their floats and lift them. When they did get up, thanks to being bounced by a friendly wave, they could not climb high enough to escape Turkish rifle fire.

Even so, Carden believed he was ready for a big assault by March 18. On the eve of it, his health collapsed, and he was replaced by his second, Admiral John de Robeck. Most of the nearer mines appeared to have been swept by now, and they intended to go inside the straits and start the grind up to the Narrows. The French claimed the position of honor, so, early in the morning, the Allied ships swept in, firing steadily, and apparently smothering the Turks on the shore.

Shortly after noon disaster struck. The ships used a wide shallow dip in the southern shore as a maneuvering area. Unknown to them, more than a week earlier, a Turkish minelayer had crept down at night and laid a line of mines there; unlike all the other lines, this one was parallel to the shore and the current. The first sign of trouble came when the French battleship *Bouvet* blew up, rolled over, and sank immediately, carrying 700 men with her. Her comrades were still unaware of the mines; they thought a plunging shell had penetrated a magazine and ignited it.

A little more than two hours later, the British battle cruiser *Inflexible* hit another mine; she limped off, out of the fight. A scant four minutes later the predreadnought *Irresistible* ran on the same line; she was abandoned, sinking. And finally, to cap it all off, as the Allies gave it up and signaled a withdrawal, the old battleship *Ocean* hit yet another mine; she foundered during the night.

The sailors had had enough; as they had already swept the area where these new mines were, they assumed the Turks were using free-floating mines, and there was absolutely no way of stopping that. De Robeck reported home that he was ready to try again, but he never had to: The government had already decided to send troops to take the Gallipoli Peninsula.

Participants and historians have argued ever since about whether or not the ships might have gotten through. Admiral Sir Roger Keyes, who fought through the whole operation, was positive they could have forced their way easily. Admiral K. G. B. Dewar was equally convinced they could not have succeeded. German officers reported that the forts had suffered surprisingly little damage and that the Turks were keen to fight again, but they also added that they were virtually out of ammunition when the Allies gave up. Still, it was the mines more than the guns that stopped the ships, and obviously some of them were still there.

Time after time in the Great War, commanders clung to the idea that "one more try" would do the trick. Almost invariably that one more try simply killed more of their own men for no result. This time one more try might just have won through, but the issue remains academic, for the problem was now handed over to the soldiers.

The army commander designated for the job had already come out. He was General Sir Ian Hamilton, and he found chaos awaiting him. The War Council had moved so gradually to the idea of a military expedition that nothing at all was ready. Hamilton had to go all the way back to Alexandria and work his way up from there. After consulting with de Robeck, he decided on an amphibious assault in mid-April and sailed off to get ready for it.

Now both sides began frantic preparations of the kind that give staff officers ulcers and cause private soldiers to curse while they load today the material they unloaded yesterday. The next four weeks was as much a credit to British ability to improvise as it was a condemnation of their lack of long-range planning. By April 21 they were back at Lemnos, ready to go, a force that consisted of a French division, the Royal Naval Division and the 29th Division, and the Australian-New Zealand Corps, the Anzacs, who had already been gathered in Egypt. In spite of the hectic weeks just past, they considered themselves the cream of the crop, and when they sailed out of Mudros harbor on the night of the 24th, the bands played and the soldiers and sailors cheered each other as they passed.

Hamilton's plan called for a series of landings. The French were to land on the Asiatic shore at Kum Kale in a feint. The Royal Naval Division was to steam up into the Gulf of Leros and demonstrate against Bulair at the root of the peninsula. The heavy assignment went to the Anzacs, who were to land about twelve miles up the outside of the peninsula and cross over to take the Narrows from the rear, and the 29th Division. The 29th was to land at five beaches right around the tip of Cape Helles, designated from the inside out, S, V, W, X, and Y. Their ultimate objective was a height called Achi Baba, six and a half miles from Cape Helles; if they got that, they were home free.

The Turks too had used the four weeks well, but they were short of supplies and heavy weapons. They had to cover all the possibilities, so they put only two divisions in the area the British were actually heading for. Even then they could not man all the beaches, so they left them lightly covered with patrols and machine gun nests and held their main forces back in the center of the peninsula, on the Khilid Bahr Plateau, ready to reinforce as necessary.

The attack began as planned on the early morning of the 25th. The French got ashore at Kum Kale and stayed there until the next day, doing their job of attracting Turks. The Royal Naval Division did the same, and Liman von Sanders thought this was the actual site of the landing, ordering troops up around Bulair.

The Anzacs landed a mile off target, being set north by an unexpected current. They met no opposition and, after sorting themselves out, began moving inland. They soon encountered Turks, however, and the Turkish divisional commander, Mustapha Kemal, who would one day be Ataturk, the father of modern Turkey, quickly rushed up reinforcements and managed to contain the invaders. By afternoon the Anzacs were fighting hard—and digging.

Meanwhile, at Cape Helles, the 29th Division had landed on its several beaches. At S Beach and at X Beach resistance was relatively light, and the troops got ashore and established themselves. At W Beach, the extreme outer end of the peninsula, the Turks were well dug in, the beach was mined, wired, and enfiladed by machine gun nests. The British had to come ashore in rowing boats, towed most of the way in by naval pinnaces, and then let go to get in to the shore. The Turks held their fire until the boats hit the beach, then opened up with machine guns. The British dashed for cover across the beach, small parties trying to get up the bluffs. In spite of very heavy casualties, they managed to get a toehold.

V Beach was to have been the center of the assault, and here the British decided to try a new wrinkle. In addition to the towing boats, they took an old coal collier, the *River Clyde*, and cut ports in her bow. They proposed to drive her ashore, put barges alongside her to bridge the gap to the beach, let down ramps from the collier to the barges, and rush troops ashore in a bunch. This was an early, improvised version of the specialized landing craft developed for World War II.

It did not work. The beach was held by only one company with four machine guns, but the Turks were waiting. The collier grounded, the barges maneuvered more or less into place, the ramps dropped, the troops poured out of the holds, and the machine guns opened up. Within moments the barges were filled with dead, dying, and wounded, their scuppers running with blood and the water turning a frothy pink around them. Still the soldiers came out of the collier, clambering down the ramps to certain death, and the Turks kept shooting them down until at last they came no more. By mid-morning, the landing here had collapsed, and a few survivors from the rowboats huddled along the shingle, trying to find shelter from the all-seeing Turks on the heights above.

General Hamilton and his staff and naval colleagues watched all this from offshore. The general in chief had allocated operational control to his divisional commanders, so though he watched the battle from a fairly close range, he did nothing to influence it. Given the shambles on his beaches and the attendant breakdown in communications, there was perhaps little he could do anyway. The sailors, who had had a total loss of fewer than 800 on their big day, including the 700 on the *Bouvet*, were absolutely appalled by the slaughter. They watched the soldiers try again and again to make ground, and de Robeck muttered unbelievingly to Keyes, "Gallant fellows, these soldiers; they always go for the thickest place in the fence . . ." By late afternoon they gave up at V Beach and finally diverted followup waves to W, where they were making slow progress.

That left Y Beach, and here the strangest thing of all happened. It was about three miles north of X Beach, and the closest of all to the commanding height. Slightly more than two battalions landed there early in the morning; their orders were to attract and hold Turkish reserves heading toward Cape Helles and the main landings, link up with X Beach to the south of them, and then as the British advance came past them, to move inland with it.

But there were no Turkish reserves to attract. In fact there were only three enemy platoons within three miles, and the troops at Y outnumbered all the Turks south of Achi Baba just by themselves. They met absolutely no opposition. About noon a party of officers strolled inland as far as the town of Krithia, halfway to Achi Baba. They encountered no one, and when they had poked around for a while they strolled back. Late in the afternoon they began to dig in. Eventually, after several hours, a few Turks showed up and began shooting at them. Adhering to their rigid orders, possibly confused by the tangled country, they had whiled away the day— and the chance to save their fellows from slaughter and win the campaign. What could be had for an idle stroll on the 25th could not be had for blood in the days thereafter.

By that evening the British had twelve and a half battalions ashore against a force that never mustered more than two battalions in contact. Yet everywhere the British were confused and in disarray, and everywhere the Turks pressed hard. The next morning the invaders evacuated their easiest beach, Y, two battalions driven off by a handful of determined men. Hamilton was upset, but since his strongest quality was an excess of tact, he sti'l hesitated to interfere in his own battle.

Within two days the front had settled down, and though the British officers did their best not to admit it, what they really had here was a microcosm of the Western Front. Both sides quickly dug trenches and then tried to lever each other out of them. Hamilton took out his frustration on his diary, complaining about the invidious nature of barbed wire and machine guns, which he thought suited the Turkish character. He was also angry with his own superiors. As did virtually every general of the time, he believed that the only real answer to trench warfare was more guns and more shells. In one revealing passage he summed up his view of the situation; it might have been written by almost any British commander in the war, and it did a great deal to show why they killed a generation winning it:

> Let me bring my lads face to face with the Turks in the open field, we *must* beat them every time because British volunteer soldiers are superior individuals to Anatolians, Syrians, or Arabs and are animated with a superior ideal and equal joy in battle. Wire and machine guns prevent this hand to hand, or rifle to rifle, style of contest. Well, then the decent thing to do is to give us shells enough to clear a fair field. [*Gallipoli Diary*, 2 vols. New York: G. H. Doran, 1920, I, 304–05.]

His real problem now, aside from the fact that the Turks stubbornly refused to acknowledge the "moral superiority" of the English, was that after the initial failure, Gallipoli rapidly became just another sideshow, another subsidiary front competing with France for men and matériel. And both were in short supply, so much so that Hamilton's failure at the Dardanelles, combined with the growing crisis over munitions shortages, contributed to a major shakeup in the government. Fisher resigned in disgust, Lloyd George became Minister of Munitions, and most important of all for the Dardanelles, Churchill was ousted from the Admiralty. He did manage to hang on to a position in the cabinet—as Chancellor of the Duchy of Lancaster.

The political scene in London may have been fierce, but it was in the gullies of the Dardanelles that men were dying. Through May and into June, Hamilton launched several attacks, always trying to take the fatal height of Achi Baba. No men made of bone and flesh and blood could have tried harder than the British and Anzacs to get forward, or the Turks to hold them. At points the trenches around Anzac Cove were but a few yards apart and had to be roofed in to prevent enemy grenades landing in them. Some of the Australians going forward to attack went berserk, blowing the roofs off the Turkish trenches and leaping down inside them, where they hacked and stabbed and died in the dark and the dust and powder smoke. The detritus of war piled up on the beaches, and the wounded came wearily back from the trenches to be taken off to hospital ships, and the Turkish dust covered the dead of both sides as they lay in grotesque attitudes, swollen and black under the Mediterranean sun. For that agony, all they had was another stalemate.

Ironically, since he was opposed to the scheme most of the way, Kitchener now became its chief supporter. He had spent most of his career outside England and at one time had regarded Egypt practically as his personal fief. Though he did not know much about the English political mind, he knew a great deal about the Oriental, and he had said early on that if the British attempted the Dardanelles, they must expect to see it through to the finish. He now decided to give Hamilton three more divisions, enough to win his campaign.

With these, Hamilton proposed to fight his way out of Cape Helles and Anzac Cove. He also thought he would put a corps ashore north of the Anzacs, at a wide, beautiful, and untouched part of the peninsula called Suvla Bay. They would advance inland, link up with the Anzacs to the south, and provide a better base. This move would also, though Hamilton did not entirely realize it at first, completely compromise the Turkish position. Suvla Bay was a potential war winner.

The attack opened on August 6. Around Cape Helles the British, French, and Turks fought one another to a standstill. At Anzac Cove the Australians and New Zealanders attacked with desperate fury, but made little gain. The country was bad, battalions and regiments got mixed up and confused, and the Turks managed to bring up local reserves. After three days the fighting died down from the soldiers' exhaustion.

Meanwhile, General Sir Frederick Stopford landed three divisions, 35,000 men, at Suvla Bay. Patrolling the area were three battalions of Turkish gendarmerie, a total of 1,800 men; the nearest reinforcements were thirty-six hours' march away, back at Bulair.

Hamilton had had his doubts of Stopford's capacity but as usual did not say anything except to his diary. The new corps commander had retired because of ill health in 1909; his last real service had been as military secretary to General Sir Redvers Buller in the South African War, fifteen years ago. But he had been recalled when the war broke out and stood at the top of the seniority list, so he got the command. The troops, on the other hand, were all new troops of Kitchener's volunteer army, good material and fairly well trained, but totally uninitiated in battle. At the top the force was old and out of touch, and at the bottom it was young and inexperienced.

The result might have been predicted. The landing went in on the morning of the 7th, and landed on air. The few Turks in the vicinity pulled back to the heights, from which they could do nothing but watch and wait. While Turkish reinforcements force-marched west from Bulair, the British got so thoroughly tangled up in their own feet that they stopped dead simply from inertia. Some unloaded supplies, some went swimming, some wandered over the flat plain back of Suvla Bay. By the afternoon of the 8th, Hamilton at last lost patience enough to order Stopford to attack —not even to attack, but just to move—but it was the morning of the 9th before the aged general could get his troops organized. And by then, it was the same old refrain; as the British went forward, the Turks were there to stop them. Suvla Bay was as bogged down as Anzac Cove or as Cape Helles or as the whole war.

That was virtually the end of the campaign. Hamilton relieved Stopford and sent him home, and then Kitchener relieved Hamilton. It was far past time, and it was too late to breathe life back into the Dardanelles. All its champions in London faded badly; Churchill went out of office and off to command an infantry battalion in France, Kitchener was in eclipse from then on. Hamilton's successor, General Sir Charles Munro, recommended evacuation, and Churchill later wrote of him, "He came, he saw, he capitulated." At the end of the year the British cleverly pulled all their troops off the beaches in the one complete success of the whole sorry story.

The Dardanelles adventure remains hanging like the grapes of

Tantalus, one of the great question marks not just of the war, but of the century. Could the Allies have won a local victory, and if they had done so, would that have led to a change in the entire complexion of the struggle? Would the western Allies have managed to get more supplies through to Russia? Had they done so, would there have been a Russian Revolution? The permutations and combinations are practically endless. One is left only with the saddest and most illusory conclusion of human affairs, the vision of what might have been. . . .

# 10. Success and Failure in the East

JUST AS THE ALLIES had their disagreements over where and how to win the war, so did the Germans. They lacked the wide range of strategic options that general command of the seas gave their enemies, yet there were still enough possibilities to generate heated argument. Their main efforts might be directed west against France and Britain, east against Russia, or rather less profitably southeast in the Balkans, or south against Italy. The latter two merely rounded out the map, for the major opportunities and dangers lay east and west. Von Falkenhayn believed, and events were to show him the more nearly correct, that the war could and should be won in the West. Hindenburg and Ludendorff wanted to win it in the East. The condition of Russia at the start of 1915 was such that it looked as if they might be right. Of the three major enemies, Russia seemed to be in the worst shape.

By now there appeared to be widespread shortages plaguing the Russian economy and war effort. The traditional picture is of an emergent industrial state buckling under the heavy pressures of a massive war. This picture has recently been challenged as a self-serving one drawn either by postrevolutionary historians or by anti-revolutionary "White" Russian writers, seeking to justify their own failures to master their situation. More modern students have claimed that what Russia was experiencing was not a crisis of collapse, but a crisis of growth. In their view there were plenty of supplies in the country, both for the needs of the war and of the civilian populace, but they were unavailable because of government ineptitude, transportation shortages, poor communications, and unequal distribution. Soldiers at the front, for example, constantly demanded more artillery shells and complained that they were not getting them. One answer to this complaint is that there were plenty of shells in the depots and fortresses, but the officers responsible for them would not release them to combat units, because they knew that if they did so, the shells would simply be fired off wastefully instead of being husbanded for when they were really needed— really needed, that is, in the view of the supply officers, not in the view of the gunners at the front.

This may be no more than arguing that the shortages were apparent rather than real, a point which makes little difference to the person at the business end of them. If a consumer cannot buy flour, he is suffering from a shortage, whether it is because there is no wheat, or because some war profiteer is holding back his grain for a higher price. If an artillery battery has no shells for a barrage, it is laboring under a shortage, whether there are in fact no shells, or several million of them back in some supply depot behind the lines. Hungry people and shell-less soldiers are not in a position to weigh the semantic niceties of the situation in a philosophic light. As far as the soldiers were concerned, there were shortages, and they were crippling Russia.

It was undeniable that the government and the war machine were inefficient. At the front the soldiers could not help but be aware of their qualitative inferiority to the Germans. Russian staff work was less competent, Russian communications did not function as well, Russian tactics were costlier in casualties; experts have assessed the Germans as anywhere from five to fifteen times more combat effective than the Russians. The army of the Tsars had made great forward strides since the Russo-Japanese War, but it still had a long way to go, and for that difference the Russian soldier paid a heavy price.

Nor was such inefficiency confined to the military ranks. It was an endemic weakness of the country; the ruling bureaucracy had not caught up with the burgeoning changes of twentieth-century society, and there was waste and weakness throughout the body of Russia.

There was also corruption. Unscrupulous businessmen, entrepreneurs, civil servants, and politicians amassed fortunes out of the war, visible fortunes that made the sufferings and the shortages of the multitudes all the harder to bear. There was unprecedented inflation, and while new fortunes were made old ones were wiped out. Foreign contractors tried, in some cases very successfully, to pick Russia clean. The government simply lacked the ability to put its own house in order under the heightened pressures of wartime —according to many authorities it lacked that ability even without those extra pressures—and as the war progressed, the rumblings of discontent and the cries for reform grew increasingly strident.

Eventually, and it did not take that long once the initial patriotic euphoria wore off, public anger focused on the royal family. The Tsar Nicholas and his wife, Alexandra, after all, were the father and mother of all the Russians; he was The Autocrat, and if things were going wrong, then it must be because Nicholas was not doing his job, or, equally bad, had fallen under evil counsels. One of the time-honored fictions of monarchical institutions is that monarchs can do no wrong—but they can be ill advised. It happened that Nicholas and Alexandra were peculiarly vulnerable on this score.

Nicholas had come to the throne in 1894 on the death of his father, Alexander III. The father had devoted his entire career to holding back the clock and preserving a rule of personal autocracy. Nicholas believed wholeheartedly in the system he inherited and tried unceasingly to resist the inroads of modernity on his government and dynasty. He was supported and sustained in this by his wife, who had been before her marriage a princess of the German principality of Hesse-Darmstadt. Indeed, with one exception, Nicholas' family line had married Germans for the last seven generations, which, for what it was worth, meant there was very little Russian blood in the Romanovs by 1914.

Blood was one of their problems, and as time went on, it took their attention virtually to the exclusion of all else. Nicholas and Alexandra had four daughters, and then they finally produced a son, Alexis. He was the hope of their dynasty, and he had hemophilia. This peculiar disease, in which the blood does not clot properly so that a normally insignificant bruise or small cut endangers life itself, appears only in males, who inherit it through their mother. There was very little that could be done about it, and it drove the royal family nearly to despair. Regrettably, they chose to hide their affliction from the country, so that instead of eliciting the sympathy that they and the boy deserved and might well have received, their silence and rumors of strange events around the throne caused consternation and dissatisfaction and seriously contributed to the loss of support they suffered as the years went on.

The appearance on the scene of Gregory, Rasputin, aggravated the situation immensely. Rasputin, which is not a name but a nickname meaning "the drunkard," was a wandering character of a type not unfamiliar in Russia, part holy man, part mystic, part charlatan. One of the women of the Tsarina's court came under his influence and convinced her mistress that Rasputin, of whose dissolute life Alexandra determinedly knew nothing, might be able to help the child. The lady-in-waiting was right; Rasputin was the only person who could calm the Tsarevitch when he was in pain, and this wandering reprobate came to have an absolutely predominant influence over the royal family. The outside world wondered what on earth was going on; vicious rumors swept the country that he was Alexandra's lover, or that she and he were in the pay of the Germans. What was a family and national tragedy was seen instead as a sordid affair, and all of it was further complicated by Nicholas' weakness and Alexandra's strength, invariably asserted at the wrong time and in the wrong direction. Whenever he faltered, as he often did, she bolstered him in his autocracy, telling him to be strong, that the Russians needed and loved the whip, and that he must not budge an inch. Since Russia still was an autocracy, since government ministers still were responsible to the Tsar, and since he and his wife remained absorbed in their family difficulties and politically trapped inside their own archaic view of monarchy, they were leading the country straight down the road to catastrophe. Weak men can influence history as much as strong ones.

Because of these problems at all levels of Russian society, the initiative in the war lay largely with the Germans. In the spring of 1915 they chose to exercise it.

Even when the Central Powers had made a decision to fight in the East, there was still the problem of where specifically to do it. Hindenburg wished to move from the north around Kovno and drive in a southerly direction. Von Falkenhayn, who possessed the largest view of the general situation, wanted to overwhelm Serbia and, he hoped, open communications through the still-neutral Balkan States to Turkey. But Austrian pleas overrode German desires. Conrad von Hötzendorf wanted an attack out of the south-central front, between the slopes of the Carpathians and the upper reaches of the Vistula. As the Germans looked over their situation, they concluded that Austria was weak and that the Russians quite possibly might have the strength to break over the Carpathian barrier in the summer. It was a case of beating the relatively weak Russians before they beat the even weaker Austrians.

To this end the Germans subordinated their entire strategy of the year. Hindenburg launched a smallish attack in Lithuania to draw Russian troops northward. That succeeded but eventually used up so many Germans that the comparative changes in strength ratios were minimized. Von Falkenhayn withdrew troops from the Western Front and fought the Battle of Second Ypres to mask their departure. Finally, around Gorlice and Tarnow the Germans built up a massive concentration of troops and guns, the whole group of armies under the command of Field Marshal August von Mackensen.

The attack opened on May 2, with a tremendous artillery barrage of an intensity previously unknown on the eastern front. The Russians were absolutely pulverized, troops driven crazy by the shellfire, units panicking, whole mobs of men wiped out or rushing to the rear. Within two days the Russian 3rd Army was completely annihilated, Mackensen had taken more than 100,000 prisoners, and his soldiers were into the open country and rolling to the northeast. The breakthrough compromised the entire Russian position in the Carpathians, and they had to go back all along the line. By the end of May they had retreated eighty miles, as far as the San and the Dniester rivers, and the immediate threat to Austria was lifted.

Early in June the German leaders sat down once more to decide what to do next. By that time Italy had declared war; Conrad now wanted German troops for his new southern front, to protect him from the Italians. Von Falkenhayn would have liked to go back with reinforcements to France, but this time Hindenburg's arguments carried the day. Even though Austria had gained a temporary reprieve, the German eastern commanders had little confidence in her ability to maintain the war if German troops were pulled out. Russia was pushed back, but not defeated. Therefore, they should continue their drives as they were.

This line of reasoning appeared the more promising as the southern Russian withdrawal had now created a large salient in Poland, with Warsaw as its point. Mackensen was still pushing ahead; he had taken the fortress of Przemsyl, and Lemberg fell in the third week of June. If the Germans mounted a similar attack from East Prussia, driving south, it ought to be possible either to drive the Russians out of Poland altogether or, even more fruitfully, to trap and destroy them while they were still there. Though this was really little more than a rehash of Hindenburg's earlier proposal, the changed situation in the south now made it more attractive, so the plan was accepted.

Mackensen, further reinforced, turned the axis of his attack northward, aiming for Brest-Litovsk, about a hundred miles due east of Warsaw, and in mid-July the Germans began a complementary drive from East Prussia, heading for Warsaw itself.

The Russians had, indeed, hoped to wreck Austria-Hungary this year, but they lacked the power to do it. Russia's overall field commander, the Grand Duke Nicholas, who was a nephew of Tsar Alexander II and therefore a cousin of Tsar Nicholas and who was also a soldier of considerable talent, had hoped to make it over the Carpathians and into the Hungarian plain. He had launched a limited offensive in the mountains late in March, but the Russians had run out of matériel by mid-April. Then before they could recoup, Mackensen's Gorlice-Tarnow offensive had hit them, and they had been backtracking ever since.

Faced with an obvious pincer attack on a large scale, the Grand Duke now responded wisely and courageously. He decided the time had come to give up Poland, and the Russians began to pull back. There were mistakes; on 1st Army's front they succumbed to the temptation of a fortress and threw themselves into Novogeorgievsk, where they were promptly surrounded, losing 1,600 guns and more than a million shells along with the garrison. The Germans brought in their experts from the Western Front and took the vaunted citadel, symbol of Russian power over the Poles, in a matter of days. Usually, however, the Russians pulled back in good time, and the Germans had to admit that their offensive gained less than they had hoped, more ground perhaps, but fewer Russians. By mid-August the salient was gone; the Russian line was back against the Pripet Marshes, and two weeks later Mackensen took Brest-Litovsk. Russian rule of Poland, which had lasted since the end of the Napoleonic wars through plot and revolution, was over—until 1944.

With fall in the air the Germans were still reluctant to stop. They spent September on the flanks, Austrians attacking south of the Pripet Marshes for little gain, and the Germans pushing farther out of the Baltic principalities. By the end of September the Russians had gone back yet another 100 miles, to a north-south line that ran through Pinsk, east of the Pripet Marshes. They had lost 2 million men, half of them prisoners. German casualties had been heavy, too, but not that heavy. The Austrians did not seem elated by the removal of the Russian threat; they still had far more men and officers reporting sick than they had incapacitated in combat, a sign that their morale remained low. It was the same old story: The front was too long, and the Tsarist Empire too big, to achieve a complete victory, and nothing short of that was meaningful. Russia was like China in the old aphorism; the Germans were wearing themselves out killing Russians.

Still, even Russia was not inexhaustible. The difficulties at home and at the front might have been bearable if they achieved victory. It was that much harder to endure them when the news was always of retreats and casualties, battles lost and fortresses surrendered. The Russians might fight stolidly, and the Germans might praise their capacity in a crisis, but morale continued to sag through 1915. It was necessary to do something to restore public confidence, and late in August, Tsar Nicholas decided on such a move. As usual, it was the wrong one. He sacked the competent, popular Grand Duke Nicholas—so popular indeed with the liberals that in some quarters his name was whispered as a possible replacement for the Tsar himself. The Grand Duke could be succeeded only by someone whose name possessed even greater power and appeal, and there was only one who qualified; on September 1, Tsar Nicholas himself assumed the supreme command of the army.

The Germans were delighted, for in truth the move was disastrous. The Grand Duke at least had been a soldier. The Tsar had no understanding of the workings or the complexity of the military system; to advise him he appointed generals because he got along well with them, not necessarily because they were competent.

The effect behind the front was potentially even more harmful. With Nicholas in the war zone, Alexandra was free to meddle in the affairs of government and to follow Rasputin's advice as to who ought to get ministries and war contracts. Incapable of running affairs herself, she was equally incapable of letting anyone else run them. The Tsar, weak though he was, had at least exercised a moderating influence on Alexandra's authoritarian tendencies, but now they were given free rein. Finally, by his move the Tsar had tied the fortunes of the dynasty to the military situation. If he won, he would be the saviour of his country, and he would go down in history as Nicholas the Conqueror as his grandfather had been Alexander the Liberator. But if he lost, he might well go down as the last of the Romanovs. By the end of 1915, it did not look like a good gamble.

As if the difficulties of the Russians were not enough to make the Allies worried, in 1915 Serbia finally succumbed as well. Through 1914 the Serbian Army had more than held its own against the Austrians, and in spite of plagues and epidemics through the winter of 1914–15, the Serbs were still full of fight when spring came around. It was at this point that von Falkenhayn wished to finish them off, but he was upstaged by Austria's larger trouble. With the heavy fighting along the Carpathians, and with the Italians hammering away on the Isonzo, isolated and relatively weak Serbia was the least of Austria's problems, and the Imperial and Royal Army left the little country alone for the first several months of the new year.

Von Falkenhayn, however, still wanted Serbia out of the way. Even more than he wanted that, he wanted Bulgaria on his side, as this would provide a secure route through to Turkey and the Dardanelles front. With Bulgaria neutral, supplies to Turkey were constantly at risk; with Bulgaria committed, there was a solid block of Central Powers' territory. Therefore, at the prodding of the Chief of the General Staff, the German government concentrated its attention on getting Bulgaria into the war.

Bulgaria had been established as a small principality, semi-autonomous but under Turkish sovereignty, after the Congress of Berlin in 1878. Its first Prince, Alexander, was a favorite nephew of the Tsar of Russia and was intended, at least by the Russians, to serve as their puppet. This was a difficult task, for as soon as they had achieved a modicum of independence the Bulgarians showed themselves to be violently anti-Russian. Alexander was driven into abdication in 1886 and replaced by Ferdinand of Saxe-Coburg-Gotha, whom the Bulgarian Assembly elected Prince. Not one of the powers recognized his rule, but for his first ten years he survived assassination attempts, plots, and coups in the best Balkan tradition. Then in 1906, at the price of having his son and heir, Boris, convert to the Orthodox faith, he achieved general recognition, and two years later he declared that Bulgaria was fully independent of Turkey and assumed the title of Tsar of Bulgaria.

A man who had survived a career such as Tsar Ferdinand's was not likely to jump into a major war without carefully weighing his chances for survival and for improving his general position. Since both the Allies and the Central Powers were frantically bidding for his support, his was a nice problem.

The diplomatic shoe was on the other foot this time, by comparison to the case of Italy. Most of what the Italians wanted was held by the Central Powers. Most of what Bulgaria wanted was held by the Allies, or if not by them directly, by states they were courting as much as they were Bulgaria, specifically Greece. The Allies offered the Bulgarians part of eastern Thrace, belonging then to Turkey, and part of Macedonia after the war, real estate at the moment under the control of the Serbs. Later they upped the offer to more of Macedonia, held by Greece, offering to compensate the Greeks with portions of Turkey around the city of Smyrna and its hinterland. None of these offers was particularly appealing, the more especially as the Greeks refused to go along with them anyway.

Meanwhile, the Germans and Austrians were bidding with greater success. They not only offered some of Turkish Thrace, but they also got the Turks to agree to it. They promised Macedonia and larger shares of coastline if the Greeks went to war; they also promised Rumanian territory if Rumania went to war.

Ferdinand remained shy, and it was not until he was certain of the success of the Gorlice-Tarnow offensive that he began to lean. He then received a push when it became obvious the Allied adventure in the Dardanelles was going to end in failure, and on September 6 he signed an alliance with Germany and Austria. The agreement called for an offensive by these two against Serbia within thirty days, and a Bulgarian attack five days after theirs opened. On September 23 Ferdinand issued mobilization orders. The French and British, still negotiating, were taken by surprise.

The Serbs were not. Field Marshal Putnik had been working all summer to rebuild the forces shattered more by sickness than by the Austrians, and he managed to gather up nearly a quarter of a million men. Soldiers were about all he had, for they lacked most of the appurtenances of modern war, and when both Russia and Italy appealed to him for attacks to take the pressure off them, he stoutly refused. He was busy with his own problems, the most pressing of which was the likelihood of a renewed invasion from Austria, coupled with a Bulgarian one. Since Bulgarians and Serbs cordially hated each other, and had for centuries, Putnik had been pretty sure whose side the Bulgarians would join. Even though he knew what was coming, about all he could do was draw up his forces along the frontiers and hope for the best. Specifically, he hoped for help from the Greeks, for Serbia had a treaty with them which stipulated that if she were attacked by Bulgaria, Greece would come to the rescue—provided Serbia put 150,000 men into the field against the Bulgars.

In the first week of October the Central Powers fell on Serbia like an avalanche. One German, one Austrian, and two Bulgarian armies—more than 300,000 men—drove across the frontiers. The Serbs were spread thin everywhere and rapidly fell back into the mountains. One of the Bulgarian forces attacked southwestward and cut the railroad up from Salonika, Serbia's lifeline to the outside world.

The Serbian government immediately called on the Greeks for aid, but the Greeks returned a cold answer. Serbia was not fulfilling her side of the treaty, that is, pitting 150,000 men against the Bulgarians, and since she was not doing this, the Greeks would not help; the treaty said nothing about Serbia being attacked by three states at once.

The Greeks did agree, however, that their place in the fighting might be taken by Allied forces, and the British and French immediately scraped up a couple of divisions and sent them out to Salonika, where they arrived just in time to find themselves cut off by the Bulgarian advance down the rail line. Greece's basic problem was that the country had a pro-German King, Constantine I, who was the Kaiser's brother-in-law, and a pro-Allied Prime Minister, Eleutherios Venizelos, who was practically an archetypal Balkan intriguer. Both King and Prime Minister wanted the same thing: the most they could get for Greece at the smallest price; but both disagreed violently on how to get it.

While the Greeks and the Allies toyed with each other, the Germans, Austrians, and Bulgarians finished off the Serbs. By the end of October half the country was gone; by the end of November the remnants of the Serbian Army had retreated over the frontier into Albania. In the midst of bitter winter weather that left men dying by the scores with sickness and frostbite, they filtered through the mountains to the coast. Eventually, Allied ships picked up the 100,000 or so who survived and took them to the island of Corfu, where they were put back together into some sort of organization.

With Serbia overrun there seemed little sense in the Allied forces, up to several divisions now, staying at Salonika. However, one of the principles of this war was that ground was never given up voluntarily, no matter how useless it was. So the Salonika front quieted down, but it did not die out. The Germans refused to let their Bulgarian allies cross the Greek frontier, as they did not want Greece more actively in the war. They also refused to let them cross into Albania, as the Austrians wanted that and especially did not want a Bulgarian coastline on the Adriatic.

The Allied commander, French General Maurice Sarrail, beaten by the Bulgarians all along the railroad line, fell back to a defensible position on the frontier, based out of Salonika. His forces were gradually built up and settled in comfortably; they called themselves "the gardeners of Salonika," and the Germans called the front "our largest internment camp." Sarrail spent his time meddling in Greek politics, which was far more congenial than fighting Germans—or even Bulgarians.

Thus 1915, as 1914 before it, came to an indecisive end. There was little to celebrate in the final days of the year and less for the Allies than for the Central Powers. Italy had come in, but Serbia had gone out; Salonika had been opened up, but the Dardanelles was closing down. The submarine remained a question mark, and as long as it did, Britain's command of the sea was tenuous. Russia was barely surviving. On the Western Front, France and Britain dashed their young men in vain against the prepared German positions, and hundreds of thousands of dead and wounded had gained them a few useless yards. The constant upgrading of artillery and the introduction of gas were plumbing new depths of frightfulness, but all to little effect.

On the other side, the picture was no more than slightly brighter. Though the Germans had everywhere held their own, and a bit more, they still had not found the magic ingredient that would bring victory. East and west they were firmly established on enemy territory, and no shells landed on the soil of Germany. It seemed to do little good; shortages were beginning to appear in German life, the British blockade was slowly tightening, and the constant news of victory here, victory there, seemed to mean only that more men and boys were drafted off to die. There was no thought of giving up, but there was as yet no sign of the desired end of the war.

In Austria-Hungary, war weariness was already well advanced. Germany had tied herself to Austria's foreign policy before the war, and in this year she had subordinated her own military desires to Austria's needs, so that once again Austria exercised the tyranny of weakness over her stronger ally. In spite of victory over Serbia and the pushing back of the Russians, there was little cause for rejoicing in Vienna. The patent weakness of the Austro-Hungarian forces made the victories hollow, and defeating neighboring Slavs still did not cure the restlessness of the minorities.

What was to be done? From London all the way east to St. Petersburg the nations were trapped in the war. Like men who had blundered into a swamp, knowing how much it had cost them to come this far, they could not bring themselves to turn about and go back the way they had come. Surely a bit more effort would see them safely through to the other side. With little thought of faltering yet, they girded themselves for an even more stupendous trial of arms. The sacrifice of those who had gone before must not be in vain. They *must* win through to victory.

# 11. "The Love Battles": Verdun and the Somme

FOR GENERAL ERICH VON FALKENHAYN, his first year as Chief of the German General Staff had been a series of unending frustrations. He had inherited the job from von Moltke, the man who had proven unable to manage the whirlwind of modern war waged according to Schlieffen. Yet though he held the offices of both Chief of the General Staff and Minister of War, an unprecedented plurality of power, he was still not a free agent. In addition to the inevitable factors of time, space, and supplies, he was hampered both by von Moltke, who retained a position of some power from which he delighted in pointing out his successor's shortcomings, and by the situation in the East, which might be summed up as a combination of Hindenburg and Ludendorff's strength and Conrad von Hötzendorf's weakness. Buffeted by all these, von Falkenhayn had been forced to watch 1915 slide by without producing the decisive victory so confidently predicted by the champions of one scheme or another.

Von Falkenhayn's view of the war was simple. As Germany had not won in the first few weeks, she was not going to do so in the foreseeable future. He saw himself, quite correctly, as the commander of a fortress, a huge one that encompassed all of central Europe, but a fortress nonetheless. He was under a siege, and the only way to win was to hold on until the besiegers were sufficiently tired to lift it. It was not a very glamorous view of the war, but it was an eminently sensible one.

Carrying the analogy into action, there are some things a besieged commander can do on his own behalf; he may make a sortie from his lines and do the enemy some damage, in this way helping along the weakening process. This the Germans had done; they

140

had pushed back the Russian siege lines, and that had given them breathing room, though it had not apparently accomplished a great deal more. They had connected with Turkey in the Balkans, but that again was less than decisive. Von Falkenhayn realized that only against the strongest members of the enemy camp, not against the weakest, could he achieve a really meaningful victory. The strongest were obviously Britain and France. With the former he could do little; he could defeat her armies, but that still would not prove definitive. He could not invade an island homeland, and unless he could it was unlikely that the British would abandon their ally. But he could fight the French. France he perceived as England's sword; hers was the mightier army, hers the land on which he was fighting. If it were possible to break France, then the British, faced with no viable alternative, would probably give up. Von Falkenhayn concentrated his attention on destroying the French Army.

By now the German chief knew what the British and French did not, that it was going to be very difficult to break through the linear defense system and re-create a war of maneuver. The advantages all lay with the defenders, and nothing as yet had come along to change that. But if von Falkenhayn were very careful, if he husbanded his resources and kept his wits about him tactically, he might well create an advantageous situation, one in which the French would have to fight, yet do so on terms so favorable to the Germans that the French Army would be virtually destroyed. As he carefully scanned his maps, Von Falkenhayn found what he was looking for: the fortress of Verdun.

This ancient city had been a focal point of Franco-German history ever since 843, when at the Treaty of Verdun the heirs of Charlemagne divided his empire into Frankish and German segments. Since then it had been fought over time and time again. Within fifty miles of it lay Chalons, where the Romans had stopped the Huns in 451; Valmy, which gave the revolution new life in 1792, and Metz and Sedan, scenes of the two great French disasters of 1870. In 1916 Verdun was largely useless, a salient in the general trench line, but one that had been consistently downgraded since the heavy fighting around it in 1914. Before the war it had been a great ring of concentric forts, but the rapid fall of such places as Liége and Maubeuge had led the French to dismantle most of the works, on the idea that they were not worth keeping up. Verdun had become a backwater of the Western Front.

Von Falkenhayn decided to change all that. Reports told him that French morale was on the wane, helped along by newspapers the Germans were subsidizing. If he now launched a major attack against a place that was vital to the French view of themselves, he might well destroy them. The red kepi had been France, the offensive had been France, Verdun was France. Von Falkenhayn decided to use that to create a mincing machine, in which he was going to grind his opponents to dust. He ordered an attack by Crown Prince Rupprecht's 5th Army for February. In his own words, he set out "to bleed France white."

The Germans were not the only ones with plans for 1916. By that time the Allies too were ready to try again. They had now overcome assorted shortages and difficulties, though not all of them, and they were ready to prosecute the war vigorously. In December of 1915 the Allied commanders met at Chantilly to discuss their plans for the coming year.

Had they deliberately sought it, the generals could hardly have found a conference site more removed from the actuality of the war, more conducive to vainglorious ideas and attitudes, than Chantilly. Dating back to the Renaissance, home of the Montmorencys and the Condés, its walls echoed France's ancient glories. The Duc d'Aumale, one of the conquerors of Algeria, lived there; the Duc d'Enghien, whom Napoleon had executed in 1804, was born there. The generals could stroll in the château's English Garden, past its Temple of Venus and its Isle of Love. Polished boots and twinkling brass competed with parquet floors and jewel collections. It was a far cry from the mud and stink of Flanders and the Chemin des Dames.

Joffre hosted the great international gathering, with Russian and Italian generals deferred to as honored visitors. Sitting around the tables in the splendid halls, they all agreed the war must be fought even more fiercely than before. After banquets they decided that there would be, for the coming year, a series of offensives. Each of them would launch all his forces, and they would coordinate their attacks, so that the Germans responding to one crisis would immediately be faced with another. The Russian delegation promised even heavier attacks than asked for, and when the conference broke up, after further feasting and mutual congratulations on a job well done, they all went off to fight the good fight.

Chantilly was mostly concerned with generalities, and two weeks later Joffre and Haig got together to do some real business. Joffre, still the senior partner, proposed a great offensive on a front of sixty miles, centered on the Somme River. As a battleground it had little to recommend it, except that it was roughly where the British and French forces joined. Haig preferred Flanders, where he still cherished a dream of breaking through and rolling up the German line, but he finally agreed; if the main purpose of the assault were simply to kill Germans, then the Somme was as good a place as any. Joffre then suggested they have a few preliminary spoiling attacks, just to keep everyone on his toes. Haig demurred; he was in the process of bringing his new troops into line, Kitchener's Army, the volunteers who were now completing training, and he thought it better to use them in one large, overwhelming offensive. Joffre agreed. They parted, sure in their minds of how the war was to progress for the next several months.

In early February signs multiplied that the Germans were up to something. Reconnaissance picked up large troop movements toward the Verdun sector. A deserter came across on the 8th and warned the French that an attack was in the offing. By the time Crown Prince Rupprecht was ready to attack on the 12th, the French were forewarned but not yet forearmed. They had done little with the reports and intelligence assessments, and though Joffre and his commanders in the area were thinking of reinforcing, they began to do so only late in the day.

Fortunately for them, the weather turned bad, and the Germans reluctantly postponed their attack from day to day. Few things are harder on troops' minds than a delayed attack. It requires an enormous effort of will to set aside all the natural impulses and steel oneself to get out of the trench and go forward when all the nerve ends scream to lie down and hide. For soldiers to work themselves up to that point, then to have an attack postponed and have to do it all over again tomorrow, drains the reserves. To have an attack postponed daily for ten days is so harrowing it is a wonder the troops can attack at all.

The wet weather that harassed the Germans helped the French, for Joffre did move reserves in. He was restoring and reinforcing his positions when the storm broke.

Verdun itself is in a hollow straddling the Meuse River. Five miles east and north of it, on the surrounding hills, was the ring made up of the outer forts, most important of them Forts Vaux and Douaumont; three to five miles beyond them lay the front line, which straggled here and there, from forest to hillock to hamlet to little country road. The entire salient was about twenty-five miles wide at its base and roughly fifteen miles deep, north and east of the town.

The German 5th Army began its assault with a twelve-hour barrage which swamped the French trench line and smothered their resistance. They then attacked on a fairly narrow front, east of the Meuse, and due south toward Verdun and its fortresses. The French fell back, fighting skillfully but steadily giving ground. In three days the Germans made a maximum penetration of three miles and had gotten through two of the French trench lines. Things began to look fairly bleak; the Germans were using a great deal of gas, introducing phosgene for the first time. Their attack appeared to be gathering momentum after a disappointing start, and worst of all, some of the French units were on the verge of collapse. One regiment held and lost 1,800 out of 2,000 men, but another fled under the heavy bombardment. With the attack from the north gaining ground, the troops in the eastern part of the salient were compromised, and the French pulled back a good five miles here, giving up a large slice of territory. Further disaster came on the 25th, when a German company filtered into the works of Fort Douaumont and found it virtually unoccupied. This brilliant coup seemed to set the seal on triumph—or disaster. The German papers hailed it as the beginning of the end, and there were those among the French who agreed with them.

They could hardly have been more mistaken. While the advance ground forward, Joffre had sent his second in command, General de Castelnau, out to have a look at what was happening. De Castelnau arrived at the local headquarters just in time to breathe life back into weary commanders who were preparing to withdraw to the west side of the Meuse, and to send orders for new reinforcements and a new commander. The French general, unknowingly, had accepted von Falkenhayn's view of what the battle should be: a slugging match, toe the mark and fight till one or the other drops. To carry out the job he called in France's foremost defensive specialist, General Pétain. The sixty-year-old bachelor was routed out of bed in a railroad hotel in Paris to receive the news of his new command. As he was not spending the night alone, he gallantly returned to bed before leaving in the morning for Verdun. So the issue was joined; von Falkenhayn had his chance to bleed France white, the French had accepted the challenge. Now it simply remained to fight it out.

The battle thus begun lasted through the entire year, ending only in December. In the first half of it the Germans pushed remorselessly forward, trying more to destroy the French armies than to take ground for its own sake. In the second half the French pushed back, trying to regain ground at whatever cost, simply because it was their ground and the thought of one small piece of territory unnecessarily under the heel of the invader was anathema—at least to the commanders who seldom were required to die retaking it.

Through March, April, May, June, and into July the Germans attacked now one place, now another. By the end of February they were fought out due north of Verdun, around Douaumont. For March they shifted their attacks to the west, to the other side of the Meuse, northwest of the town. Here Pétain had built up two particular strongpoints, Hill 304 and another one ominously—and aptly—named Le Mort Homme. Progress was slow and fighting bitter. For two months the Germans tried to take Le Mort Homme, sending over pulverizing artillery barrages, followed by assaults that used up six divisions. When the shelling stopped, the Germans surged forward, and the French came up out of their holes—there were no more trench lines, the ground was too battered for that— and beat them back with machine gun, rifle butt, and pick handle. Then the Germans went to ground, the French artillery opened up, and after a few hours, the French came charging down the slopes, and the Germans came out of their holes and beat *them* back. At the end of two months 89,000 Frenchmen had died around the Dead Man Hill alone, and so had 82,000 Germans, and observers might well ask who was bleeding whom.

Late in March the Germans tried east of the Meuse again, and on the last day of the month they finally took Fort Vaux, after horrible fighting in its subterranean galleys. On April 9 they opened a mass attack on both sides of the Meuse, but again the French held on to their shattered lines, and again the Germans failed.

Pétain's hand was felt everywhere. There were many individual displays of incredible heroism, and here and there one man or another was the soul of this attack or that defense, but overall it was Pétain's battle, and his name became irrevocably linked with it. Whatever he might be in another age and another war, he was still "the hero of Verdun." His big problem was supply, relief for the fighting troops, reinforcements. There was but one main road leading up to the city, from Bar le Duc, and a single, inadequate, railroad line. Pétain organized the logistics, so that there was an endless chain of trucks going up the road. It collapsed under the traffic, and thousands of men stood alongside it, shoveling dirt and fill into the mudholes to keep the trucks going. Twenty-four hours a day, with bonfires lighting the work and the way at night, the trucks rolled, carrying men to their deaths and maiming, and carrying the supplies to keep them at it. The French called it *la voie sacrée*, "the Sacred Way," and it aroused the same emotions as those ceremonial paths by which the ancients led their sacrifices toward the altar; indeed it served the same purpose. Pétain instituted a system of troop rotation, so that his weary men could get some rest. It is estimated that 70 percent of the French Army fought at Verdun at one point or another during the course of the battle, and their slogan *Ils ne passeront pas*, "They shall not pass," symbolized France's effort in this most brutal battle of all her many wars.

As did the war, the battle took on a life of its own. Von Falkenhayn knew when he had had enough. By mid-April he was fought out, ready to quit. But now Crown Prince Rupprecht, dismayed at the thought of giving up when his men had fought so hard for their as-yet insignificant gains, demanded that they keep on, and not only that, but that they enlarge the battle on either side of the salient. The Chief of the General Staff gave in; Crown Princes occupied a position slightly different from that of other generals. Though he refused to widen the battle von Falkenhayn said Rupprecht might continue it.

So they did, and they very nearly broke through. Attacking from Douaumont toward Verdun, they reached the ridge line that commanded the town. Pétain had had enough, and he asked Joffre if he could pull back; that was in the last week of June. Joffre said hold on, for the British were about to attack on the Somme. Pétain held. On July 11 the Germans nearly did it again, but that was their last gasp. Exhausted, they gave up; even the Crown Prince had to admit he was not going to take Verdun, and he was ready to let the battle die out.

Unfortunately for Rupprecht and his soldiers, the decision to end the battle did not rest with them alone. They had started it, and the French had fought it on German terms; but they could not end it just by wanting to. Rupprecht reluctantly went on the defensive, and the front quieted temporarily, while the Somme battle was begun and Germans went off to rescue Austria from Russia's last offensive. But in the fall the French decided it was their turn and they attacked as fiercely as the Germans had done in the spring. Pétain and his subordinates, General Nivelle as the planner and General Charles Mangin as the executor, were determined to do the job correctly. They carefully built up supplies, especially of artillery, more than 650 cannon and more than 15,000 tons of shells. The preliminary bombardment opened on October 19, and the French began to move forward on the 23rd. Anxious hours followed, in which the fog of battle was compounded by a literal fog lying over the desolate ground. Units advanced in some cases by compass-bearings; the Germans fought hard in pockets, disappeared or surrendered dejectedly in others. In the chancy weather and swirling mist no one could be sure what was happening. Then a French reconnaissance plane— they were up in spite of the weather—swooped over headquarters and dropped a map with a line scrawled even with Fort Douaumont and a penciled notation, "*La Gauloise* [Division] 16:30. *Vive la France.*" Late on the afternoon of the 24th the sun broke through and momentarily lit up the largest cupola of Douaumont. There, silhouetted in the lowering rays, were three Moroccan soldiers, triumphantly waving their rifles in the air. It reminded watchers of the famous "sun of Austerlitz."

Early in November the French fought their way into and past Fort Vaux. The Germans, who had trumpeted the taking of the forts earlier in the year, now tried to brush them away as of no importance, but the army could not be fooled. Morale plummeted; even Hindenburg was in despair. Nor were the *poilus* finished yet. In December, as bitter weather closed in, they launched yet another drive that carried them a good two miles beyond the forts. Pétain was developing his own theories of the attack: careful preparation and training, matériel superiority, limited objectives, and stop as soon as resistance thickened and the casualty balance threatened to turn against you. His success was notable, and when the attacks stopped in the third week of December, the French, if they had not regained all their territory, had rendered Verdun secure once more. They had won a clear moral victory.

How much more they won is debatable. By the time the casualties were totaled up, the French had lost about 542,000 men, and the Germans 434,000. Von Falkenhayn had not quite succeeded in bleeding France white, though as events of the next year would show, he had come fairly close to it. Unfortunately for him, he had also nearly bled Germany white in the process, and that had not been part of his plan at all. In the short run it appeared that the concept of the Verdun battle had been a failure, for which von Falkenhayn paid with his job. Late in August he was relieved, and Hindenburg replaced him as Chief of the General Staff, with Ludendorff as his assistant.

The Battle of Verdun interrupted Joffre's proposed spring offensive and indeed the concurrent offensives of all of the Allies. So brutal was the German attack, so dangerous the threat, that the French had to appeal to all their allies for an even greater effort. The Italians and Russians loyally responded, both with attacks for which they were ill prepared. The largest burden fell on the British, however. Joffre's plan for a joint Franco-British assault on the Somme was now converted into a British attack with French support on one flank. On July 1, 1916, the volunteer armies of Great Britain clambered up out of their trenches to face the single worst day in the entire military history of their country.

The Somme is an unimpressive little stream, about halfway between Paris and the Flanders coast. The front line crossed it in a north-south direction between Peronne and Amiens, the former behind the German line, the latter behind the British. Joffre had chosen this location not for any strategic significance, because it possessed none, but rather for administrative convenience, the fact that the French and British armies met here.

As more and more French were drawn into the holocaust at Verdun, the impending attack became increasingly British in complexion. The French 6th Army, under General Fayolle, was to attack on the Allied right flank, with two corps south of the Somme and one north of it, in the direction of Peronne. On the left flank General Allenby's British 3rd Army was to mount a diversionary attack around Gommecourt, where the Germans held a small salient some fifteen miles north of the river. The main attack was to be made between Fayolle and Allenby, and it fell to General Sir Henry Rawlinson's 4th Army. Along their front the line ran roughly south from Gommecourt to Beaumont-Hamel, then past Thiepval, to Ovillers, La Boisselle, and Fricourt. From there it trended roughly east past Mametz and Mametz Wood, then bent southerly again to Maricourt where it met the French sector. General Sir Douglas Haig's directive to his army commanders called for a breakthrough between Maricourt and Fricourt, followed by an advance of several miles; after that the British would shore up their flanks and, if all went well, filter their cavalry through the gap and into the enemy's rear. The most optimistic forecasts saw the cavalry exploiting forward to Cambrai and Douai. Cambrai was twenty-five miles behind the front line; Douai was more than thirty from the point of attack. Haig was a cavalryman, as were many of the British higher commanders, and they were all concerned by the failure of cavalry thus far on the battlefield to serve its allotted role.

The details of the breakthrough itself, which of course had to be provided by the infantry and the artillery, Haig left to his subordinate, Rawlinson. This was only proper, as it was Rawlinson's army that was going to carry out the attack, and he was the responsible commander. Rawlinson was an infantryman, unlike Haig or Allenby or General Gough, who commanded the cavalry reserve slated for the exploitative role. He thought it was going to be a tough job breaking the German trench line—in fact breaking three of them, for the Germans were deeply dug in in this quiet sector—without a lot of additional foolishness. Infantrymen tend, after all, to regard cavalry with a somewhat jaundiced eye, and nothing so far in the war had lessened that basic skepticism. He therefore concentrated on his particular difficulties and left the cavalry to its own devices.

His plan called for heavy artillery preparation, an intensive barrage of a week's duration. He proposed to paralyze the German defenses, to smother them with fire. When his gunners were through battering the Germans, there should be little for the infantry to do but climb out of the trenches, walk over, and take possession of the German lines. It required an immense expenditure of shell, but Rawlinson believed it was absolutely necessary for a peculiar reason: He did not think his infantry was capable of any more sophisticated effort than this.

It was not the quality of the matériel Rawlinson distrusted, for the British soldiers who attacked on the Somme in 1916 were probably the finest body of men Britain had ever put in uniform, the mother country's equivalent of the Canadians who had held the line at Second Ypres or the Anzacs who had fought so well at Gallipoli. Before the war, soldiers had not ranked high on the social scale in Britain, the one major European country with no conscription, but these men were volunteers, men who had willingly, eagerly, answered the call to defend their country and what they perceived as the virtues of western civilization. The old regular army, the "old sweats," was mostly gone now, either dead or wounded or dispersed through the volunteer formations to give some training and steadying to these brand-new innocents.

Their units reflected their recent peacetime lives and attitudes. They had enlisted locally, with their friends or their working pals from offices and loading sheds; some were seventeen, some only fifteen, who lied about their ages to get in with the rest of the members of their rugby team. Some were past fifty, and they had lied, too, rather than miss the great adventure. The government called their units one thing; the soldiers called them another: The 16th Middlesex was the Public Schools Battalion; the 10th Lincolns, the Grimsby Chums. Glasgow produced three whole battalions for the Highland Light Infantry, and Yorkshire and Lancashire recruited thirteen. The Ulster Volunteer Force, an illegal formation that before the war had been dedicated to keeping Northern Ireland Protestant and British, had been asked for four battalions and had recruited twelve. All in all, the middle classes of Britain had responded with a loyalty and enthusiasm that the government had never before even attempted to tap. Now Douglas Haig in his first big battle as commander-in-chief of the B. E. F. was going to launch these men against the German line on the Somme.

They had been training for a year and had gradually been filtered into quiet spots in the lines, but Rawlinson still had his doubts about their ability to handle a major battle. The thinking of the early twentieth century was that it took years of drill to produce a regular soldier, and that anything less than that yielded an inferior product. Enthusiasm and intelligence were not adequate substitutes, and Rawlinson's plan therefore left as little to chance, and to the infantry, as he could possibly manage. The artillery barrage would cut the German wire and pulverize the German trenches. At the right moment, the guns would shift from a general to a zoned barrage, firing on a given line and then lifting and moving slowly forward at intervals. Behind this barrage the infantry would advance, clearing up the few surviving Germans, taking over their blasted strongpoints, and keeping to a very precise and careful timetable. All the men had to do was follow instructions, and, so they were assured, it would be a walkover.

After the fact, it appeared as if all the generals involved had been blind fools or, even worse, callous brutes who sacrificed their men absolutely unfeelingly. That was hardly true. Rawlinson especially, but Haig and the other commanders as well, prepared as best they could given their preconceptions of what the battle would be like. A more realistic charge than callousness is that after nearly two years of war, they should have had a lot better idea of what a battle actually was all about than they did. But by their lights at the time, they worked diligently to fight the best battle they were capable of. The Royal Flying Corps managed to acquire air superiority over the intended battle zone. The artillery massed more than 1,500 guns on an eighteen-mile front; in the French area the ratio of guns to ground was even higher. Thousands of tons of shells and supplies were brought in; several hospital trains were readied to take the expected wounded. Rawlinson actually asked for more than he got, because the medical authorities drastically downgraded his estimate of the number of casualties.

On the other side, the Germans could hardly avoid knowing something was going to happen on the Somme. General von Below's 2nd Army might not have air superiority, but the preparations were still impossible to disguise completely; they were simply too massive for that. The Somme had until now been a quiet sector, and the Germans had had ample time to build and improve their defenses. Their lines were three deep, and their dugouts, in some cases thirty feet underground, were all but impervious to even the heaviest fire. The British employed imaginative deception plans and did manage to convince the enemy that the attack would probably come a bit farther north, a notion assisted by the German belief that the French, exhausted at Verdun, were incapable of any offensive effort at all.

Haig scheduled his grand assault for June 29, and the preliminary artillery barrage began on the 24th. The British guns fired off thousands of rounds of shells, the attacking troops slowly filtered forward to their jump-off positions—and the weather turned bad. For two days the barrage had to be stretched out, while the green troops fretted and worried and lay uncomfortably in their assembly areas. Finally it cleared, and at 7:30 on the morning of July 1 the great attack began. Haig, Rawlinson, all the other commanders, had done all they could for better or worse. Their success or failure and their place in the history books now depended on young men with no braid on their shoulders.

On the right flank the French did well. Fayolle's troops were skillful in their use of cover and their heavy barrage. They made impressive gains, indeed they got farthest of anyone on the first day, and their push astride the Somme was the clearest success of the operation. On the left Allenby's men attacking the Gomme-court salient had mixed fortunes to begin with. Allenby had been extremely unhappy about a prebattle deception plan that led the enemy to believe the attack was coming right where his men *were* due to make their drive, and he approached the Gommecourt attack with a good deal of caution. One of his battalions did reach its objectives and get well into the salient, but others were held at the front line and made little or no penetration. The forces that did get into the German lines were driven back with heavy losses, and the Gommecourt attack did little to divert the Germans from the main battle itself.

The first great battle of the New Army turned into an unmiti-gated disaster. As the artillery shifted into its rolling barrage phase, the troops clambered up out of their trenches. To reach the German positions they had to go through their own wire, where lanes had been cleared for their passage, cross no-man's land, go through the German wire, which the barrage was to have flattened, and then get into and through the German trench system. The shellfire, now falling on the enemy front positions, was to shelter them while they did this, and they were given so many minutes to make their passage. Then as they neared the German line the barrage was to lift to the second trench system, and so on.

It did not work that way. Most units got through their own wire all right—a few, with either more daring or more innovative com-manders, had made their way out into no-man's land under cover of darkness—but almost immediately things began to go wrong. These can best be summed up by saying that on the one hand the troops took longer than schedules allowed to reach given positions, and thus lost the protection of the barrage, and on the other, the barrage failed to work anyway. The battalions came out through their own wire and then found two frightful things: The German wire was uncut in most places, and the German machine gunners in their deep dugouts had survived the bombardment. Taken together these were absolutely catastrophic. As the British rushed across no-man's land the Germans set up their guns, and soon the heavy chatter of rapid fire was drowning the noise of the barrage as it got farther and farther ahead of the increasingly exposed infantry. When the survivors of the rushes got up to the German wire, they found in most cases that their wirecutters were too light to cut the heavy wire, which was stronger than British wire. Now they were pinned in the open, with no support; they could not get forward, they could hardly even get communications back to the rear. Wounded were hit and hit again. Their position was clearly impossible. Better, more knowledgeable troops would have given up; worse ones certainly would have fled to the rear. But these were Britain's best young men, ignorant of war, full of sublime faith in their leaders, determined to "play the game," and if this was how it was played, so be it. They scuttled up and down the wire, looking for breaks, they tore at it with their hands, here and there they got through and into the trenches; in most places they fought heroically and died stoically.

There were some little successes and many large failures. The XIIIth Corps, on the right flank of 4th Army, laid on a different barrage schedule for its assault. In most areas, the barrage lifted so many yards at a time, so that the infantry rapidly fell behind and the Germans were not bothered in the zones where the barrage did not actually land. Thirteenth Corps put on a barrage that simply rolled over the ground, lifting but a few paces at a time. In this area some of the troops had also cleared their own wire during the night. With these two minor variations on the plan, the corps made good progress; it was also aided by the French advance on its right. The corps took its objectives as assigned.

At the other end of the scale, whole battalions were ruined for little or nothing. Though this was almost exclusively a metropolitan British battle, the experience of one of the two imperial infantry formations in it was peculiarly tragic. In 1914, Newfoundland was a thinly settled frontier land of fishing villages and lumber camps; having remained aloof from Canadian confederation, it considered itself the Dominion of Newfoundland and clung to its ties with Britain. At the outbreak of war, the colony had decided to raise 500 men; instead it raised a thousand, and they went off to fight as the 1st Newfoundland Regiment.

On July 1 the Newfoundlanders were in a reserve trench on the 29th Division front, waiting to reinforce the first-line units when these had cleared the German trenches and took Beaumont-Hamel. Of the eight battalions who made up the initial attack, not one formation got successfully through to the German lines. The higher commanders, not believing this and attributing their lack of news to a communications breakdown, ordered that the Newfoundlanders and the 1st Essex attack straight from their reserve trench. The Essex moved up the already clogged communication trenches to get to the British front line and attacked late. The Newfoundlanders went over the top instead. When they came up out of their trench they had several bands of British wire to get through, then no-man's land to cross, then the German wire, then the German trenches. There was no barrage; it was mid-morning; they had to go about half a mile in full view of absolutely undisturbed German machine gunners.

The Germans picked them up as they got out of their own trench; they slaughtered them as they bunched up to come through the cut lanes in the British wire. Still they kept on, and a few made it to no-man's land. Some of them got as far as the German wire, still uncut and littered with the remains of the eight battalions of the earlier wave. No Newfoundlander cleared the German wire. Forty minutes after it started, the attack was over. Of the 752 Newfoundlanders who clambered out of the reserve trench, all twenty-six officers and 658 men were dead or wounded, a casualty rate of 91 percent. The effect of that forty minutes on the subsequent history of Newfoundland would be very difficult to overestimate.

Even that was not the worst calamity of the day. The dubious distinction of having the highest casualty rate went to the 10th Battalion of the West Yorkshires. After crossing the first German trench line, but not stopping to mop up, it was caught on a rising slope from front, flank, and rear. In a long day, pinned down in the open, it lost twenty-two officers and 688 men, more than 60 percent of them killed, and many wounded several times. A battalion normally had from 700 to 800 men, and thirty-two battalions each had more than 500 casualties on the first day of the Somme battle. By nightfall the British Army had suffered 57,470 casualties, more than 19,000 of them killed. In most places they had not even reached their first objectives.

Yet the communications mixup was so complete that the generals from the corps level up thought it had all gone not too badly. Perhaps not as well as they might have hoped, but still, these things happened in war. Nothing could be done, obviously, for the next few days. These were given over to clearing the battle area, rescuing the wounded, by day if the Germans allowed, which they occasionally did, by night if they did not. Many men died alone, some were brought in as much as a week later. The dead were buried in abandoned or unused trenches. At one forward position soldiers buried a large group of men and put up a board saying "The Devonshires held this trench: The Devonshires hold it still."

As soon as the British had had a chance to recoup, the battle resumed. Haig was determined that he had had a success, and he was further determined to exploit it. He no longer possessed enough battleworthy formations to fight all along the front, so he concentrated his attacks on the south, where the initial gains had been made. For two more weeks the British ground forward, with the French helping south of the stream. On July 14, Bastille Day, they delivered a major assault and got through the second German line —one of the objectives for the first day of the battle—around Delville Wood. For a moment it looked as if they might break through entirely, and they shook loose a little cavalry toward High Wood. But as usual the reinforcements came up too slowly over the battered terrain, while the Germans rushed up reserves, and the chance, however real it may have been, passed by. Von Falkenhayn had ordered up massive reserves from the Verdun sector and ordered all the lost ground retaken, which forced the Germans into counterattacks that were as costly for them as the British attacks.

The Somme had now become another Verdun, a Frankenstein whose cost exceeded any conceivable gain, a battle to be fought simply because it had already cost so much. Through August and into September the fighting went on. On September 15 Haig delivered his third big attack, and introduced a surprise for the Germans.

This was a machine called a "landship." The problem of providing machine gun or heavy weapon support for advancing troops had become obvious at a very early stage of the war. A partial answer to it already existed, in the shape of the heavy tractors equipped with caterpillar treads to tow large guns. If some armor plating and a machine gun could be mounted on such an instrument, then it ought to be able to maneuver over broken ground, providing the attacking infantry with the close support they desperately needed.

The idea was a very simple one, but like many simple ideas, it took a long time to catch on. Initially the brainchild of Colonel Ernest Swinton, it was rejected by the War Office in Great Britain. Churchill at the Admiralty picked it up, and the first landships were built for the Royal Navy, painted battleship gray, and christened "H. M. S. Landship Number . . ." Since the term "landship" or "armored fighting vehicle" both tended to give the secret away, the less revealing camouflage name of "tank" was adopted for them. The first forty-seven of them were now carefully brought forward for their debut in battle.

Senior commanders were as usual skeptical. They did not expect much of the new weapon, and unfortunately they were right. The tanks were slow, seriously underpowered, and mechanically quite unreliable. Of the forty-seven, only about a dozen survived the approach march and actually got into battle. These achieved some success, mostly because of their surprise effect at this point, but by the end of the day they had all broken down, too. It was apparent to all that they needed a great deal more refinement before they might become effective on the field of battle.

Still the fighting continued, with another major effort on the 25th. Again the British gained a little ground at paralyzing costs. The French once more supported with flanking attacks. By late October, with the weather getting bad, Haig was ready at last to quit; Joffre asked him to keep going. The Germans were now desperately holding on to improvised lines. Finally, a few days of good weather in mid-November allowed the British to extend their bulge northwards and take the village of Beaumont-Hamel. That was the end. Haig finally acknowledged exhaustion, and the battle died down at last.

The toll was enormous. The British New Army was no longer new; they had sustained 420,000 casualties. The French had lost 195,000 supporting them, and the Germans, with their costly counterattacks, had lost 650,000 stopping them.

# 12. "Another Such Victory and We Are Lost..."

THE COMMANDERS MEETING at Chantilly and agreeing on their coordinated offensives for 1916 did not take into account that the enemy might have his plans as well, and when von Falkenhayn opened the Verdun battle he knocked all their careful timetables into a cocked hat. The French immediately began appealing for help, wherever they might get it. As in the past, their weaker allies responded loyally, winning some small victories at great cost and thus furthering their own weakness. Success in this war was so indefinite and so costly that it was almost as damaging as defeat.

In Italy, General Cadorna had agreed that he would attack the Austrians in March; now, with French pleas ringing in his ears, he did so, in spite of the fact that bitter Alpine winter weather still hung over the fighting front. On March 9 he opened the Fifth Battle of the Isonzo, and it lasted for a little more than a week. Its results were the same as the preceding four battles in the same place: Both sides had heavy casualties, the Italians worse than the defending Austrians, and there was no significant change in the front line.

Cadorna was not the only man with ambitions, however. On the other side Conrad von Hötzendorf wanted to achieve something of his own, and at the same time that Cadorna was planning his offensives, Conrad was trying to pry troops from von Falkenhayn. He asked for Germans to use in an offensive out of the Trentino, hoping to knock the Italians out of the entire northern salient. The German chief refused; he was at the moment totally preoccupied with his forthcoming Verdun battle, and he thought it would be just another useless diversion to subtract units from it for what was just another secondary effort.

The Austrians were tired of playing second fiddle to the Germans anyway, so Conrad decided to do the job all by himself. He began carefully pulling formations out of the line all along the Isonzo and from the Russian front as well and shifting them westward to the Trentino. By careful redistribution he managed to build up a striking force of fifteen divisions, which he designated the 11th Army and put under the command of the Archduke Eugene, who had done so well over on the Isonzo front. He massed these in the mountains south of Trent. Their objective was the town of Padua, forty-five miles away. That was a long way to go, but the stakes were high. Padua was less than twenty miles from the sea. Even more important, it was the easternmost rail line leading to the Isonzo. If the Austrians managed to take it, Italy's capacity to carry on the war would be virtually ended.

The movement of fifteen divisions across the entire war zone could not be successfully disguised, especially in an Austria where many members of the population were antagonistic to the ruling regime. Cadorna soon knew that an offensive against him was planned, and he had a very good idea where it would hit. He ordered his 1st Army commander, General Brusato, to take precautions. Brusato simply disregarded his orders; he felt he knew more about his front than the high command did. This was a quiet area anyway, and given the nature of the terrain he saw no need to disturb the troops unduly by forcing them to prepare defensive positions in depth.

When Eugene launched his attack on May 15 he caught the 1st Army completely unprepared. After a heavy artillery preparation, the Austrians drove across the mountains on a front that ran from Riva in the west, at the head of Lake Garda, to the Aviso River in the east. It was terribly difficult terrain, though not perhaps quite as bad as the Isonzo area. The rough going, the problems of supplying forward over the mountains, and the arrival of reinforcements gradually slowed the Austrians down. Nonetheless, by the end of the month they took the town of Asiago, which gave the battle its name. By the first of June they were still going, and Cadorna was desperately appealing to the Russians to help out by an offensive of their own in Galicia. Still Eugene's men pushed their way forward, and the town of Arsiero fell to them in mid-June. They were nearly out of the mountains, but they were still more than thirty miles from Padua.

At that point Russian pressure began to tell, and Conrad was forced to give up his offensive. He had lost about 100,000 men; so had the Italians, but neither had achieved anything decisive.

Cadorna, eternal optimist, thought he saw an opportunity knocking in the midst of all this travail, and he quickly regrouped as soon as the Austrian drive began to slow. He pulled units out of the Asiago front and raced them back to the Isonzo. Given his interior lines, he had to move just over 100 miles between the two fronts, while the Austrians had to cover more than 200 to get from one area to the other. By early August the fighting in the Trentino was dying out, and the Austrians had pulled back to defensible lines once again, with the Italians up against them; all was back to normal. Also by early August, Cadorna was ready to fight on the eastern front. On the 6th he launched the Sixth Battle of the Isonzo.

This battle is also known as the Battle of Gorizia, for now at last the Italians made some progress. Against the weakened Austrian defenses they pushed forward about three miles and took that town. Three miles did not sound like much, but it was significant on a front where previous gains were measured in yards or meters.

Regrettably, that was as far as they got. There was nothing in back of Gorizia but more hills just as steep as those in front of it. The nearest conceivable objective after that was Trieste, more than ten miles down the coast; it might as well have been on the moon. There was nothing north or east that was remotely worth the effort it would take to reach it. Cadorna therefore settled down to enlarging his bridgehead across the Isonzo. In September, October, and November he fought the Seventh, Eighth, and Ninth Battles of the Isonzo. The only effect was to kill a lot of Austrians and even more Italians. If ever there were a useless waste in this most wasteful of all wars, the Isonzo was it.

The Russians too were put under pressure by French calls for assistance. After their disastrous retreats of 1915, Russian armies had spent the winter rebuilding and reequipping. Morale had somewhat recovered, and now under the leadership of the Tsar himself, they hoped, perhaps unrealistically, to achieve some significant victories in the spring. They were not quite ready for it when the Verdun storm broke, but they responded by beginning a drive north of the Pripet Marshes around Lake Narotch. This opened on

March 18, but in less than two weeks it was bogged down in the mud of the spring thaw, and with nothing to show for their effort but heavy casualties, the Russians called it off.

Then they went back to preparation, but once again events forestalled them. When the Austrians opened the Trentino attack, it was the Italians' turn to shout for help. As Austrian troops had been pulled out of the southern end of the Eastern Front for Eugene's offensive, Russian pressure here ought to have a direct influence on the Italo-Austrian situation. When the Tsar talked this over with his commanders, however, they were distinctly unwilling to go to Italy's aid. They had throughout the war subordinated their own timetables to those of their allies, and the results had been uniformly bad. Invariably, they ran out of men or matériel prematurely. Whether this was in fact true or whether it was a useful way for Russian generals to explain away their own deficiencies was debatable, but in any case the higher commanders now explained to the Tsar that they simply were not ready to make any attacks. The Italians would have to wait.

There was one exception to this opinion. General Alexei Brusilov, commander of the Southwest Front ("Front" being the Russian designation for what we today call an "army group"), disagreed with his colleagues of the West and the North fronts. Brusilov said he could and would attack on June 4. Faced with this, the other front commanders reluctantly agreed to attack a few days later, in support of Brusilov's drive.

Brusilov was a new man; he had just recently replaced the previous Southwest Front commander, General Ivanov, whose inability to produce results had finally outrun his popularity. With Brusilov's advent new men began to come into positions of power and influence at the staff and intermediate command levels of this army group. They had studied their earlier attempts and had reached some startling conclusions. Up to this point tactical failure had been virtually absolute: In not one major battle of the entire war had the attackers demonstrated sufficient tactical skill to achieve a strategic victory. To the nonprofessional, tactics, the art of actually fighting the enemy on the battlefield, is a dull subject and one best avoided. Yet what happens "up at the sharp end" is as vital to the success or failure of a campaign as strategy or the greater combinations beloved of historians. Given the undeniable strength of defensive field fortifications, generals had so far fallen back on matériel as the answer to their tactical problems. As

General Hamilton had written at the Dardanelles, "give us enough shells" to clear the way. Thus the constant calls throughout the preceding months of the war: more guns, more shells, more men. For virtually the first time in history, generals were given unlimited amounts of men and matériel; they were deferred to as experts, told they could have as much as they wanted of whatever they wanted, and so far, they had not even been called to account for their lack of results. They were practically drowning in an outpouring of national wealth.

The simple fact that Brusilov's people stumbled upon—and they did not see it entirely clearly, as events proved—was that this massive *materialschlact,* or battle of matériel, was ultimately self-defeating. Why could a commander never get reserves and supplies through the battle areas to sustain a break? Because he had made such a mess creating that break that it was impossible to maneuver past it. The Somme was a case in point; there the British barrage had so pulverized the ground that neither horsed cavalry nor even tanks could get through it into the open country beyond. Or at least the attackers could not get through the broken terrain of the battle zone faster than the defenders could bring up reserves over as yet unbroken ground.

The only way to achieve tactical success, then, and to turn it into strategic success, was to find some way for the attackers, and especially their reserves, to achieve mobility equal or superior to that of the defenders and *their* reserves. The ultimate answer to this in the West, with its great productive capacity, was the tank, and finally the tank-and-aircraft combination. But the Russians lacked that productive capacity. To a certain extent, so did the Germans, for they had been initially surprised by the tank and had then decided after its poor performance on the Somme that it was really nothing to bother with.

There was a simpler way to restore mobility than inventing the tank and producing it in large numbers, however, and that was just to avoid messing up the battlefield in the first place. Suppose it was possible to break through into open country without destroying the road network, and indeed turning the whole battle zone into a quagmire, so that reserves and supplies could be brought forward without chaos and filtered in as necessary. What broke down the roads and the soil? Artillery. Artillery had become the key element in the battle, but seen in this light it had become self-defeating. Even if you could absolutely wipe out the defenders and their trench system by shelling them, you caused so much havoc doing it that you still could not get through the line with any residual mobility.

Now the problem was how to break the defense system without using superfluous amounts of artillery, and it was this problem to which Brusilov and his staff turned their attention. They did not, indeed, go through this exercise in military logic; the initial problem with which they had been faced was simply a shortage of artillery for their early drive. Working from that, they began to look for answers.

What they got was just a restatement of one of the oldest principles of war. Up to now everyone had opted for the principle of mass; instead of that they rediscovered the principle of surprise. Earlier attacks were preceded by bombardments that lasted first for hours, then for days, then for weeks. By the time the attack actually jumped off, the defenders knew all about it and were already bringing up their reserves. Now the Russians planned to make a virtue of necessity: careful reconnaissance and spotting of targets; a short hurricane bombardment, laid on to specific strongpoints rather than hitting indiscriminately. Then they went further. Instead of sending out masses of men to get slaughtered, hoping to overwhelm the defenders with human waves, they took carefully selected troops and trained and briefed them thoroughly, specialist teams slated to knock out certain targets or types of targets. These were the genesis of the shock troops, who would open the way for the masses of infantry to follow. It might well work; since they had no real alternative, it was worth a try.

The Russians were not the only ones thinking along these lines. Germans too were analyzing their tactical papers and deciding that there must be a better way to fight. Pétain was developing new ideas of limited attacks for the Verdun battle as well, though generally speaking, the westerners remained more preoccupied with matériel answers than did the people farther east.

In the first week of June, Brusilov put the new ideas into practice. He commanded four armies on a front that ran more than 200 miles from the southern end of the Pripet Marshes to the Rumanian frontier. He accumulated what stores and supplies he could get—his colleagues were not at all forthcoming in shaving their own allotments in his favor—but he avoided any large-scale massing of troops that might telegraph his intentions to the Austrians. The two sides were about evenly matched in numbers,

Austrians with thirty-seven infantry and nine cavalry divisions against thirty-six and eleven for the Russians, so the attackers were also forfeiting the normal numerical advantage so far thought necessary for an attack. Brusilov did manage a careful preattack phase, though, with approach trenches and assembly areas more thoroughly prepared and better camouflaged than had ever been the case in a Russian attack before. When the troops jumped off after a short hurricane bombardment, they did achieve surprise all along the line.

The Austrian lines were torn apart, not by a huge bombardment, but by a short one and by the rapid infiltration of specialist teams. Having seen few of the usual signs of a big attack, and having disregarded those they had seen, they did not have reserves ready to meet the crisis, and it rapidly escalated to one of major proportions. The Russians broke the front just below the Pripet Marshes for a length of sixty miles and within a week had advanced twenty-five miles. In the south they cracked the enemy line on both sides of the Dniester River and advanced toward the ancient Polish holy city of Czernowitz. Then things began to creak all along the Austrian front; by the end of the month the important rail town of Kowel was threatened in the north, the center was falling back, and in the south the Russians were getting near the Carpathian foothills again. The Austrians urgently requested German help to shore up their collapsing line.

Several developments now began to work against Brusilov. His fellow front commanders had promised to launch their own complementary drives a few days after his; this was to keep the Germans busy while he pummeled the Austrians. They failed to deliver. Even though they usually outnumbered the Germans opposite them by about two to one, they complained that the minuscule diversion of reserves to Brusilov had left them seriously under strength and that they could not advance. When ordered to do so, they wasted time by shifting targets and wrangling about supplies. At one point the West Front commander, Ewarth, refused to attack because it was unholy to do so on Trinity Sunday. When they finally did move, well on into July, it was obvious their hearts were not in it, and the Germans easily contained them. Even with the subtractions of troops for Verdun and the Somme, the Germans still did not budge in the north.

Therefore, von Falkenhayn was able to reinforce the Austrians, though the first scattered units he sent down were simply lost in the maelstrom. Gradually, however, the normal equilibrium of a battle asserted itself. As the Austrians fell back and the Germans arrived, the danger lessened. The farther the Russians advanced, the more they had to devote to supply, and the less momentum they had for fighting. The Tsar overrode his other generals and allocated reserves and supplies to Brusilov, but the Russians were working forward over a bad communications system, while the Germans were sending their troops down over a good one. By the end of July, some sort of stability was approaching.

At this point Brusilov and his people revealed that they were not entirely sure what had caused their thus-far spectacular succes. Had they known, they would have stopped and regrouped and built up for another advantageous moment. Instead they decided to keep going. Neglecting the careful preparation and the surprise that had won them their victory, they now fell back on the old method of heavy artillery bombardment and mass attacks. It was the old one-more-try syndrome, pursued with the old faulty methods. Brusilov kept pushing on through August and September, and his offensive degenerated into another battle of attrition, with the losses mounting alarmingly. As Russian losses climbed, those of Austria and Germany lessened—the Russians had taken nearly 200,000 prisoners in the first week of the drive—and as Russian morale dropped, the enemy's recovered.

By the third week in September the Russian armies collapsed from exhaustion. Both sides had lost about a million men. In terms of territory gained, this was Russia's greatest success of the war, and it just about finished her. Brusilov's offensive was pregnant with consequences.

It did manage to weaken the German position in France, and the Austrian in Italy. Both had to divert men to meet this threatening Russian drive. Neither diversion was critical, except for von Falkenhayn. This new demonstration of continued Russian capacity, plus the Somme, which seemed to show that his great Verdun plan had failed, put the finishing touch on his career as Chief of the General Staff. Dismissed at the end of August, he went off to fight Rumanians, which he did with characteristic capability.

Another side effect of Brusilov's offensive was that it brought Rumania into the war. The Rumanians were the last of the Balkan States to succumb to the siren song. As were Italy and Bulgaria, their southern neighbor, they were wooed by both sides. As in the case of Greece, their decision depended to a great extent upon the monarchy. Until October of 1914 the King of Rumania was actually a German of the House of Hohenzollern. King Carol I had been born at Sigmaringen; until his death he was naturally pro-German, though his government was not. Indeed, his death was widely attributed to heartbreak because the government declared its neutrality instead of honoring a treaty with Austria. His successor, Ferdinand I, who was his nephew, was also a German. Ferdinand's wife, however, was a granddaughter of Queen Victoria on one side, and of Alexander II of Russia on the other. Ferdinand was primarily interested in botany but he had had some military experience, and he was no fool; his country was relatively prosperous, possessing both grain and oil, and it had a respectable if not very modern or fully equipped army.

Most of the things Rumania wanted were already held by the Central Powers, which meant the Allies were able to offer better deals than the Germans were. When they eventually decided on war, the Rumanians insisted on receiving large slices of Austro-Hungarian Transylvania as their reward, and when the Allies agreed to this, they declared war on Austria late in August.

Two things ruined them. First was timing. Brusilov's offensive in June finally made up their minds for them, but then they spent nearly three months holding out for better deals from the Allies. The Allies promised them 300 tons of supplies a day from Russia, though in the event they never got more than a tenth of that. More important, by the time they finally declared war, the Brusilov offensive was over, and the Central Powers were able to move forces against them.

The second thing that ruined the Rumanians was greed. The Allied idea was that Rumania, upon entering the war, should stand on the defensive in the west, where the mountainous ring of the Transylvanian Alps shut her off from Austria-Hungary, and attack south across the Danube into Bulgaria. The end product of this drive was to be a link-up with the Allied forces in Salonika and a cutting of the Berlin-Baghdad railway, Turkey's lifeline. Had this been done and done at the right time, in conjunction with Brusilov's drive into Galicia, something substantial might well have been achieved.

The Rumanians wanted to play it their own way, however, and they wanted Transylvania now. They did not declare war on

Bulgaria, but rather on Austria, and they attacked not south but west, across the mountains. All of the concerned Central Powers were ready and waiting for this. Von Falkenhayn, watching the Rumanian juggling act, had already sent Field Marshal von Mackensen down to Bulgaria to organize a Danube army there for a drive to the north, and the Austrians had two armies in Transylvania, one of which von Falkenhayn himself took over after being relieved from his General Staff command. Rumania's geographic situation was chancy at best; given her vacillation and her short-sighted military strategy, it was disastrous. Her drives through the mountains to the westward were easily contained. Then, with the Rumanian Army fully committed on that front, the Bulgarians drove up from the south, first taking Rumania's only seaport and then pushing across the Danube. At the same time, von Falkenhayn's 9th Army got through the southwestern passes in the mountains and linked up with Mackensen's left flank. The Austro-German-Bulgarian forces then simply rolled up the Rumanians. By January of 1917 Rumania was for practical purposes occupied and out of the war, her resources greedily plundered by her enemies; she had had 300,000 to 400,000 casualties, the Central Powers less than a quarter of that. Seldom had the superiority of German methods been more crushingly demonstrated, and seldom had the Allies been more openly embarrassed.

The Austrian failure to contain Brusilov unaided, coupled with von Falkenhayn's lopsided victory over Rumania, brought into the open a further development of the war, the increasing domination of the Germans as the senior partner of the Central Powers. It was patently obvious now to the most casual observer that Austria was failing, and in 1916, she was not even able to influence Germany by her weakness as she had the year before. When the Austrians now complained or asked for help, the Germans simply sent down the men and plans and took over the Austrian armies and ran them as their own. Hindenburg as the new Chief of the General Staff and Ludendorff as his Quartermaster General were not only running their own armies but their allies' as well. Very soon now, such was the dominance they were assuming, they would be running the respective governments, too. The Kaiser might call himself the Supreme War Lord or the All-Highest, but it was rapidly becoming Hindenburg and Ludendorff's war.

Finally, and most ironic of all, Brusilov's success just about finished Russia; more correctly speaking, the cost of that success, coupled with its ultimate indecisive degeneration into a battle of attrition, carried Russia to the end of her rope. The 1916 summer offensive was the last great attempt of Tsarist Russia to master its fate, and it was a failure. With more than a million men gone, the Russian armies were reeling. Morale was down, desertions up. Discontent was endemic, treason openly muttered in the ranks, despair the order of the day at home. The Tsar did not know what to do, Alexandra, ever more firmly under the spell of Rasputin, counseled only the wrong things. As the cold of winter settled over the Eastern Front, the cold of death infected the limbs of the Romanov dynasty. By late 1916, the shadows were palpably gathering.

# 13. The Navy Gets Its Chance

FOR NEARLY TWO LONG YEARS the Royal Navy had waited for the Germans to come out. Grand Fleet and High Seas Fleet, they sat on either side of the North Sea like bristly dogs, neither one quite ready to try conclusions with the other. The advantages of strength and position were all with the British, and so was time. They controlled the seas, they managed the blockade, and if they waited it out, it might take twenty years, but in the end Germany would collapse.

The problem was that they could not wait twenty years. Public opinion would not stand for it. That had been all right in the Napoleonic wars, when public opinion had not counted for much, and more especially when most of Britain's fighting was being done by subsidized European allies. But it was not all right in 1915 and 1916, when virtually every home in Britain was receiving the telegrams expressing the War Office's regrets, and when a generation of young Britons was dying on the battlefields of France. The public wanted action, and the government wanted action. So did the sailors, but the enlisted men got it largely through fighting soldiers who made insulting remarks, and the officers got it trying to explain to politicians that they could not fight an enemy who refused to put to sea.

Therein lay the rub. The Germans simply would not come out. They sent their U-boats into the Atlantic to harass merchant shipping, with substantial effect, but their main battle fleet stubbornly sat behind its sandbanks and its minefields and thumbed its nose at the enemy. It was not that the Germans were disinclined to fight; they too had spent a great deal of money on a navy, and their sailors were as proud of their short naval heritage as the

168

British were of their long one. The Kaiser refused to let his sailors risk his ships; there was no sense fighting a battle on British terms.

So the Germans sat there and fretted, and across the narrow sea the British sat and fretted, too, the names of their ships reeking of imperial glories—*Conqueror, Temeraire, Agincourt*—and mocking this new generation in its apparent impotence. It was a stalemate which could not last.

The commander of the High Seas Fleet, Admiral von Pohl, had carefully followed the Kaiser's orders through 1915: He had done nothing and done it very well. Then at Christmas, about the time the Allied generals were meeting at Chantilly, von Falkenhayn produced a memorandum which in its criticism of the navy brought about major changes. The Chief of the General Staff pointed out that Britain was playing her age-old game, exhausting a continental enemy while herself subsisting on the resources of the entire world. As the German Navy had been unable to prevent this, it was up to the army to win the war alone—by fighting Verdun. The naval leaders quite naturally resented such remarks and were quick to point out that it was not *their* fault they had not been allowed to meet the Royal Navy. When von Pohl gave up his command because of ill health in January of 1916, he was replaced by Admiral Reinhardt Scheer; the navy collectively sighed with relief and tightened its belt with eagerness, for Scheer was known to be a fighter, and at the same time he took command the Kaiser was persuaded to loosen his prohibitions a bit: the High Seas Fleet might now go adventuring. Indeed, by this time, with blockade and stalemate on land, the Germans had little to lose and possibly much to gain.

The only people happier with the thought of the Germans coming out than the Germans were the British. They had worked their Grand Fleet up to a finely tuned pitch of organization and readiness. Their dispositions were long refined and practiced. They thought they were set.

The spring weather of 1916 brought some preliminary sparring and a growing sense of great things about to happen. In April the Germans sent out battle cruisers under their Scouting Group commander, Admiral Hipper, and they threw some shells in at Lowestoft on the British east coast. Bad weather prevented a follow-up shelling of Yarmouth. Early in May the British tried to lure the Germans with a seaplane attack, but again the weather was uncooperative. About the same time the Germans were forced by American pressure to agree to the "*Sussex* pledge," stating that their U-boats would operate only under the limits of international law, which made them virtually useless. They responded by recalling the submarines and using them as adjuncts to the battle fleet. Stationing his U-boats off the British coast, Scheer planned a bombardment of Sunderland for late May. Again the weather was bad, and it delayed his move past the operational limit for the subs. He then decided on a sweep into southern Norwegian waters with the High Seas Fleet, to harass any naval and merchant shipping he might encounter. By chance, Sir John Jellicoe was considering the same thing in the same waters, as a possibility of luring the Germans out. These two independent decisions set the stage for the greatest battleship encounter in the world's history.

The two fleets about to meet in the swirling fogs and mists of the North Sea represented the highest pitch of human technology. The dreadnought-type battleship was a perfect embodiment of the expertise, the virtues, and the failings of western society. Huge, ponderous yet graceful, those floating cities were massive machines made up of a combination of brute power and the finest instruments the mind of man had yet devised. They could spot a target twenty miles away, and they could hurl at it with pinpoint accuracy a shell that weighed more than a ton. Manned by highly trained and determined technicians, they seemed indestructible. They were dedicated to destruction, and destined for it.

The British were at two and a half hours' steaming notice for Jellicoe's proposed North Sea sweep when Admiralty intercepts informed them that something was going on. By now the radio operators of both sides had been listening to each other for so long that they felt as if they were old friends. The sudden increase in German signals tipped the British that they were about to sail, and Jellicoe was informed from London that the Germans were coming out. When the High Seas Fleet did go to sea, Scheer's custom was to have the guardship at Jade Bay acknowledge all incoming signals with the call sign of the addressed ship, so the British listening service could not say for sure when the Germans had left, only that a sortie was imminent.

When he received this news, Jellicoe changed his plans. Just as the Germans hoped to draw him into a mine or submarine ambush, he hoped to catch them in the open where the superior British weight of gunfire might overwhelm them. Now he issued orders for his various fleet units to sail. Jellicoe himself left Scapa Flow with the main body of the Battle Fleet, and Admiral Jerram left Cromarty Firth with the rest of it. When they rendezvoused nearly 150 miles out at sea, Jellicoe had twenty-four dreadnoughts, three battle cruisers, eight armored and eleven light cruisers, and fifty-three destroyers.

The main fleet cleared Scapa Flow at 9:30 P.M. on May 30. Forty-five minutes later Admiral Sir David Beatty, Jellicoe's scouting commander, left Rosyth with the Battle Cruiser Force. Beatty had four brand-new super-dreadnoughts of the *Queen Elizabeth* class, plus six battle cruisers of his own, screened by fourteen light cruisers and twenty-seven destroyers. Jellicoe's dispositions were such that at 2:00 P.M. on the next day, the 31st, he would be about seventy-five miles southwest of the Norwegian coast, and Beatty would be about seventy miles south-southeast of him. Then they would join together and sweep down toward the German coast.

The Germans sortied from Jade Bay before daylight on the morning of May 31. First out was Admiral Hipper's Scouting Force: five battle cruisers, five light cruisers, and thirty destroyers. Then, some fifty miles behind them, came Scheer's Main Body, sixteen dreadnoughts, six old predreadnought battleships, six light cruisers, and thirty-one destroyers. Making a speed of advance of sixteen knots, they steered just west of north, up past the coast of Denmark. They were to pass about fifty miles to seaward of the western shoreline of the Danish peninsula, known as Jutland.

As they maneuvered in the open sea, the British squadrons passed through the German screen of lookout submarines, who reported occasional sightings but did not succeed in making any successful torpedo attacks. Though Scheer received the sighting reports, they tended to be either confusing or contradictory, so he disregarded them. Scheer's first hope, then, that he might weaken the Grand Fleet by drawing it over a torpedo trap, was gone. He was about to meet a fleet that was almost double his in size, that fired twice the weight of shell his did, and that had a good knot or more speed superiority.

Great events often turn on small incidents. Beatty was on the point of turning back to take up his afternoon steaming station with Jellicoe, but he delayed a few minutes because his scouts had taken time to examine some fishing trawlers, and he believed he was slightly out of position. Keeping on those few extra minutes brought the cruiser *Galatea* in sight of a Danish merchant ship, stopped and blowing off steam. As that was an unusual thing to be doing in the open sea, *Galatea* closed to investigate; upon doing so, she saw a German destroyer slip off from alongside the Dane and dash away. When Beatty got the report he had so long awaited, "Enemy in sight," he led the whole Battle Cruiser Force off after the German. One authority has written that this chance sighting probably cost the Royal Navy a decisive victory, for if Beatty had turned back on time, the British and Germans would have met much farther north, with the British more concentrated and the Germans critically farther from home.

Racing across the sea, the British soon spotted the distinctive pole masts and heavy funnels of German battle cruisers. Beatty signaled the joyous news and bore on into range. But Admiral Hipper had already spotted the British and had promptly turned back, planning to lead the enemy down onto the guns of Scheer's main body. Hipper was forty-seven miles from Scheer, going toward him, and Beatty was fifty-some from Jellicoe, going away from him. Each battle cruiser commander, Beatty in *Lion* and Hipper in *Lützow*, knew his own main fleet was out, but neither knew the other's main fleet was out.

The run south, as this first phase of the action is known, lasted just over an hour. The heavy ships engaged in a long-range gunnery duel while the light units scampered about them, seeking an opportunity for a close-in attack. Unfortunately for Beatty, his ships were poorly disposed; he had been changing positions for a turn north to meet Jellicoe when the Germans were sighted, and this meant that his newest and most powerful ships, Admiral Evan-Thomas' Fifth Battle Squadron of super-dreadnoughts, were now trailing behind, the last to come into action. Therefore, though the odds were with the British, the points were scored by the Germans.

Both lines charged along at high speed, the huge battle ensigns whipping out from the masts, the guns reaching out toward one another. Their respective equipment was such that the Germans, with better range finders, were likely to score hits first, but the British, with better fire control and correction, were likely to hit more steadily once they got on target. Fire was opened at 3:49 P.M., and within moments the two lines were wreathed in smoke and shell splashes, going at it hammer and tongs, and sailing through the geysers of misses and near-misses, punctuated every few moments by the dull red glow of a hit on one ship or another. *Lion* was an early casualty when a plunging shell hit her midships turret; only a sacrificial flooding of her magazine by trapped crew members saved her from being blown apart. The Germans were suffering heavily, the fire of some of their ships becoming increasingly erratic. Then, at four minutes after four, the battle cruiser H. M. S. *Indefatigable* was hit on her forward turret. For seconds she steamed on apparently unharmed, then a huge explosion blew her up. There was a sheet of flame, dense gouts of smoke, her steam picket boat danced 200 feet in the air, and she was gone, with a thousand men. Two ratings from the spotting top were later picked up.

As Beatty turned slightly to open the range Evan-Thomas and the Fifth Battle Squadron at last were able to catch up and come into action. *Barham, Warspite, Valiant,* and *Malaya,* these were superb ships whose long careers went from Jutland, their first action, right through to the end of the Second World War; they have been well called the most cost-effective warships ever built, and now their huge fifteen-inch guns began to punish the German line severely.

Yet the Germans still fired rapidly, and twenty minutes after *Indefatigable* blew up a salvo hit *Queen Mary, Lion*'s sister ship. She too disappeared in a frightening burst of flame and cloud of smoke. Beatty turned to his flag captain, Chatfield, and remarked, "There seems to be something wrong with our bloody ships today," and at *Lion*'s yard they hoisted the signal, "Engage the enemy more closely," and turned to close the range. A few moments later Hipper turned away; the Germans, none of them sunk but all of them hard hit, had had enough. Besides, Hipper knew what Beatty did not. As Hipper fled east, Commodore Goodenough in the cruiser *Southampton,* out ahead of the pack, signaled, "Battleships to southeast." Hipper had led the British down onto the main body of the German fleet.

Now it was Beatty's turn to play hare to the German hounds, and he ordered his ships to reverse course and head back north. As he turned, he did so in succession rather than all together, which had the unfortunate effect of forcing Evan-Thomas to continue steaming south until he reached the turning point, then swinging his ships around one by one. The last of them, *Warspite* and *Malaya,* came under heavy fire from both Hipper's ships and

Scheer's van, but still scored hits on a ratio of five to one in those few anxious moments.

The second phase of the battle, the run north, now began, with Beatty leading the Germans back to Jellicoe. These were incredibly anxious moments for Jellicoe, for he had his ships in a steaming formation of six columns. It was vital that at just the right moment he should deploy them into line, so that they could all open fire on the Germans. Yet if Jellicoe deployed to the wrong flank, or too early or too late, he would miss his golden chance. Everything depended on exactly where Beatty was relative to Jellicoe, and where the Germans were relative to Beatty. None of them knew their exact position; none of them knew the exact relationship between one force and the other. To compound it all, Beatty was so involved in his own battle that his signals to Jellicoe only served to increase the latter's anxiety and frustration.

Yet Jellicoe chose wisely. A later cadet in the Royal Navy wrote that after studying the problem for a week, with all the data laid before them, his class reached the same answer Jellicoe did in minutes in the middle of the battle. At six o'clock Jellicoe on *Iron Duke* sighted Beatty on *Lion*. Fifteen minutes later the British admiral deployed his main fleet into line ahead. A scant few minutes after that, Hipper and then Scheer steamed out of the late afternoon fog and mist—to find thirty-two British battleships and battle cruisers steaming right across their line of advance, an arc of fire-tipped steel that extended from horizon to horizon. It was the classic naval battle situation of "crossing the T," having your own ships in a line where all guns could bear while the enemy could bring only his forward guns into action, and even those were masked by his own leading ships. For both sides, it was an awesome sight, and for many of the officers and men involved it represented the culmination of their entire professional careers. Few of those who lived through Jutland would ever know a moment such as this one again.

There were officers who believed that Jellicoe was basically wrong in his approach to modern naval warfare. He had insisted in his whole period of command that he wished to exercise a very tight tactical control. The days when "no captain can go very far wrong who lays his ship alongside an enemy" were gone, but there were still ship captains in the Royal Navy who did not recognize that. They were proven wrong by what happened to part of Jellicoe's First and Second Cruiser squadrons. The eight ships of these formations were armored cruisers, too small for the line of battle, too big and slow to work well with the destroyers. Functioning as outriders for the battle fleet, their job was now to get out of the way and clear the range for the big ships. Most of them did so, but two, *Defence* and *Warrior*, were caught on the engaged side of the British deployment, and as the Germans swept by, every ship in the line took a shot at them. In moments *Warrior* was reduced to a shattered hulk, wallowing in the waves, and *Defence* blew up with her entire crew.

None of that made any difference to the general picture, for two armored cruisers were as nothing compared to that long gray line that now opened fire on the German van, engulfing the leading ships with shell splashes, scoring hit after hit. The Germans were firing back; there were targets everywhere, and at 6:34 they found another one of the British battle cruisers: *Invincible.* A shell hit her midships turret, there was the same flashback into the magazines as had sunk the other battle cruisers, and she blew up and broke in half. As the main fleet sped by, there she was, bow and stern both standing high in the air, her broken midships resting on the bottom. Those few still alive cheered the rest of the British line rushing by, and six men lived to be rescued.

But now Scheer was well and truly trapped, and the enemy battle line bore around in a great arc, seeking to cut him off from the route home. Hipper's battle cruisers were virtually out of action; leading the German line, in heavy combat ever since the first moments of the battle, they had been steadily worn down. One by one their guns fell silent; it was *Derfflinger's* last shot that killed *Invincible*. *Lützow* was half-sinking, her guns at crazy angles, her torpedo handling rooms and magazines flooded. Hipper was forced to shift his flag and spent several hours on a destroyer, racing about trying to find a battleworthy ship from which he could fight.

If Scheer kept on he was doomed, and the High Seas Fleet with him. Another hour of this and there would be British battleships shelling the Pomeranian coast by next week. Fortunately for Scheer, the Germans had an ace up their sleeve, and now they played it. Suddenly the British saw, through the smoke and fog, that the Germans were no longer there; they had disappeared.

What they had done was a maneuver called a "battle turn away together," in which each ship in the line turned simultaneously, so that the rear suddenly became the van, and the entire line was heading in the opposite direction. The British had thought that could not be done under battle conditions and had never tried it; the Germans thought it could and had practiced it. Now it paid off. Covering their retirement with smoke and a torpedo attack by light units, they sped off to the westward.

Their sudden turn was compounded by the light-unit attack, for the standard British tactic for dealing with such a threatened torpedo attack was a turn *away* from it by their battle line, while their own light units dealt with the enemy. The average battleship was something around 600 feet long and just less than 100 wide; it was therefore six times smaller a target for a stern shot than it was for a beam shot. It was also, of course, six times smaller for a bow shot, and turning *toward* instead of away from a torpedo attack would have reduced the odds in the same way. But it would also have brought the enemy attacking units into position for a beam shot that much faster and reduced the time available to the British light units to deal with them. Added to that, a hit on the bow would have the additional impact of the ship's forward motion, while a hit on the stern would have its impact lessened by the ship's speed going away. So as Scheer's torpedo boats and destroyers came out, the British came to meet them, and Jellicoe turned his battle line away. There was a bitter fight among the small ships, while the big guns fell silent.

Leaving the carnage behind him, Scheer made off to the westward. That was not the direction he really wanted to go, however, so after twenty minutes he turned back to an easterly course again, thinking perhaps the British had split their line or gone home or that he might somehow get through unspotted. He did not, and a few minutes after seven, there he was again, plowing toward certain death for the second time. The light was going now, both sides nearly invisible in the gathering haze and dusk. Had it been a Coronel day, with the Germans clear against the afterglow, the subsequent history of the twentieth century might have been different. But it was not; Scheer took more punishment, turned away together again, and this time sent not only his light units but his battle cruisers as well on a death-or-glory ride against the British line. Jellicoe sheered off again, and once more the main units lost contact while the small ships barked at one another. The main fleet action was over.

Scheer was still in deep trouble, because Jellicoe was between

him and home, and if the High Seas Fleet were caught at sea on
the morning of June 1, it would never see June 2. The British
admiral knew that as well as Scheer did, and shortly after nine,
Jellicoe took up a night steaming position, course a little east
of south, with his heavy ships forward and his smaller units aft.
He intended to be between the Germans and their swept channels
in the morning.

Scheer was forced now to desperate measures. He called for air-
ship support off the entrances to his minefields at first light; this
was picked up by the Admiralty and gave away his intention but
was not passed on to Jellicoe. Then Scheer simply ordered his
ships to make for home, crossing through the British line, don't
spare the horses, devil take the hindmost, and good luck to us
all. That was about all he could order, and it was all he did.

The result was that as the Grand Fleet promenaded south,
binding up its wounds and waiting for an early dawn, the Germans successfully fought their way through the lighter British
forces in the rear. Jellicoe did not particularly want a night action,
where the odds tend to favor the smaller side, and he did not get
one. Many of his cruiser and destroyer men did, however, as they
blundered into Germans and fought desperate little flaring battles
in the dark. Ships crashed into one another, threw torpedoes at
friend and foe alike, and exchanged gunfire with shadows barely
glimpsed in the night. Incredibly, no one told Jellicoe what was
happening in the rear—the few ships who tried had their fre-
quencies jammed by the Germans—and neither Jellicoe nor any
of his senior unit commanders displayed what might have been
thought a reasonable amount of curiosity about the intermittent
noise and flashes astern of them. It was all casually dismissed as
bickering among light units. When daylight came the Royal Navy
steamed serenely on an ocean empty of all but the flotsam of
sunken ships, dead sailors, and lost opportunities.

The ensuing backbiting, assessment and misassessment, analysis,
and propaganda went on so long and so furiously that it has come
to be known as "the battle of the battle of Jutland." The earliest
question that had to be answered was who won, a question that
indeed might have been applied to the entire war. As the Germans
had been so inferior numerically, merely surviving the battle could
be called a victory; by contrast, British expectations had been so
great that anything short of annihilation of the Germans seemed

a defeat. The Germans were first into print, being nearer their home bases, and they claimed they had won a great victory in the Battle of the Skagerrak, as they called it. They trumpeted that they had been outnumbered by eight to five, but had inflicted losses on the British in precisely that ratio, eight to five. The British had lost three battle cruisers, three armored cruisers, and eight destroyers. The Germans lost one predreadnought, one battle cruiser, four light cruisers, and five destroyers. Therefore, the German papers said, we won. The British pointed out that losses mattered less than possession of the field and that on the next morning they were at sea ready to fight again, while the Germans were scurrying for home. Indeed, on balance, it was perhaps a material victory for the Germans, but it was a tactical and strategic one for the British. One writer commented that the High Seas Fleet had assaulted its jailers, but was now safely back behind bars. The whole might be summarized by saying that Jutland was not a battle that changed world history, but one that prevented world history from being changed. The strategic balance remained with the Royal Navy; sea power could continue to do its work of slow strangulation, and the next time the two fleets met was when the High Seas Fleet sailed into Scapa Flow to be interned at the end of the war.

This still-distant conclusion was not apparent to a shocked British public which read on June 1 that a great naval battle had at last been fought in the North Sea and that the Royal Navy had suffered heavy casualties. The public expected the schooner *Pickle* beating up the Channel with news of another super Trafalgar; casualties, yes, but where was the victory? The restrained and somber Admiralty communiqué sounded as if it were a thinly disguised defeat, and the disappointment was bitter; it took months and even years for the man in the street to realize that this was not 1805, and indeed to realize that the Royal Navy had won a victory after all.

Meanwhile, the navy now made good the defects that should have been remedied after the Dogger Bank; better armor-piercing shells were designed, better protection for turrets and magazines and horizontal surfaces. Beatty replaced Jellicoe in November and turned his attention to developing more aggressive tactics. Jellicoe, upstairs at the Admiralty, worked on improvements in communications and fleet handling. The post-Jutland navy was a less complacent and better navy than it had been before.

That made little difference to World War I; the issue had been tried and decided. Jutland was the end of an era. Lepanto in 1571 had finished galley warfare; Trafalgar in 1805 was the last great fleet action under sail. Jutland was the last and greatest naval action fought on the open sea between surface vessels alone; none of the available submarines, airships, or seaplanes had intervened in the battle. By the next time battle fleets met at sea, war would have become three-dimensional. Jutland was like every other major battle of the first war; the complexities were just a little too great for anyone to be able to deal with them. Both sides made shocking mistakes and misassessments, some made in the heat of battle, some going back for years into the past. Once again the cumulative effect of them had been to produce an indecisive conclusion. There was still no way out.

# 14. Imperial Wars and Colonial Campaigns

IT WAS FORTUNATE FOR THE ALLIES, in a contradictory way, that the Ottoman Empire had joined in with their enemies. For without her as a selling point, they would have been hard pressed to find promises with which to buy more allies of their own. One of the great contributory factors to prewar rivalries had been the imperialist race that divided up most of the world among the major European powers. Fortunes and lives were spent to acquire odd bits of territory, and as the pickings got leaner, the bidding rose higher. By the decade before the war, there were major diplomatic crises over fly-ridden backwaters that no one would have wanted a half century earlier.

World War I by no means ended this urge to possess; indeed it intensified it, and aside from the initial belligerents and the United States, most of the countries drawn into the war came in because they hoped to gain territories here or there, either adjacent to them, as in the case of Bulgaria and Rumania, or in some colonial enclave, as did Japan, or both, as with Italy and eventually Greece. The cutting up of the imperial pie reached its height at the Peace of Versailles.

Both sides spent a good deal of the war, as far as diplomacy went, dividing up the potential spoils. Before they could take legal possession of them, however, they had to win them, and that was not as easy as it looked.

The German situation was a strange one, and once again it depended upon that most elusive but important of all attributes of great power status, sea power. The impressive German prewar colonial empire had been built up, not as a natural outgrowth of economic expansion in the sense of the British or even French empires, but by Germans throwing their weight around in Europe and making nuisances of themselves every time there was a colonial problem or an international conference. From the mid-seventies on, Germany was always there with her hand out, and as usual, if you do that often enough, someone will eventually put something in it.

When war finally came, however, these German territories were mere hostages to fortune. Lacking a navy that could assert command of the seas—and even Tirpitz had never seen it doing that—the Germans were forced to let their colonies fend for themselves. Their claims to postwar empire, and they had very far-reaching ones, were based not on what they hoped to conquer overseas, but on the position they expected to occupy on the Continent at the end of the war. Having replaced France as the main continental power, they now pursued the same long-range diplomatic and military course that France had followed in the series of great Anglo-French wars of the seventeenth and eighteenth centuries: They believed their bargaining position on the Continent would be so strong it would offset their weaknesses and losses overseas.

The British, on the other hand—and most of the colonial cleaning up was done by them, the French being almost completely absorbed in the Western Front—were able to play the role they had always played. In spite of the demands of Douglas Haig and the "westerners" they managed to produce troops, ships, and matériel for a whole series of colonial campaigns that they ran as an adjunct to their main war in Flanders. They tried to gather in the German overseas empire, and they tried to break up the Ottoman Empire. In neither case did events work out entirely satisfactorily.

German Pacific territories were dotted around the map of the China coast and islands here and there. All of these fell early in the war to a race between the Japanese and the Australians. Japan, who was not obligated by the Anglo-Japanese Alliance of 1902 to enter this war, immediately did so, not because Britain asked her to, but because she saw opportunities for herself to gain the German colonies. This was resented in Australia, where people feared the "yellow peril" a great deal more than they feared Germany. The upshot of it all was that the New Zealanders took Samoa, the Australians moved up into the Bismarck Archipelago, the islands just east of New Guinea, and also occupied northeastern New Guinea, otherwise known as Kaiser-Wilhelmsland. As there were fewer than 2,000 German nationals spread all over the South Pacific, there was not much to all this.

The major German holding in the Far East was up on the China coast, the port of Tsingtao on Kiaochow Bay. Here the Germans had built a substantial fortress and garrisoned it with 4,000 marines. When Japan declared war on Germany on August 23, 1914, she immediately landed troops near the place and opened a regular siege. The British sent up forces from Hong Kong to join in, and eventually, the two had about 25,000 men surrounding the Germans. The latter, completely cut off, bombarded from the sea and bombed from the air by the Japanese, a startling innovation at the time, surrendered on November 7. For 700 casualties of their own they had inflicted more than 1,800 on the attackers. At the same time, Japanese expeditions picked up German islands in the North Pacific, the Marshalls, Marianas, and Carolines. By the end of 1914 the German empire in this part of the world was already gone, and the occupiers were squabbling over the spoils.

In Africa it was rather different. Here the Germans possessed four holdings. The smallest of them, Togoland, was sandwiched in between French and British territory on the Guinea coast. Just above the equator where the west African hump bends off to the south was the Cameroons, again flanked by enemies, this time by British Nigeria and the French Congo. Farther down was German Southwest Africa, between Portuguese Angola and the Union of South Africa. Finally, Tanganyika or German East Africa was midway up the east coast.

Three of these went fairly rapidly. In Togoland the garrison consisted of 200 Germans and about 1,000 native troops, Askaris. A joint Anglo-French expedition pinned them down and they surrendered on August 26, 1914. The captors divided the colony between them.

British imperial forces invaded the Cameroons late in August as well. As in most such campaigns the chief problem was logistics rather than actual fighting, and here the British had jumped in prematurely, poorly prepared and in the middle of the rainy season. The Germans let them get thoroughly bogged down, then counterattacked and drove them over the border early in September. But they came back later in the month, this time both British and French, and with naval support, and by late September they had taken Duala and driven the Germans into the back country.

Eventually, the Germans fell back to Yaunde, on high ground, and planned to hang on there until the soon-expected victory in Europe. The Allies were therefore constrained to mount a campaign against them, and they spent a terribly difficult time wallowing through swamps and bogs, fighting mosquitoes, heat, and occasional Germans. It took the British until New Year's Day of 1916 to reach Yaunde, and when they did the Germans were gone. The garrison trekked more than 100 miles across the frontier into neutral territory, the Spanish enclave of Rio Muni, where they were interned. The 8,000 German troops, most of them Askaris, had tied up 24,000 British, French, and Belgians, and 40,000 native porters, thousands of whom were ruined by dysentery.

German Southwest Africa had been thought absolutely useless when the Germans occupied it in 1884; even they themselves took it only because it looked good on the map. Then they found that they had struck it rich, for the area contained the fabled diamond coast. The best port there was already held by the British, at Walvis Bay, but the Germans built ports at Lüderitz and Swakopmund, and ran a rail line into the capital at Windhoek.

The Allies decided that the South Africans could take care of this by themselves, and that all they need do was take the two ports and leave the rest of the colony to rot; its 300,000 square miles were mostly desert, with a thin population of about 15,000 Europeans and a scant 100,000 natives.

In mid-September a South African force landed and occupied Lüderitz, but then the British found themselves in trouble. The South Africans were little more than a decade away from the Boer War, and many of the Afrikaners felt better disposed toward the Germans than they did toward the British. Disaffection spread rapidly, some of the Afrikaners rose up independently, and a substantial number joined the Germans, who for a moment threatened to invade the Union of South Africa itself. It took 30,000 British and loyal South African troops to put down the rising, but the famous Boer commandos could not compete with early armored cars, and by the start of the new year, the Union was quiet again.

After that, South African General Louis Botha led a converging attack on Windhoek. Columns moved inland from both the German ports and crossed the interior frontiers as well. It was incredibly difficult going, and even the water had to be brought up by wagon, but the tribes rose to a man against the Germans, who had been hated overlords and taskmasters, and the South Africans made good use of the natives as carriers and workers. Levered finally out of Windhoek, the surrounded Germans made a last stand at Otavi, and in July of 1915 they surrendered. It was a neat little campaign and proved far less troublesome than South Africa's subsequent determination to hold on to the territory.

That left only German East Africa, and here was played out one of those epic little affairs that attract attention far beyond their importance to the larger scene. The colony was one of the great prizes of imperialism, covering the area between the coast on the east, Lake Victoria on the north, Lake Tanganyika on the west, and Lake Nyasa on the south, the modern country of Tanzania. Not only was it valuable territory in its own right, but its possession by Germany had spoiled Cecil Rhodes' dream of an all-British Cape-to-Cairo railway. In 1914 the colony had a population of about 8 million, 5,500 of them European. The German garrison was under the command of a colonel, later general, Paul von Lettow-Vorbeck, and consisted at its peak strength of about 3,500 white and 12,000 native troops.

The war here got off to a slow start, as there were few enemy troops for the Germans to fight. Von Lettow-Vorbeck raided into Rhodesia to the southwest and made threatening gestures toward the British rail lines. The Royal Navy sent landing parties ashore to destroy the docking and wireless facilities at Dar es Salaam. Meanwhile, the British were deciding to do the job right, and they assigned the task to the government of India; the colony was, after all, more readily accessible from India than from Europe, and the Indian Army was a very respectable force, with a mystique and aura all its own.

Unhappily, mystique and aura were no more a substitute for efficiency in Africa than they were on the fields of France, and the troops slated to overrun German East Africa quickly stubbed their toes. In October a mixed force of about 8,000 men, a tenth or one battalion of them British, sailed from India and stopped at Mombasa, up the coast in British East Africa. From there they moved to the little German port of Tanga. The British force commander, General Aitken, wanted to sail in and land at the jetty, but the Royal Navy refused to do so because they were afraid of mines, even though their ships had been visiting the harbor under a flag of truce ever since the war began. Aitken therefore agreed to make a landing on a peninsula south of town.

The peninsula turned out to be a swamp; the soldiers, who had been confined aboard their troopships for a month, were forced to wade ashore through breast-high water with full kits. When they finally got organized and advanced in line into the swamp, it took them two hours to go a thousand yards. They then met Germans, one whole company, which forced several of the Indian battalions to break under machine-gun fire. The two units that did get into the town were driven out again by their own supporting fire from the navy offshore, which managed to hit only the British and the local hospital. The Germans finally gave up the town, but the British, not knowing that, gave it up, too. They re-embarked and sailed back to Mombasa, where the troops were off-loaded. Before being allowed ashore, they were assessed for customs duties on the few supplies they had managed to rescue from the beach at Tanga.

After this rather inauspicious beginning, the campaign settled down. British from north and southwest, Belgians from the west, and eventually Portuguese from the southwest, all tried to strangle von Lettow-Vorbeck and his little band by a series of converging drives, but by the end of 1915 there were still German troops holding portions of the British railways, and there were still no Allied troops on German soil.

When German Southwest Africa was finally overrun, the South Africans took a hand in the matter, and General Jan Christian Smuts came up from the Union with more troops. They finally cleared the Germans off the railroad in Uganda and in March of 1916 took the enemy base at Moshi. Von Lettow-Vorbeck fell back south of the Rufiji River and hung on. In early 1917 Smuts, about to go off to an imperial conference, decided that European and Indian troops simply were not suited to the campaign. His forces were decimated by diseases of one kind or another, so he gradually brought in Nigerians and other African units. By November of 1917 Smuts' successor had captured the major portion of the Germans, about 5,000 of them, but von Lettow-Vorbeck got away and with the remainder of his men slipped over the border into Portuguese Mozambique. The Allies chased him all the way to the southern border of this colony, whereupon he eluded them and went back north again. From there he ducked over into Northern Rhodesia, and it was not until the last of November, 1918, two weeks after the war in Europe ended, that he finally surrendered. He still had 1,300 men under arms and had been considering crossing the continent and operating in Portuguese Angola when the news that the war was over reached him. He had kept 300,000 Allied soldiers and porters busy throughout the war and caused 700,000 more to become casualties through disease—there were but 15,000 battle losses—and he had cost the enemy nearly half a billion dollars. His became one of the great personal triumphs of the entire war.

Turkey was far more important to the course of the war in Europe than the German colonies were and in addition to the Dardanelles campaigns, the Allies pecked at the outlying provinces of the empire, feebly in terms of results, wastefully in terms of manpower and matériel employed. There were three frontiers on which Turkey was attacked, two of them British, one of them Russian.

The Russians and Turks fought practically a separate war up in the Caucasus Mountains, between the Black and Caspian seas and around the Russian province of Georgia. For nearly three years the battle seesawed back and forth, with the Turks driving forward into the mountains and the Russians, as soon as they recovered, driving southwest back out of them. The Turks were incredibly hampered by their overall commander, Enver Pasha, who could not resist making grandiose plans according to the map rather than realistic ones according to the country. They were further disadvantaged by their propensity for turning aside to slaughter noncombatants, especially Armenians, and finally by the fact that on this peripheral front the Russians produced an extremely able general, Nikolai Yudenich, who knew both his business and his troops. In many ways this was an old-fashioned war that had been going on for generations between Cossack and Turk, and there were few of the refinements of modern technology and weaponry employed elsewhere. Except for machine guns and smallish amounts of up-to-date artillery, this was still nineteenth-century warfare.

The first Turkish drive had opened in the winter of 1914, and the Russians stopped it at the fiercely fought battle of Sarikamis. Much of the maneuvering and fighting was done in temperatures that went to fifty-five degrees below freezing, and few wounded lasted long in that. The Turkish field army ended the campaign reduced from 95,000 to 18,000. The Russians followed up this victory by advancing in the spring. They got as far as Malazgirt, where the Turks turned the tables on them and pummeled them back to their own territory; then the Turks too overextended once again, and the year ended with both sides fought out.

By 1916 the Turks were able to reinforce with battle-tested troops freed by the British evacuation of Gallipoli. In spite of this Yudenich gained the jump on them and advanced as far as Erzerum, which he stormed in the middle of bitter February weather. A Russian amphibious operation at the same time took the fabled port city of Trebizond. The thought of this was anathema to Enver Pasha, and he ordered his generals to clear the Russians out. Before they could do so, however, Yudenich struck forward again. His troops broke the Turkish lines south of Trebizond, and the Cossacks harried one Turkish army out of existence. Only farther south did steady men from the Dardanelles under the command of Mustafa Kemal hold fast, but the Russians ended 1916 well ahead on points.

That was as far as they got, for with the spring the Russian armies began to disintegrate. An able commander such as Yudenich held his troops together better than most, but slowly they recoiled. The Turks followed them up and ended the campaign largely as they had begun it, moving into the mountains and massacring the unfortunate Armenians, more than half a million of whom fell before Turkish guns and bayonets in the midst of of shameful scenes of carnage.

The second theater of operations for the Allies in the Turkish Empire was in the Persian Gulf. The gulf coast had for centuries been the home of fiercely independent and unceasingly quarrelsome sheikhs, who lived by piracy and raiding their neighbors. In the nineteenth century, as an adjunct to their Indian trade and the necessity of protecting its marine aspects, the British had moved into the gulf, had established naval patrols, and had succeeded in getting the sheikhs to sign truces saying they would behave themselves. The southern shore eventually became known as the Trucial Coast. The northern shore was under the control of Persia, an area so coveted by both Britain and Russia that neither could countenance the other controlling it, and this standoff allowed Persia to retain its independence during the period. The development of oil as an energy source and the discovery of it in the gulf sharpened British interests there; much of the debate about shifting from coal to oil for warships, for example, centered around the problem of security of fuel supply. So when Turkey declared war, the British naturally looked to the gulf, and the India Office took measures, initially defensive in character, which soon involved them in a mess of trouble.

Their first move was the dispatch of troops to garrison the Anglo-Persian Oil Company installations on Adaban Island, right at the head of the gulf. These occupied the island against negligible opposition, then moved upriver to Basra, the main town of the area, which they took after fairly heavy fighting against the Turkish garrisons; there they established a base.

Officers who can be content with achieving easily what they have been ordered to do are nearly as rare as politicians who, ignorant of military problems, can avoid the temptation to grab something on the cheap. The senior commander in Basra, General Sir John Nixon, and General C. V. F. Townshend, his fire-eating subordinate, were anxious to go forward and to improve their situation, though how far forward they would have to go to do that was problematical. The officials of the India Office and the Colonial Office agreed with them, and before anyone was sure why it had developed, or what it was actually supposed to achieve, there was a full-scale campaign afloat in Mesopotamia. By the end of July in 1915 the Anglo-Indians had secured their oil pipeline from Persia and had advanced up both the Tigris and Euphrates rivers, reaching Amara on the former and Nasiriya on the latter.

Though there was occasionally heavy fighting, the Turks were really not in the area in strength, and the major British problem was supply; the rivers were shallow, even drying up in the hot seasons. The temperature was appalling, disease was rife, and the conditions were generally primitive and nasty for everyone. The British made a considerable attempt, not entirely successful at first, to convince both the Turks and the Arabs in the area that the invaders were their friends, and that the Turkish government had fallen prey to the wiles of the Germans, forgetting the true interests of its own people.

The next leap forward was up the Tigris as far as Kut al Amara. This was halfway to Baghdad, the major city of Mesopotamia and the only possible objective of the campaign, once the British had committed themselves to something more than hanging on to the oil fields. Townshend as the field commander was keen to advance as far as Kut, even though it meant going out on a fairly thin limb for his communications, with a shallow and chancy river behind him. The Turks made a serious attempt to stop him, but he levered them out of their positions before Kut, very nearly cut their line of retreat, and won for himself a neat little victory on September 28.

At this point politics once more intruded, and the India Office decided to try for Baghdad, as a counter to the now-obvious failure at Gallipoli. All Townshend's earlier pushing came home to haunt him; he said he had gone as far as it was reasonable to go. His superiors, both military and political, wanted to know why on earth he had gone that far if he intended going no farther. They ordered him on.

Townshend therefore trimmed down his force, leaving behind at Kut everything that could be regarded as superfluous, and some things that could not, such as medical personnel, and set off for Baghdad. He found the Turks entrenched at Ctesiphon, seventy-odd miles upstream and but twenty short of the city. Here he attacked them vigorously but unsuccessfully on November 22. They were carefully dug in, they were as numerous as their attackers, and they fought hard and well. With considerable losses and no place else to go, Townshend fell back to Kut.

He was now in real trouble. The Turks followed him, and it was obvious to all the local inhabitants that the tide had turned. The British and Indian troops were thoroughly exhausted by the campaign, and the seventy miles back from Ctesiphon had been agony for the wounded. The river was low. With plenty of supplies in Kut, enough for two months if necessary, Townshend began digging trenches and fortifying his lines. He was ready for a siege.

So were the Turks. They soon had his lines invested, and the Germans obligingly sent down General Baron von der Goltz, a specialist in siege warfare, to help them out with technical advice. By the first week in December, Townshend was well and truly boxed in and calling for rescue.

The British made three attempts to fight their way through, but the Turks fortified the river below the town and created formidable lines with their flanks anchored on marshes, canals, or the river itself. In January of 1916 the first relief attempt was turned back at the battle of Shaikh Sa'ad, with 6,000 casualties. A second try in March failed again, with another 3,500 men lost. By this time the troops in Kut were eating horses and mules.

In April the British made their last effort, under the command of General G. F. Gorringe, who was probably the best soldier in the theater at the time. A careful and meticulous worker, he managed to lever the Turks out of two positions, but then stuck at the third and failed to breach the Turkish line at Sannaiyat. Fought out, the British had to give up relief attempts for the foreseeable future. Townshend opened negotiations, and on April 29 he surrendered the surviving 10,000 men of his garrison.

Coming as it did more or less on the heels of the evacuation at Gallipoli, Townshend's fall was a severe blow to the pride and sense of self of Great Britain. It was up to that time the largest surrender of British troops on the field of battle; by contrast, Cornwallis at Yorktown had surrendered about 8,000 men, and Townshend's men were exceeded in numbers only by the surrender of the British at Singapore in 1942. To be beaten by the Turks, whom Britain professed to despise, both here and at the Dardanelles, further rubbed salt in the wound, as well as making it very bad for the poor soldiers, who were treated with the utmost brutality by their captors. Faces were very red at home, and the India Office found its control of the campaign usurped by the War Office; Nixon was relieved and replaced eventually by General F. S. Maude, who settled down to rebuild his army and do some serious soldiering.

There were, finally, bickerings in the Sinai Desert around the frontier of Egypt. The British as always were extremely sensitive to the security of the Suez Canal, the jugular vein of empire, and they assembled a large force in Egypt under the command of General Sir John Maxwell to protect it. Maxwell was so busy demanding more troops that he did little with the ones he had, and in January of 1915 an audacious Turkish force led by the German Baron Kress von Kressenstein actually raided the canal and got a few troops across to the west bank of it before being chased out.

The British then began to play that time-honored military game which says that one line will be secured if you hold another forward of it. In this case the refrain ran: Suez will be safe if we take Sinai; Sinai will be safe if we hold Palestine; Palestine will be secure if we take Constantinople. Most of 1915, however, was devoted to cleaning up a revolt among the Senussi tribesmen in the Nile Delta and west of there. The term "revolt" may be something of a misnomer, for the British had secured their political position in Egypt by the deposition of the pro-Turkish ruler and his replacement by one more congenial to themselves.

It was 1916 before they got ready to move into the Sinai Desert. Maxwell went home, replaced by General Sir Archibald Murray, who moved up along the coast, building a rail line and a water pipe as he went. The Turks contested the British advance, and Kress even got some German field artillery and mortar companies sent down to help him out, but by the end of 1916, Sinai was cleared, and the British were up to the Palestinian frontier and ready to try for Gaza.

Everything now went wrong. On his first try at Gaza, the field commander, General C. M. Dobell, got well inside the Turkish works and then abandoned his successes because of poor staff work and confusing reports. Murray nonetheless reported this home as a victory and was therefore told to continue on and take Jerusalem. That was in March of 1917. In April, Dobell again failed to take Gaza, losing casualties of three to one for the Turks. Needless to say, this rather surprised the authorities in London; Murray sacked Dobell and London sacked Murray. They sent down General Sir Edmund Allenby from the Western Front and told him to get on with the job. But by the middle of 1917, here they were still stalled on another front, and the only thing to encourage their sagging hopes was the fact that several of the desert Arab tribes were in revolt against the Turks, assisted by a rather bizarre English character named T. E. Lawrence. Most responsible British soldiers thought he was crazy.

The inability of British generals to overthrow the Turkish Empire did not in any way inhibit British and other Allied politicians from carving it up on their maps. Who was to get what out of Turkey became the great diplomatic parlor game of the war. It seemed good sense at the time, and few in positions of responsibility could foresee the endless trouble they were creating for themselves and their successors.

Taking them in chronological order, the Government of India— that is, the India Office in London—recognized Sheikh Ibn Saud, the leader of the puritanical sect of the Wahabi Moslems, as King of several of the Persian Gulf territories. That was in December of 1915.

At the same time the Anglo-Indian diplomats were dealing with Ibn Saud, the Egyptian government—that is, the Anglo-Egyptians

—were dealing with his rival, a man named Hussein, who was Sherif of Mecca. In June of 1916 he proclaimed an Arab revolt against the Turks, in return for which the British had promised independence for the Arabs, with certain rights and territories reserved for themselves. Hussein followed up the revolt by declaring himself "King of the Arabs" in October. Since this cut across the position already announced by Ibn Saud, and accepted by the British, they had to reply, rather shamefacedly, that they could recognize Hussein only as King of the Hejaz, roughly the Arabian coast of the Red Sea. In the long run Ibn Saud ended up ruling Saudi Arabia, and Hussein got the Transjordan.

Meanwhile, back in April of 1916, the British, French, and Russians all got together and agreed that each of them should have special spheres of influence in the postwar independent Arab states. One of the great ironies of World War I is that after spending a century keeping Russia away from the Dardanelles and the Middle East, as soon as war started, the western Allies were eager to promise Russia Constantinople and almost anything else to keep her in the fight.

Both British and French soon had second thoughts about this agreement, so the next month, in May, in what became known as the Sykes-Picot Agreement, they decided that they should not only have spheres of influence, but that they should have as well direct control of some specific areas within those spheres. They left the Russians out of that one.

Unfortunately, they also left the Italians out, and when word began to seep out, the Italians wanted to improve their position as well. So Britain and France, in the St. Jean de Maurienne agreement, conceded that Italy should have an enlargement of her territory in the Turkish province of Adalia and around the city of Smyrna. That was in April of 1917. The noted diplomatic historian William L. Langer summed all these up by saying, "These agreements were not entirely compatible with other agreements made with Arab chieftains, agreements which, indeed, were not compatible with each other."

Even that was not the end of the story, for in November of 1917 Arthur Balfour, the British Foreign Secretary, issued a document which became known as the Balfour Declaration. In it His Majesty's Government announced that it favored "the establishment in Palestine of a national home for the Jewish people." The move was partly a play for support from the Zionist movement, and partly, it has always been suspected, a means of interposing a buffer between the postwar French sphere of influence and the Suez Canal. The British spent the next twenty-five years trying to explain what they meant by "a national home," and why a national home was not a state—for to the Jews the term meant a state, which they passionately wanted, and to the Arabs it meant a state, which they passionately did not want. As so often happens, carefully chosen diplomatic ambiguities were eventually interpreted by men with blunter weapons. The pen is not always mightier than the sword.

In fairness to the politicians, "the frocks" as the soldiers contemptuously termed them, it must be pointed out that such a bald summation of deals does considerable violence to the confusion and the cross-purposes of the times. There certainly was chicanery and double-dealing, much of it indefensible. But the deals were usually made by different men working from different circumstances, and motivated by different points of view. By the time these agreements were made, almost every other consideration had paled before the overriding necessity of winning the war. The Central Powers made the same kind of promises to the same people, but fortunately for their subsequent records, they never had to deliver. For the Allies, a certain degree of disingenuousness, as they then saw it, with feudal tribal chieftains was a small price to pay if it led, in however tangential a way, to the end of the war.

# 15. The Nadir of the War

THE WINTER OF 1916–17 was known in Europe as the "turnip winter"; until that time turnips were for animals, but now they were eaten by people, who were glad to get them. Shortages were endemic, and long lines for goods a hallmark of the season. War is an immense consumer, without any corresponding production, and this war was more of a consumer than any before it. It ate up huge quantities of raw materials; iron that would have made streetcars or stoves went to make guns and shells instead. It ate up men; eighteen- and nineteen-year-olds who would have gone into factories or farms went into the trenches and did not return. European civilization had become a cannibal, gobbling up its own flesh and blood and crying unceasingly for more.

By mid-winter the war had lasted twenty-nine months, more than the number of days predicted by some optimists at the beginning of it. The situation remained unrelievedly gloomy. By Christmas of 1916, after Jutland, the Somme, Verdun, the Isonzo, and Brusilov's offensive, there was hardly a family in Europe that had not lost someone.

The greater the sacrifices demanded, the farther away peace seemed to be. As the war cost more and seemed worth less, it was pursued ever more desperately. The more insatiable the monster grew, the more moderate men were shunted aside for those willing to face the test. In all the major belligerents, there was a shift away from the leaders who had initially directed the war toward those who wanted to wage it more vigorously.

To be more accurate, the shift was toward those who wanted others to wage it more vigorously, for one of the peculiarities of this war was the opening of a vast schism between those who were fighting it and all the rest of society. Most of the hate was concentrated behind the front lines, and the soldiers in the trenches felt a perverse sympathy for the man in the trench across the way. That did not at all prevent them from trying to kill each other with a vicious abandon, but it meant that all frontline soldiers, no matter what their uniforms, were victims of the system that had put them where they were. Many a soldier wished he could take a machine gun or rifle butt not to the Frenchman or German fifty yards away, but to the well-fed staff officers who sent up ridiculous orders or to the complacent and fiercely patriotic civilian he met on his occasional leave. Never before had the conditions of war been more brutal, and never before had they been so heavily concentrated on the heads of the "poor bloody infantry." This was but one more of the many schizophrenias produced by the war. Had they been given a choice, which of course they were not, few of those who went off so eagerly and innocently to war would have stayed in it.

In Paris, London, and Berlin, however, there was still plenty of martial resolve. All over the Continent those whom the war found lacking were ignored. "Give me men to match my mountains," the poet said, but the war said, "Give me men to match my appetites."

By the time the counteroffensive at Verdun ended late in 1916, the French were near the end of their resources. The losses had been astronomical, the most productive industrial areas still lay under German control, discontent and war-weariness were widespread. In 1914, under President Raymond Poincaré and Premier René Viviani, France had joined in a massive surge of national unity. Bitter political hatreds dating at least from the establishment of the Third Republic in 1871 or from the Dreyfus Affair, which ended in 1906, were set aside, and all parties joined in a national front known as the *union sacrée*. The government had adopted a military and an economic war plan that was predicated on a short war, and there was a massive temporary dislocation of French industry and commerce. Banks, businesses, even factories producing war matériel shut down for the anticipated duration of the war.

Reality hit hard when it dawned on them that the war was not to be short, and the whole public approach had to be reworked. Half a million men were demobilized from the army and sent back to work in the armaments factories. Yet government controls and demands remained spotty. If industry was remarkably reshaped, public expression was not, and assorted papers in France continued to be subsidized by the German government, spreading defeatist propaganda throughout the country. By late 1916 criticism of Premier Briand, who had replaced Viviani in the fall of 1915, was becoming more and more overt. Few French Premiers in modern times have avoided overt criticism, but what was more startling than that, voices were raised against the military leadership of the General Staff and even against Papa Joffre himself. The saviour of France two years ago now appeared a bumbler with only one idea, and that not a good one. In December of 1916 Briand carried out the kind of musical chairs Cabinet shuffle that enables French politicians to continue making a living as French politicians whether they are doing anything or not. It gained his government a few more months of life, but the opposition continued to grow in stridency, led by the man who was to become the embodiment of the Republic.

Georges Clemenceau had been born in the Vendée, that home of lost causes, in 1841. A physician, he had lived in the United States for some years after the American Civil War. In the 1870's he had associated with the extreme radical left in the Chamber of Deputies. As a brilliant journalist he had founded the paper *L'Aurore*, and it was in this that Emile Zola published the famous *J'accuse* letter in 1898. In French political life Clemenceau was called "The Tiger," or the "destroyer of ministries"—and that was what people who liked him called him. From 1906 to 1909 he was Premier of France. He vividly remembered 1870 and France's humiliating defeat by Prussia, and his most consistent attitude was utter hatred of things German. With his laments for Alsace-Lorraine, and his demands that the growing might of Germany must be destroyed, he played Cato the Elder to the Third Republic. French political journalism has never been known for dignified restraint, and as 1916 ended, Clemenceau's vituperation rose to new crescendos: The war must be won, and nothing and no one else mattered.

This type of pressure finally caused Poincaré to issue a decree kicking Joffre upstairs. He became commander-in-chief, directly under the Minister of War, which left him free to fiddle with ration returns and not much else. He resigned in December, whereupon the government made him a Marshal of France. At the business end, General Robert Nivelle, last involved in the work around Verdun, succeeded him as commander of the French armies on the

Western Front. Nivelle and the politicians got along well.

Even this sort of shuffling about did not satisfy the critics, and in March of 1917 Briand finally quit. His replacement was the septuagenarian Alexandre Ribot, no better and no worse than a dozen other political gentlemen. Paul Painlevé accepted the Ministry of War, and these two, basking in the happy optimism of General Nivelle, heard plans for a new offensive. France had already suffered more than 3 million casualties, nearly a million of them dead. To the Tiger's cries for action Nivelle returned a cunning smile: He was going to win the war.

He very nearly did—for Germany.

The British had never expected to fight a large-scale continental war; they had little experience of it and no desire to acquire any. In spite of the glorious traditions of Wellington and Marlborough, Britain had not made the major military contribution to any of the great coalition wars of modern history. Her role had been to control the seas and loosen the purse strings. The demands of this new kind of war necessitated a rapid adjustment. Still, British institutions possessed the stability and the flexibility of long practice, and without perhaps entirely realizing what they were involved in, the British turned their minds to this new and horrific reality.

The Liberal government, more or less firmly in power since 1906, did not see the need for taking the opposition into office with them at first, unlike the French with the *union sacrée*. Their only real change was the appointment of Kitchener as Secretary of State for War. By May of 1915, however, it was so obvious that the war was following a course different from the one projected for it that a coalition became necessary. In the face of stalemate in France and the new stalemate at the Dardanelles the government took in Conservative members and formed what is known as Asquith's Coalition Cabinet. There was also a streamlining of the major members into a War Committee.

Coalition governments are usually regarded as a retrograde step in the parliamentary system and indicate the nature of the adjustment required of Britain. But there were other, more profound shocks in store than that. In 1916 Ireland broke out in rebellion.

Ever since 1171, when King Henry II of England first landed in Ireland and asserted his sovereignty over it, the British and Irish had been at daggers drawn. By the late nineteenth century many leaders in England were reluctantly coming to the conclusion that virtual independence for Ireland or some form of Home Rule was the only real answer to the problem. Unfortunately, by this time the British had compounded their difficulties through the settlement of Protestant colonies, especially in the north of the island, so that solving the Irish Question meant aggravating the Northern Irish Question. They had created the classic historical situation of an unsolvable dilemma. By 1914, as the Parliament at Westminster moved hesitantly toward Home Rule for Ireland, the Protestant North moved unhesitantly toward armed assertion of its own case.

The war temporarily sidetracked these problems, but not for long. There were inevitably Irish leaders, patriots they called themselves, traitors the British called them, who saw opportunity knocking while Britain was embroiled in war. Just as some of them had sought aid from Revolutionary France and Napoleon in the last general war, now some sought it from Germany. On April 20, 1916, Sir Roger Casement, who had been knighted in 1911 for his work in the consular service, landed from a German submarine. The rebellion had been long in the making; Casement, ironically, had come to call it off, for he had found the Germans were not serious in their offers of help. As often happens, however, the situation first hung fire, then flared up almost by accident. A small minority of Irish extremists took up arms in Dublin on Easter Sunday, seized the post office, and proclaimed the Irish Republic. Four days later they were in prison, and four months after that their leaders were hanged. The Irish Problem was pushed back underground.

Yet military disaster piled on political mistake finally undid Asquith. General Townshend surrendered at Kut soon after the Easter Rising; the government brought in conscription; Kitchener, out of favor, went off on an inspection trip to Russia and was drowned when the cruiser *Hampshire* hit a mine. The criticisms rose on all sides. The war demanded firmer measures, said David Lloyd George, the fierce and formerly radical Welsh politician, and Lloyd George knew just who the man was to apply them. In December of 1916 a tired Asquith gave up, and Lloyd George replaced him with a coalition of radical Liberals and hard-line Conservatives. The new Prime Minister was a complete disbeliever in Douglas Haig, as he had been in the now dead Kitchener. So in both Britain and France, there was growing agreement among leading politicians that the war must be fought more intensely, and also that the generals, hitherto unchecked, were not entirely the men for the job.

The ongoing stress of war meant stronger men in Russia, too, but not of the type that was emerging in western Europe. In February of 1916 Tsar Nicholas appointed Boris Stürmer as chief of the Cabinet. Stürmer was an arch-Conservative, and he was widely suspected of being pro-German. Naturally, his name did not help, but a great many Russians, especially of the governmental class, had foreign names derived from marriages in Germany or from the three-centuries-old Russian habit of importing western experts to modernize the country. Stürmer's real claim to power was that he was acceptable to the Tsarina Alexandra and to her mentor, Rasputin, with whom he was reported to confer nightly about affairs of state.

In July, Stürmer dismissed Foreign Minister Sazonov and took over the ministry himself. This was regarded as bad news in the West, for Sazonov was notably pro-Allied, while Stürmer was both disliked and distrusted. Stürmer's answer to all of Russia's problems was simply more governmental repression. He soon found it impossible to stifle all of the discontent, for it would have meant putting virtually the entire country in prison. In November the Duma threw off its generally ineffectual mantle long enough to protest against the way the government was conducting affairs, and Nicholas at last dismissed Stürmer. As was his custom, the Tsar accompanied his step forward by one backward, for he now appointed as chief minister Alexander Trepov, and Trepov believed in repression as the answer to everything even more than Stürmer did.

By the end of the year the Russians were in despair. There was talk of regicide, not only among the radical and extremist underground but also among the members of the aristocracy itself. The army was in disarray, desertions were mounting, shortages were felt everywhere, the communications network was near collapse, the cities torn by strikes and riots. Successive call-ups of soldiers had left essential industries and services undermanned, and there was a general sense of the country collapsing under the strain. Under the circumstances, it is not surprising that some Russians hitherto supportive of the monarchy took drastic action; it is more surprising that they waited as long as they did.

People close to the throne had long known the Tsar was weak, but no one believed him evil. They now concluded that if he were to stay, the malign influences over him must go. Prince Felix Yusupov and some of his aristocratic colleagues decided to assassinate Rasputin. In the midst of a war in which millions of young men were being killed in peculiarly beastly conditions, the death of one man, and that not a very good one, may seem of little import. To say that is to underestimate the mental effort required for a group of nobles, in a country where, though casual brutality was endemic, the death penalty was hardly ever enforced, to decide actually to commit murder.

On the night of December 29–30 Yusupov invited Rasputin to his palace to dine. The conspirators plied him with cakes and wine, both poisoned, and watched in horror as he happily stuffed himself and asked for more. Finally, in near terror, they pulled out revolvers and shot him repeatedly. Still refusing to die, he began to crawl out of the palace, while they beat him with revolver butts and hacked at him with their sabers. At last they stuffed him under the ice of the Neva River. Later when the Tsarina had his corpse recovered, the doctors found he had died of drowning.

The conspirators were kept under guard but not tried. The Tsar and Tsarina went into private mourning. If Russia heaved a sigh of relief at the end of evil counsels in the dynasty, it was short-lived; Alexandra and Nicholas, feeling betrayed, deserted, and fearful, could think of nothing better than to continue as before. One of Rasputin's prophecies preyed on the Tsarina's mind: "If I die or you desert me, your son and your throne will not last six months."

Yet another of the great actors passed from the scene before the end of 1916, for the Emperor Franz Josef died on November 21. As his empire was doing, he himself had faded into the shadows, reduced both by his own great age and the pressure of events to little more than a figurehead. The politicians and soldiers had assumed more and more of the power he had wielded so diligently, as shown by his often-quoted remark to a supplicant: "I can do nothing for you; don't you know a sergeant-major with influence?"

Franz Josef was succeeded on the throne by his grand-nephew, Charles; there had been earlier Charleses on the Hapsburg throne, but their titles had been different, so this Charles took the number "I"; there was not likely to be a "II." His wife, the Empress Zita, came from the family of Parma, one of the few in Europe that considered itself every bit the social peers of the Hapsburgs. Together they made a striking couple, both of them handsome and regal looking; unfortunately, he was weak though well intentioned, and she was a bit of a schemer and not much more.

Charles desperately wished to get out of a struggle that he could see no way of winning. As far as his empire was concerned, the war had long lost its original purpose of quelling minority demands and putting Austria's neighbors in their place. The state was threatening to break up under the imperial feet. A month before the old Emperor's death the Prime Minister had been assassinated; his successor had seen nothing to do but to remodel the war organization of the country along German lines and to accept increasing German domination of Austria's internal life. His military counterparts had already done the same thing. The most august and ancient dynasty in Europe had become a mere satellite of a bunch of upstart Prussians, whose rulers had been border-runners when the Hapsburgs were Holy Roman Emperors. However well-meaning he might be, Charles was not the man to cross swords with the Germans. The Austrian government had drafted a peace proposal which Franz Josef had accepted before he died. But by the time it was cleared with Berlin, it was reduced to meaningless verbiage, a red herring which the Allies were bound to refuse. Charles could only sigh and pray that he and his family might survive the disaster he could see looming in the future.

If Austria wanted peace at virtually any price, the Germans, as did the Allies, wanted it only with victory. They had fought too hard and gained too much to give up the struggle without a tangible acknowledgment that they had won it. They had, after all, kept practically the rest of the world at bay for two years now; their troops firmly held large portions of France and Russia, and virtually all of Belgium, Rumania, and Serbia. Who could doubt that they were the winners?

But there was doubt and there was worry. Though they might look good on the maps, the Germans had not won the war until their opponents admitted they had done so, and in spite of lost territory the Allies seemed disinclined to such an admission. Germany's problem then was that even she could not sustain the current situation indefinitely. The indirect pressure of the blockade—such an insidiously British weapon; just like them!—was slowly strangling her. The question now was how to alter the balance even farther in Germany's favor, and the answer here was provided not by the civilian politicians as in France and Britain, but by the soldiers. On the other side they might think that "war was too serious to be left to generals" in Clemenceau's phrase; in Germany they thought everything ought to be left to generals, and Hindenburg and Ludendorf fully agreed with this view.

The pair were by now unchallenged masters of the German Empire. Chancellor Bethmann-Hollweg had been upstaged, and civilian and diplomatic moves were cleared with the General Staff before anything was done. A War Materials Organization under the direction of Walther Rathenau, formerly head of the largest industrial combine in Europe, had already fully mobilized the economy of the Reich, subordinating all else to the demands of the war effort. The Kaiser was reduced to the role of funnel; ideas and policies went through his hands, but he had minimal control over them. Hindenburg and Ludendorff made the decisions, and at the end of 1916 they made a momentous one. Eventually it cost them the war.

Given the necessity of ending the stalemate, something had to be done, for even Germany was war-weary. At the start of October, 30,000 workers in Frankfurt held a mass meeting and demanded peace on the basis of the prewar situation. Mass meetings were not exactly officially approved in Wilhelmine Germany, where the Kaiser himself had openly looked forward to the day when he could, as he liked to say, clear out the Reichstag with the bayonet. Later in the month the Reichstag itself barked, voting to examine foreign policy and the conduct of the war. Since Germany was constitutionally about where Great Britain had been in the eighteenth century, and both these areas of national activity were still a matter of the sovereign's prerogatives, this was practically a revolution. Some new direction was clearly needed.

A major problem for a state at war is the accurate assessment of the enemy. Spies may report what they pick up, but they know little of the whole, and they may even report what their masters want to hear rather than what they really see. Once the normal intercourse of society breaks down, antagonists are forced to create intelligence pictures which may or may not be very accurate. Had the German leaders in late 1916 correctly assumed that Great Britain, the paymaster of the Allies, was coming fairly close to bankruptcy, or had they read aright the signs of impending collapse in Russia, they might well have chosen to act differently than they did. Constrained by that limit from which only historians are free—that they could not see the future—the Germans played their last card.

That card was the submarine. Through the closing months of the year, discussion centered more and more around the navy and submarine warfare. The generals reached this by a gradual elimination of other alternatives. The army was at full stretch, yet able to achieve only a stalemate east and west. It could do no more than it was already doing. The civilian economy was equally fully extended; there was nothing more that could be done behind the front lines to give the soldiers a decisive edge. There was thus only one remaining area in which restraint might be significantly loosened, with war-winning results. The soldiers suggested that the navy throw off its self-imposed shackles and go all out for victory. Bethmann-Hollweg, with a wider view than that acquired in barracks, thought the adoption of a policy of unrestricted submarine warfare would be disastrous; it would probably lead to war with the United States, for one thing, and he was not at all sure Germany could stand that. The Admiralty disagreed; they guaranteed they could sink 600,000 tons of Allied shipping per month, and that that would knock Britain out of the war within six months. On October 7, the leaders of the Catholic Center Party in the Reichstag announced that if Hindenburg favored unrestricted submarine warfare, and Bethmann-Hollweg did not, they would vote against the Chancellor. The military men were firmly in the saddle.

Out of this debate came the German peace offer at the end of the year 1916. On December 12 the Germans announced, through the United States, that they were prepared to talk peace. They refused to mention any specific terms, though after their performance in the last twelve months, and especially the conquest of Rumania, they could only be thinking of a highly favorable settlement. The Allies indignantly rejected their offer. Meanwhile, President Wilson, newly reelected and still hoping to play a role as mediator, asked the belligerents to state their terms for opening negotiations. The Central Powers all responded with a reiteration of their vague offer but again refused specifics. The Allies responded with particular claims which were not too far different from the ones actually enforced at Versailles. To bring in such terms to a defeated enemy in 1919 was one thing; to suggest them to a near victorious enemy at the beginning of 1917 was blatantly insulting. Even Wilson was shocked and angered by the Allied claims, and the whole possibility of a negotiated peace immediately fell apart.

That may have been what the German leaders wanted all along anyway; the Allied terms were announced on January 10. Two days earlier, at a meeting held at Pless, the Germans had made the decision for unrestricted submarine warfare. It would probably make the United States enter the war, but the Admiralty stated the three premises for its case: Britain, as already assessed, would be knocked out in six months; the Americans could not build up an army in that time; even if they somehow could, the submarines would prevent its getting to Europe anyway.

Bethmann-Hollweg was not so sure the soldiers and sailors were right. Unfortunately, he had nothing to offer as an alternative. It was indeed the last card Germany had to play. The only other option was to go to the peace table, and obviously, no one who counted was yet ready to do that.

# 16. The Collapse of Russia

IN THE SIXTEENTH CENTURY the great humanist Erasmus observed that just when mankind had reached a level where it had the ability to abolish suffering and poverty and provide a good life for everyone, its rulers found a way to get rid of the possibility: They discovered the delights of war. Though this was an overly fond view of history, none of the advances of four more centuries had altered that situation. Spanish Hapsburgs and French Bourbons had been laid low by their expensive indulgence in war; it was, ironically, the accumulated debt of financing the War of the American Revolution that finally brought about the French Revolution. And now the Romanovs were to go the same way. The archaic state organization of Russia was simply not up to the demands of a western European-style war. The Tsars had had difficulties after the Crimean War, they had had a near revolution in the Russo-Japanese War, and in 1917 the cup finally ran over.

The Eastern Front had been relatively quiet after Brusilov's offensive collapsed late in 1916. The exhausted Russians could do no more, and the Central Powers, with Austria equally worn out, managed to overrun Rumania but left Russia alone while they did it. Little happened during the winter, and as the new year went on, neither side seemed inclined to break the uneasy calm blanketing the front. Before either could undertake a major military move, the soldiers were upstaged by events behind the line in Russia.

The revolution was not a plot; indeed, at first it did not even look like a revolution, it looked like a food riot. On March 8, 1917, the populace of Petrograd, the patriotic name since 1914 for the too-German sounding St. Petersburg, rose up demanding food. A demonstration, originally called to celebrate International Women's Day, began to get out of control. Petrograd and Moscow were the great industrial centers of Russia, and in them was concentrated all the misery of an emergent industrial society: slum housing, long hours, poor and criminally unequal distribution of goods and services. There had been shortages and long lines of hopeful customers ever since the war began, but by 1917 the hope was gone; only the long lines remained, and they were fertile breeding grounds for rumor and discontent. A thousand isolated individuals are just that, but a thousand people brought together by a common need or grievance are a pressure group—or a mob.

The food riots of March 8 might have remained a low-level disturbance if other conditions had not contributed to put them over the edge. Crowds continued to gather the next day, and March 10 was crucial. On that day the military garrison of the city, instead of suppressing the demonstrations as ordered, went over to the rioters. The Cossacks, the most hated and feared government instrument of crowd control, even turned their guns on the police, and by nightfall of this third day, there was shooting in the streets. The capital was slipping out of control.

Yet there still was no revolution as such. Allied Ambassadors in Petrograd reporting on the event did not think it would go too far. They estimated that Russia still had plenty of men left, that her war supplies were by no means exhausted, and that in some categories they were even now increasing, helped by the long lull on the front and the arrival at the northern ports and at Vladivostok of matériel from Russia's allies. The government would of course try to take firm measures, but if it took wise ones as well, the situation was not beyond redemption.

On the 11th the Romanovs moved to deal with the problem. The soldiers were now in open mutiny, led by the Pavlovsky Regiment of the Imperial Guard. Premier Golitsyn issued a decree from the Tsar dissolving the Duma, but the members of the assembly simply went from one hall to another, where they reestablished themselves and set up a Temporary Committee. In fact, the Duma was as irresolute as the government, and these moves meant little. Neither was the sort of development that on the one hand would have quelled rebellion, or on the other have controlled it.

Now the affair began to gather momentum. By the 12th, regiment after regiment was going over to the mob, and the soldiers of the garrison were out of control, turning on their officers, deserting, or setting up their own leaders—soldiers' councils or "soviets," as they called them. The Duma now moved to establish a Provisional Government, headed initially by Prince George Lvov; the most important member of the new Cabinet was the only Socialist in it, Alexander Kerensky, who became Minister of Justice. At the same time a potential rival was being organized in the form of the Council of Workers and Soldiers Representatives, or as it soon became known, the Petrograd Soviet.

Two rival claimants to power were two too many for Nicholas, and he responded characteristically; on the 15th he abdicated, in his own name and that of his son the Tsarevich. Not only was the abdication characteristic, but so was the manner of it, for Nicholas could not conceive of a clean break with the monarchical tradition. He gave the throne over to his brother, the Grand Duke Michael. This latter at least had a clearer view of events and in his one move on the historical stage he too abdicated, on the next day, the 16th, this time in favor of the Provisional Government, pending the meeting of a constituent assembly and an election.

Within little more than a week, it looked as if the "revolution" were over. In fact, a good four years of bloodshed, civil war, and terror Red and White was just beginning. The Provisional Government lasted from March until November—or from February until October, if one used the older Russian calendar—and it made a valiant effort to be a western-style parliamentary government.

It proclaimed a host of civil liberties and the abolition of social, racial, and religious discrimination. It recognized the independence of Finland within the Russian federation, and it acknowledged the total independence of Poland. Both of these were worthy concessions to the principle of nationality; neither meant much, as Finland was breaking away of its own accord, and virtually all of Poland was at the moment occupied by the Germans. Late in March the new government announced the confiscation of imperial and monastic lands and said it would distribute them to the peasantry. It was also going to undertake a vast program of social reform.

Regrettably, none of these measures was as convincing as might have been desired. Try as it might, the Provisional Government was still lumped in the popular mind with the old regime. The politicians of the Duma, after all, had not been generally perceived as being in the forefront of demands for reform. But the largest albatross around the government's collective neck remained the war.

The new leaders had loyally announced that they would continue fighting and would honor their obligations and their treaties with the Allies. The move, which of course was warmly welcomed in the

West, had the effect of making them appear the lineal descendants of the Romanov policies, and Russia had already had enough of those. Support of the war more than any other single factor may have doomed parliamentary government in Russia. To keep Russia's word to the Allies the dynamic Kerensky assumed the portfolio of Minister of War in May, and with General Brusilov he began planning a great offensive for July, designed both to defeat Russia's enemies and to galvanize support among the people for the new government and its policies.

The assumption that by the adoption of new political principles losers would be magically transformed into winners was unfortunately illusory. For while Kerensky and his party were trying to keep the war going, the soviets were trying much more successfully to stop it, by the simple but effective expedient of destroying the Russian Army. In addressing the men in the ranks, the soviets had several advantages not enjoyed by the Provisional Government. Where the latter represented the politicians and the minority of politically conscious Russians, the former became the real focus of power, uniting the urban civilian working class and the rural peasant soldiery. They were further blessed in having no responsibility; everything that went wrong—and that included nearly everything in Russia at the moment—the soviets could blame on the Provisional Government. The men who made up the soviets were not after all babes in the wilderness; they were tough veterans from the dark side of politics, thwarted union organizers, shop stewards, barrackroom lawyers, professional agitators, some confessed revolutionaries, members of the Communist party. They had learned their business in a hard school, and if they made a great many mistakes they had an instinct for the jugular that put them light years ahead of the Provisional Government when it came to the sharp end of politics, getting the man or woman in the street to do what they wanted.

Their unwitting destruction of the army began early, when the Petrograd Soviet issued Order No. 1 on March 14, even before the Tsar abdicated. Prompted by fear that the officers would soon attempt a counterrevolutionary coup, the order "democratized" the army, destroying the rank hierarchy and abolishing officers' privileges and their authority along with it. Listening to an order that said no more saluting, no more guard duty if one chose not to do it, few soldiers stopped to ask about the legitimacy of the issuing body. A committee system was immediately established to deal with supply and administration, and orders from the Provisional Government attempting to countermand the soviet move were completely ignored. Desertions skyrocketed, whole formed units of troops marched where they chose, officers either went along with them, were left behind, or were shot or bayoneted.

Memoirists have left intriguing accounts of units trying to decide what to do. Old noncommissioned officers would speak to the men, pleading for loyalty and obedience; meanwhile, members of the soviets moved through the masses, muttering the magic phrase, "Peace, land, bread . . ." like an incantation. It seldom failed to work. The army dissolved in chaos.

At the beginning of July, Brusilov, now the Chief of Staff, launched Russia's last offensive of the war. It was Russian in name only, for the troops that could be trusted to advance were mostly Finns and Poles, with a few nonpolitical Siberians, and smatterings of other troops drawn from the imperial fringes. They made a good start. Attacking around Lemberg, they pushed the Germans and Austrians back for nearly thirty miles. Their left flank, under General Kornilov, made especially good progress, but they could not sustain it. Within a week the troops had refused to go any farther, and the offensive was over. The Germans prepared a major riposte, opened it on July 19, and by August had driven the Russians back to the border of Galicia, a good seventy-five miles from where they had originally started. Not only did the failure of the effort mark Russia's last offensive in the war, it brought the first overt attempt to overthrow the Provisional Government. The Bolsheviks led by Nikolai Lenin had their first try at seizing power.

Vladimir Ilyich Ulyanov, who called himself Lenin, was born in 1870, a member of the minor intelligentsia in the provincial Russian town of Simbirsk. Before he was out of his teens he had become a committed revolutionary and an ardent student of Karl Marx. His activities and his opinions cost him three years in Siberia, after which he left Russia and took up residence in Switzerland. That was in 1900; three years later he became the leader of the minority wing of the Russian Communist party, known as "Bolsheviks." They had split from the majority, the "Mensheviks," over the issue of proper interpretation of the Marxist gospel. The Mensheviks thought that the Communist state could be brought into being by gradual pressure and by insinuating themselves into the ranks of parliamentary government. Castigating this as "bourgeois reformism," Lenin and the Bolsheviks insisted that only violence, as predicated by Marx, would bring about the true classless society.

In 1905, at the time of the abortive unrest in Russia, Lenin returned home, but found that conditions were not yet ripe. Disgruntled and unhappy, he returned to Switzerland once again, where he and his wife and a small group of true believers continued to eke out a fragile existence, writing tracts, smuggling funds into and out of Russia, waiting and working and hoping for the great day. It came in April of 1917.

The Germans knew of Lenin's situation, and in one of the most fateful decisions of the century they decided he was just what they needed. The new government in Russia was making noises about its determination to remain in the war; from the Germans' point of view, any further deterioration of the Russian scene was all to the good. It has been written that the Germans injected Lenin into Russia like a plague bacillus. Discreet contacts were made, and Lenin allowed that he was quite willing to accept German assistance and German money in the pursuit of his own aims. If the capitalist states were fool enough to help him work toward their own ultimate destruction, that merely seemed to confirm Marx's view of the finally self-destructive nature of capitalism. The Germans provided a sealed train for Lenin and his companions. Boarding it in Switzerland, they were carried through Germany to the Baltic, and traveled from there to Finland.

As soon as he arrived in Petrograd, Lenin set to work. He declared that the "bourgeois" revolution was but a passing phase and that all efforts must be bent to bringing about the "true" and "proletarian" revolution. Up until this time the Communists had more or less worked with the other parties, but now Lenin rigorously followed his own course. His organization and his dynamism soon made him a power to be counted in the Russian scheme of things. He was close to breaking apart the fragile unity that the other parties had so far achieved under the aegis of the Provisional Government.

Lenin was not of course alone. There was the small following he had brought with him from Switzerland, there were Bolsheviks in Russia already, who now came to the fore in the hurly-burly of revolutionary politics, and there were other exiles who saw their chance to make a mark at last. One of them, for example, was working in the post office in New York City when the revolution broke out. His name was Lev Bronstein, a Jew from the Ukraine with much the same background as Lenin's. He started for home, was arrested in Halifax, Nova Scotia, imprisoned for a while by Canadian authorities, and then released upon application by the Russians through the British. He got home to become Lenin's right-hand man, the creator of the Red Army, and very nearly Lenin's successor. His revolutionary name was Leon Trotsky, and he ended up in Mexico in 1940, murdered by an assassin who buried a geologist's pick in his skull.

The tragic dilemma of revolutions now developed, that it is all but impossible to be moderate in a situation created by extremes. Under pressure from left, right, and the Germans, the Provisional Government began the fatal oscillation that has signaled the imminent fall of post-revolutionary parliamentary governments in the past. The German counteroffensive in July seemed to Lenin to herald the ripening of his schemes, and in the middle of the month he attempted to seize full power in Petrograd. It turned out to be a mistake; the government still had more reserve strength than Lenin had assumed, and after two days the coup fizzled. Lenin and some of his immediate supporters were forced to go into temporary exile across the border in Finland.

The abortive coup was only one of several pressing problems. In the space of a few days the Finns announced their complete independence, the Ukraine was also threatening to break away, and even the Cossacks were establishing their own regime led by their traditional hetman. Under these blows Prince Lvov resigned, and Kerensky, by now acknowledged as the real force in the government, became Prime Minister. He and his Cabinet were torn between the demands of the people, sick to death of the war and the shortages and cleverly played upon by the Bolsheviks, and the equally vociferous demands of the rightist groups, especially some of the army officers, led by General Kornilov, who wanted a firmer hand with the Bolsheviks.

In September, Kornilov made his move. Dismissed by Kerensky for insubordination, the general instead gathered up his forces and ordered them to march on Petrograd. Before he got there, his attempt, too, collapsed; many of the soldiers deserted, the railway workers refused to transport them, or did it so reluctantly that organization broke down, and the government mobilized popular support to stop the army. It managed that, however, only by turning to the Bolsheviks, Trotsky, in prison since Lenin's July coup, was released, and stopping the right threw the government into the hands of the left. Kornilov had achieved exactly what he had set out to prevent. In October the Bolsheviks became the majority party in the Petrograd Soviet, and Trotsky was elected chairman. Lenin, back in the capital once more, timed his move more carefully now, and on November 6, in a scuffle that was far less dramatic than it deserved to be, given its historical importance, the Bolsheviks seized power. It was October 24 in the old calendar, so in Russian history this is called the October Revolution. Kerensky got away to a distinguished career as an exile in the United States. The next day the Second All-Russian Congress of Soviets ratified the coup. The Socialists gave up, and the Bolsheviks assumed full power. Throughout Russia they were soon engaged in civil war and fighting for their lives.

It was not part of Lenin's plan to fight Germany. The war was nearly but not quite held in abeyance while the Russians worked out their own salvation or damnation. Almost immediately after he had seized power, Lenin offered the Germans an armistice.

Up to that point German pressure, light though it was, had been of major assistance to the Bolsheviks. A factor in the decline of the Kerensky government had been the German offensive around Riga in September. Though it was a limited affair, and the only real German advance between the summer of 1917 and their final moves, it was significant both in its effect on Kerensky and Lenin, and in its own right as a military operation, for it introduced the "Hutier tactics," which were to come close to winning the war for Germany.

General Oscar von Hutier was commander of 8th Army, on the northern end of the German line along the Baltic coast. For two years the Germans had been making occasional attempts to take the fortress of Riga, all without success. Wishing to capitalize on Russia's internal difficulties, the Germans decided to exert more pressure on them; the taking of Riga might make them ask for an armistice.

By now the technicians and theorists of the General Staff had made a thorough study of the tactical impasse on the fighting fronts. They had carefully analyzed the successes and the failures of both sides. They noted the way some of the British units had made an initial gain on the Somme, how their own troops had attacked at Verdun, and how the French had riposted; they studied Brusilov's tactics in his great offensive as well. They came to essentially the conclusion that Brusilov and his staff had reached. The vital difference was that the Germans knew why they had reached it, whereas Brusilov had largely stumbled on it by the accident of ammunition shortage and discarded it as soon as the shortages were made up. Brusilov's lucky shot became Germany's tactical doctrine.

The Riga offensive contained all the new elements: last-minute approach of fully briefed and highly trained troops, specialized units assigned to given tasks, short preliminary barrage that did not give the attack away, close coordination and support for infantry by carefully controlled artillery fire, and advance and infiltration that bypassed strongpoints and flowed through weak spots.

The drive opened suddenly on September 1. Two days later Riga was German and the Baltic coast wide open. A week after that Kornilov attempted his coup. In the next month the Germans went on to overrun Latvia and the Baltic islands, creating an obvious threat to Petrograd, and in November Lenin seized power. Three weeks later he asked for an armistice.

It took the Germans a week to reply, but hostilities along the Eastern Front were suspended in early December. The representatives of the Central Powers and of the Bolsheviks met at Brest-Litovsk in Poland on December 3 to discuss a peace settlement. Trotsky, ultimately representing the Soviets, was in a poor bargaining position. His government had already broadcast to the world a request for an immediate peace without annexations or war indemnities, which had been utterly ignored in the chancellories of the belligerents. The Allies regarded the Bolsheviks as traitors to the great cause and were already considering how they might be brought down and Russia kept in the war. The Central Powers, having won at least this part of their war, were in no mood to listen to what they considered sophomoric and utopian schemes from their victims. In addition, the Bolsheviks' domestic position was far from secure. If they gave in too much to the Germans, they might well be overthrown at home; indeed, their power base was so insecure that they were still receiving financial support from Germany, and the Germans were still paying it because they wanted to keep the Bolsheviks afloat long enough to get their peace treaty negotiated.

The desirability of propping up the Leninist regime did not extend to giving it favorable peace terms. Germany's demands were formulated largely by the General Staff and were indeed considered unduly harsh by Richard von Kuhlmann, the diplomat sent to negotiate them. When Trotsky received these proposals he blanched and tried desperately to stall for time. Time, however, was running strongly against the Bolsheviks. Finland was gone, the Ukraine going, the Cossacks in arms, Bessarabia declared its independence, the Baltic States were in an uproar, and the heart of Russia itself was in complete chaos.

What the Germans wanted was independence for all the border states of the Russian Empire: Finland, Poland, the Baltic provinces, Moldavia, Galicia, and even Armenia. Though the terms demanded varied from one proposal to another, and even from day to day, they essentially included pushing Russia back several hundred miles and replacing the Russian with a German sphere of economic and political influence in eastern Europe. Publication of the demands both horrified the Russians and hardened the western allies, who took them as indicative of the kind of claims the Germans would make in any peace discussions that preceded complete victory.

Negotiations dragged on into the new year. Twist and turn as they might, the Russians could not get the Germans to lessen their demands; in fact, the more intransigent the Russians were, the more the Germans upped their claims. On the first of February they recognized the independence of the Ukraine.

Under such pressure, Lenin and Trotsky hit on a new device. On February 10 Trotsky simply and loftily announced that the Russian government considered the war over. Since the Germans would not agree to a reasonable peace settlement, there would be none. He unilaterally declared the peace discussions and the war were over. Initially mildly bemused by this novel approach, the Germans soon decided they would show the Bolsheviks what the real world was like, and they ordered their armed forces into motion once again. Along the front from the Pripet Marshes north, they advanced about a hundred miles. On the Baltic coast this brought them from Riga to Lake Peipus, or more than halfway to Petrograd. In the south they moved even farther and still kept on after the Russians hastily came back to the peace table.

For the Russians of course did come back. They had no trustworthy armed forces left with which to halt the German advance, and they were absolutely helpless in any real sense. At the end of February, Trotsky reappeared once more and humbly said he was ready to talk. By that time the Germans were getting impatient—they had other things to do besides deal with recalcitrant Russians

—and they upped their demands yet again. They kept their troops going right into the Ukraine and down to and past the Crimea. They demanded Russian locomotives and rolling stock, artillery pieces and machine guns, rifles and ammunition, wheat and oil, economic concessions and territorial bits, and they got them all. On March 3, 1918, Trotsky agreed to everything, and the peace was signed. The war with Russia was over.

Two and a half weeks later the Germans opened their great spring offensive against the western Allies. It was designed to end the war and do it quickly, for now the Americans were in it, and it might be that the Germans had waited a bit too long. Their determination to get the pound of Russian flesh kept them involved months longer than absolutely necessary. A compromise peace, or even a temporary one, might have freed them to win the war in the West as well as in the East. For their U-boat policies had at last brought the great neutral into the fight against them.

# 17. The Submarine Campaign; The United States Enters the War

BY LATE 1916 the Germans believed two things: They were winning the war; they were not doing it rapidly enough. They possessed the one weapon that had so far shown itself capable of altering the military balance to a significant degree and up to now they had been willingly hamstrung in their application of it. That weapon was the submarine, and the Germans had accepted the restrictions imposed upon its use by the United States. A coldly analytical view was that President Wilson and the United States had not won the war for the Allies, but they had by their interference prevented the Allies from losing it.

The soldiers who now dominated German thinking asked themselves why this should be so and could find no reasonable answer to the question. When they reviewed the submarine campaign, it was obvious that only the United States' attitude was saving the British from disaster. When they reviewed the military strength of the United States, they could not see why they paid any attention to it.

The first period of the submarine crisis had reached its high point in 1915. The *Lusitania* had been sunk in May and had caused a near explosion in the United States. In spite of that the Germans continued their sinkings for about another four months. In August the White Star liner *Arabic* was torpedoed, and three more Americans were killed. Wilson protested once again to the German government, and the German Ambassador in Washington, Count von

Bernstorff, finally convinced Berlin that this time the Americans meant business and there was a genuine danger of their entering the war. In September of 1915 the Germans decided they were really not ready to risk that, so they issued new orders on the policy to be followed for sinking liners or ships containing passengers. They would no longer attack them without warning, and they would make some provision, whenever they could, to see that passengers got off safely, as long as the ships stopped and did not try to escape or ram or otherwise fight back.

These guidelines worked fairly well for the rest of the year and into 1916. The situation was also eased by the German decision to shift the major focus of submarine operations to the Mediterranean, where they embarrassed the British operations around the Dardanelles. Unfortunately for the advocates of restraint, it was just about this time that the British blockade began to show dividends; business with neutrals suspected of supplying Germany dropped dramatically, and other British measures of economic warfare took effect as well. It was difficult for the Germans to avoid lumping all of these factors together, even though not all of them were connected with the submarine issue itself.

By early in 1916, then, German official opinion was veering back to the desirability of unrestricted submarine warfare once more. German leaders knew of an American note to Great Britain that suggested the arming of British merchantmen was forcing the German hand, and they took this as a sign of some sympathy for their point of view—which it was not—and began pressing the Kaiser, who still retained a firm interest in naval matters, to allow greater freedom of action. He eventually agreed to a compromise, that there might be unrestricted submarine attacks in certain limited areas. Admiral von Tirpitz was so offended by the timidness of the decision that he resigned in a huff.

Yet a mere two weeks later the Germans and the Americans were squabbling again. On March 24, UB-29 torpedoed and sank the French cross-Channel steamer *Sussex*. She was carrying a few American passengers at the time and the response from Washington was forceful: Unless Germany called off the submarine campaign, the United States would sever diplomatic relations. As that was the first step to war, the Germans backed off once more and issued what came to be known as the "*Sussex* pledge," agreeing that, in effect, they would go back to prewar rules for submarines. Such a limitation made them all but useless as commerce destroyers, and for the next six months the submarines operated either in the Mediterranean, where there were few Americans to get in the way, or as adjuncts to the battle fleet, which was what made them available, if not effective, for the operations that culminated in Jutland.

The conditions that had pertained in 1915 were even more in evidence in 1916. The British blockade was cutting increasingly deeply into Germany's life and her ability to wage war. By contrast, German sinkings of British and Allied shipping had increased enormously during the few months when the submarines operated unrestricted; they were sinking fifteen merchantmen for every sub lost, five times better than they had done earlier in the war. They also had a large number of new, improved vessels coming into service as a result of the building programs undertaken at the start of the war. Here was a potential war winner, and the Germans were denying themselves the use of it, largely at the behest of the United States.

To military and naval leaders this policy was the more incomprehensible when they examined the power of the Americans, for as a power the United States was negligible, at least by European standards. In 1898 the United States Army had had an active strength of 210,000 men. That was the year of the Spanish-American War. Since then it had sunk to a low of 64,000 in 1907, roughly equivalent to the British casualty list on the first day of the Somme. In 1914 it was back to 98,000, and another 10,000 had been added by 1916. The German General Staff did not regard an army of 110,000 men on the other side of the Atlantic as an insurmountably formidable force. During that year the Americans had been at full stretch to contain the activities of a Mexican bandit named Pancho Villa, who had shot up a couple of towns in Texas. A punitive expedition under the command of John J. Pershing had marched into the Mexican hills and wandered around there for a while, without achieving much more than annoying the Mexican government.

There had been some development of a citizen-soldier movement called "preparedness," but as far as the Germans could tell it had not gone very far. There seemed to be perpetual squabbles over federal versus state troops, and other arcane matters of interest only to American Congressmen. The United States Army was known to be utterly deficient in all the weapons and matériel of modern war. There was enough artillery and ammunition, on a prewar scale, to support about five divisions. The air service of the army owned fifty-five airplanes, none of them modern by Western Front standards. The United States Army had never seen a tank.

The navy was more formidable, as the traditional "first line of defense." Admiral Mahan's parent service, presided over by the hero of Manila Bay, Admiral Dewey, it was a firm believer in the battle fleet theory and consisted of an impressive force of both pre- and dreadnought-type battleships and supporting cruisers. However, only a third of the vessels were supplied up to operational standards, and the navy possessed but 10 percent of its general manpower requirements. It was also deficient in exactly the type of vessels needed for the war, antisubmarine and escort forces. The 1916 building program would have given the United States the greatest navy in the world, but here again it was aimed mostly at a battle fleet, and many of the ships begun before the American entry were subsequently left on the stocks for the duration of the war, while shipyards turned out destroyers and submarine chasers instead.

There were no plans for war, as the American General Staff was a skeleton body not entirely trusted by the government. When President Wilson heard it was producing war plans for use against Germany, that is, developing exactly the type of contingency operational plan a general staff is supposed to develop, he angrily ordered the work stopped. If it were impossible to be prepared without being provocative, he seemed to prefer not to be prepared.

The Germans could see this perfectly well, for as usual in the United States, things that were closely guarded secrets elsewhere were discussed in full view and at great length. Democracy does not lend itself to secrecy any more than it does to military preparedness, and the German diplomatic services were able to keep their government fully apprised of what was going on, or, in this case, not going on in America.

The problem with experts is that they cannot be universal in their expertise. The German Army leaders could assess the United States as negligible. Militarily they ranked it with Denmark and Holland and Chile. Neither their training nor their inclinations led them to look beyond the immediate military scene. They did not consider the reserve strength or adaptability of American industry, for they believed, to the extent that they did bother with it, that the victory would be won before that strength could be turned to war production. Even at this stage they tended to underestimate the vigor with which an aroused people might throw themselves into the war, and here again, they believed the American people totally lacking in the military virtues anyway. Above all, they failed to consider what unlocking the reserves of American financial credit would do for the Allies. In their view Germany and the Allies were two giants locked in mortal combat; one of the giants was fighting with all its might, the other was fighting with one arm only, letting the other arm be held back by a weak child who possessed no strength of its own, but exerted pressure only because of the giant's good will and restraint. That giant, Germany, could no longer afford such a policy. On January 31, 1917, the Imperial German Government notified the United States government that it would begin unrestricted submarine warfare on February 1.

President Wilson had gradually moved to a position where, by the time he received the German note, he was at the end of his patience with Europeans. He had consistently tried to arrange for some form of negotiation or mediation; he had sent his close friend and advisor, "Colonel" Edward House, around Europe plugging a set of peace proposals which were basically sympathetic to the Allies, but House found even the Allies, let alone the Central Powers, unwilling to accept them. European governments had now sunk so far in the mire that nothing short of total victory would satisfy them. As their attitudes hardened, so did Wilson's. With the United States not in the war, he could see only that they were completely under the sway of some sort of bloody-minded intransigence. He continued his efforts to find a way out, but every escalation of the fighting, or of the demands and conditions put forward by either side for peace, served to reinforce his growing belief that he was the only sane leader in a world gone mad.

By and large his country tended to agree with him. There was some desire for intervention, especially in the eastern states, which remained more susceptible to the pull of Europe than the rest of the country. Numbers of American young men continued to drift across the border and end up in Canadian or British units, wearing kilts or the jauntily tipped cap of the Royal Flying Corps. But these were isolated acts by those who still believed war romantic or who had succumbed to the idea that the world must be saved from the Hun. The country as a whole tended to support the Allied side, but not to the extent of sending its sons to die for them.

In the United States, 1916 was a presidential election year, and Wilson campaigned on a somewhat contradictory platform of non-intervention in the war and preparedness for it; the two were sufficiently watered down that they did not appear blatantly incompatible. The phrase that caught the voters was "He kept us out of war." Fortunately for Wilson, the Republicans could not disagree with his proposals and had to confine themselves to picking at the edges of them. They also produced a lackluster candidate, Charles Evans Hughes. Teddy Roosevelt noted that he was a "professional prohibitionist," implying that such could hardly be anything but lackluster, and the Democratic papers called him "Chilly Charlie, the human icicle." Though Wilson lost the East, he carried the rest of the country and won by a fairly narrow margin of 600,000 votes out of a total of more than 17 million.

Safely returned for another four years, the President who "kept us out of war" was now about to take the United States into it. Presented with the German note on January 31, he broke off diplomatic relations on February 3. He decided, however, that he must have an unchallengeable, overt act of hostility before he could declare war. He very nearly got it within the next month over the bizarre affair of the Zimmermann note.

Arthur Zimmermann was Germany's Foreign Secretary. On January 16 British naval intelligence intercepted a coded message from him to the German Ambassador in Mexico. In it he stated that if Germany and the United States were to go to war, Germany would offer Mexico assistance in recovering Texas, New Mexico, and Arizona, in return for her aid against the Americans. The Germans were also going to offer Japan pieces of the American West if she switched her alliance. The British decided to sit on this juicy bit of stupidity until the time was ripe, and they released it to the Americans on February 25. In terms of making the hitherto lukewarm western states prointervention it was tailor-made, and it caused the expected furor in the United States.

Still Wilson held off; how divided American opinion remained is shown by the fact that when he tried to get Congressional authority to arm American merchant vessels, his proposal was filibustered to death. Eventually he did it by executive order. The outbreak of the revolution in Russia removed any lingering qualms that the Americans might be supporting autocracy in one country by fighting it in another. Finally, in the middle of March, German submarines sank four unarmed and clearly marked American merchant ships; thirty-six lives were lost, and a no-longer reluctant Wilson decided to go to Congress.

On April 2 he spoke to a joint session of House and Senate,

asking them to vote a declaration of war. "The world," he said, "must be made safe for democracy." Two days later the Senate agreed by a vote of eighty-two to six; two days after that the House voted 373 to fifty, and on the afternoon of April 6, the United States of America was at war with the German Empire. The immediate effects were startling: German submarine sinkings increased alarmingly, and the Americans found they had joined the losing end of the war.

The Germans now had about 120 submarines, of which, with newer types and better operational techniques, they could keep perhaps two thirds operating at any one time. They believed that was enough to drive Great Britain into starvation, bankruptcy, and financial collapse, and in early 1917 they were right. Their previous unrestricted sinking campaigns had netted 120,000 tons a month, with a mere nine boats on station to do the work, and they had then doubled that before adopting the *Sussex* pledge. Just half a dozen boats were sinking 400,000 tons monthly in the confined waters of the Mediterranean. So far in the war, Allied shipping had had a net loss of about 700,000 tons more sunk than launched, or a diminution of about 5 percent.

The latest effort opened on February 1. By the end of the month more than a half a million tons had gone to the bottom. In March the Germans upped that figure to three quarters of a million, and estimates for April were that it would top a million; in fact it reached 875,000 tons. One ship in four that left the British Isles in the first quarter of 1917 did not return. Early in April, when American Rear Admiral Sims, sent ahead to coordinate his country's effort with the British Admiralty, was shown the sinking figures he remarked, aghast, "But this means we are losing the war." His British opposite number coldly answered, "That's right —and there's nothing we can do about it."

In this, however, he was mistaken. During all the great Anglo-French wars of the eighteenth century, the British had been forced by the pressure of privateers and raiders to convoy their merchant ships, especially around the British Isles themselves, where the proximity of the Continent provided more than ample bases for the enemy. There was now in the Admiralty a group of younger officers who had long been advocating the introduction of such a convoy system. In the early stages of the war the senior commanders had insisted that this was impossible; the complexities of organizing loading and unloading facilities would simply clog the ports, and the entire economy would break down. Like most ideas, and especially ones involving human lives, this one came to be defended more vehemently the more vigorously it was attacked. Certain officers had staked their expertise, and therefore their professional careers, on the thesis that convoy of modern vessels could not be done. The chances of the junior, proconvoy people were greatly enhanced when Admiral Sims, mulling over the catastrophic sinking figures, asked, disarmingly, "Why don't you convoy?"

Between Sims, its own people, and the fulminations of the Prime Minister himself, the Admiralty at last reluctantly agreed to an experimental attempt. On May 20 the first convoy arrived safely in Britain from Gibraltar. By September the system was generally accepted, and sinkings by U-boat fell off dramatically. In addition, the British developed depth charges and hydrophones to pick up the sounds of approaching submarines. What made the convoy system effective, though, was the fact that tempting vessels were no longer scattered unescorted all over the ocean. The submarine now had to come to the target, and when it did, it had to get by the escorts to make its attack.

Provision of escorts was crucial, and as fast as the British turned them out, they needed still more. It was this need that made the Americans set aside their building program for major units and concentrate on a host of wooden sub chasers and light destroyers, the famous flush-decked four pipers. They rolled on wet grass and they were incredibly uncomfortable, but they served well through the end of the war, and many of them went on to do yeoman service under American, British, and Canadian colors in the Second World War.

By the end of the year a variety of means had mastered the U-boat threat. British and French patrols sealed the Channel and created a mine barrage across it. In April of 1918, in a daring and gallant raid, the British tried, with some success, to block the submarine base at Zeebrugge on the Belgian coast. The Allies also strung a mine barrage all the way from Scotland across the North Sea to Norwegian waters and at enormous cost discouraged the subs from using this route. The last major area of successful operation for the Germans was in the Mediterranean, where their boats worked out of Austrian bases at the head of the Adriatic. Here again the Allies sealed them in, setting up a mine barrage and patrol fleet out of Otranto, down on the heel of the Italian boot.

Between one thing and another, the U-boats were confined, and the German Admiralty proved wrong in its first assertion, that it could sink 600,000 tons a month and drive Britain out of the war. It is always dangerous to assume that if your side initiates a change, the other side will not do so, too.

One aspect of American entry into the war that the German military and naval leaders had not even remotely considered was the effect it might have on the financial situation of the various belligerents. The costs of the war were absolutely astronomical and had forced governments into measures they had never before considered. These were far more sophisticated than the forced loans, debased coinage, and arbitrary declarations of bankruptcy resorted to by governments of the premodern period, though on examination, there is perhaps more difference in form than in substance between a forced loan and an income tax, or between obligatory labor service and military conscription.

Shortly after the war ended, the Carnegie Endowment for International Peace put together an extensive picture of the costs of the war. It estimated that until 1918 the fighting of the war cost $123,000,000 a day, and that in 1918 it rose to $224,000,000 a day—and that in 1920 dollars. At that time the major nations of the world were still basing their currency on gold as a fixed medium of exchange, and there was then enough gold in the world to have fought the war for approximately fifty days. In that sense Ivan Bloch had been correct. If everyone had had to fight on cash, the world financial scene would have collapsed before the end of September, 1914. What Bloch forgot was the possibility of fighting the war on credit.

Income taxes were particularly associated with war. Great Britain had introduced one in 1798 to help fight revolutionary France, but it had been dropped during the nineteenth century and reintroduced early in the twentieth. In 1915 it was increased to three shillings sixpence a pound, or 17½ percent, and an excess profits tax was also imposed, as a means of getting at war profiteers. During the war Britain's national debt rose from £625,000,000 to £7,809,000,000. The United States had had an income tax during the Civil War, but that was regarded as a peculiarity of wartime conditions. The government attempted to reimpose such a tax in 1894, at the rate of 2 percent on incomes of more than $4,000 dollars a year, but the Supreme Court declared it to be unconstitutional. In 1913 a constitutional amendment put the Supreme Court in its place, and since then the income tax has become one of the less blessed, if more necessary, features of American life. In France the introduction of an income tax had been one of the few things Frenchmen could unite against, and it was not until 1913 that increasing military expenditures at last made it unavoidable. Even then it was not until 1917 that a general income tax was brought in. By and large the French politicians preferred not to tax for the war, which enabled their Cabinets to survive during it—and contributed to France's instability after it ended.

Faced with the awesome costs of waging war, the governments were all forced to borrow, either from their own citizens or from their allies. Japan loaned money to Russia, France loaned a billion and a half dollars to her allies, Britain loaned more than two billion to France and six and a half billion to the other allies, and the United States advancd nearly nine and a half billion to the allies after entering the war. The immediate availability of American credit may have been even more important to the Allies early in 1917 than was dealing with the submarine problem, for at that time the British were as close to bankruptcy as they were to starvation. But the concerns of national finance had been completely beyond the ken of the men in Germany who chose a course of action they knew would lead to American belligerency.

Certainly American money was of far more immediate help than American manpower, for that was slow in getting to the war, and untrained when it got there. The first Americans to reach France in June were on the staff of Major General John J. Pershing, late chaser of Pancho Villa, now commander-in-chief of the American Expeditionary Force. But it was October before the 1st Division was considered ready to filter into a quiet sector of the line. Though the division was a regular army one, it had come to France with large numbers of new enlistees, and most of the men landed with no more than the rudiments of military training. Pershing's efforts were devoted about equally to bringing them up to some kind of useful standard, and to fighting off French and British attempts to steal his raw material. Both the major Allies were by now so depleted for manpower that they looked with longing at the fresh Americans and tried everything they could think of to get Americans filtered into their own formations as replacements. The heart of Pershing's policies was that his troops were going to fight in and as American units, and he clung to that through all kinds of hazards. It was undoubtedly a correct policy from the point of view of national self-esteem, but it caused a great deal of acrimony. That was readily understandable, for while the Americans were getting ready to win the war, the French and British came perilously close to losing it.

# 18. The Western Front, 1917

THE SHUFFLING OF POLITICAL AND MILITARY leadership among the Allies at the end of 1916 came right in the midst of planning for the spring campaign. In November there had been the by now traditional meeting at Joffre's headquarters, and the assembled worthies there had reached the by now equally traditional conclusions. In the coming year they would fight the war more vigorously; they would carry out coordinated attacks in France, on the Eastern Front, and in Italy, Salonika, and Palestine, and they would make their main effort once again on the Western Front. General Joffre proposed that the French should make a major attack on the Oise River, and when this had achieved success—and who could doubt that it would?—the British would follow with an offensive that should clear the Belgian coast.

The miasma of war did not hang unduly heavily over the heads of the planners. True, they had lost Rumania, but Rumania did not appear especially important to them. General Joffre was convinced he had won a great victory at Verdun, and General Haig was equally convinced he had done well on the Somme, and so selective is human intelligence and memory that most observers agreed with them. Throughout the entire war the Allied leaders happily convinced themselves that they had inflicted disproportionately heavy casualties on the enemy—this delusion is of course a common one in war and has been repeated in all the wars of the twentieth century—and since their strategic sense had now been reduced to a rock bottom war of attrition, they were perfectly content merely to grind ahead. In the seventeenth century, Turenne, the great marshal-general of France, had believed that victory could be achieved by the arts of maneuver, perhaps without even fighting bloody battles, and he had actually done so. But the World War I generals were made of sterner stuff and could read casualty lists and even tour hospitals without flinching. One of the necessary facets of the art of war is to know how to expend human lives wisely and to be willing to do so. These generals certainly knew how to expend lives and were equally willing to do so; in spite of the efforts of some apologist historians, their wisdom still does not appear to have been their dominant quality.

As soon as they had decided on this hackneyed plan of attack, they were shocked by political changes. Lloyd George became Prime Minister in Britain, and he was vocally anti-Western Front and especially anti-Western Front generals. He made no secret that he thought Douglas Haig was inept, and he probably would have fired him had he dared. Unfortunately for him, Haig's name was by now so completely identified with the B. E. F. and the war effort that to relieve him was unthinkable. If the Germans could not dig him out of his entrenchments, a mere Prime Minister was not going to do so. Nonetheless, Lloyd George immediately announced his preference for action on subsidiary fronts and began meddling with the possibilities of downgrading the British effort in France. He exerted pressure on General Sir William Robertson, Chief of the Imperial General Staff and ostensibly Haig's superior. But Robertson and Haig were hand in hand, Haig the aristocrat and Robertson the dour Scot who had enlisted as a private soldier and made his way up the ranks through sheer brains, bravery, and dogged hard work. Whenever Lloyd George sent around a particularly scathing memorandum, "Wully" Robertson would growl to his aides, "Get 'aig." Had not the country been locked in a life-and-death struggle it would have presented an amusing music-hall act, two canny Scots versus one mercurial Welshman.

Lloyd George's rise to chief political office coincided roughly with the disappearance of Joffre and his replacement by General Robert Nivelle. Nivelle was the very embodiment of the dashing French officer, with a brilliant career behind him in various subordinate positions. His springy walk and jaunty smile were in startling contrast to the hulking Joffre, who at his most active resembled a bear about to hibernate for the winter. The important thing about Nivelle was that he was a good talker and he could meet the politicians on their own ground; that presumably was what got him his job as Joffre's replacement, for there were in the French Army many men with claims as good as his, and some with better. Nonetheless, Nivelle got the top office, and he then unrolled before the dazzled eyes of the politicians a plan to win the war. He suggested that the British mount a diversionary attack in the north, after which the French would break through the German lines along the Chemin des Dames on the Aisne. He believed he could crack the enemy positions in twenty-four to forty-eight hours. Asked how he would do it, he replied, "with violence, brutality, and rapidity."

The skeptic might suggest that the French for more than two years now had been applying whatever rapidity they could manage and certainly had not been lacking in violence and brutality, but no one seems to have splashed this sort of cold water on Nivelle. Not only did French politicians accept him at face value, so did British. For when Lloyd George, the arch foe of the Western Front, visited Nivelle's headquarters, he was so enraptured that he agreed completely with the Frenchman and in addition said he would put the whole B. E. F. at France's disposal for the offensive.

This was utter anathema to Haig and Robertson and nearly every other responsible British commander, for they had all spent the last two years diligently avoiding any French direction of their affairs. It reversed their entire policy of fighting an independent war, and of course it also showed that Lloyd George's military ideas were founded on nothing more substantial than personal dislike for British generals, which was what they had suspected all along. They immediately carried out one of their better campaigns of the war, to water down Lloyd George's promises to the point where the British agreed only to conform to French moves, that is, to the point where they were virtually free to go their own way once again. After all, Nivelle was not the only one planning to win the war; Haig had his plans as well.

The British commander did not think the French were going to win the war in the spring. He therefore planned to do it himself in the fall, and he resented any French moves that would involve his troops and detract from his preparations. His own idea was that there should be a great British attack in Flanders, up around the Ypres salient, that would break the German line and lever them away from the coast. To do this he had to throw the Germans off guard by a preliminary attack somewhere else along his front. The result of Haig's and Nivelle's concurrent plans was that there were three Allied attacks in the spring and early summer. First, Haig launched at Arras in early April an attack that was his contribution to Nivelle's plan. Just as that ended, Nivelle opened his own great operation on the Chemin des Dames. It ran until about mid-May, and shortly after that Haig began his second drive, at the Messines Ridge, which was the preliminary to Britain's major operation of the year.

As the western Allies were engaging in all this planning and preparing, the Germans were making some adjustments of their own. About to embark on their submarine campaign and certain that it was going to win the war, they decided to stand even more completely on the defensive in France and Belgium. To this end they chose to shorten and strengthen their lines, creating a more thoroughly fortified system, and also freeing troops from holding the line to serve as a general reserve. They retreated out of the westernmost bulge of the line, along a fifty-mile front from Arras down to Soissons. Twenty-five miles to the rear, they created a thick defensive system which they called the Siegfried Zone, but which came to be known to the Allies as the Hindenburg Line. In the abandoned territory they completely devastated the land, blowing bridges and culverts, burning buildings, poisoning wells; as it was enemy territory, they had no compunction about leaving an utter wasteland behind them. The new line was prepared at leisure and at great expense. It was, naturally, especially strong where it joined in with the old front line, for here there were both prepared positions plus the long-developed original trench system. These two hinges, Arras in the north and the Chemin des Dames-Aisne River feature in the south, were exactly what the British and the French were proposing to hit in their first two offensives.

This was not entirely coincidental. By the time the Germans were back in the Hindenburg Line, they were pretty well aware of what was happening, and by the time the Allied attacks opened, they knew almost as much about them as the Allies did. For Nivelle talked so charmingly that everyone wanted to hear what he had to say; faced with such an appreciative audience, he told them of his plans at great length. He was so proud of his new scheme that he even discussed it with the newspaper reporters. They of course could not be privy to all the little details, but the Germans got these anyway from the numerous copies of the operation orders that the French left lying around everywhere, even in their frontline trenches where raiders picked them up gratefully if somewhat skeptically. So when the attacks opened, there were to be some surprises all right, but not exactly the ones Nivelle had so fondly and so publicly anticipated.

Haig's attack at Arras was first off the mark. It was a difficult target, for the Germans had been in the line here a long time and were well dug in; even worse, five miles behind their main position was a northward extension or spur of the new Hindenburg Line. Haig hoped to take them both. His chief problem was to get the dominant terrain feature, a long rolling hill north of Arras called Vimy Ridge, the scene of bitter fighting in earlier attacks in the war, for from its crest the whole Douai Plain lay open to observation.

There was one thing in Haig's favor. The Germans had by now developed a three-tiered defense system, with light posts forward and reserves held well back, ready to respond to any emergency. On Vimy the area commander had ignored this defense in depth and put most of his troops up close to the front line, highly vulnerable to the British barrage. The British plan called for General Allenby—not yet sent off to Egypt—and his 3rd Army to advance forward from Arras, and for General Horne's 1st Army to take Vimy Ridge. Horne gave the job to the Canadian Corps, now four divisions strong.

During the course of World War I, Canada's sons built up a reputation as an elite fighting force. With a population of barely 8 million people, she sent 600,000 troops overseas in the course of the war, virtually all volunteers. Two thirds of them were casualties of one kind or another, and one in ten never came home again. They started the war in divisional strength and ended it with a strong corps with their own Canadian commander, Sir Arthur Currie, a solid militiaman who was the kind of warrior for the workaday world that the other dominions produced in New Zealand General Sir Bernard Freyberg and Australian General Sir John Monash. To the extent that Canadians were able, they followed their own independent path and preserved their separate identity. Before their first attack at Festubert they protested the stupidity of the British tactical plan, and later in the war Currie had the corps transferred from one British army whose commander he thought incompetent to another whose commander he trusted. The attack on Vimy was the high point of the war for the C. E. F. and holds the same hallowed place in

Canadian annals as Anzac Cove in Australian, or St. Mihiel and the Argonne Forest in American. It is not too imaginative to say that Canada became a nation on the slopes of Vimy Ridge.

For one thing, Vimy was all Canadian. The 1st Army commander, Horne, left the details to the corps commander, at that time General Sir Julian Byng, who later became a Governor-General of Canada. His staff produced a meticulous battle plan which took full account of the possible contingencies. The attack jumped off at daybreak on April 9, an intermittently rainy, foggy day of swirling mist and poor visibility. There had been a thorough five-day preliminary bombardment, which had hit the German trenches hard and, as it lifted, the young men of the Maritimes and Ontario and the prairies clambered up out of their trenches and went forward with bayonets and grenades to drive the enemy out of positions he had held against all comers for two and a half years. At the end of the day the Canadians stood on the crest of the ridge, looking eastward past the slag heaps toward Douai. In later years, after the slaughter was over and the grass had done its work, Canada put the most graceful of all World War I monuments on the top of Vimy Ridge, and sheep graze now on some of the most richly fertilized terrain in human history.

The taking of Vimy Ridge was the one clear-cut tactical success of the larger battle of Arras. To the south of the ridge, before the town itself, the British made a quick couple of miles up the little valley of the Scarpe River, courtesy of the German mistake in massing well forward. Then the weather turned bad, "German weather," the troops grumbled, speculating that the intense artillery barrages caused rain to fall, making them even more self-defeating than usual. The Germans shored up their defenses, as always, and the British attacks made less and less progress at more and more cost. Haig did not wish to get too deeply committed here, as he was looking forward to Messines Ridge and his autumn battle; after about a week he let the fight wear itself out.

The end of the Arras offensive coincided with the opening of Nivelle's great affair, known as the Second Battle of the Aisne. Strategically, the spot was well chosen, for if the French were to succeed in breaking through the German positions, they would cut in behind the southern flank of the Hindenburg Line, cutting enemy communications through Laon and compromising him extensively to the westward.

Tactically, however, the terrain could hardly have been worse. The French had fought here before, and it was very difficult country. From just east of Soissons to Reims, the front line lay either along the valley of the Aisne and the parallel canal that made it navigable, or mounted to the heights of the Chemin des Dames overlooking the river from the north. From the Aisne ten miles north to Laon, the country consisted of rank on rank of rolling, tumbled hills, steep cuts, and wooded slopes. The French would have to fight for every yard.

Difficulties notwithstanding, Nivelle was supremely confident of success, and he managed to communicate this to his troops. They were sure, pathetically sure as it happened, that they were going to win the war on this one; they were also inspired by the news that the United States had just come into the war, and though that meant little in an immediate sense, it was surely a good omen for the future. The troops on their approach marches showed a spirit and dash that had not been seen since 1914, and from the footsoldiers' view, things looked good. There were guns everywhere, more than 7,000 of them, as the infantry threaded their way up to the foreward trenches. Some 200 tanks were scattered about in the rear, waiting to go forward in support of the infantry. By the night of April 15, Nivelle had 1,200,000 soldiers ready to assault at dawn on a forty-mile front from Soissons to Reims. The weather had been bad, and the ground was wet and slippery.

There were signs other than meteorological that Nivelle was in trouble. Behind him there was yet another government shuffle, and the politicians, once they started talking to generals besides Nivelle, began to harbor serious doubts about the great offensive. On April 5 Nivelle offered to resign rather than modify his preparations or his aims, but in view of the hopes he had aroused, the government did not dare accept his offer. He did go on to say that he would immediately cancel the attack if it did not live up to advance billing.

At six on the morning of April 16 the barrage shifted; the preliminary bombardment was over, and the gunners began walking their fire up the ridges. Dashing out of their trenches, the *poilus* ran forward to mount the heights. For a few short moments it looked like 1914 all over again. Then things began to go wrong.

Well aware that the attack was coming, the Germans had made thorough preparations. Now their fighter and scout aircraft were all over the sky, driving the French artillery spotters out of it and covering their own. The French gunners began to fire blind by timetable, with no way of correcting their shooting. German guns deluged the advancing infantry with shrapnel and high explosive. Their batteries, informed by radio from aircraft and well-positioned spotters on the heights, raked the columns of advancing tanks, many of which were knocked out while still on the approach to the battlefield.

Meanwhile, the French infantry, heavily laden with their big blue overcoats and all the extra impedimenta of battle, were trying desperately to keep up with their own barrage. Relentlessly it moved up the hills above the Aisne, while behind it the infantry slipped and slithered and cursed on the steep slopes. And in the growing gap between shells and soldiers, the Germans came out of their dugouts and set up their machine guns. Still, this was the battle that was to bring victory at last, and the French kept on coming. They carried the first German line and pushed on, into the cuttings and reentrants, where both sides fought blindly, blundering into each other and lashing out viciously.

The attack continued the next day. Casualties were heavier than expected, but Nivelle, with that fatal confidence that infected World War I generals, was certain he was making great progress, that the Germans were about to crack. He ordered the troops to push on. Behind him the government wavered. When Nivelle scheduled yet another attack, by 10th Army, for April 20, the politicians reminded him of his promise not to continue if he did not achieve immediate successes. Obstinately he clung to his idea; violence, brutality, and rapidity would win through. The politicians called up Pétain and installed him as Chief of the General Staff; Pétain ordered Nivelle to confine himself to limited attacks of the kind that had brought success at Verdun. But Nivelle kept on. On May 5 a last attack cleared the crest of the Chemin des Dames Ridge. It was merely Nivelle's first objective; behind it lay another, higher ridge, and another and another.

The troops were worn out. Where now the crashing victory they had been so casually promised? They had done all they could, and more. They had lost 120,000 men, a tenth of their attacking force, and now reinforcements going up to the line were sullen and slow. Passing their generals they baa-ed, imitating the noises of sheep being led to a slaughterhouse. On May 15 Pétain relieved and replaced Nivelle, taking over command of the armies himself. He was just in time. The infantry had at last had enough. Disaffection spread like fire from one regiment to another, and Pétain suddenly found himself commanding men who were in a state of mutiny. After two and a half years of wanton slaughter, the French Army had broken at last.

As with the Russians now in revolt, the wonder was not so much that the French soldiers had refused duty as that it had taken them so long to reach this point. Their conditions were truly appalling. The men of France were conscripted into their army, but that was not unusual; by now even Britain had introduced conscription, and in all the continental states it had long been an accepted fact of life. But in 1917 the French Army consisted of older men and veterans—men in their thirties who had already been wounded and patched up one or more times—and young boys recently called up ahead of their conscription years to make up gaps in the ranks. The prewar officer class had been nearly wiped out, and its survivors had by now, if they displayed a minimum of ability, been promoted to positions where they had little contact with the troops. Their places had been taken by former noncommissioned officers who, as a general rule, were primarily concerned to preserve the distance from their former colleagues. The French officers performed incredible feats of courage and leadership in the heat of battle; the rest of the time they ignored their men.

Discipline was savage, harsher than in the British or even the German army; amenities were nonexistent. It was bad enough in the stinking filth of the trenches, where life was expected to be miserable, but neither the military hierarchy nor the government took any interest in the welfare of the troops out of the line. There were few rest camps, fewer canteens, and totally inadequate leave facilities. When a soldier did get leave, if he were lucky enough to have time to get home on the wretched railways, he often found his wife and his children destitute, for the state paid him a miserable five sous a day, less than his daily bread cost, and made no real provision for his dependents at all. Much of this misery was matched by a similar lack of social services in civilian life, but republican political philosophy held that it was the citizen's duty, even privilege, to serve his country, and that therefore his country was not obligated to take any particular care of him or his family while he did so. The result was that in or out of the line, on service or on leave, the soldier's lot was a disgrace. There were only two ways to get free of his troubles: to get killed or to get drunk. There was plenty of rough red wine, and soldiers in what were nominally rear areas were practically encouraged to drink themselves into insensibility; it was about the only thing they had to do. It was highly significant that the mutinies broke out behind the lines.

Through the end of May and into June the reports came in; eventually half the army was refusing duty. The outbursts were sporadic; here a battalion turned on its officers, there one refused to go up in the line, in another place a regiment threatened to march on Paris. The government blamed it all on paid agitators, but Pétain knew better; bitterly he told his political masters that yes, they should censor those newspapers who cried peace and were supported by German funds, but beyond that, they should wake up to the needs of common humanity. The troops should have better leave systems, better pay, some provision for their dependents. They should have some creature comforts behind the lines. They should, in sum, be treated as human beings who deserved well of their country, not as cattle who existed merely to die for some abstraction called The State. Finally, Pétain did have his way, and conditions did improve. He went among the troops, talking to the men in their units, and he managed to convince them that there really was after all someone in authority who cared for them and looked out for their interests.

That was later. Immediately, the problem was to restore order, and Pétain moved in a firm way to do it. Loyal troops were ordered to put down mutinous ones and did so. In a couple of cases there were practically pitched battles between French units. In most cases after scuffles and high words the mutineers were disarmed, or surrounded and herded back into camps. Officers were ordered to take a firm stance, and those unable to do so were sacked. By mid-June the crisis was past; outbreaks of mutiny dropped off rapidly after the tenth of the month, and order was restored throughout the army. Summary courts-martial dealt with offenses, and eventually more than 23,000 soldiers were found guilty of some breach of discipline or other. That was roughly one in every hundred men. Death sentences were passed on 432, though only fifty-five were actually shot, the rest being sent to penal colonies. Of those punished, some were guilty of grave offenses, some of none at all, but happened to be unlucky, men in the wrong place at the wrong time. Surely that phrase could have applied to every frontline soldier in the war.

The most amazing thing about the entire mutiny, which was really but the military aspect of widespread discontent throughout the whole country, was that the Germans never found out about it. Pétain, the other army commanders, and the politicians were in mortal fear that if the Germans discovered what was going on and mounted an offensive, France would collapse completely. Yet on the fronts the soldiers continued to hold their lines; they simply refused to go on any more suicidal attacks. And in the rear a rigorous censorship and suppression of press reports succeeded in keeping news of the revolts from seeping out. The Germans did not find out about it in time to do anything.

The result was favorable for them anyway, for the outbreak finally did what the Germans themselves had not been able to do: It destroyed the offensive capacity of the French Army for the foreseeable future. Though he disguised it well, Pétain was deeply disturbed by the army he now commanded. Never a brilliant intellect, he possessed perhaps more than any other French leader of the war a dour, uncluttered mind that was attuned to his soldiers. He had always been close to his men and in his youth was an extremely popular junior officer, for his thought processes ran in the same channels as the ordinary soldier's. Now he knew the army was all but finished; as supreme commander, his guiding principle for the rest of the war was simply to hang on. Joffre's sangfroid and Nivelle's flights of fancy were both finished now. When asked how he proposed to conduct the war, Pétain replied that France could do no more; she must hold out and wait for the Americans.

Douglas Haig shared Pétain's view of the diminished capacity of the French, but he was determined to win the war with the British Army this fall. The French leader's requests that Haig take an active role in keeping the Germans busy while the French recuperated fitted in nicely with what Haig was planning to do anyway. His Messines battle was fought in late May and early June, while his allies were in the midst of their difficulties, and then he went right on with his next operations.

Messines Ridge was a necessary preliminary to fighting another major battle around Ypres, for it was a long, arcing terrain feature, the dominant high ground two to three miles to the south of the old town. The German positions on the ridge ran out past the little town of Wytschaete, forming a German salient which balanced the British salient to the north in front of Ypres. The line looked therefore like a backward "S," with the British holding the top bulge and the Germans holding the bottom. Unhappily, as was usual on the Western Front, the British bulge was in the low ground, and the German on the high. The ridge was held by a corps-strength formation known as "Group Wytschaete," five divisions strong.

The task of taking this was given to General Sir Herbert Plumer's 2nd Army. "Daddy" Plumer looked like a caricature of Colonel Blimp, with a pot belly, a round face, and a little white walrus moustache; he was in fact a first-class soldier, and he was also one of the few army commanders whose soldiers genuinely liked and admired him, which was why he had earned his nickname. Faced with the ridge, he hit on a novel solution; among his troops were several Welsh units, drawn from the coal mining valleys of Wales. He put these to work with his engineers, and they fell to with enthusiasm. They decided they would blow the ridge right off the map.

Digging tunnels under enemy positions and packing them with high explosives calls for steady nerves, but the British worked carefully, with fully developed deception plans. The attack was set for June 7, with the preliminary barrage beginning as early as May 21. Meanwhile, nineteen mines were driven under the the German front positions, and packed with close to a million pounds of high explosive.

The mines were exploded at 3:10 on the morning of June 7. Tremendous columns of smoke, dirt, and flame climbed into the sky; the sound of the blast was clearly heard in England, seventy miles away. Around Wytschaete and Messines, in the two or three miles where the mines were most thickly concentrated, the ridge simply disappeared in a great blast. Into the smoke and drifting dust dashed the full strength of Plumer's army, nine divisions strong.

The surprise and the success were complete. The German lines were obliterated, their few surviving soldiers shocked out of their senses. Preceded by a barrage laid on scientifically and planned to be 700 yards deep, the infantry quickly reached the crest of the ridge, past the former German line. By dark the German salient was gone, and the line south of Ypres straightened out. German counterattacks were hesitant at first, but increased in intensity over the next few days, and the front stabilized within a week. It was a limited operation, but for once a clear-cut tactical success. Coming as it did soon after the equally successful taking of Vimy Ridge, it improved the British outlook considerably. The Germans could be broken after all, and things looked good for the forthcoming battle, which was to be known officially as Third Ypres, but which came usually to be called after a little village a few miles to the east, Passchendaele.

It took the British six weeks to get ready for this next big battle, but Haig was determined to do it right. Pétain was still asking for British help and was happy to leave the initiative to those whom the French had always regarded as the junior partners of the alliance. He did offer a French army, the 1st, and it was transported up north and levered in between the B. E. F. and the Belgians to the left of them. Haig's plan for the attack was in many ways his version of what Nivelle had just tried, except of course that he did not intend to fail—neither did Nivelle, but the British disregarded that.

The battle was to be fought in three phases. In the first the British would score a major breakthrough around Ypres. In the second phase they were going to mount an amphibious landing on the coast behind the German flank, toward Ostend. Finally, there was to be a pursuit and exploitation phase, pushing toward Ghent, which was slightly more than forty miles east northeast of Ypres, or rather farther, a pessimist might note, than Cambrai and Douai had been from the Somme.

Ypres itself was in the area controlled by Plumer's 2nd Army, and Plumer had just done well at Messines. Haig believed, however, that the next task needed someone a bit less methodical, someone with a bit more of the dash that cavalrymen liked to see in their juniors. He gave the job to General Sir Hubert Gough and sandwiched his 5th Army in between Plumer and the newly arrived French. Gough did not know the terrain as well as Plumer did, but considering what kind of terrain it was, perhaps that was just as well.

The ground around Ypres was truly a monstrous place to fight a battle. Even though they had cleared the Messines Ridge, the British were still going to have to fight their way uphill, for the ridge ran off to the northeast from Messines to Passchendaele, beyond which it tailed off into the generally featureless plain. It was indeed not much of a ridge, just enough, as usual, to give the Germans an edge. So all the way from Ypres to Passchendaele, the British would have to go forward with rising ground to their right front, and it was on this rising ground that Gough planned to mount his major thrust.

Even the soil was bad. Soil may not be thought to be of much importance in military operations, but it is one of the supreme conditions of the soldier's life, as he has to spend a great deal of his time digging in it, putting it in sandbags, and moving it from this spot to that spot. As if to emphasize the miserable quality of life in the war, the Ypres soil was peculiarly nasty. It was heavy and clayey. Before the war the peasant farmers of the area had managed to work it only by building up, over the course of years, extensive and sophisticated drainage systems, so that the water would run off during the rainy season. Unless the drains were kept up, the rain lay on the ground, and the clay dissolved into a clinging mud, thick, glutinous, and all-conquering. With more rain, it became a nauseous semi-liquid. Even without the presence of an enemy, it was a struggle merely to stay alive in the mud around Ypres during the wet season.

The battles over the years had long since destroyed the carefully built-up drainage system, so there was some danger that if the weather should break early, the British would be in trouble. June was a good month for preparation, however, and July was not bad, though there were some rainy days and nights that made life a bit wet. The gun batteries came up and took their positions, the ammunition dumps behind the lines grew and grew and grew; soldiers in the rear areas, ostensibly resting for the big attack, spent night after night humping supplies and materials forward. Haig asked the Royal Flying Corps to gain him air superiority, and they did it, at considerable cost. The Germans were chased out of the sky, and British fighters and observation planes flew their daily missions up and down over the lines. Reports looked pretty good. Haig's intelligence people told him German morale was way down; intelligence gathering is rather like paying someone to do a survey: You tell him what you want to think, and he will tell you that what you want to think is correct. British military intelligence was not all that accurate during the war.

The attack was due to begin on July 31 at first light. The preliminary bombardment opened on July 18. Obviously the British generals had not yet considered that artillery might not be a war-winner, and they were still entranced by the battle of matériel. Surely if you bombarded an enemy position for an entire fortnight, there would be little left of it when you finally assaulted. The guns were the idols of the First World War. Day and night, night and day, they poked their ugly snouts into the heavens and coughed up death for men on earth. Around them in the blazing sun or the frigid night toiled their priests and servants, from the gunnery officers with their soft voices and their precision instruments that told them the slight adjustments of life or death, to the hustling, cursing gunners, manhandling their huge loads, shells and explosive, working with a frenzied precision that had all the coordination of a ballet and a hell of a lot more purpose. For two weeks the infantry listened to the mutter or shriek of the guns, both sides knowing full well what they portended.

As July went on and the guns kept at it, the weather turned chancy. There were occasional heavy rains, and the shell holes of the battlefield—and there was little of it that was not pockmarked with them—began to accumulate water. The soil became slippery. But with the end of the month all was ready, the great plan was complete. Gough had eighteen divisions packed into the Ypres salient; Plumer had twelve more to support him on his right flank, and the French, with little role to play, another six on his left. Directly opposite Gough, in Group Ypres, the Germans had only five divisions immediately to their front, but they were not worried; maybe they knew it was going to rain.

With the first pale glimmerings of light in the eastern sky on the morning of July 31, the British began to move forward. The guns kept up their hideous noise, and the infantry climbed painfully out of their trenches—no one leaps to the attack with sixty to eighty pounds of gear on his back—and began to advance. The first day was not too bad as battles went in this war. Pressing against the elastic German defense, the British infantry made about two miles. German counterattacks were heavy, but they were contained, and the infantry crept on. By nightfall it looked pretty good.

The next day, August 1, it began to rain, not a sudden summer shower that leaves the trees sparkling and the birds singing, but a steady, drenching, continuous downpour. It rained on the second and the third; it rained for two solid weeks. The soil got more slippery, then it began to dissolve. The shell holes filled up; the landscape looked like the craters of the moon, with water in them. Sappers and engineers tried to build up paths that threaded their way tortuously through and around the holes. Soldiers in ammunition- or ration-carrying parties slipped off the paths and into the holes and drowned, sinking into the mud under their loads before they could claw their way out. All the time the attack kept on. The shells churned the mud into more mud; the Germans, almost as miserable as the British but at least not attacking, held on relentlessly. Soldiers could not move through the mud, so at night the carrying parties went out and laid duckboards in front of the British line, and in the morning the troops came up and balanced and slithered on the wet boards. The Germans shot them off and they fell into the mud and died and drowned. Wounded could not be got back and guns could not be got forward. The entire world was mud-colored and doomed to wallow in it until it drowned. Still the attack went on; they slept between sheets at corps headquarters and lamented that the infantry did not show more offensive spirit. Gough gave up, and Haig shifted the advance south and let Plumer do it. August gave way to September; still the rain fell. Daddy Plumer was careful, and he kept his attacks limited, with plenty of support. Slowly his troops gained ground; the Menin Road, Polygon Wood, just a few shattered treetrunks now. The Germans used mustard gas, and the British kept on. As September and October waned, Haig had to withdraw troops for the disasters on the Italian Front, but he continued his attacks, not now to win through to victory, but just to gain what he considered a defensible line for the winter. He got it. The Canadians finally took and held the village of Passchendaele. The great advance to Ghent, Third Ypres, had gained the British a salient of four and a half miles. It had cost a quarter of a million casualties.

The British military historian and critic, Basil Liddell Hart, in his history of the war, tells the story of a staff officer who came up to see the battlefield after it was all quiet again. He gazed out over the sea of mud, then said half to himself, "My God, did we send men to advance in that?", after which he broke down weeping and his escort led him away. Staff officers, distinguished by red tabs on their collars, often complained that infantrymen failed to salute them.

\* \* \*

Passchendaele was the end of an era in warfare. There were contradictory reasons for this, positive and negative. The positive ones were that the nature of the war was changing, and within a few months of the slaughter in Flanders new techniques, new weapons, and new tactics would make Haig's great battle nearly as obsolete as Waterloo or Balaclava. These things did not happen overnight; they had been years in the making and took a long time to work out. Nor did they mean that men would cease to die uselessly in battle; that particular human failing seems an intrinsic part of the race. But the next big battles of World War I were to be quite different from those that had gone before.

On the negative side, there was not to be another Battle of Ypres because European civilization simply could not stand any more. In *Tender Is the Night* Scott Fitzgerald wrote that Verdun and the Somme and Passchendaele were "love battles," and that the only people who could fight them were those who possessed a sublime faith in their countries, their institutions, and their own unquestioned value systems. Only that kind of security, that kind of unthinking confidence, armored men sufficiently to endure the hell of such battles. Now those men were gone; either they lay rotting in the mud of France, or, if they still lived, they no longer possessed the faith of those pathetically innocent times. The German Army consisted of old men who had already dreamed their dreams or young boys who had never had time to see visions. The French Army had already mutinied. In Britain they no longer allowed soldiers to take their rifles home on leave with them, for men returning to the front took pot shots at London houses as they rode by on the trains, in a futile but revealing expression of their frustrations. The whole sickening horror had simply gone on too long.

Yet it still had another year to run. The new methods and weapons that were changing the practice of war and altering the balance of forces were operative for Germans as well as Allies. Both sides therefore believed that they would win if only they could hold on long enough, or act quickly enough. In that sense the basic equation had not changed at all. The equilibrium of force still prevailed; the Clausewitzian extension of violence had proceeded farther than ever before, but had still not achieved a victory. Until one side or the other acknowledged defeat and bowed to the will of the stronger, the war must continue. Indeed, in that sense, it did not even end in 1918; it lasted until 1945.

# 19. Change and Continuity

"THE MORE THINGS CHANGE, the more they remain the same," as the old French proverb has it. Such cynicism certainly applied to the political and military situation late in 1917. Both sides thought they could see victory just down the road, and it apparently escaped those who saw it that they had seen the same thing in August of 1914. Generals and politicians were quite willing to fight on; to surrender now, after all the sacrifices they had made—caused to be made—was unthinkable. Clemenceau in France, Lloyd George in Britain, Orlando in Italy, all were determined to have their pound of flesh, and Foch and Pétain, Haig and Cadorna were anxious to deliver it to them. All the old Allies were in parlous state, but that was the more reason to hang on, for the Americans were coming. During the height of the crisis about to burst on them, Foch was to remark calmly that if the Allies could last until 1919, they could go on the offensive in 1920 and win in 1921.

From the German side it looked a bit different. The leaders there recognized that it was purely a matter of time, almost on a mathematical equation. Though no one publicly acknowledged it, it was now obvious that their unrestricted submarine warfare campaign had been a disastrous mistake. It had been wrong in all three of its fundamental premises: Britain had not been starved into submission in six months; that being the case, the American military intervention was going to have significant effect; and finally, the Americans were getting to France after all. The Germans still did not think much of American fighting potential, but even so they could not ignore the growing flood of healthy young men steaming into French ports day after day. The Americans might or might not be any good, but the Allies would win by sheer weight of numbers if the war lasted too much longer.

American intervention, however, was balanced by Russian collapse. The Provisional Government there had tried to stay in the war, but from mid-1917 on it was clear that Russia was no longer a major factor, and the Germans began shifting troops westward. For a short while they were going to have a fair superiority of men and matériel on the Western Front; they should be able to win the war in the spring of 1918; if they could not, then they were going to lose it.

Through late 1917 then, both sides, equally aware that the war was balanced on a knife edge, undertook a series of operations. It is easier now than it was then to see this as a point of departure. New weapons and new ideas came into play at last, too late for perfection in this war, and too late for the generation that fought it. All the participants could tell was that the war was approaching a crescendo of violence. The opening of this new phase was marked by a disaster for Allied arms in Italy.

The Austro-Hungarian Empire, which had appeared on the verge of collapse in August of 1914, still looked to be in the same condition three years later. This is less surprising than it seems at first glance, for both Austrians and their enemies had been predicting the imminent breakdown of the empire ever since the end of the Thirty Years' War in 1648, so under its apparently ramshackle exterior there was a good deal of residual resilience. The German General Staff, which had gradually taken over Austria as it had everything else, did not pay too much attention to the cries and mutterings of disaster that constantly assailed them from their now-junior partner.

By the fall of 1917 it was obvious to Ludendorff, who now had taken over most of the military planning, Hindenburg being reduced even more to the role of front man, that something must be done about the Italo-Austrian front. He acknowledged at last the calamitous state of affairs there and found time to deal with it.

The Italians were in marginally better shape than their opponents, but no more than that. Early in 1917 General Luigi Cadorna had asked the British and French to send him a stiffening of men and matériel, estimating, probably correctly, that he could knock Austria out at last if he had a little help. Both Lloyd George and a reemergent General Foch in France thought this was a good idea, the former because of his anti-Western Front bias, the latter because, with no immediate command responsibility on the front, he could take a longer view. Unfortunately for Italy, this sympathy was promptly scuttled by Haig; the British commander was contemplating his own Flanders offensive and wanted no sidetracking of his troops that might diminish his strength. The best Foch and Cadorna could do was to work out some of the preliminary staff planning for the dispatch of Allied troops to Italy in the event of an emergency.

Armed with this cold comfort, the Italians fought the Tenth Battle of the Isonzo from mid-May to early June. It had the usual result, small gains and heavy losses. Cadorna then recouped his strength for what he considered his major effort of the year, and from August 18 to September 15 fought the Eleventh Isonzo. Again the losses were heavy, but this time the Italian troops actually made some ground. They attacked fifty-one divisions strong, supported by more than 5,000 guns, and they succeeded in pushing the Austrians back for perhaps five miles. Though it was five miles that was useless in a terrain sense, it put tremendous strain on the Austrian resources, and the only thing that saved them from a complete break was that the attackers outran their guns and their supply capacity.

At this Ludendorff finally awoke to the danger in the south. He was busy with the Riga offensive on the Eastern Front, and with stopping third Ypres in the West. The Emperor Charles asked if he might not bring home Austrian troops from Russia and Rumania, where some desultory mopping-up operations were still going on, but Ludendorff preemptorily refused the Austrians their own troops. Instead he decided to organize a new army, the 14th, under the German general Otto von Below; he assigned to it five German divisions and sent it down to be the spearhead of a major attack.

Von Below brought his force into the line just north of the latest Italian gains, facing the town of Caporetto on the upper Isonzo River. He planned a straightforward drive, using the new Hutier tactics, and he believed that with a little luck the offensive might well go as far as the line of the Tagliamento River, twenty-five miles ahead of him. As the entire front had shifted less than ten miles so far in the war, this was certainly ambitious.

Cadorna knew something was coming. He was not entirely certain what, but he was happy enough to go momentarily on the defensive. His troops were better armed and equipped than they had yet been in the war, thanks both to Italy's own efforts and the assistance of her allies, but their morale was low, sapped by

Bolshevik agitation and unceasing complaints from the civilian population. The war had eaten deeply into the always fragile structure of the Italian economy and political life, and so far there was precious little to show for it. When he ordered a defensive stance, Cadorna did not object unduly that his army commander facing Caporetto chose not to obey that order. Both agreed that the area was unsuited for heavy operations and expected the attack to come farther south, where they themselves had fought their Isonzo battles.

The Austro-Germans thus achieved complete surprise when they jumped off on the morning of October 24. After a six-hour bombardment, compared with Haig's thirteen days at Third Ypres, the infantry dashed forward, covered by smoke and by gas shells. Highly trained assault teams infiltrated the Italian lines; what they could not quickly overcome they isolated and kept on going. Behind them the regular infantry units pushed on, finishing off the strong points. Italian battlefield communications quickly collapsed, and the 2nd Army commander lost control of his battle within hours. It was the first big breakthrough on the Italian front, and by nightfall the Germans and Austrians were rolling. To the south, the Italian 3rd Army and Cadorna's reserves were forced into a pell-mell rush to the rear to avoid being encircled. To the north, most of the Carnic Force was trapped as the attackers rapidly pinched off the poor tracks and roads into the mountains. In four days Gorizia was gone, fruit of two years' work, and the Austro-Germans were as far as Udine, along the lateral railroad that fed the whole Isonzo front. Three days after that they were at the Tagliamento. Both Cadorna and von Below expected the attack to run down here, but both were mistaken. On the night of November 2–3 German mountain troops got across the river at its upper reaches, and again the Italians were levered off their line. Back they went once more, and the retreat continued for another week, long columns of tired troops, bumper-to-bumper trucks, guns, and animals. Traffic piled up at bridges and crossings, and the enemy constantly cut off stragglers and shattered units. At Longarone, a lieutenant Erwin Rommel captured 8,000 prisoners in one day. Rommel's entire battalion lost fewer than twenty men in the whole advance. By the time Cadorna pulled his weary army together, he was on the Piave River, seventy-five miles from Caporetto—and fewer than twenty from Venice. Forty thousand Italians were killed or wounded, more than a quarter of a million had been taken prisoner, many of them glad to be out of it; 2,500 artillery pieces were captured, and the Austrians and Germans were pleased to find themselves in possession of mountains of supplies. In Vienna they gave thanks for the last great victory of the Hapsburg Empire.

Dr. Johnson wrote that nothing concentrates the mind like the imminent prospect of being hanged. Faced with their dismal record for the year, and the disaster of Caporetto piled on top of it, the Allies decided they must mend their ways of running the war. It at last became obvious even to them that they could no longer bumble along, assuring each other of their support while going their separate ways. Foch came down to Italy with six Anglo-French divisions as reinforcements for the front, and at a meeting held at Rapallo the Allies agreed to establish a Supreme War Council to sit in Paris and coordinate operations in the coming months. It was a weak weapon to pit against the single-minded obstinacy of a Haig or a Pétain, but it was a necessary first step to a logical prosecution of the war. There was here some glimmer of hope in all the gloom.

The disaster in Italy aside, the year ended on a slightly better note for the Allies than might have been expected. November 20, 1917, was the commencement exercise of the tank. The Germans, with their fine military tradition, had answered the problem of the World War I battlefield with new tactics and techniques; the Allies, with their inventive and industrial genius, answered it with new machines.

The gestation period of the armored fighting vehicle had been long and frustrating. Supporters of the new weapon had to fight against conventional military thinking, which preferred to bet on the horses, and they also had to fight the unreliability of their own creations. The earliest tanks had performed poorly at the Somme, leading to a widespread "I told you so" attitude among the traditionalists. A year later, at Second Aisne, Nivelle's disastrous offensive, the tanks had done no better. The terrain had been unfavorable for them, and the majority had been destroyed in their approach marches; that was more the result of German control of the air and observation points than of inherent shortcomings in the tanks, but it did not make them look any better.

Nonetheless, development had continued, and by the time of the Battle of Cambrai, the British had a tank force consisting of between 300 and 400 tanks. Though incredibly clumsy and awkward, they were far advanced over the machines used on the Somme fifteen months earlier. They could cross over ditches and climb parapets, as long as they were not too wide or too high. Some tanks were fitted to carry fascines, bundles of brush which they dropped into trenches to make a rough bridge for following infantry to cross over. The Tank Corps staff officer, Lieutenant Colonel J. F. C. Fuller, had drawn up a detailed tactical plan for tank and infantry cooperation, and it was he who had suggested Cambrai as a suitable battleground for the new kind of attack he envisaged.

That was in June of 1917, but at that time Haig was still busy with preparations for Third Ypres, and the proposal was kept on the shelf. As it became apparent that the war was not going to be won in Flanders, the Cambrai plan was brought out and refurbished. The town lay just south of Arras, behind the northern part of the Hindenburg Line. The terrain here was more favorable for tank operations than it was farther north and seemed to promise significant results. The burden of the attack was given to Byng's 3rd Army, and he was told he could have the entire Tank Corps to work with.

An even more startling innovation was that Byng decided to go without any preliminary barrage. With the tanks to flatten the German wire and provide close fire support, a lengthy preattack bombardment was unnecessary. The gunners were told instead to wait for the start of the attack, and then provide covering fire for the infantry, and counterbattery fire against the Germans. New techniques were in evidence here, too, for the British were developing methods of sound-ranging and flash-spotting; rather than being forced to fire a wasteful and indiscriminate area barrage, they could now hit the enemy's guns with increased accuracy.

The plan called for the British to break over the St. Quentin Canal, which formed the right flank boundary of their attack and then bent north in front of them. They were to take the village of Flesquieres to their center, and their left was to seize a strategic feature called Bourlon Wood, which was just high enough to dominate the ground to and past Cambrai. Byng hoped to score a clean breakthrough and had the cavalry standing by to exploit forward once the tanks and infantry had done their job. Haig, for once more realistic, expected only a local success.

It did not go quite as well as anticipated, though the first hours of the attack looked good. As the monsters rolled forward, many German soldiers threw down their weapons and fled to the rear. On much of the attack, the German line burst wide open. Unfortunately for the British, the division slated to attack Flesquieres, the 51st Highland Division, had substituted its own tactics for Fuller's; instead of passing in files through the lanes torn in the wire by the tanks, its infantry deployed in line and got hung up. A wide gap opened between tanks and infantry, and the Germans, well dug in around the village, knocked out many tanks unhampered by British infantry; without closely interlocking mutual support, the trick did not work, and the heroic defense of Flesquieres upset the entire attack plan.

Nevertheless, on November 23 the government in Britain ordered the church bells sounded for a victory, the only time in the entire war this happened before its actual end. The British did carry Bourlon Wood, and in a couple of places they got across the St. Quentin Canal. But the infantry reserves were low, because of losses up in Flanders and units drafted off to shore up the Italians, and Byng lacked the depth to keep his affair going. By the 26th the British were fought out.

The Germans then riposted with a surprise of their own. Using the tactics now proven at Riga and at Caporetto, they counterattacked on November 30. Ludendorff had been hard pressed to scrape up reserves, but his attack was a bit wider than the British, and the Germans hit the new salient and the old line to the south of it. Attacking with surprise, they recovered most of their original losses and in some cases penetrated as much as three miles back into the original British positions. The village of Gouzeaucourt was saved only by British tanks counterattacking the German assault units, so here was the new warfare in earnest, a far cry from Passchendaele and a foreshadowing of coming events for 1918. By the first week of December the battle had burned down, with both sides eyeing each other with wary respect. Clearly something was brewing.

An increasingly important factor of the new warfare was that it was now three-dimensional. The submarine had taken it under water, and the airplane had lifted it above the ground. Just as with the tank, the airplane took a long time to become effective, partly because of its own limitations, and partly because of the conservatism with which it was regarded by those in authority. But by 1917 it was impossible to ignore the effect of the airplane on operations; command of the air, as had command of the sea, had emerged as a necessity of war.

The effect of the war on aircraft was far greater than the effect of aircraft on the war. As soon as military men discovered that the airplane was something more than a mere toy, they demanded better and better planes, and throughout the war there was an incredibly rapid developmental spiral. The earliest military use of aircraft had been just before World War I; the Italians had employed a few in Libya in their campaigns against the desert tribes, and in the Balkan wars an American pilot had hired himself out to fly reconnaissance missions. Airplanes at this time were not armed, and most military men who paid them any attention at all saw them as observation machines. In the first weeks of the war, a German aviator had flown over Paris and dropped a few hand-held bombs, but that was a mere gesture; far more significant was the discovery of Kluck's turn away from Paris by a British spotting plane. Both sides soon discovered the usefulness of having aircraft for general observation, and more especially for artillery spotting, in spite of the deficiencies of early signaling and communication methods.

As soon as the airplane had a legitimate military use, it became desirable to deny that use to the other side. One way was to shoot the plane down from the ground, and both sides developed extensive antiaircraft armaments, far more sophisticated than the early method of simply digging in the trail of the gun so that its barrel pointed up in the air. But the big leap forward came when airplanes themselves could be armed.

At the very beginning, pilots saw one another as members of a select club, and German and Allied fliers waved at each other as they flew by on their lawful occasions, rather congratulating themselves that were literally and figuratively above the sordid things being done on the ground. Fairly soon, however, they started carrying rifles and pistols and taking pot shots at each other. Next, an imaginative French pilot fitted the propeller blades of his aircraft with deflector plates, a crude mechanism that allowed him to fire a machine gun through the arc of the whirling propeller and enabled him to shoot down Germans at an impressive rate. Unfortunately, he made a forced landing behind enemy lines, and his secret was discovered by the Germans. They took the idea to a Dutch aircraft engineer and manufacturer named Anthony

Fokker and asked him to duplicate it. Fokker said he could do much better, and he and his designers installed a simple interrupter gear, synchronized so that the machine gun would fire only at such a rate and time that its bullets would pass through the propeller arc without hitting the blades. The idea had been around since before the war, but had to this point been ignored. Armed with the new mechanism, the German pilots temporarily swept the skies early in 1916, and this time was known as the period of the "Fokker scourge." The Allies were utterly at a loss to counter it, simple though the idea was, and they produced a series of aircraft, looking more or less like powered birdcages, with the engines behind a nacelle in which the crew rode. These "pusher" types were fairly sound aerodynamically, but did have limitations. In desperation the French hit on a particularly bizarre answer; they took a conventional airplane and mounted a sort of crow's nest affair on a frame in front of the propeller, and in this a gunner stood and took his chances. Needless to say, it was not a popular assignment or a very effective answer to the Germans.

One counter to the Fokkers was to mount the machine gun on top of the upper wing of the biplane, so that it fired over the propeller arc. Unhappily, since the guns carried their ammunition in a drum, the pilot had practically to climb out of the plane to reload his gun. One pilot, faced with a jammed drum, ended up balancing with his feet on the cockpit fairing and beating at the drum with his hands to try to free it. Under this strange distribution of weight, the plane flipped upside down, and the pilot found himself hanging in space, now hoping the drum would not release after all. Finally, the aircraft, which seemed to possess a mind of its own, turned right side up again, and the shaken flier climbed back into his cockpit and flew home. Such episodes were made more exciting by the fact that Allied leaders refused to allow their pilots to wear parachutes, on the thesis, obviously formulated by people on the ground, that parachutes would make pilots reluctant to try to save their planes if they could abandon them. Hundreds of young men suffered horrible deaths by burning or crashing because of such official stupidity.

Eventually the Allies, too, developed an interrupter gear, and air fighting came into its own by mid-1916 or so. As the airplane advanced in sophistication, specialist types developed. There was the basic two-seater artillery observation or reconnaissance plane, and day after day these poor creatures flew up and down the lines, spotting for the guns and serving as targets for the other side. Then there was the "scout" or "fighting scout" or "fighter" as it eventually came to be called. These were the prima donnas of the air war, and the great names of air fighting were associated with them. There were for the Germans Baron von Richthofen with his red Fokker Triplane, which gave rise to the "Red Baron" nickname, or the lesser ace Hermann Goering, who flew a white Fokker D.VII. The French aces Guynemer and Nungesser flew Nieuport "Scouts," and these planes were such nice little machines that every air force in the war flew them, even the Germans and Austrians, who copied the design for themselves. The best British fighters came later in the war, in the S.E. 5 and especially the Sopwith Camel, so called because its guns were mounted in a hump behind the engine. The leading ace for them was a Canadian, William Bishop. From late 1916 on this kind of plane was increasingly important to the war as air leaders discovered their own doctrines about commanding the air space over the battlefields.

Bombing aircraft developed as well. The medium-range and -weight day bomber was used to support attacks, rather more by the Allies than by the Central Powers. There were real limitations on what these planes could do; an early one, the De Havilland 6, could either carry an observer or bombs, but not both, and it was widely unpopular with crews who called it "the Clutching Hand." Perhaps some measure of the reliability of these aircraft is shown by the fact that De Havilland 4, universally regarded as the best bomber of its class in the war, was equally universally known by its crews as "the Flaming Coffin."

The Germans had long championed the lighter-than-air ship and possessed several rigid-structure Zeppelins at the outbreak of the war. The Allies tended to concentrate on nonrigid airships, which they used for anti-submarine patrols, while the Germans turned their Zeppelins into bombers. Coasting high above the reach of British fighters, the Zeppelins carried out what was for the time a terrifying bombing campaign against Britain. Eventually, the British got fighters which could reach the Zeppelins' altitude, and as the Germans used flammable gas in their airships, this soon put a stop to their raids. Both sides then tried to develop large bombers, and the Germans eventually produced the Gotha-type bombers, while the British made Handley Pages. The former could carry nearly half a ton, the latter three quarters of a ton, of bombs. By 1918 the British were initiating a bombing campaign directed against German heavy industry, but it had just barely begun to function when the war ended.

The vision of airplanes having a strategic effect on war remained just that, but by 1917 and 1918 the airplane had become a vital element at the tactical level, and both sides made strenuous efforts to dominate the air. The British followed the most aggressive and the most costly policies, seeking out the Germans in their own airspace and fighting them behind German lines. Though the French had led aircraft development before the war, the British put more emphasis on it later, and on April 1, 1918, the Royal Air Force was officially born, out of an amalgamation of the old Royal Flying Corps and the Royal Naval Air Service. The scornful might note that April Fools' Day was appropriate, but air power was here to stay. Man's age-old dream of conquering the skies had reached fruition; he could now kill in the air as well as on the ground and on or under the water.

Two additional signs of change were noticeable at the end of the year: The Allies made some progress against Turkey, and in France the first American units entered the fighting. Both events held out some small hope for the coming year.

When General Sir Edmund Allenby left France after his victory at Arras and took over the campaign in Egypt and the Sinai Desert, he began a shake-up of British methods and men that ran like a fresh wind through the hot and desultory theater. Under Maxwell and Murray the British had fought a war in the good old imperial style, bumbling along on the tried-and-true idea that the British bulldog would always win in the end. Allenby changed all that; Lloyd George had sent him off with the parting admonition that he wanted Jerusalem taken by Christmas, and the new general proposed to deliver the goods.

Even so, it took him most of the summer to get ready. He got the command in June, moved out into the desert where the British still had their lines before Gaza, and started to work. He asked for, and got, three more divisions plus support troops; Lloyd George was quite willing to send men anywhere but to Haig on the Western Front, and by late October, Allenby was set to go.

The key to the Gaza line was its inland flank, which by now the Turks had strongly fortified at Beersheba. They had about 35,000 men on the whole line and thought they could hold it with no real difficulty. At this particular time, late 1917, the Turks were not in too bad a shape. They had used some of their troops to help overrun Rumania, but those units had now been recovered. The revolt in the desert of Arabia was a nuisance, but as yet little more than that. In Mesopotamia the British under General Maude had taken Baghdad in March. Unfortunately, Maude, the most popular of all British generals, had died of cholera, ironically in the same house where Baron von der Goltz had also died of it, and after that the campaign had tailed off into political maneuvering. Palestine appeared the most difficult front, and the Germans sent General von Falkenhayn, ex-Chief of the General Staff, fresh from the conquest of Rumania, down to handle the matter. He arrived in Jerusalem on November 1; by then he was a few days too late.

Allenby, who outnumbered his enemy by better than two to one, made all the open moves for yet another attack against Gaza. Meanwhile, he carefully marched four infantry and two horsed cavalry divisions inland, taking real chances with his water supply, and concentrated them around the two Turkish divisions dug in at Beersheba. In spite of his precautions, the Turks picked up the move, but not knowing its strength, thought it was not a serious threat. On October 31 Allenby struck.

Taken by surprise at the weight of the attack, the Turks nonetheless fought with their usual tenacity. The British infantrymen broke through their outer positions and began to work in toward the town. Late in the day the battle was decided by a pell-mell charge of the Australian Cavalry Division, which captured the town's water supply and broke into Beersheba itself. The Turks began reluctantly to pull back to the northwest.

The next day Allenby opened the second prong of his drive, along the seacoast, against Gaza. For four days the Turks threw back the British assaults, but on November 6 the British broke through the general line out at Tel Esh Sheria, between Gaza and Beersheba. That did the trick; in danger of being cut off now, the Gaza defenders had to pull out. They went back thirty miles to Junction Station, a position on their rail line that was almost as far north as Jerusalem. The British followed them up, but lack of water reduced them to a crawl, and the Turks largely made it back to their new line. They were digging in by November 11; meanwhile, over in the east in the Judean Hills, the Turks stopped at Hebron, about twenty miles south of Jerusalem.

Allenby kept on; he was up to Junction Station on the 13th,

and he threw his troops right at it. The Turks were pressured out in a day and once again went back all along the line. Now Allenby shifted his attention over to his right and put his emphasis on the troops going from Hebron to Jerusalem. Here von Falkenhayn managed to give him a bloody nose, and he was forced to stop and prepare a proper full-scale attack.

By the first week of December the Turks were disposed in a long thin line that ran from Bethlehem north in front of Jerusalem and then bent off northwest to meet the seacoast above Jaffa. The Turks lacked the strength to hold in depth, and on the 7th Allenby pushed his fired-up troops across the Jaffa road. Once again the Turks were levered out and had to give up Jerusalem or be trapped in it. Back they went, and on December 9 Allenby marched on foot into the holy city.

Falkenhayn tried to get it back a few days later, but what he could not hold he could not retake, and the British not only contained his attack but also beat him back several miles. By the end of the year he was on a line running from Jericho to the sea. Allenby asked Lloyd George for more men, hoping to finish things off. Instead, he lost troops because of what was happening in France. Setting that aside for future consideration, Allenby had done as ordered, and Jerusalem, though it was not Berlin or even Brussels, made a morale-boosting Christmas present for the Allied nations.

By the time that Allenby's dusty but triumphant soldiers made their way into Jerusalem, there were a quarter of a million American soldiers in France. They celebrated Christmas in the fine old style, with turkeys and cranberry sauce and presents for the local village children around their camps. The only thing wrong with them was that they had not yet done much fighting, and the only reason they hadn't was that they still did not know how to do it.

The Germans had been mistaken in their assessment that Americans were not sufficiently warlike to fight, but they had been correct in assuming that they were totally unprepared to do it. The Americans had manpower, but that was all they had. Their government, as usual, had gotten itself into a war without any real consideration of whether or not it was prepared to wage it. Back in the States the new men were drilling with broomsticks; in France they used French artillery pieces and French and British aircraft. In spite of all the hopes of the U. S. Army and all the war production for the Allies, they did not produce any of their own indigenously designed heavy weapons in time for the war.

But they did have men. The 1st Division had arrived in midsummer, the 2nd was formed in France. Next over were National Guard divisions, the 26th from New England and the 42nd, called the Rainbow Division because its men came from all over the country. As these late comers practiced the strange business of trench-fighting in the fields around Chaumont, the 1st Division, the "Big Red One," 20,000 strong, twice the size of a British or French division and called by Pershing "the best damned division in any army in the world," went into the line around Luneville, up near Verdun.

This was a quiet sector; both the Germans and the French on either side of the newcomers were too exhausted to make difficulties, and the whole exercise was just to give the Americans a little firsthand experience. The Yanks were all eager curiosity, and the Germans obliged by several trench raids to teach them their manners. Both sides did a little scrappy patrolling, and after a month the division went back out of the line. Eventually, the other new divisions went through the same kind of process, but by the spring of 1918, a year after the United States had entered the war, its troops had still taken no significant part in the holding of the Western Front. Indeed, the hottest American action yet had been Pershing's fights to preserve the autonomy of his own forces from his allies. From the British and French point of view, the Americans were in, which was good, but had done little, which was bad. The tired Allies heard of the German troops moving west from the Russian Front, and as the first signs of spring came in 1918, they girded their loins for the storm about to hit them. American help or not, they were by no means certain of weathering it.

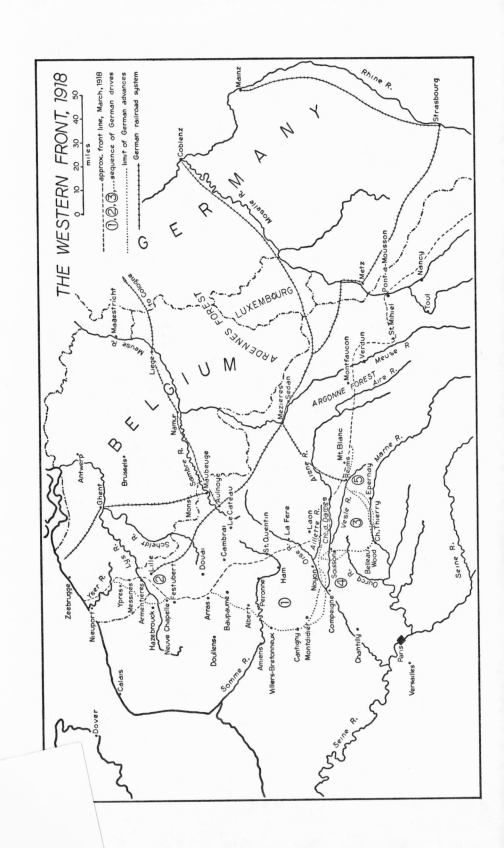

THE WESTERN FRONT, 1918

miles
0  10  20  30  40  50

------- approx. front line, March, 1918
①,②,③ ... sequence of German drives
••••••• limit of German advances
------- German railroad system

# 20. The German Spring Offensives, 1918

IT WAS THE FOURTH SPRING OF THE WAR, and the atmosphere of the moment depended almost entirely upon one's geography. East to west, people ran the gamut from utter despair to vaulting optimism. In Russia they were now out of it. The Bolshevik rulers waited for the capitalists to destroy themselves, after which the world revolution would obviously begin. Lenin and his cohorts had few other causes for satisfaction, however, for the Cossacks had declared against them, and the Ukraine was asserting itself, supported by German troops who overran the whole vast territory. The Allies were getting ready to land troops in the north, and the Japanese had already sent men into Vladivostok. It did not look as if it were going to be a good year for Russia.

In Central Europe things were almost as bad. Poles were declaring their independence, and the various minorities of Austria-Hungary were more and more restive, supported by Allied money and propaganda. In southeast Europe, in the Balkans and Turkey, war-weariness was endemic. The Germans were still determined to carry things to a successful conclusion, but the margin was ever more narrow. In spite of the incredibly successful mobilization—a euphemism for plundering—of the resources of their partners and their conquests, the country was living on next to nothing. The war had consumed Germany, taking off older and older men and younger boys, as indeed it was doing to all the major long-term belligerents, and starving the nation for the most basic of consumer goods. By now only the politicians and the industrialists seemed to be doing well from the war; unfortunately, they were the ones who counted in the scheme of things.

It was the same in France and Britain. The French countryside appeared peculiarly deserted to travelers, as if some selective plague had taken away all the healthy men. Women, oldsters, and children were all that were left. They went to the factories or the fields each morning, they came home to empty houses at night; some sort of half-life went on. But the industries kept producing the guns and the shells, and somewhere the men were found to use them. The army was recovering its equilibrium; Pétain knew his business, and his business was to survive until the Americans took over, an unglamorous concept of war completely at odds with 1914, but one with which there was now little argument.

In Britain, too, the iron had sunk deep. Conscription had been introduced in 1916, against the bitter opposition of organized labor; the national debt had increased nearly ten times, but there was still little sign of flagging. Late in 1917, when the politician Lord Lansdowne managed to get a letter published in the *Daily Telegraph* urging a negotiated peace—a letter which the *Times* had refused to publish as defeatist—he was mobbed by irate Londoners. Though some Englishmen wanted a settlement at the expense of Russia, a potential imperial pie whose pieces ought to satisfy everyone, most wanted to keep on in spite of hardships. There certainly were significant changes taking place: Parliament gave the vote to women and early in 1918 introduced food rationing. Yet the British felt they had been through this before; in 1811 the Chancellor of the Exchequer had introduced a budget which, he proudly announced, would enable Britain to fight Napoleon "forever"; now the same attitude prevailed, despite the cruelly significant fact that Britain had lost three times as many men on the first day of the Somme as she had lost in combat during the entire twenty-two years with France and Napoleon. The empire was still with them, though British handling of military operations had allowed the white dominions to insinuate their way into a greater share of political say on the war. The general outlook was dour but remained determined.

Across the Atlantic, by comparison, the Americans, even after nearly a year, were still enjoying the excitement of new belligerency. They had seen little combat as yet, and therefore suffered few losses, so the war was still a great game of bonfires and patriotic rallies, bellicose speeches and John Philip Sousa's fabulous marches, a sort of super Spanish-American War. Members of the Home Guard dressed up self-consciously in bits of uniform and patrolled the reservoir in Ansonia, Connecticut, to keep democracy safe from German saboteurs, and sauerkraut became "liberty cabbage." It was just a matter of time; Uncle Sam was rolling up his sleeves, and as soon as he was ready, he'd show all those people how things ought to be done!

America's was the optimism of youth and innocence, and if it was a bit ebullient for European tastes, it was a sorely needed corrective to the terribly tired peoples of France and Britain and Italy. For the final storm was about to break; the war might go on for years yet, but whether it was won or lost was going to be decided in the next few months. Foch, Haig, and Pétain knew that as well as Ludendorff and Hindenburg. A mighty passage of arms was in the offing.

The initiative lay with Germany. Day after day the troop trains came back from Russia and Poland, bringing the veterans to shore up the Western Front. For the first time in years, the German General Staff was going to have a manpower superiority to play with. On the Allied side the Supreme War Council decreed that they should create a thirty-division reserve, a fire brigade to be used wherever the storm struck. Haig refused. He wanted his troops for his line, and he thought, correctly as it turned out, that the French would be far more eager to take his units away from him than to give him theirs when the time came. Besides, after Passchendaele, Lloyd George was refusing to send him any more cannon fodder. So there was to be no general reserve; the soldiers dug and wired, the generals tried to create fall-back positions, and everyone hoped for the best. By March there were 325,000 Americans in France, and still more on the way.

The calendar moved inexorably; Napoleon had once remarked, "Ask me for anything but time." Ludendorff was as conscious of those Americans coming by ships as the Allies were of the Germans coming by train. It was imperative that he attack early, but where should he do it and to what end? There were three possibilities, pretty much the same as they had been throughout the entire war. He could attack around Verdun, on the Somme front, or up in Flanders. Of the three, Verdun was the roughest territory, hard to fight through. Even more important, it had behind it nothing that Ludendorff considered a major strategic objective. If he pushed the French back from Verdun, they would simply dig another line and he would then have to push them back all over again; he could not afford to do that indefinitely.

Flanders was potentially far more profitable. Less than fifty miles behind the front line lay the Channel ports, and the Germans had gone farther than that at Riga and Caporetto. The difficulty about Flanders was the mud; what had cost so many lives was now going to preserve at least a few. It was impossible to undertake heavy mobile operations in the north until the terrain dried up, and it would not do that until mid-summer. Ludendorff could not wait that long.

That left the Somme front, not quite midway between the other two. The chief difficulty about operations there was that, again, nothing of any great significance lay behind it, no one vital capital or port or rail junction the loss of which would seriously compromise the entire Allied position. Ludendorff's assessments of his enemies, however, led him to desire to defeat the British. He believed they were far less skillful in defense than the French. He acknowledged that they were far more tenacious, and that they would hold the line until they died where they were; in a sense, that was exactly what he wanted them to do. He further believed that if the British were beaten, the French would collapse, whereas if the French were knocked out, the British probably would not give up. On balance, then, the Somme it was.

Preparations, as usual, were thorough, methodical, and well concealed. Ludendorff assigned the attack to three armies, significantly Hutier's 18th, von der Marwitz' 2nd, and von Below's 17th, so he had the veterans of the new tactics on each of his flanks. He confidently expected to make as good progress as he had in both those earlier battles, and when staff officers pointed out that the country was different here and that the British, skilled or not, might not be quite like war-weary Russians or Italians, he paid little attention. The attack was to center around Peronne, on a front of just over forty miles that ran from Arras down to the Oise where the French took over. The Germans were going all the way. Ludendorff, though he started planning for a subsidiary attack in the north, essentially put his money on the big breakthrough, the magic moment when troops broke into the enemy's rear areas and he began the process of quick disintegration that would lead to total collapse for one side, victory for the other. Morale among the troops was high; they were going to win the war.

Knowing an attack was coming and having a pretty good idea where, the British could still do little about it. Byng's 3rd Army was well dug in in front of Arras, with fourteen divisions covering a front of twenty-eight miles. Gough's 5th Army to his right had only fifteen divisions, and some authorities give it even fewer, to cover a front of just over forty miles. Even worse than this imbalance was the fact that Gough had extended south to take over a line previously held by the French. The French defense system was much more fluid than the British, for the former tended to rely on heavy artillery support to break up attacks, while the British put their faith in infantry weapons, both more or less following out in this respect the attitudes with which they had entered the war. The British problem was that they now lacked the artillery to back up a French-style trench system and did not have a trench system suited to their own kind of fighting. On such ostensibly minor technicalities the lives of men depended.

The British situation was made even more difficult by the fact that they did not possess the labor force to create adequate fall-back positions. Wanting to build a three-stage line, they were able to build only the forward outposts and the main battle position, but not the third, final defense system. The want of men to do this was directly attributable to Lloyd George's dislike of Haig and his refusal to send him any more reinforcements. On one occasion during the Second World War, when Churchill refused to support General Auchinleck in the Western Desert, he was told, "You must back him or sack him!" Lloyd George could not sack Haig, or at least he did not think it politic to do so, but he would not back him either. He should have done one or the other.

Ludendorff's plan called for Hutier, on his left flank with twenty-five divisions, to break through Gough's line and then swing left and anchor on the Somme River, preventing the arrival of French reinforcements or any interference with the battle from the south. Von Below, on the other flank, was to break through from Arras to Cambrai and move forward, taking Baupaume near the bottom of Byng's front. He would then turn northward, partly rolling up the British line, partly holding the shoulder of the break and preventing its being squeezed shut. Finally, in the middle, von der Marwitz' 2nd Army was to dash through Gough's broken positions for Peronne, then wheel half-right and take off to the northwest, toward Doullens, about fifty miles behind the front lines.

The morning of March 21 was thick with fog, German weather that grounded the Allied planes. At 0440 the German guns opened up, 6,000 of them firing a saturation barrage on the British positions. Precisely five hours later they switched to selected targets, and the gray-clad infantry came up out of their trenches and started forward. The fog was still so heavy that visibility was near zero, and it was made worse by gas. A gas mask has to be one of the least comfortable items of clothing or equipment ever devised by man; the wearer itches and sweats, the Plexiglas lenses fog up, and even on a bright clear day, sight is severely impaired. Now between the fog, the gas, and the gas masks, soldiers groped blindly for one another. Little rushes of men loomed up out of the fog, indistinguishable as friend or enemy, and disappeared; machine guns and rifles were fired almost blindly; the artillery kept on battering, the Germans firing on map coordinates and time schedules, the British simply firing off furiously into the void. In this kind of melee, the careful preparation and training of the German assault teams paid handsome dividends. They infiltrated into the trench system, moved along it with bayonets and grenades and flamethrowers. When they had cleared a section of trench they kept on going; when they found the British grouped together and full of fight, they dropped squads to keep them busy and kept on moving forward. The follow-up waves took out the strongpoints one by one. Within hours the British line was a line no longer, and Gough had lost touch with his battle. At corps headquarters, where generals had been comfortably ensconced miles behind the line and hitherto happily safe from reality, the phone lines went dead. Cooks and clerks suddenly found themselves attacked and fighting back. Confusion hung over the battlefield even more thickly than the fog.

Toward midday the weather began to clear, and the British got their aircraft up. For the rest of the day the squadrons made valiant efforts to slow the Germans down. They wrested domination of the air from the German pilots, and then they went down close to the ground to strafe and bomb. But they could do only so much. The front had suddenly become fluid, and for everyone involved this was a brand-new experience. Often pilots dared not strafe because they were uncertain whether the little scurrying targets were their own side or the enemy.

By midday Gough knew he was in real trouble. He had two divisions in his rear areas in General Headquarters reserve; he asked for and got them. At the same time Haig gave two more to Byng, but by nightfall the news was either uniformly bad or nonexistent—which was the same thing.

The morning of the 22nd was foggy again, and the Germans kept coming; the sky cleared a bit earlier than the day before, but the best efforts of the air squadrons still could not stop the advance. By late afternoon Hutier had broken his men through into the clear; they had got past the last positions and were heading full-tilt for Ham, the Somme, and the Canal du Nord. Byng was still holding stubbornly in front of Baupaume, and von der Marwitz was still stuck in the deeper British trench system in the center. The French were sending up six divisions to help Gough, but they were not going to arrive in time to be of immediate assistance, and even when they did, they would be little use until their guns and supply units caught up with them.

Faced with the fact that the battle had imposed its own logic on him, Ludendorff now changed his mind about it. Instead of directing the attack to the northwest, he decided to go with Hutier's success and push to the southwest instead. His general target became Amiens instead of Doullens. The next day Hutier's troops followed Gough's so fast they captured bridges across the Somme before the engineers could blow them, and suddenly it looked like the first weeks of the war all over again.

This made the Allies face some harsh realities. Though there was no great strategic prize behind the Somme battle, there was one element that was fraught with danger for the Anglo-French, and with opportunity for the Germans. Ludendorff had hit the point where the two allies' lines joined. Breaking it here brought into stark clarity the fact that they would respond differently to pressure: The British would fall back northwest to cover the Channel ports and their communications, and if necessary, their line of retreat; the French would pull back southwest, to cover Paris. Unless someone were prepared to make some sacrifices, then, the line might be completely ruptured, and the always fragile coalition might fall apart.

It was this sort of possibility that the Supreme War Council, set up at Rapallo, was supposed to prevent. Over the few months of its existence, however, it had become little more than a clearing house and a debating society. Now, on the 26th, while German troops were rampaging a full thirty miles in the rear of Gough's original line, the British and French leaders met at Doullens. President Poincaré himself chaired the meeting, along with Clemenceau, Premier since last November; Pétain; Foch; and various other ministers and generals. The British sent over Lord Milner, Secretary of State for War; Sir Henry Wilson, who in February had replaced Robertson as Chief of the Imperial General Staff; Haig; and assorted officers from Haig's staff. The session opened in gloom. Haig was appalled at the look of Pétain; previously the two had gotten along well, Pétain's French peasant stolidity appealing to Haig's dour Scots Presbyterian outlook. Pétain now seemed to think the war was all but lost and said so openly to Clemenceau; in his opinion, the British were a broken reed.

Foch, however, disagreed; his official position at that time was Chief of the General Staff at the Ministry of War, which made him more or less equal to the British Chief of the Imperial General Staff, with responsibilities basically administrative and policy-making rather than operational. It was a great boost for the French when Wilson, notably francophile, had replaced Robertson, who was neither pro- nor anti-French, but tended to be uncritically supportive of Haig. Soon after seeing Pétain at the beginning of the meeting, Haig had muttered to Wilson that they needed a supreme commander, and it had better be "Foch or some other French general who will fight." The qualifier was important, in view of Pétain's obvious attitude, and when Foch argued forcibly for fighting, in front of Amiens, everywhere and anywhere, Haig finally said what had needed saying for a long time: "If General Foch will give me his advice, I will gladly follow it."

Subsequent events were to show that Haig did not always "gladly" follow Foch's advice, and that often Foch's advice was not terribly good anyway, but at that dark moment on March 26, both men deserved well of their countries and their cause.

The agreed formula was rather less than a clear mandate and far from a stirring call to arms. It said, "General Foch is charged by the British and French governments with the coordination of the action of the Allied armies on the Western Front. He will make arrangements to this effect with the two generals-in-chief, who are invited to furnish him with the necessary information." It was a start, however, and in early April at Beauvais, Foch was given the "strategic direction" of operations. By the middle of that month he was formally named general-in-chief of the Allied armies.

At the moment a great deal more depended on tired men slogging along with rifles on their shoulders than on generals and their papers. The day after the Doullens meeting, Hutier's troops leaped another dozen miles and got possession of the town of Montdidier. For a few short hours there was nothing ahead of them. The French were desperately trucking reserves up from the south but were able only to shore up the shoulder of the battle; Sir Henry Rawlinson, taking over command from Gough, whose 5th Army had now been destroyed, was trying to hold along the Somme Valley with a cavalry screen, which at the moment was all he had.

But Hutier's men had done their best and could do no more. They had driven forty miles, much of it over the old Somme battlefields of 1916 and over the territory they themselves had devastated in the retreat to the Hindenburg Line. They had outrun their supplies, and trucks and guns could not get forward through the devastation. Casualties among the assault groups had been heavy. To the north, von Below remained stuck before Arras; there the British had held hard and successfully. By April 1 it was all but over. French troops filled the gap in front of Montdidier, linking up with Rawlinson's men, and the golden opportunity, more illusory than real, was gone. Ludendorff had won a great tactical victory; he had scared his enemies so much they had finally resolved their differences and combined their aims. His tactical success was thus in the long run a strategic setback of the first order. By April 4 the line was stabilized.

Ludendorff was now in something of a quandary. Where should he attack next, and to what end? He still believed his original intention had been correct, that it was desirable to break the British and beat them out of the war. The success, limited though it was, of the first drive had shown up the possibilities of thrusting the two allies' fronts apart. But he could not try the same attack immediately in the same place; he decided, therefore, to attack up in the north, an area in which he had already made some preparations as a cover for the March offensive. He hoped that a second attack would break the British; if it did not, it should at least distract them sufficiently to allow him then to return to the other end of their front and finish off the job. The terrain was still bad and of itself necessitated limited objectives. About this second German offensive, therefore, there was an air of not being entirely certain what its goal was, or exactly how to achieve it.

The area he chose was just below Ypres, around the town of Armentières, and either side of the valley of the Lys River, and it was the Lys that gave its name to the battle. Ludendorff had sixty-one divisions in Arnim's 4th Army, north of the river, and in 6th Army, south of it, though in fact only about thirty-five were capable of use as assault formations. On the British side Plumer's 2nd

Army, thirteen divisions strong, faced 4th Army from the hard-won positions along the Messines Ridge. To its right, General Horne's 1st Army had sixteen divisions running south from the Lys to Festubert and Givenchy, a front of about fifteen miles. The name Festubert recalled memories of 1915, but few of the men now in Horne's line went back that far; not many infantrymen lived through three years of combat. One of Horne's weaker divisions, for example, was the 2nd Portuguese.

Portugal traced its alliance with England back to the Treaty of Windsor in 1386. In 1914 the country had voted to go to war with Germany, but the declaration was delayed by a coup led by pro-German officers. Though the resulting military dictatorship was overthrown after a few months, the new government maintained its neutrality until March of 1916. Then when Portugal seized German ships in Lisbon, the German government declared war on Portugal. The Portuguese, already involved in hostilities with the German colonial forces in Africa, decided to send two divisions to fight alongside the Allies on the Western Front. The two were integrated into the British sector and, from their arrival on, largely left to fend for themselves. They were something like a small Portuguese raft adrift in a sea of misery, and they suffered immense hardships, which they bore stoically, fighting in a war the causes of which most of them must have been utterly ignorant.

On the morning of April 9 Horne had only four divisions holding his front, with the 2nd Portuguese covering a long stretch on either side of Neuve Chapelle. They were completely unprepared for the storm that hit them, when, after a short hurricane bombardment, five German divisions using the new tactics burst through their line. The Portuguese split apart like an overripe melon, and the Germans went right on, scarcely pausing. It was late in the day before the British could pull themselves together, and by the time they did so, the Germans had gained a full three miles and were slowed only by the Lys, some of its tributary streams, and a stout if hasty reaction by flanking British units. Horne sent up anguished yells for help, and Plumer moved some of his troops south to bail out his colleague.

This proved to be a mistake, for the next day the Germans hit Plumer in the same way and rudely shoved his divisions back a mile, off the Messines Ridge and in the direction of Mt. Kemmel. That day the Germans took Armentières and crossed the Lys on Horne's front. Haig was thoroughly shaken; he had no more reserves to commit. The Germans were clearly heading for the rail junction at Hazebrouck, and if they got there, the front would be so seriously dislocated that they might well go through to the coast. Foch came up to have a look that evening and said he was assembling French reinforcements around Amiens. Haig said they should come up as fast as possible, but Foch went away thinking things were not quite as bad as Haig himself thought. The British commander was sufficiently alarmed to issue an order of the day which ended, "With our backs to the wall and believing in the justice of our cause each one must fight on to the end. The safety of our homes and the freedom of mankind alike depend upon the conduct of each one of us at this critical moment." Those were fairly strong words from a general who was not notably concerned with troop morale or public relations. Haig tended, like England, to expect that every man will do his duty, and not to say much about it.

It was going to take more than exhortation, however, to stop the Germans. By April 12 they had taken the town of Messines on Plumer's front and penetrated more than seven miles on Horne's. That day heavy air attacks slowed them down, and they looked as if they might be getting tired. For two more days the attacks came on, but on the 17th when they tried to take Mt. Kemmel the British threw them back in ferocious fighting. Daddy Plumer had taken over the whole front now, and he was plugging gaps here and shoring up weaknesses there. The same day the Germans tried to extend the attack northward against the Belgians, whom they had pretty much left alone since 1914, and they took a severe beating for their pains, the Belgians not budging an inch. Meanwhile, Foch was moving reinforcements north but keeping them back as much as he could while doing so, still generally confident that the B. E. F. could hold its own if necessary. Four French divisions finally reached the front on the 21st. By then Haig's short-lived trust in Foch was nearly gone. On the 27th the new French divisions lost Mt. Kemmel, which the tired British had held so doggedly.

But Foch brought up even more French, and when the Germans made a last effort on the 29th, both of the Allies bore up under heavy pressure. By now the French formations were fully organized and dug in for this new front, and they did well. The British, short on manpower—Lloyd George's distrust of his generals again—and desperately weary, held their line with divisions reduced to the size of brigades. As before, the Germans did not have quite enough power to turn a dent into a breakthrough, and though it was a very close affair, once again Ludendorff had to admit failure, or only partial success, which was for practical purposes the same thing.

Both sides were now at a crisis point. Ludendorff was fighting with one eye over his shoulder, for he had promised to win the war, and no one knew better than he that if he did not deliver, all was over for Germany. In a perverse way it looked as if even his limited successes were telling against him. The troops brought over from the Eastern Front had been unpleasantly surprised by the firmness of the British resistance. They had been equally dismayed by what they found behind the British lines. Haig might complain that his soldiers were on their last legs, but the Germans, when they got into British rear areas, were astounded and appalled by the wealth of matériel, rations, clothes, and general sense of well-being that they found. They knew Germany was close to starvation. They had been told by their leaders that the Allies were in even worse shape, but now they found that they had been deceived. The British took as a matter of course items that had not been seen by a German soldier for two or three years. In this way even their success led to doubts and fears, and while they gorged themselves on captured delicacies, they asked how such things could be and found no satisfactory answers.

The French were equally downcast. Though they had not yet been directly attacked, they expected that they soon would be. Pétain's fears in this regard had made him more and more miserly with his own troops, so that Foch was caught in a tug of war between the French and the British army commanders. Things were bad behind the lines, and at the height of the first German offensive, the French government insisted that four divisions be distributed among industrial centers to prevent strikes and demands for the end of the war. Clemenceau was not going to stand for such nonsense as that. Foch sent cavalry divisions, for impressing civilians was about all mounted cavalry had proven good for in the war thus far.

Foch and Ludendorff and Haig might well have sympathized with one another, and if they had met on neutral ground, probably all three would have agreed that their major problems were their civilian masters, for Lloyd George was at it again, too. He now wanted to downgrade the Western Front effort entirely and had talked at the turn of the year of taking some of Haig's best divisions away from him and sending them off to Palestine, as he had already sent some to Italy. In the end it was Foch and not Haig who got him to change his mind, and the British government reluctantly agreed to rebuild half a dozen divisions that had been so run down as to be disbanded by now. The men they sent over were conscripts, or those who had previously been rejected as physically unfit, but by now the B. E. F. was a ghost of what it had been two years ago, when it boasted of being a volunteer army of the finest material in the world.

Few things illustrate the bizarre nature of warfare better than the 1918 offensives. Ludendorff still thought he was right and that it was the British he should beat. He therefore decided to attack the French next. His thinking, in this as in his other moves, was all perfectly logical: Twice he had all but defeated the British; both times they had been saved, at least in his view, by the timely arrival of French reinforcements. That was obviously not the British view, but it was Ludendorff's, and that, at the moment, was what mattered. His opponent, Foch, had pulled troops out of the French sector and sent them off north, where many of them remained. This had two effects. It must have weakened the French sector somewhere, and it made Ludendorff think that if he were to break the British completely, he must prevent the further dispatch of French troops to rescue them. The appropriate thing to do, therefore, was to attack the French and teach them to stay where they were. Having done that, he could then go on to attack and defeat the British without fear of intervention from their allies. As an exercise in logic, it was impeccable; as an experiment in human affairs, it was not quite that good.

The Germans were already annoying the French in a novel and nasty way. On the morning of March 23, when the first offensive was at its height, shells began to land in Paris! This was so astonishing that initially the French thought the blasts were some sort of accidental explosion. The front at that moment was seventy miles away. The fact was that the Germans had been working ever since 1916 to create huge long-range guns capable of shelling the French capital from an immense distance. The guns had originally been designed to fire fifty miles, so the whole scheme had to be reworked when the German field forces withdrew to the Hindenburg line. Now they were ready, installed in a forest near Laon.

The guns themselves were marvels of technical ingenuity. The Germans had put a smaller gun barrel inside a larger one, and added a sleeve to the muzzle to increase range. They had even calculated the wear of the firing and assumed that the gun could fire sixty-five times before the barrel was so worn it had to be rebored; they therefore prepared sixty-five separate shells and powder charges, each a little larger than the last, so they could be used in sequence. Fired at a steep angle into the air, the shells rose to a height of twenty-four miles before descending, and they took nearly three minutes to reach their target.

The shelling lasted intermittently from March 23 to August 9; the Germans fired more than forty separate bombardments, using nearly four hundred shells. At a price of several million marks, they inflicted almost 900 casualties on Paris. The most terrible stroke came on March 29, Good Friday, when a shell landed on the Church of St. Gervais, causing the medieval vault to collapse. Seventy-five people were killed, nearly a hundred more injured. Militarily, the results of the bombardment were negligible, but if anything further were needed to harden French hearts against the Boche, the shelling served that purpose admirably. It was the First World War's equivalent of Hitler's V-1 and V-2 Blitz of 1944.

Ludendorff was still concerned with weightier matters as he planned his third offensive. Looking over his maps of the French front for a suitable target, he decided on the Chemin des Dames, along the Aisne. It was strong defensive territory, as he well knew from defeating Nivelle there; all the more reason to attack it. The thinly stretched French were known to be relying on the natural features to hold the position, rather than manning it heavily. Indeed, so secure was the area considered that at the moment it was held by weak French divisions and by several exhausted and decimated British divisions that had been sent down from the Somme Front for a rest. So tactically, this looked like a good proposition. Strategically, it was equally inviting, for it was close to Paris, and a break here, or even the threat of one, was sure to throw the French into a panic. All the Germans needed was a limited success to keep the French minding their manners, while Ludendorff then went on to his major objective, the crushing of the B. E. F. The third German drive was really nothing more than a pinning attack on a large canvas.

By now the Germans had their techniques down to a well-ordered routine. Ludendorff called for his gunnery specialist, Colonel Bruchmüller, called "*Durchbruch*-müller," "Breakthrough Müller," by the troops, with his bombardment artillery. He massed eleven divisions in General von Boehn's 7th Army secretly along a front of roughly twenty miles. Thirty more were brought in and carefully hidden in the woods and along the ridges in immediate reserve. Deception plans convinced Foch that yet another attack was about to hit the British; Pétain was still more concerned about Verdun than the central part of his line. The French therefore remained absolutely ignorant of what was about to hit them until two days before the attack, when a couple of German prisoners told them an assault was due within twenty-four to forty-eight hours.

By then it was nearly too late to do anything. The French front was extraordinarily ill prepared for any real defense. The area commander, General Duchesne of 6th Army, had relied chiefly upon the terrain to protect him. Even with it in his favor, he had made most of the mistakes it was possible to make. The Chemin des Dames was a very steep, narrow ridge, dropping away on the northern or German side to the valley of the Aillette River, and on the southern or French side to the valley of the Aisne. The two rivers are a mere five miles apart, a long way by 1916 standards, but not much by those of 1918. South of the Aisne was another rising bit of ground, after which the terrain dropped again to the valley of the Vesle. Instead of putting his outposts on the Chemin des Dames and his main line of resistance behind the Aisne, Duchesne insisted on holding everything right up on the crest of the forward ridge. Even though the British commanders moving into the area protested this sort of position, he nonetheless insisted that the ridge, which had cost the French so much to gain, was going to be held, and all his superior commanders, right up to Foch, on whose staff he had formerly served, either agreed with him, or at least did not disagree with him. The result was that the Germans were presented with a heaven-sent opportunity.

Bruchmüller's bombardment opened shortly after midnight on the morning of May 27. It landed among the heavily packed French and British troops on the crest of the Chemin des Dames, and for three hours the Germans fired away madly. A little before four their assault platoons swarmed across the little stream of the Aillette and began climbing up the steep side of the ridge. They arrived on the top to find utter chaos, the trench line in a shambles,

some French and British completely broken by the barrage, cower-
ing and whimpering in their holes or walking about completely
stunned and oblivious to the German advance. Resistance was
sporadic, and those soldiers with enough presence of mind left to
fight were quickly killed or rounded up. By sunup the left-hand
British division and its French neighbor had disappeared. For ten
miles the crest of the Chemin des Dames was a smoking, desolate
wilderness, and through it and over it poured regiment after regiment of German infantry.

On they came, loping down the gentler reverse slope of the
Chemin des Dames. To their left a second British division, taken
in flank, was hastily brushed aside and began going back; to their
right the same thing happened to the French formations. By noon-
time German units in route march column were clumping across
the unblown bridges of the Aisne, and they kept on going. There
was unalloyed panic in the French rear areas. Surely a line could
be held on the Vesle, but it was not, and by dusk of the first day,
the Germans were across that, too, and not just here and there,
but for nine miles along the length of the river. As a limited attack,
it was an almost unlimited success—thirteen miles in just one day!

Nor could they be stopped yet. By the evening of the next day
they had passed through Soissons, which had not seen armed Germans since 1914, and they were a mere two miles from Reims, the
ancient resting place of the Kings of France. The French 5th
Army moved in and shored up the line before that city and held,
keeping the Germans out of it, but to the west the Germans flowed
out over the open country. By June 1 they reached the Ourcq,
where Kluck and Maunoury had fought back when the war was
still young and men still believed in it, and three days later they
were on the Marne. Ludendorff had far exceeded his ideas and expectations, and his troops were now outrunning supplies, guns, and
everything else. Yet Paris was only eighty miles from the Chemin
des Dames, and the gray-clad troops were halfway there. How
could they be stopped now?

Three things brought them to a halt. Far the most important, in
an immediate sense, was the simple arithmetic of a World War I
battle, the same thing that had stopped Brusilov in Galicia or von
Below at the Piave or Ludendorff on the Somme a few weeks ago:
The advance ran out of steam. The natural equilibrium between
attackers moving forward over poor communications and defenders reacting over good ones reasserted itself. A forty-mile advance

was stupendous, but it was simply impossible at this stage, not only of the war but also of the development of industrial society, to turn it into a complete victory. The Germans were worn out just by the effort it took to get to the Marne.

Secondly, the French reacted well once the initial panic and shock subsided. They and the reinforced British divisions on the eastern side of the breach managed to hold their ground and channel the Germans off without allowing them to widen their penetration. On the western side of it, though they lost Soissons, they held equally hard along the edge of the great Forest of Villers-Cotterets, and again the German advance was restrained rather than widened. Even before his men reached the Marne, Ludendorff was worried that his new salient was too deep for its width.

The third element appeared when the attack was already past its peak and when the Germans had all but stopped anyway. Nonetheless, it was the most important in a long-term sense. As the Germans reached the Marne and seized a small bridgehead around Château-Thierry, they ran into Americans.

United States troops were already in action. The 1st Division had been sent up to the Somme to help stop Ludendorff's first drive, had gone into the line around Montdidier with the French, and had even put in a nice little attack at Cantigny, which elated the division and cheered its allies. But the A. E. F.'s commander, General Pershing, found himself in a serious disagreement with his British and French colleagues. At the height of the first German drive, he had offered troops to help out and found Pétain curiously unresponsive. Reading between the lines, it was possible to deduce that Pétain was not all that interested in helping out the British, because he was completely preoccupied with the battle he expected to break over his own front. He neither wanted American units to go off to help his allies, nor did he especially want green Americans replacing his own veteran troops so they could go help them.

Foch and Haig, on the other hand, and their political masters as well, tried to use the crisis to get as many Americans as they could. Pershing's problem was the one he had faced ever since his arrival in France: He wanted to build up an independent American army, his colleagues wanted to use his men in their own forces; if they had their way, the A. E. F. would be little more than a replacement pool for the British and the French. Now they used the crisis to ask that America send over only fighting men, infantry and machine-gunners; no logistics support, no technicians, just fresh bodies. The truth was that though they desperately wanted American manpower, they did not really want any American share in the direction of the war. Looking ahead to the end of the war, which the generals did not do but the politicians did, the British and French believed that they had fought the war, as indeed they had, and that they ought to dictate its future course and not be upstaged by some naive, innocent junior member of the coalition who happened along at the last minute.

Pershing, on the business end of the partnership, was far more conscious of this problem than his political superiors at home, and he fought an uphill battle to preserve and enhance American status. Allied friendship nearly foundered on the British and French attempt to make a profit out of their difficulties and Pershing's efforts to maintain his independence. When the Supreme War Council met at Versailles on June 1 and 2, the matter came to a head. Foch angrily asked if Pershing were going to risk a total Allied collapse just to get his men together, and Pershing replied that he was. If the Allies broke and made a separate peace, the United States would still build an army, and when it had done so, it would win the war. Pershing was from Missouri, whose sons have traditionally prided themselves on plain speaking, and by this time he was thoroughly fed up with inter-allied fiddling while Rome burned. Finally Foch, Haig, and company realized Pershing was not going to settle for their views of how the Americans ought to be used, and they began to act a bit more sensibly.

Pershing's position was immeasurably strengthened by the performance of his troops as they got into action. The Americans wanted to attack; they were impatient with Pétain's insistence that they learn only trench fighting, for Pershing wanted them to be trained in assault tactics and moving in the open. In combat they took heavy casualties, but they learned fast and they kept coming back for more. Allied generals who observed them were amazed at how full of fight they were; they had not had the long years of grinding effort in the mud that had all but broken the manpower of Britain and France. Alongside the Americans' noisy self-confidence, the tired and warworn French and British took new heart, and the Germans who met them lost faith in victory. As the American divisions came into the line along the Marne, the Germans halted their offensive anyway. Young doughboys were soon writing home that they had met the enemy and stopped him cold.

In fact, they had found the Germans, even when running down

of their own accord, pretty tough. At a place called Belleau Wood the marines of the 2nd Division had walked into German machine-gun crossfire and been slaughtered in the best 1914 style. They expected to clear the wood and the little village of Bouresches in a few minutes. It took them twenty days and 5,200 casualties and turned into a small-scale Verdun. The wood was useless, but the Germans had it, and the Americans were determined to prove they were good enough to take it away from them, and in the end they did. Meanwhile, the 3rd Division held the Marne crossings around Château-Thierry, and Ludendorff decided he had better win his war quickly or he was not going to win at all.

What to do next? The German leader was beginning to run out of ideas. He had won three tactical victories, at a cost of roughly 600,000 casualties that he could ill afford. He had not really altered the general picture of the war; in fact, though his success looked much more impressive on the map than von Falkenhayn's work at Verdun, it was having about the same effect, and the terri-torial gains were more illusory than real. All he had really done was punch three large salients in the Allied line, and, setting aside the casualties incurred, he had depleted the number of assault troops available by lengthening the line he must garrison.

He decided to clear out one of the salients. His line bulged inward from Montdidier, fruit of the first drive, to Château-Thierry, the end of the third drive. Communications with the latter town were extremely vulnerable, for the only rail line into his Marne salient ran south through Soissons, within easy reach of the Allied line. If he could drive forward along the line Montdidier–Château-Thierry as far as Compiègne, he would link up his two big salients, shorten his line, clear his communications, and threaten Paris directly, all in one operation. He had actually seen this early on and had planned it more or less as a second stage of his Chemin des Dames operation. The fourth German offensive, therefore, was not really independent in its own right, as the previous three had been; it was more like drive number three-and-a-half.

Ludendorff chose this time to attack from Montdidier to Noyon, a front of roughly twenty miles. He gave the task to Hutier's 18th Army, with a target date of June 9. Things did not go as well as they had before. The Germans had to hurry their preparations, they were far less successful in their deception attempts, and the whole impending operation was so obvious that for a while the

French believed it must be just a cover plan for the attack Foch and Haig, and for that matter Ludendorff, still expected up in Flanders. Deserters gave away the timetable a couple of days before the offensive, and the French were ready and waiting. Fifteen minutes before the German barrage was scheduled to start, the French guns opened up, deluging the German batteries and assault positions. In spite of this, the enemy attack, when it began, still had sufficient cohesion and force to break into the French line, overrunning both the outposts and the main line of resistance. The French were thrown back on their support positions, but there they held on. By nightfall of the 10th, after two days of battering, the Germans had gained perhaps six miles. The next day French and American troops launched a counterattack that gained little ground, both sides fighting bitterly and losing heavy casualties. On the 12th the Germans launched a supplementary attack over near Soissons, to give them more breathing space and to pressure the French holding up Hutier. Again they gained a bit of ground, but again they were unable to convert it to anything substantial, and within forty-eight hours they were digging in. The fourth drive was finished.

The equilibrium was patently shifting now. More and more Americans were arriving in France and appearing in the front lines as the long gestation period of the buildup began at last to produce trained formations. The influenza epidemic that was to reach its height during the coming fall and winter made an early appearance, and it hit especially hard in Germany, where the population was generally reduced to inadequate rations by the effectiveness of the Allied blockade. This worldwide sickness, almost ignored by most histories of the period, was one of the deadliest events of the century; in India alone it killed more than 6 million people. In Berlin, 1,700 died on one single day in October. It seemed as if all the Furies were unleashed on a suffering but stubborn world.

Still General Ludendorff clung desperately to the conviction that he could win the war in one final, cataclysmic operation. He still believed in the great Flanders offensive, and he still believed that he needed one more distraction before he launched it. He chose to attack the French front one last time, to make sure they stayed where he wanted them. His fifth offensive was scheduled for either side of the city of Reims, and after that was completed, he would launch the sixth, war-winning battle and destroy the British Expeditionary Force.

Once more the job was entrusted to von Boehn's 7th Army, attacking along the Marne and up the eastern face of the Marne bulge to Reims. Mudra's 1st Army would support by attacking Mont Blanc, east of the city. Fifty-two German divisions should have little trouble breaking the Allied line and reaching Châlons, twenty miles in the rear. July 15 was the date, and as soon as the Germans had won this limited battle and taught the French to stay put, it was off to Flanders and victory!

Foch and Pétain had a mixed bag with which to hold the impending drive. Along the front there were thirty-six Allied divisions, twenty-three French, two British, two Italian, and nine American. The over-sized United States divisions were still pretty green, but numerically they were equal to eighteen Allied divisions, so they represented a major addition, untried or not.

Even more important than numbers was the fact that German morale was cracking now, and the most obvious manifestation of this was a steady trickle of deserters, who obligingly told their captors all about the coming attack, its timing, its direction, its strength, and everything else the Allies wanted to know. Deserters are so eager to please that they are not always reliable as sources of information, but there were enough of them now, and they told sufficiently coherent pieces of the story, for the Allies to know all about it.

Therefore, just as with the fourth offensive, the counterbarrage began before the German barrage started and raked the attacking troops as they moved up to their jumping-off positions. Foch was also able to prepare a small counteroffensive force to use when he believed the Germans had passed the crest of their attack. They still fought well, however. Along the Marne they crossed the river and made a few bridgeheads; they hit the American 3rd Division from front, left, and right, and the division, with its flanking units pushed back, found itself fighting on three sides at once, one of its regiments earning the nickname, "the Rock of the Marne." To the east, nearer Reims, the Italians were driven back, but British divisions came in and helped stiffen the line. Over on the 1st Army's sector, in the supporting attack, the Germans got nowhere, and they gave it up before noon of the first day. On the Marne and around Epernay, they were fought out by the 19th and sullenly gave over. The fifth great German offensive ended in near despair; there was not to be a sixth.

Through all these months of furious activity Ludendorff had been the dominant intelligence. Though Hindenburg was officially Chief of the General Staff, it was Ludendorff in his post as quartermaster-general who planned the attacks, controlled them, and indeed directed the larger issues of German policy and war-making. The aged field marshal had contented himself with grumping around headquarters, looking at maps and fiddling with troop strength figures. Now, as Ludendorff's last offensive was sputtering out and as Foch's first counteroffensive was beginning, Ludendorff went to talk to Hindenburg. He got cold comfort; he asked what Germany ought to do now. "Do? do!" Hindenburg bellowed. "Make peace, you idiot!"

# 21. Allied Counteroffensive

FOR MORE THAN THREE YEARS the Germans, with substantial help from their friends, had stood the world on its ear. It was a stupendous feat of arms, but now their race was nearly run. In early 1917 they had played what they then thought was their last card, the submarine, and they had lost the hand. The Russian Revolution and the development of the Hutier tactics had given them yet another card, and they had now played that, too, and lost again. This time they lost the game as well. There was no last-minute fortuitous discovery now to change the course of events. The best they could hope for was to stave off disaster long enough to win some sort of compromise peace. In the event, by trying to hang on to too much, they failed even in that. With the collapse of Ludendorff's hopes for a conquered settlement, the Allies swung over to the attack. Foch, though he had had caution forced upon him during the war, still believed in the offensive, everywhere the offensive, and now the Allies were strong enough to make it work. The balance had finally tipped.

Even while the French were sustaining the fourth and fifth German drives, Foch was planning his response. Before the last attack he let General Charles Mangin open a limited offensive around the Soissons bulge, in which American and French colonial troops made good progress against second-line troops. If there was one short period in which the tide of war definitively turned, it was probably the third week of July. On the 18th the fifth German drive was breaking down, the Allies launched their first counteroffensive, and Ludendorff, up in Flanders and still determinedly making preparations for his last big offensive, had to send reserves, carefully collected and husbanded for the attack, south to shore up the Soissons front. Two days later he finally canceled the Flanders offensive and moved, temporarily he hoped, to the defensive.

Foch's plans went beyond a mere limited advance now. Bolstered by Pershing, whose troops were rapidly becoming a major factor, and who was anxious to keep the initiative, Foch looked over the maps and planned how he would fight the rest of the war. He produced a straightforward, no-nonsense scheme that had about it none of the frantic scurrying hither and yon of Ludendorff's plans. For once an Allied idea made simple, sound military sense.

The first stage was the clearing of three bothersome salients held by the Germans. In each of these cases several ends were to be served. The bulge along the Marne, fruit of the third German drive, overlooked the main rail line feeding the entire eastern sector of the French front. Driving the Germans back out of this bulge was therefore not only useful in its own right, it would also have a beneficial effect on the supply situation. The second salient was up around Amiens, where the first German drive had again come close to the railroad from Paris north. Clearing that, too, would be highly advantageous, and though Foch would have preferred to attack farther north, he accepted the wisdom of Haig's suggestion on this one. Finally, there was a third salient, over east of Verdun, a deep narrow penetration at St. Mihiel that had been there ever since the lines had stabilized in 1914. The French had attacked this unsuccessfully in 1915 and had left it alone since then. It put pressure on the rail line from Paris east to Nancy, so even though this was a quiet sector of the front, it was something that called for attention. After these three irregularities were straightened out, then the Allies could move to the second stage of their general scheme.

The attack on the Marne, opened on July 18, was notable for three things. It was an inter-Allied venture, and the same troops that had stopped the German advance—French, British, Italian, and American—now went over to the offensive and made steady if not very exhilarating progress. The French employed well over 300 tanks in this operation, so it became, as it happened, their largest tank battle of the war. This time things did not go wrong as they had a year ago; the tanks came into action successfully and plowed along, supporting and supported by the infantry, and the two in concert proved a winning combination. Where in years past a single machine-gun nest might wipe out a whole battalion, now such a strongpoint could be masked until a tank came up and blasted it out of existence. The Germans, so good with submarine, aircraft, and artillery technology, had made a major mistake on the tank. Seeing it in action for the first time, they had assessed it on its early performance and decided it was not really worth bothering with. They did eventually develop armored fighting vehicles of their own; the first tank-to-tank battle was fought around Villers-Bretonneaux at the end of Ludendorff's Somme offensive, in April. But generally they had dismissed the tank as unreliable and a waste of effort, a mistake they did not correct until the next generation.

Finally, Foch's Aisne-Marne offensive, as it came to be called, was used as a training ground for the Americans. The eight divisions that took part in it had all been around for some time, some had had shorter or longer periods in the line, but all needed the actual process of sustained combat to shake them down and make them fully battleworthy. Training, no matter how realistic it is made, is still just that, and there is regrettably no substitute for the real thing. The Germans proved admirable if unwilling teachers. They fought careful rear guards, they did their demolition work thoroughly; wherever the terrain was favorable they stuck hard and had to be dislodged by nasty, close-in fighting. The fresh Americans took relatively heavy casualties, paying the price for their lesson.

By August 3 the salient was pinched out; the Germans were back on the Vesle, and there they stopped. The whole action provided the first bright spot on the Allied horizon for the year. Foch was given his baton and became a Marshal of France, and Pershing got his reward, too, in the formation of the 1st United States Army; he no longer had to fear any pressures to break up his troops and use them as feeders for British and French units.

Attention turned next to the Amiens salient. This was to be a joint Anglo-French attack, and the comparative strengths between the German defenders and the Allied attackers give the best idea of how the war was now trending. The British on this front had seventeen infantry divisions, significantly including four Canadian and five Australian, about 600 tanks, more than 2,000 guns, and 800 aircraft to give them cover and observation. The French, though they had few tanks there, had 1,100 aircraft and ten infantry divisions. Against these twenty-seven Allied divisions the Germans could muster only twenty thin formations, a handful of tanks, and fewer than 400 aircraft. Their morale was weak, their units rotted by sickness, and their strength suffering from a slow but steady seepage of desertion. As the Franco-American offensive from the Marne to the Aisne had slowed down, Ludendorff had offered his opinion that the Allies would now need time to regroup, and that the Germans would have a breather through August, but he was about to be disabused of that delusion.

The attack jumped off on August 8. The French, with not many tanks, put in a conventional assault with short but heavy artillery preparation. The British 4th Army, Rawlinson's, using tanks, Canadians and Australians, opted for surprise and crashed into the German line with no early warning at daybreak. Fog delayed the air support and also served to confuse both attackers and defenders, but as the day went on, it was obvious that a major event was taking place. By nightfall the British and French were in some places nine miles into and past the German trench line, several divisions had completely broken, men streaming to the rear or, even more significantly, throwing down their weapons and stumbling out to meet the Tommies and the *poilus* with their hands in the air. Sixteen thousand surrendered on the first day alone. Ludendorff was stunned by the news, and he was later to say that August 8 was "the black day" for the German armies, not just because of the ground they had lost, but because in the manner of their losing it he could see the first signs of impending disintegration.

Nonetheless, the Germans managed to put a new line together, in some cases with officers herding their troops into positions at gun-point. Both sides battered away in a confused fashion on the 10th, with most of the tanks now broken down, and the Germans able to regain their balance a bit. On the 11th they even launched a limited counterattack. This scared Haig and led to disagreement with Foch; the new Marshal of France was back to his old 1914 tricks again, and to every fluctuation in the tactical situation his answer was always "Attack!" Haig felt he was caught between a manic Foch and a depressive Pétain, and wished French generals would be a bit less mercurial; he decided to extend his attack by letting loose Byng's 3rd Army twenty miles north of the battleground. The promise of an attack should both placate Foch and produce greater results than were to be expected in front of Amiens.

Byng began probing on the 11th, and for ten days the British and the Germans sparred ineffectually. Then on the 21st the battle flared up again. Byng drove in five miles, the French to the south of Amiens joined in as well, Rawlinson started his tired men forward once more, and on the 26th Horne's 1st Army advanced up around Arras itself. The Germans, battered along a front of eighty miles, simply lacked the strength to hold. Ludendorff ordered a general retreat in front of Amiens to a depth of nearly twenty miles. Even that was not enough. In full cry the Australians got across the upper Somme and burst through Peronne; the Canadians, moved north, made a major thrust forward on Horne's front, and Ludendorff gave orders to go back yet again. By the first part of September all the Germans' spring successes were gone. Desperate for troops to hold his shaking lines, Ludendorff retreated up around the Lys as well and began pulling men out of the St. Mihiel salient away over to the east, shuffling units about wherever he could find them. Morale took yet another nose dive, and the latest advances cost Germany a further hundred thousand casualties in wounded, killed, prisoners, and deserters, the figures for the last two categories ominously rising.

The St. Mihiel operation, though it was the easiest of the three in terms of actual fighting, was the most portentous for the future, because it was basically American. The U. S. 1st Army, formally organized on August 10, took over its assigned sector of the front at the end of the month. The Americans went into the line holding about fifty miles, from just east of Verdun down as far as Pont-à-Mousson. In a straight line this would have been only twenty-five miles, but the existence of the St. Mihiel salient in the middle of it doubled the frontage. Pershing had had his eye on the area for some time, as it nicely suited the American operational needs at that particular point. It was fairly quiet, which meant the newcomers could complete their training; it was, in spite of that, strategically situated, so that if the war opened up, as now appeared likely, the American training in open-field warfare might pay handsome dividends. Finally, it was a good section of the front from the point of view of the American supply situation; using ports on the Bay of Biscay, the Americans could run their own logistics operation without crowding the French north of them, or the British up in the far north.

Pershing intended to do more than simply work his force up gradually. Even before the activation of 1st Army he was busily planning the reduction of the St. Mihiel area, and he was looking beyond that, too. His idea was for an initial assault that would clear the salient, then a major drive forward in the direction of

Metz. Metz was in German territory, at least since 1871, and taking it would allow exploitation forward in the valley of the Moselle River and toward the German iron-ore fields around Briey. No one could say Pershing was not thinking big; even before he had a real army, he was considering fifty-mile advances and strategic objectives that had been far beyond the capacity of his allies for four years.

In the event he was denied his chance here, Haig was planning an attack toward Cambrai, and he convinced Foch that Pershing ought to be redirected in such a way that the Germans in France might be pinched out by threats to their rail communications. Haig's ideas became the basis of Foch's approach in the next stage of the fighting, and Pershing's plans had to be reshaped to conform. The St. Mihiel operation thus reverted to its more limited original concept, a straightforward clearing of the salient. This was possibly a mistake, for in the long run Pershing's proposal might have offered more real gains than did Haig's.

Pershing, with three American corps and the French IInd Colonial Corps attached, was ready to go by September 12. The Americans were long on infantry units, short on everything else; so, much of their artillery support, armor, logistics, and air power was supplied by the French. Nevertheless, Pershing's staff planned a fairly sophisticated attack, with the French waiting along the bottom of the salient while the Americans attacked it at its bases; there had been some criticism of Foch's Aisne-Marne offensive as a simple pushing job, when he might have achieved better results by cutting off the Germans at their base line. Pershing proposed to do just that.

His potential haul of prisoners was lessened, but his task eased, by the fact that the Germans were in the process of abandoning the salient just as he struck. They started pulling out their heavy weapons on the 11th and were already well under way when the Americans jumped off early the next morning. The Americans attacked in some confusion, between a heavy fog, their own newness to battle, and the fact that the Germans were not doing what they were supposed to be doing, but there were equal difficulties on the German side, for few things are more disconcerting to an army than being pressed when it is in the process of a retreat anyway.

Confusion aside, the operation went pretty well as planned. A mixed Allied air force, commanded by an American, Colonel Billy Mitchell, did substantial work in breaking up German formations, and the Americans hit the faces of the salient while the French pinned its point. There was steady progress, and within twelve hours the mouth of the salient was pressed in from nearly twenty miles to only five. The Germans scuttled out as fast as they could, and by the end of the next day the salient was gone, about 15,000 prisoners and, more significantly, 250 guns along with it. Pursuant to their orders from on high, the Americans then stopped, to the intense gratitude of the Germans, who found themselves wondering with relief why the attack had not been pressed, for in fact there was very little to prevent a major thrust at this point had Foch put one in.

It was now mid-September. With the three salients cleared, Foch was ready to turn to the next stage of his plan. He was escalating his ideas, for when he conceived the salient clearing in July, he did not think the war could be won in 1918. Now he was having second thoughts. The St. Mihiel operation had shown him the Americans could be used freely, and that the Germans were getting ragged. This latter fact had been even more convincingly revealed by Haig's battles around Amiens, and the near-breakdown of German fighting strength there. Things were definitely looking up at last.

The problem, as Foch now perceived it, was how to defeat the Germans quickly; it was highly desirable that they not be allowed to get back to the German frontier, devastating northern France as they went and reaching their own territory with sufficient cohesion to hold on there for the winter. No one on the Allied side wished to see the war go on into the spring if it could possibly be avoided. The whole thing was a matter of railroads. It had always been that, of course, for this most massive of wars could not have been fought without the rail lines and their arterial flow of goods to the fronts. Now particularly, if Foch could deprive the Germans of their rail system, they were doomed.

The railroads that had fed the German armies throughout the war in France looked like a misshapen "E." The vertical stroke of the "E" was a line that ran roughly 250 miles from Strasbourg northwest to Lille. A second line extended this stroke even farther northwest, up as far as the coast at Zeebrugge. The vertical stroke supported feeder lines going forward to the front and was itself sustained by the three bars of the "E": At the bottom, a line ran up the Rhine from Mainz to Strasbourg; the middle bar was from

Coblenz on the Rhine, running through Luxembourg to the stroke near Montmédy; the upper bar ran from Cologne along the Meuse and the Sambre to Maubeuge and Aulnoye, where it joined the stroke. If Foch could get any one of these lines at the various terminal points, then the Germans were bound to lose vast amounts of matériel; if he could get two, especially the more vital northern two, the German armies might collapse completely.

The two vital points were Aulnoye, at the top, and Mézières, near Sedan, roughly in the center of the whole system. Seizure of the former meant the ruin of the two northern German army groups, Rupprecht's and von Boehn's; taking Mézières meant the same for the central army group under the Crown Prince. From their lines before Cambrai the British might drive directly east the thirty miles to Aulnoye; the French and Americans, moving north-northwest from the Verdun sector, had about forty-some miles to go to reach Mézières.

The Germans were even more aware of the possibilities inherent in the situation than were the Allies, for they knew as the enemy did not how close to the edge they actually were. The Kaiser was convinced by August that a negotiated peace must be sought immediately and gained as soon as possible. Ludendorff himself was very close to nervous collapse, and by late in the month he finally agreed with his Emperor, though for the next few weeks his moods fluctuated wildly; with every Allied advance, he urged a precipitate peace, and with every momentary German recovery, he hardened the terms he thought Germany might get. The chief concern of the military commanders, as the end neared, was that they should shift the burden of defeat and surrender onto some other shoulders than their own, and in this they were, regrettably, all too successful.

Meanwhile, the war still had to be fought. The diplomats who had trooped off the stage in 1914 were once more gathering in the wings, but the soldiers' act was not entirely over yet. The General Staff proposed a fighting withdrawal out of France. The two most critical areas were up near the seacoast in Flanders, where the communications tended to be marginal, and the southwesternmost portion of their front, the "Laon bulge," where they were farthest from their own frontier. It was this bulge that Foch intended to amputate, with his converging drives on Aulnoye and Mézières. The field commanders in the German lines could see this coming, and there were proposals for a hasty retreat back to the Meuse, but

Ludendorff vetoed it because it would cost supplies the Germans simply could not afford to lose if they hoped to sustain the war effort long enough to gain a negotiated peace.

Foch was ready by mid-September; the Allies now enjoyed a clear superiority in men, matériel, and the quality of their troops. The Allied commander-in-chief had 220 divisions; he put 160 of them in the line and allowed himself the luxury of a sixty-division reserve. By nationality these were made up of 102 French divisions, sixty British, forty-two Americans, still equal numerically to twice that many in other armies, twelve Belgian, two Italian, and two Portuguese. The Germans officially mustered 197 divisions, 113 in the line and eighty-four in reserve, but these figures were illusory, for a mere fifty divisions were actually considered, even by their own assessment, combatworthy. Faced with such a pleasant disparity, Foch planned attacks all along the line, essentially leading to Aulnoye and Mézières, but varied in time and place so that the German reserves would be exhausted running here and there. Somewhat simplified, the fighting for the remainder of the war worked out to four interlocking Allied drives.

The first of these was the southern prong of the pincer that aimed to cut off the Germans. It was a Franco-American affair, launched on September 26, known as the Battle of the Meuse-Argonne, and it gave the Americans the hardest fighting of the war, with the possible exception of the much smaller action at Belleau Wood. Fought just above and west of Verdun, the battle covered some very difficult territory, and since a major breakthrough here would have been fatal to German hopes, they held on hard.

The eastern boundary of the attack was the Heights of the Meuse, those murderous hills where the French and German armies had all but bled each other to death two long years ago. Moving westward the front line crossed the valley of the Meuse itself, then climbed another, lower ridge line, on top of which sat the town of Montfaucon. Then it dipped again into the valley of the Aire River, a tributary of the Aisne. Next it ran through the dense tangle of the Argonne Forest, roughly a hundred square miles of wood straddling the trenches on a north-south axis, and after that the front ran on westward to Reims. The assault plan called for Pershing's 1st Army to drive north, essentially up the Meuse and Aire valleys, with one flank on the Heights of the

Meuse and the other in the Argonne Forest. To their left General Gourard's 4th French Army would also drive north. Something more than ten miles would carry them clear of both the forest and the ridge line between the two rivers, after which they were to wheel off to the right, clearing the Heights of the Meuse, and continuing up along the river to Sedan and Mézières.

Again the Americans were strong in infantry and weak in supporting arms. The timetable and the necessity of shifting fronts from St. Mihiel to the west of Verdun meant that the battle-tried American divisions were squeezed out, and much of the offensive was undertaken by virtually green troops. Fortunately, the French cooperated valiantly, and Pétain did his best to get the Americans extra artillery and air power, while 4th Army kept in step as the doughboys fought their way up along the valleys and ridge lines. This, however, was an area vital to the Germans, unlike the St. Mihiel salient, and they were not going to be levered out without a fight. The terrain was naturally strong defensively, with numerous little hamlets, each of which could be turned into a stronghold. The Argonne Forest itself was a large wilderness, giving rise to the incident, famous in American annals, of the so-called Lost Battalion.

On October 2 two battalions of the 308th Infantry of the 77th Division attacked and broke into a major German position. They soon disappeared into the heavy woods and the tangle of ravines that made up their front. Ordered to go forward and let their flanks take care of themselves, the formations did so, and nightfall found them, merged together now, completely alone a couple of miles deep in German territory. During the night they were surrounded and for the next several days, frantic efforts to fight a way through to them were turned back. Meanwhile, the remnants of the two battalions hunkered down in a ravine, fighting off Germans from all sides and dodging barrages of grenades lobbed down the slopes at them. After five days the Germans sent them a very courteous letter suggesting they surrender, to which the response was a profane chorus of "Come and get us!" The Germans tried and failed, and on the 8th the American advance finally caught up with the survivors, many of whom spent the rest of their days telling friends back home that they were not all from one battalion, and as far as they were concerned, they were never lost either.

Progress was generally slow and very costly. The Americans kept grinding ahead, bringing in new divisions to take over from tired ones. It was October 10 before they finally reached the northern end of the Argonne Forest; by then they and the French were also taking ground along the Heights of the Meuse. A dissatisfied Clemenceau at one point suggested to Foch that perhaps he should relieve Pershing from command for not pressing on fast enough, a rather strange suggestion from such a consummate politician, and one that probably reflected his haste to wrap things up rather than anything more profound. Given what politicians had put up with from generals over the last few years, the suggestion was unfortunate, to say the least, and Foch quickly brushed it aside.

Pershing was doing better and better, anyway. On October 12 he organized the 2nd U. S. Army and became an army group commander. The heavy slogging continued, and by early November, the Germans began to break at last. Gourard's men got to and over the Aisne, the Americans cleared the ridge between the Meuse and the Aire, and the weary but elated troops began their right wheel —toward the Meuse, toward Sedan and Mézières, toward victory at last.

The western pincer of Foch's great attack was run by Haig, and it pitted one French and three British armies against some extremely difficult country, including the St. Quentin canal, and the same kind of dogged German resistance the Franco-Americans were meeting in the east. Haig opened his drive on September 27, the day after Pershing jumped off, and his soldiers made slow but steady progress. The Germans could not hold on; they were trying to pull back under their own control. But they refused to be hurried, and they constantly held up the British by using the best troops remaining to them, especially their artillery and their machine-gun companies. The main thrust of the British attack was east, toward Cambrai and Le Cateau. On the first day they made a good dent in the German line, but the threat here was so patently obvious that Ludendorff had to hold it back, and he managed to do so. For three weeks the British ground slowly forward, tanks, artillery, and groundstrafing aircraft supporting and encouraging the infantry as it overran one machine-gun nest after another. It was a painful business, and many a soldier who had already lived through his share of suffering died in these closing weeks of a war that was clearly running down. By mid-October, the Germans were all but finished. Desertions were skyrocketing, and units trudging back from contact with the enemy were jeering at soldiers going up to the front, accusing them of deliberately prolonging the war. The generals and politicians knew it was all over but still wanted to stall for time and better conditions; the soldiers knew it was all over, too, and no one wanted to be the last man killed in a lost war.

Still the German field commanders could not be panicked or broken, and even while the country behind them collapsed into chaos, and the General Staff above them dissolved in defeat, they kept their heads. The British achieved considerable advances, but nowhere did they achieve a clearcut breakthrough that enabled them to get into open country among a completely demoralized foe. The Germans carried out demolition work thoroughly even now, they fell back in an orderly way, and the front never completely broke. The British got past Le Cateau, where General Smith-Dorrien and the "Old Contemptibles" had made the Germans eat their words so long ago. They took Aulnoye and cut the vital rail line, and they got up to Maubeuge, where the northern spur ran off to feed the German armies on the seacoast. By the second week of November they were moving up the valley of the Sambre to the Belgian border.

The other two final offensives were far less important to the ultimate course of the war, if not to the men who were involved in them. On September 28, a day after Haig's big offensive began, he opened yet another one, farther north in Flanders. One British, one French, and one Belgian army began to attack over the old battlefields up around Ypres, Messines, the valley of the Lys, and on toward the coast. There was little the Germans could do about this. With their communications so severely threatened to the south, they must go back anyway, and now they did. The Allied soldiers advanced over ground that had literally run with blood a year ago, and now the most difficult opposition they faced was the rain. It rained almost as hard as it had during the Battle of Third Ypres, and the troops moved through an eerie, fog-shrouded wasteland populated chiefly with ghosts.

The final attack was in the center of the long line, the Laon bulge, as the Germans called it. This front was held by the French, and they put in a series of pinning attacks, designed less to gain ground than to hold the Germans in place so they could be cut off by the southern and western pincer attacks. But again the Germans fell back. They gave up La Fere, where young Bonaparte had done garrison duty, and Laon, where the big gun had shelled Paris and the Chemin des Dames, which held as many ghosts as Ypres did. The horizon-blue uniforms entered villages that had seen only field gray for four years, and the few inhabitants who had not fled or been chased away came out and stared in disbelief. The frantic rejoicing would come later. For the moment the mind and heart could not comprehend that it might all be over. The Central Powers were collapsing at last. On the morning of November 11, Canadian patrols marched into Mons.

# 22. The Collapse of the Central Powers

GERMANY WAS THE LAST to give in. By the fall of 1918, all the Central Powers were collapsing. They had fought for as long as they could, they had demanded and cheerfully received sacrifices from their populations virtually unknown since the days when Louis XIV's subjects starved to save him from a dishonorable peace, two centuries earlier. Now people had had enough; governments fell, and chaos prevailed over central Europe.

Bulgaria was the first to topple, the pressure applied by the "gardeners of Salonika." This front had been inconclusive ever since it was first established, and through most of 1916 and 1917, the Allied commanders there had been more occupied with badgering the Greeks than with fighting the Bulgarians. After several indecisive encounters on the front, they convinced themselves that their success in the Balkans depended upon their altering the Greek political scene, and in June of 1917 they forced King Constantine to abdicate, replacing him with someone more amenable to them and also putting in the pro-Allied Venizelos as Premier. The new Greek government obligingly declared war on the Central Powers.

This did not make as much difference as the Allied political commanders had hoped, and the position there received more of a tangible boost from the forces buildup encouraged by Lloyd George than it did from maneuvering in Greek back rooms. The Allies sent down a new commander for the front, General Louis Guillaumat, and in the fashion of new commanders he convinced his bosses that his was the vital area and that his numbers should be substantially increased. By early 1918 he had twenty-nine divisions, something over 700,000 men under him, with Franchet d'Esperey as his field commander. Having built up the front and prepared a great assault, Guillaumat was then recalled to France, leaving Franchet d'Esperey to gather in the fruit of his labors. The troops were a mixed bag—French, British, Italians, Czechoslovaks in the French Army; and Serbs, Greeks, and assorted exotic Balkan units—but when they finally began to advance in mid-September, they were more than enough. The Bulgarian front fell apart almost immediately.

Bulgaria had already been trying to find a way out of the war for three months. In June her pro-German government had been replaced by a Cabinet determined to open negotiations. For a while the Bulgarians tried to play both sides of the fence at once. King Ferdinand journeyed to Vienna to plead for more troops for his front and to demand more concessions as a price for staying in the war. The Austrians were hardly in a position to help, even had they wanted to, and neither the pleas nor the demands had any result. Within a fortnight of opening their drive, the Allied armies had advanced nearly a hundred miles over the frontier. The Bulgarian Army fell apart before them; the German units stiffening the front were left to make their way north as best they could.

The Bulgarian government hurriedly asked for terms, and negotiations were opened by Franchet d'Esperey. The armistice was signed at Salonika on September 29, and the last of the Central Powers to join the war was the first out. The terms were strict: the Bulgarian Army was to be completely and immediately demobilized, which was easy enough as the individual soldiers were taking care of that on their own initiative anyway; Greek and Serbian territory still occupied was to be evacuated. That meant almost all of Serbia and the little bit of Macedonian Thrace the Bulgars had held since 1916. Rather more important, the Allies were to be allowed to continue their advance freely until a general armistice ended the war. This meant that, in spite of some supply and communications difficulties, Franchet d'Esperey was free to push his troops into Bulgaria as far and as fast as he could, in the hope of cutting off the Turks from their European allies. Through the next two weeks Allied columns dashed for various vital spots in the Balkans; the Italians pushed up through Albania to Scutari, and Allied forces raced into Serbia and up to Belgrade. They also drove into the interior of Bulgaria itself, reaching Sofia, cutting the rail line through the Maritza Valley, and then they ran on to get into Rumania, and nearly reached Bucharest by November 11.

King Ferdinand abdicated, giving the throne to his son, Boris, and the Bulgarians, recognizing that they had not only backed but also gone down with the wrong side, could only await the pleasure of the victors. Given the intensity of Balkan politics, their future did not look bright.

Turkey, now isolated, was the next to fall apart. Her hinterlands had gradually been whittled away. Baghdad was gone, and the British firmly in possession of the whole of Mesopotamia. The revolt of the Arabian desert tribes had finally gotten out of hand, with railways blown up, Turkish garrisons cut off or ambushed, and the Arabs, who had hated the Turks ever since the Ottomans first arrived on the scene, taking revenge for years of misgovernment and oppression. Even more crucial was the front in Palestine. After the taking of Jerusalem in December of 1917, General Allenby had hoped for a quick advance into the area of Lebanon and perhaps across the Taurus Mountains to Asia Minor itself. Crisis on the Western Front had deprived him of the means for such an offensive, and it was not until fall of 1918 that fighting flared up once more.

The front was still where it had been nine months earlier, running from the seacoast above Jaffa inland to Jericho. It was now commanded by Liman von Sanders, the victor of Gallipoli, who had replaced von Falkenhayn after the latter had lost Jerusalem. Arab raids on von Sanders' left flank and across the Jordan led him to place more of his troops than really necessary inland, and this allowed Allenby to mass unsuspected near the seacoast. Early on the morning of September 19 the British launched a furious attack which in three hours burst the Turkish line wide open. Through the gap poured mounted cavalry, supported by numerous aircraft, and as the Turks fled to the rear, the horsemen herded them eastward, away from the seacoast, away from their line of retreat. With an eye on the history books, Allenby named his battle after a town some miles to the north, Megiddo, scene of the earliest battle in recorded history, where Thutmose III of Egypt defeated the armies of the city of Kadesh in 1479 B.C. Megiddo is often considered the site of Armageddon, so Allenby's choice of names may well have had a double edge to it.

Thoroughly beaten, the Turks and their German allies retreated across the Jordan, to no water and the hostile arms of the Arabs. The whole affair cost them 75,000 casualties, and their army began to fall to pieces. Allenby's dusty Indian cavalry entered Damascus on October 2, and within three weeks leaped forward another 200 miles as far as Aleppo. By then French sailors and marines had landed at Beirut. The Sultan since July, Mohammed VI, dismissed the Young Turk ministers who had entered, fought, and now lost the war, and the next day, October 14, the new Cabinet asked President Wilson to arrange an armistice. Wilson as a belligerent was a somewhat awkward choice, and when he did not bother to reply, the Turks released General Townshend, their prisoner since the disaster at Kut el Amara, and sent him to the nearest British ship to ask for terms.

The armistice was signed at Mudros on October 30, and again the Allied conditions were stern. The Dardanelles were to be opened immediately to Allied shipping. The Turks must demobilize their armies, release prisoners, and place their territory at the disposal of the conquerors, officially for further military operations. In fact, the Allied troops sent here and there throughout the Ottoman Empire were the vanguard of the partitioners; the ancient empire was soon to disappear. On November 12, a massive Allied armada passed the Dardanelles and sailed majestically up through the Narrows and into the Sea of Marmora. The next day they anchored off the Golden Horn, where they had so confidently expected to be three and a half years earlier.

Even the impending breakup of the Ottoman Empire was of less moment than the strange events taking place in Austria-Hungary. The threatened dissolution of that dynastic anachronism had been the proximate cause of the war, and for the Hapsburgs, keeping the minorities in their places was what the whole thing was all about. The process of war, far from cementing the empire, had only accelerated its decline, and national units of all the minorities had been formed in the Allied armies. Foremost among them were the Poles and Czechs. In the eighteenth century, Poland had been partitioned out of existence, the nation divided up among Russia, Prussia, and Austria. At the beginning of the war, then, Poles were fighting against each other in the uniforms of their three conquerors. To compound the matter, by ironic circumstance, Polish prisoners were often drafted into the army that had captured them. So Poles who had been taken from the Austrian Army donned Russian uniforms and joined their fellow nationals, already in the service of the Tsar, while other Poles went in exactly the opposite direction. As if that were not enough, thousands of Poles in the west, responding to France's role as the traditional friend of Poland, joined the Foreign Legion and fought under French colors. By 1918 there were three strong Polish divisions of the French Army. After the Russian Revolution, thousands more Poles deserted from Austrian and German units and joined their comrades in Russia, and these and the Poles in France became the genesis of a new, postwar Polish Army to sustain the revived Polish state.

The Czechs went the same way. From the start of the war in 1914, thousands deserted the Austro-Hungarian armies and joined the Russians, where they eventually formed probably the most famous of these seminational forces, the Czech Legion. Becoming a virtually independent body during the revolution, the legion moved here and there through Russia, back and forth on the Trans-Siberian railway, going through adventures which, if they have never found a modern Xenophon, rivaled the march of his 10,000 Greeks. Similar though less famous legions of Czechs were formed in both France and Italy.

The central Europeans not only fought for their independence, they propagandized and bargained for it throughout the war. Especially after the American entry into the fighting, and the ostensible escalation of Allied war aims to some sort of crusade, all the minorities became vocal in demanding their own states. In April of 1918 the Congress of Oppressed Nationalities met in Rome, and Poles, Czechs, Yugoslavs, and Rumanians all joined in denouncing the Hapsburg monarchy as a villain. That spring the Czechoslovak National Committee, led by Thomas Masaryk, called for the independence of its country in a convention held in Pittsburgh, Pennsylvania, and in June, France and Italy officially recognized this. The British and the Americans shortly followed suit, though no one was exactly sure what Czechoslovakia was or where it ought to be.

The Austrians, apparently determined to make again the same mistake that had started the war, decided a military victory would restore their sagging hopes, and in mid-June they attacked the Italian armies along the Piave River. They succeeded in getting across the river, where for nine days they and the Italians fought desperately to tip the balance. In the end the Austrians had had enough and gave up, after the battle had cost them 150,000 casualties. Their armies rapidly began to go to pieces. It was late October before the Italians were sufficiently restored to respond in kind, but on the 24th General Diaz opened an attack all along the line from the Trentino to the sea. The Austrians on their left cracked wide open, and the battle of Vittorio Veneto became a Caporetto in reverse. Though some units kept on fighting, the Austrians could not go back rapidly enough to keep a line together; hundreds deserted, thousands surrendered, and by the first week of November the fighting was turning into a race for territory. An Italian naval expedition sailed into Trieste on the 3rd, and on the 5th they got troops to Fiume.

Diplomatically, the Austrians did no better than they were doing militarily. They had attempted to open negotiations as early as September, appealing to President Wilson, who refused to deal with such a government as that of the Dual Monarchy. In October, Emperor Charles proclaimed his willingness to transform the state into a federal union giving all the minorities a degree of autonomy within it. This was roughly equivalent to trying to stop a flood with a tablespoon, though some might reflect that had the Hapsburgs possessed foresight enough to do that five years earlier, there might have been no World War I. Now it was all too late. The Czechoslovaks formally declared their independence on October 21, followed by the Yugoslavs on the 29th. In the next two days the Hungarians and the Austrians, whom everyone else regarded as the oppressors and the villains of the empire, seceded from their own state. When the imperial government managed at last to sign an armistice with the Allies on November 3, it signed for an empire which in fact no longer existed. Nine days later, slightly late as usual, Charles abdicated. By then he was back-page news.

For many months now Germany had been kept in the war only by the will of the Kaiser and, more important, the domination the military leaders had assumed over virtually all aspects of national life. Even they had found themselves pressured by the increasingly overt dissatisfactions of the people at home, and as early as mid-1917, they were faced with near-revolt in the Reichstag.

Chancellor Bethmann-Hollweg had retired on July 14 of that year, having long outlived his mandate with just about everyone. His replacement was a nonentity named Georg Michaelis, whose sole claim to political power was that Ludendorff regarded him as an acceptable front man. That was not sufficient to tame a Parliament which had so far not been noted for its independence, and five days after Michaelis assumed office, the Catholic Center Party, led by Matthias Erzberger, succeeded in passing a peace resolution. By a vote of 212 to 126, the centrists and liberals combined against the nationalists and conservatives to demand a peace without annexations.

The only effect of this on the General Staff was to convince it that Michaelis was not the man they thought he was, and he went from office at the end of the month, replaced in turn by Count Georg von Hertling, who did nothing much and did it quite successfully for about a year. It was not, outside the Reichstag, a very happy period. There were widespread strikes and civil disorders of one kind or another in January of 1918, and the calls for peace grew ever more strident. In that same month, however, the Germans were finishing with the Russians and sending men to the Western Front. They were convinced that if they could keep the country quiet, they could win the war. The generals, in the best German military tradition, were totally unsympathetic to the woes of the civilian segment of society. Their views were about as advanced as those of Frederick the Great, who thought civilians ought to mind their own business, their business being to produce goods and conscripts, and pay taxes so the army could do as it wished.

Spring came and went, and with it the chance of victory. By August, Ludendorff and Hindenburg were ready to admit the game was up and were at last counseling a negotiated peace. This was not going to be easy, for as the war moved toward a close, it was clear that there were not only the two sides, Allies and Central Powers, but numerous factions to both of them, and each faction within the larger whole had its own aims and ambitions. There were thus several leaders, each claiming to speak for his entire side, making offers, hedging them with conditions, and contradicting not only one another, but even themselves from one proposal to the next.

Setting aside the completely abortive suggestions and proposals for negotiation that had circulated during the entire course of the war, the considerations that had real bearing on the end of it surfaced in January of 1918. On January 5 Prime Minister Lloyd George publicly announced the conditions on which Great Britain would be willing to make peace. He called for evacuation by the Central Powers of Belgium, Serbia, Rumania, and Montenegro, and the territory on which they were fighting in France and Italy. France's claims to Alsace and Lorraine must be reopened, which in effect meant she should get the lost provinces back. Poland was to be reestablished, self-government given to all the nationalities of the Austro-Hungarian Empire, Rumania and Italy to have their territorial claims fulfilled, and the Ottoman Empire was to be broken up into separate entities. Finally, there was to be some form of supranational organization to limit armaments and prevent future wars. The speech was delivered to the meeting of the British Trades Union Congress, so it naturally received wide coverage and was regarded as the official statement of British war aims. It took into account neither what the French might want, nor the fact that at that moment Germany still looked as if she might win the war. Most of all it neglected Woodrow Wilson.

The British leader's position was different from the American's. Lloyd George, though he had long been well known in British politics, had come on the world stage by his wartime policies. He more than any other politician in the United Kingdom had advanced to world fame by his advocacy of a harder-fought war. He was far more comparable to Clemenceau than he was to Wilson. For the American, though he had taken his country into the war, had done so with a reluctance that had received attention everywhere; the whole world knew of his hesitations and delays and his attempts to find some ground for mediation or negotiation. He was widely regarded as something of a secular messiah, with a message of peace and justice for all. Of the major Allied leaders, Wilson said, "I bring you peace," and it was Lloyd George and Clemenceau who added, "not peace but a sword."

While Lloyd George was considering his terms, then, Wilson was doing the same, and when he went before Congress on January 8, just three days after the British leader had spoken, he delivered his own set of proposals, in part designed to dissociate the United States from the sordid diplomatic deals he suspected the Allies of making before and during the war, in part to reassert what he saw as his primacy over Lloyd George. Wilson's past career and the character it displayed were not such that he was going to ride along happily in the wake of the British ship of state.

Wilson's speech consisted of, and has been known ever since as, the Fourteen Points. Discussion of these and of their fulfillment or nonfulfillment has provided one of the great academic arguments of the twentieth century. Taken as a group, they showed both what Wilson thought had caused the war and what had dragged the United States into it and also how he proposed to resolve Europe's problems for the foreseeable future. The first point was "open covenants, openly arrived at," reflecting his distrust of the secret diplomacy that was widely believed, especially in the United States, responsible for the alliance network that had transformed an insignificant Balkan contretemps into a world war. Secondly, he wanted absolute freedom of the seas, in both peace and war; the relevance of this to a country that had entered the fighting over submarine attacks was obvious, but its acceptability to a Britain whose claim to great power status depended upon her command of the sea was doubtful. The third and fourth points were removal of trade barriers, eminently agreeable to a country who was now the world's greatest economic power, and reduction of armaments, with which no one could reasonably argue. Point five was likely to cause trouble: impartial adjustment of all colonial claims, with due regard for the interests of peoples as well as of colonial governments. The next eight points were all more or less specific territorial ones, and included: evacuation of and nonintervention in Russia; restoration of Belgium; and of France; adjustment of the Italian frontier; autonomous development for the various national groups of the Austro-Hungarian Empire; restoration of Rumania, Serbia, and Montenegro; a general settlement in the Ottoman Empire that included self-determination for the subject peoples; and reestablishment of Poland with access to the sea. Finally, the fourteenth point called for the setting up of some sort of association of nations to resolve future difficulties and prevent general war.

The specific territorial items of the Fourteen Points were not too far removed from what Lloyd George wanted; the more general ones went beyond anything the British had envisaged, but since at that point the war was by no means won, the incompatibilities might be safely left, it was thought, for future discussion.

The Germans of course rejected both Lloyd George's and Wilson's ideas out of hand. Those of the Fourteen Points in which they did express some interest were the general ones, and these they suggested might be used more against Britain than against themselves. Their idea of freedom of the seas, for example, was that the British ought to give up Gibraltar, Malta, Aden, Hong Kong, the Falklands, and virtually all the other bases that held the empire together.

Though the subsequent course of the war made German ideas of the peace entirely academic, it is worth noting the kind of terms they would have demanded had they won the war. In the west they wanted Belgium, Luxembourg, and the Longwy-Briey ore-field area incorporated into Germany proper; Holland and France would both become economic satellites and eventually succumb to a greater German Empire. In the east, where they were dictating peace to the Russians, they wanted Courland, Livonia, Estonia, Lithuania, and all of Poland incorporated into Germany; Austria-Hungary as a satellite state—so much for allies; Rumania, Bulgaria, and Turkey tied to and subordinate to Germany. They expected to dominate the eastern Mediterranean, the Aegean, the Black, and the Baltic seas and turn all the lands bordering them into dependents. What remained of Russia was to be an economic colony of Germany. They wanted a huge central African empire and command of all the sea routes to it, and economic penetration and naval domination of South America. In Asia they wanted New Guinea and Samoa back and a better deal in China, and they were willing to replace Britain as the ally, and partner in exploitation, of Japan. Their peace, had they won it, would have been more of a "Diktat" than they subsequently accused the Allies of. The victors do not always write the history books.

It was one thing to dismiss Allied proposals contemptuously in January, when the Germans thought they were on the verge of winning the war, and rather another thing to deal with them by September, when they belatedly acknowledged that they were losing it. The hammer blows on the Western Front practically ruined Ludendorff, and the news of Bulgaria's surrender finished him off. The day that Bulgaria signed her armistice he demanded that immediate negotiations be opened, while the army was still capable of keeping a front together. The next day Chancellor Hertling resigned, to be replaced on October 4 by Prince Max of Baden, widely known to have a liberal point of view. Max took both the Chancellor's and the Foreign Minister's portfolios, and appointed a Cabinet of moderates. His first official act was to appeal to President Wilson for an armistice, explicitly accepting the Fourteen Points as a basis for peace negotiations.

There followed a very curious period of some weeks, during which both the Allies, represented solely by Wilson, and the Germans trimmed their sails. In the best diplomatic tradition, they sent each other a series of clarifications the chief result of which was to darken the waters of international understanding. The simple fact was that Wilson's attitudes had considerably hardened between January and October; it was one thing to take a view of lofty impartiality when the United States was not doing any of the fighting; it was quite another matter when American boys were getting killed—a point which any of the other belligerents would have been delighted to have made to Wilson during the last four years. Now he was not entirely sure how magnanimously he wished to deal with Germany after all.

On the 8th, therefore, Wilson returned a note to the German government in which he inquired if Max of Baden spoke for the German people or merely for the Kaiser and his crew. To the former political science professor, this may have seemed a legitimate question; in fact it was an insult of the grossest kind, and the Germans would have been perfectly justified in asking if a man elected by a margin of 600,000 votes on a record of staying out of the war truly represented *his* people either. Unfortunately for the Germans, they were not in a position to trade insults. After this "first exchange of notes" they consulted what to do and on October 12 initiated the "second exchange of notes."

The German government now repeated that they accepted the Fourteen Points as a basis for discussion and added that they did indeed represent the people of their country, that is, that they were responsible to the Reichstag and not to the Kaiser. To this, Wilson replied with a four-point bucket of cold water. He stated that the armistice conditions would have to be agreed to not by the diplomats but by the military commanders of the Allied forces, and that any such conditions must provide for the continuation of the by-then obvious Allied military superiority. In other words, the Allies were not going to allow the Germans any sort of breathing space in which to recoup their shattered formations. He insisted that all submarine operations cease immediately. Building on the previous points this meant that while the Germans might not use an armistice to improve their situation, the Allies would use it to improve theirs. Finally, and "curiouser and curiouser," he said that the German government must produce some evidence that it had reformed.

The Germans hardly knew what to make of this. Ludendorff, shown the note, now decided he and the army could fight on, and he did a sudden about-face and demanded the war continue. The end result of this pitiful business was a tongue-lashing by the Kaiser, who asserted himself for one of the last times in his life, and Ludendorff resigned on October 27. The German Admiralty too wanted to continue the struggle and balked at the submarine stop order, but eventually gave in. That left the last point, and Prince Max still did not know what to do about it, except to stress that his ministry did consist of moderates and that they did represent the will of the German people.

On the 20th, therefore, the Germans sent back a third note, agreeing to Wilson's conditions, and three days later he replied that in view of their acquiescence, he was asking the other Allied leaders to discuss an armistice. But he repeated his demands for conditions which should guarantee Allied victory and also in even stronger language reiterated his disinclination to deal with "military masters and monarchical autocrats." While all this was going on, Turkey and Austria-Hungary were collapsing, and the Allied armies were advancing all along the Western Front.

On the 27th, Max's government replied yet again, telling Wilson that far-reaching changes were being introduced in the German constitution, and that it was trustingly awaiting terms which would lead to a general peace with justice for all. That was on the day of Ludendorff's resignation; the next day the German Admiralty, determined on a final act of defiance, ordered the High Seas Fleet out to do battle in one last Götterdämmerung. Instead of sailing as ordered, the fleet broke out in mutiny. Its best officers and men were long gone, drafted off to submarines or artillery units, and for months now it had been left in festering inactivity. The mutiny spread rapidly and was matched by a similar breakdown of civilian authority over all of northern Germany. Spokesmen for the sailors demanded the Kaiser's abdication, peace, amnesty for everyone, and the vote. The entire country was dissolving; his authority completely repudiated, the Kaiser went to army headquarters at Spa, where he waited passively for something, anything, to happen.

By November 8 Germany was in the midst of a full-scale revolution, with crowds out in all the major cities, and various factions shooting at one another. Government buildings were stormed and officials mobbed, records were destroyed, soldiers were deserting in huge numbers, and the situation was completely out of control. The King of Bavaria abdicated on that day. At Spa it was still fairly quiet, but the rot was seeping in. Staff personnel are not noted for their fiery natures, but by the 8th some of the soldiers had stopped saluting their officers, and there were rumors that a few of the noncommissioned officers had even set up a soldiers' council. That evening the new Quartermaster-General, Wilhelm Groener, a brilliant officer with an impeccable career, talked with Hindenburg in the army headquarters, ironically located in the Hotel Britannique. The Kaiser was staying at the Château de la Fraineuse, insulated as always by his immediate entourage from the full impact of bad news. He must be made to abdicate, and only the army leaders could get him to do it. Hindenburg, an utterly devoted monarchist, could hardly face the fact.

Groener and Hindenburg went to see Wilhelm the next morning and argued and cajoled for hours. He simply would not face reality; he would put himself at the command of his loyal troops and reconquer Germany, he would put himself at the head of loyal troops and die fighting the British—not a bad idea that—but eventually they convinced him there were no loyal troops, and it was all over. "What of their oath to the colors, to me as Warlord?" he asked bitterly, and Groener replied with equal disgust, "Oath to the colors? Warlord? These are just words today." Finally, Wilhelm gave in and signed his act of abdication. The next day he got on a train and crossed the frontier into neutral Holland. He stayed there the rest of his life, living quietly even after the Nazis had taken over his host country, and he died, an all-but-forgotten relic of another age, in 1942.

The abdication was little more than a footnote to the anarchy in Germany; it is difficult after the fact to see why anyone at the time thought it would make a great deal of difference to the course of events. On the 8th a German armistice commission, led by Matthias Erzberger, leader of the Catholic Centrists, arrived outside the Allied Headquarters at Compiègne. Marshal Foch was not disposed to bandy courtesies with the representatives of the Hun, and the terms he presented were such as to make it utterly impossible for Germany to resume the war after an armistice. The Germans were required immediately to evacuate all territory west of the Rhine, and the Allies were to take three bridgeheads across the great river: the French around Mainz, the Americans at Coblenz, and the British at Cologne. German troops were to be pulled back at once from Turkey, Rumania, Austria-Hungary, and finally Russia, and the Eastern treaties renounced. In the west, Germany must surrender 5,000 trucks, 5,000 railway engines, 150,000 railroad cars, and heavy guns and aircraft. Major warships were to be interned in a British base, and 160 submarines were to be surrendered. The Germans blanched at such terms, but Foch was unbending, and Erzberger, far more conscious than his military colleagues of the chaos behind him, insisted that the conditions be accepted. Very early on the morning of the 11th the Germans filed into Foch's railway command car, sat down quietly, and signed the papers. The ceasefire came into effect at eleven o'clock that morning.

# 23. Peacemaking

WITH THE SIGNING of the armistice, the soldiers yielded first place to the diplomats. It was more than a century since there had been a general resettlement of European problems after a period of major upheaval; the last great conference, setting aside a couple of meetings in Bismarckian Berlin, had been the Congress of Vienna in 1815. Then it had been France rather than Germany who was the international disturber of the peace. The French, however, had attended the congress, and under the wily maneuverings of that supreme politician, Talleyrand, had even ended up dominating the proceedings.

No such thing was likely to happen this time, and not just because Germany did not possess a Talleyrand; the victors simply refused to let the vanquished attend. In 1815, though the French Revolution and Napoleon had stood all Europe on its head for a quarter of a century, the peacemakers still acknowledged that France was an integral part of the world scene, and that it was impossible to get along without her, for better or worse. There was a monarchy, if recently restored, in France, and by pretending they were dealing with it, the men of Vienna could still handle a world that existed in ordered and familiar terms. Even though defeated, France was like the old Holy Roman Empire: If she did not exist it would be necessary to invent her.

This relatively benign point of view had been destroyed by the immense conflict that had just come to a halt. An initial intention that Germany should eventually participate in the conference was soon discarded. The fighting and the price for it had been so bitter that there was little spirit of magnanimity among the peacemakers. The war had gone beyond politics and had become a matter of faith; it had ceased to be seen as another of the long series of convulsions in which Europe periodically indulged, a sort of bloodsport "King of the Mountain." Because of the intensity of the fighting and the absolute necessity to enforce or otherwise obtain public backing for it, the war had been transformed into a struggle for humanity. Both sides appealed to a God who indeed did not seem to be overly interested, and both insisted to their subjects or citizens that they alone had a monopoly on goodness, justice, and humanity. The other side became not just a political rival, not a contender for economic hegemony, but a personification of evil. He was the Hun, who raped nuns and bayoneted babies, or the vicious English sea captain, who gloried in keeping the blockade going after the armistice, so that German children still starved in 1919. Having created this mythical beast, the enemy, the victors could not then, even if some of them had wanted to do so, sit down calmly as civilized gentlemen and talk terms with him.

This general feeling was further compounded by the strange position of Woodrow Wilson. He was the very embodiment of the thesis that the voice of the people is the voice of God. As a fervent believer in the most complete kind of democracy, he yet had a Cromwellian ability to conclude that whatever he himself wanted was what democracy wanted. He brought to the conference all sorts of emotional and philosophical baggage which made him an extraordinarily difficult colleague for the other delegates to deal with. Wherever he went, he was hailed as a modern messiah, and he tended to take this as no more than his due. The second new secular messiah, Lenin, was busy at home with civil war and revolution, so Wilson at Versailles occupied a unique, and to his fellow heads of government, a maddening, position.

The others all had bills to call in or scores to settle. The costs of the war had been so incredible that their main task at the conference was to take home something that would make it all look worthwhile. Trying to figure out exactly what the war did cost was in some respects ludicrous, for the estimates were necessarily imprecise and incomplete. The Carnegie Endowment for International Peace in 1920 stated that the war had cost, directly and indirectly, a total of $337,980,579,560. This figure, whatever it meant, was arrived at by juggling the cost against the benefits of the war, estimating what each life was worth, how much merchant shipping and property damage there was, and adding up various other figures. It assumed all reparations would be paid, and it made a series of value judgments about intangibles. For example, the compilers had to assign some monetary value to lives; they decided an American life was worth $4,720, a French life $2,900, a Russian life $2,020. The compilers were Americans, and others might disagree with their assessments, though they were based as carefully as might be managed on the productive capacity of an individual balanced against the amount he would consume in his estimated lifetime.

Such figures were an interesting exercise, but for any practical purpose they were meaningless. A rather better idea of the cost of the war—and the bitterness of the survivors—can be interpolated from a brief review of the casualty figures.

All the Allies together mobilized a total of just over 42 million men. They counted as casualties those who had been killed or died while in service, wounded, prisoners, and missing. The total of these was slightly more than 22 million, or about 52 percent. The casualties had of course been extremely unevenly distributed. Russia, which was not represented at the peace conference, led this ghastly parade. She had mobilized 12 million men and had had 9,150,000 casualties, or 76 percent. The British Empire had mobilized 8,904,000 and suffered more than 3 million casualties, about 36 percent. Italy had 39 percent losses among her 5.5 million servicemen. France, by contrast, had put under arms half a million fewer than the British Empire, 8,400,000, but had had a far higher ratio of losses, over 6 million, or 73 percent, the highest of any of the surviving states.

The United States on the other hand, the only other Allied belligerent to put more than a million men under arms, mobilized 4,355,000, and had losses of 364,000, a casualty rate of just 8 percent. Wilson's magnanimity had not stood up under even such relatively light American losses, and had his country gone through what France had, it is safe to assume his peace terms would have been every bit as draconian as Clemenceau's were to be.

The Central Powers sacrificed as many men losing the war as the Allies did winning it. Of 23 million men mobilized they had 15 million casualties, 15 percent more than the Allies. Germany lost more than 7 million of her 11 million fighting men. The worst record for the entire war was Austria-Hungary's, for she mobilized 7,800,000 and lost 7 million of them, an astonishing ratio of 90 percent, and though her numbers of prisoners and missing were high, perhaps reflecting the dissolution of the state at the end, they were not inordinately so. As the vanquished no less than the victors thought they had been fighting for truth and justice, there was some feeling among them that the peace negotiations should be carried out in a spirit of general sorrow and amity. The vanquished, of course, always think that, after they are vanquished.

The victors do not think that way, particularly the victors at Versailles. When the conference opened on January 18, 1919, the delegates for the twenty-seven Allied and associated powers were determined to gain what they regarded as a meaningful reward for their labors. Only later would thinking men realize that absolutely nothing they could possibly have brought home from the negotiating table was worth the cost incurred in gaining it.

The actual process of peacemaking was extremely complex, and it was also unfortunately hurried. Commentators have pointed out how much wiser it would have been to have ended the fighting, the blockade, and all the suffering—as much as it could ever have been ended—and then have sat down to a general European or world conference and discuss the residual difficulties of the upheaval. This was not done at the time, though it had been intended and a few saw that it should have been done. For better or worse, the delegates simply battered ahead with one problem after another, and sometimes with several at once.

The full sessions of the conference amounted to little. The importunities of the Portuguese and the desires of the Chinese to be heard were hastily brushed aside. The great powers quickly formed a Supreme Council of Ten, consisting of the heads of government and the Foreign Ministers of the five big states: Britain, France, Italy, Japan, and the United States. Even this proved marginally unwieldy, so the Supreme Council eventually thinned down to four men who counted: Wilson, Lloyd George, Clemenceau, and Premier Orlando of Italy. Relying, or in some cases not relying, on their technical staffs and advisors, they then got to work.

Each of the four had his own problems and his own point of view. Wilson was at the outset the most influential, as the one with the highest public standing, though in the later sessions of the conference his position was remarkably eroded by political troubles at home. Nonetheless he had already got the Allies to concede that the basis for discussion would be the Fourteen Points, and that gave him an initial edge in steering the conference the way he hoped it might go. Lloyd George was in a peculiar position, for his public pronouncements contradicted his private convictions. Germany had been Great Britain's best prewar customer, and the revival of British prosperity, he thought, depended upon a generous peace with the enemy. He would have liked to restore Germany and what he thought of as a normal world situation as quickly as possible. Unfortunately, he had just fought an election and publicly committed himself to a harsh peace, to making Britain a "land fit for heroes," and to making Germany pay for the transformation. He also came to the conference burdened with the various colonial promises Britain had broadcast during the course of the war.

Clemenceau's and Orlando's situations were more clearcut. The Italian government had entered the war because there were certain things it wished to possess, and it had been promised them for its participation. Orlando's function at Versailles was that of national bill collector, pure and simple. Clemenceau's view was equally single-minded. France's prosperity did not depend on the rehabilitation of the Germany economy, rather the contrary. He had but one purpose: He was still fighting the war.

The chief aim of the French was in fact to ensure their national security. The older generation could remember the German invasion of 1870 as well as of 1914, and in both wars the fighting had been bitter, and the German attitudes harsh. It took a far longer view of history than individuals were capable of to recollect that this was simply part of an ongoing European process, and that the great "middle kingdom," the land between the Meuse and the Rhine, had been fought over ever since Charlemagne's grandchildren had divided his empire among them, giving the middle to Lothar, whose name had gradually been transformed into Lorraine. Frank and Teuton, French and German, had battled in this area for a thousand years; both wanted the fighting stopped, but only on their own terms. Now the French demanded that Germany west of the Rhine be broken up and a separate Rhenish republic established, essentially setting the clock back before 1870. They did not get that; the British and the Americans would not go along with it and offered instead a mutual defense treaty for the next generation. The French settled for the treaty, which the United States Senate then refused to support, and in the end France got neither the buffer state nor the alliance.

The conference tried in an indirect way to deal with the question of Russia as well. The Communists, however, were not thought fit company for a great international gathering, so there was an attempt to set up a meeting on an island in the Baltic, a suitably out-of-the-way spot. The Bolsheviks would have attended, but the leading counterrevolutionary generals, who at the moment were making considerable progress against the Reds, refused to talk; hindsight reveals that they should have done so while they had the chance. As it was, the Russian Civil War continued its lamentable course. The Allies, after some ineffectual interference, drifted back out of Russia, and the revolution survived, though it never quite fulfilled Marx's predictions. A dictatorship of the proletariat remained a dictatorship, whatever its slogans and propaganda.

In Woodrow Wilson's mind the supremely important item for discussion was the League of Nations, and it was to this project that he directed his main energies. Unhappily for him, other things kept getting in the way. The British, for example, immediately rejected his point on the freedom of the seas. It was as important for them to command the seas as it was for France to command the Rhineland, and they were not going to give that up in the name of some vague principle. As his own navy thoroughly agreed with Britain on this one, Wilson soon let that point drop.

Nor could he obtain any agreement on the question of war damages and reparations. All the Big Five could manage there was to set it aside for future consideration. Even then Wilson was unable to proceed to the League, for next the question of the disposition of German colonies arose. This completely deadlocked the conference. Wilson had wanted a general adjustment of colonial questions; the Allies wanted the territories they had conquered. The Gordian knot was finally cut by the South African, Jan Christian Smuts, who suggested the "mandate" system. The German territories should be transferred to the League of Nations, which should in turn assign or "mandate" them to states who would administer and hold them in trust for the League, presenting a yearly accounting of their stewardship. It was a beautiful formula, for it allowed the conference and the League to have the name while allowing the conquerors to have the game. It was rather like Henry VIII's dissolution of the monasteries, of which it was said that it was a rare situation which allowed a man to satisfy both his conscience and his pocketbook at the same time.

Having either resolved or set aside these difficulties, the peacemakers moved on to the covenant of the League of Nations. The chief difficulty about this, since everyone perforce had to agree that it was a good idea in itself, was that the French wanted the

League to have a general staff and an army. Only when the Americans and British promised the subsequently stillborn mutual defense treaty did they give it up.

Wilson then returned home to the United States during a short recess while all the major leaders attended to domestic problems. He found himself faced with a revolt in Congress, where a Republican Senate was violently hostile both to him and to the kind of commitments the League might entail. When Wilson returned to Versailles, therefore, his position was very much weakened, and he was forced to ask for a series of amendments watering down the League covenant. This allowed virtually everyone else to grind his own ax, and there was yet a further move away from any possibility of general reconciliation. The three major areas of disagreement eventually turned out to be reparations, the frontiers of Germany, and plums for the Italians.

The reparations question not only dogged the conference, it remained one of the major bones of international contention until at least the Depression, and in a sense right up until the Second World War. Various commissions had striven mightily to deal with it at Versailles. The tradition of paying war damages was well established, and France had been forced to do this both in 1815 and again in 1870. Never before, however, had the damage been so tremendous or the costs so high. The problem centered around what should be counted as a war cost, and views ranged from those who wanted Germany to pay for reconstruction of damaged buildings and sunken shipping, to those who wanted her to pay widow's and children's pensions, all the costs of defeating her, and everything else they could think of. Even by the time the treaty was signed there was no agreement, and the Germans were constrained to accept the fact that they would pay a sum to be determined later. The whole question eventually tailed off into those esoteric realms of high finance that are incomprehensible to normal persons, where it got tangled up with Allied war debts to one another and especially to the United States, and it never was satisfactorily resolved.

There was more agreement on the question of German frontiers, for virtually everyone was united on the idea that border states should be enhanced and Germany diminished. Many of these frontier questions were already touched upon in the territorial provisions of the Fourteen Points. They were also resolved by the independent action taken by claimants to statehood in the dying days of the war, so in spite of the peacemakers' efforts to establish fair and viable frontiers, they often found themselves merely accepting what had already been accomplished. They ended up with a large Poland, giving it access to the sea through the valley of the Vistula. This cut off East Prussia from Germany proper and became a constant complaint of later German leaders. In fact such a settlement was historically and ethnically just; until the partitions of the late eighteenth century, East Prussia had always been so detached from Germany. In a concession to German feelings, the city of Danzig at the mouth of the Vistula was organized as a free city and not united with Poland. The gesture of good will ultimately backfired, for Danzig became a major stalking point for Hitler later on.

That could in fact be said of most of the territorial provisions of the Peace of Versailles, for the same was true of the Sudetenland, ethnically German but incorporated into the new state of Czechoslovakia, or of the Rhineland, demilitarized as a gesture of security to France. The French were still not happy, even with Alsace-Lorraine back and the Rhineland demilitarized, and for some years they meddled in Rhenish politics, attempting to engineer a separatist movement there without any real result other than to discredit themselves with their former allies.

The Italians were among the most obdurate of the various claimants at the peace treaty. Premier Orlando insisted that Italy receive everything she had been promised in the Treaty of London in 1915, plus the city of Fiume at the head of the Adriatic as a bonus. He refused to consider that it might not be fair to punish the successor state of Yugoslavia for the sins of Austria-Hungary. The Italians eventually left the conference in a huff, returning only to sign the last documents, and they rapidly developed into one of the powers constantly demanding revision of the treaty, "revision" being a high-sounding name for "more for me."

In spite of all these conflicting ambitions and difficulties, the treaties were eventually prepared and signed. There were five of them that made up the entire package, one with each of the Central Powers or their successor states. Each treaty was named after a separate suburb of Paris, suggesting that France was still the heart of the diplomatic world. The major one was of course the Treaty of Versailles, with Germany. The original idea of a second, general conference had disappeared. As the Allies could not even agree among themselves, they could hardly be expected to do so with their enemies, and the idea was lost in the shuffle. On May 7 the German government was given the draft of the treaty. It returned its comments and protests three weeks later, all but a few of which were summarily rejected. The Germans therefore refused to sign the treaty, objecting especially to Article 231, in which they acknowledged their sole guilt and responsibility for the war. Upon receipt of this refusal, the Allied armies made preparations for a further advance into Germany from their Rhine bridgeheads, and on June 28 the German government finally did sign, protesting that it did so "under threat of force."

The Germans were not the only ones who balked. The United States Senate refused to ratify the treaty as well. Not until July of 1921 did the American Congress simply pass a resolution saying the war was over.

The Treaty of St. Germaine-en-Laye was signed with Austria in September, and the Treaty of the Trianon with Hungary in June of 1920. Both of these officially did little more than recognize that the Hapsburg monarchy was dead. They did, however, saddle Austria, and to a somewhat lesser extent Hungary, with the sins of the parent Dual Monarchy. Czechoslovakia and Yugoslavia, the latter formed of Serbia and the southern territories of the empire, were just as much successor states of the old empire as were Austria and Hungary, but, presumably simply because of their names, these latter two became the residual villains of the story, while all the other minorities became the heroes, except when they interfered with the trans-Adriatic ambitions of Italy.

The Treaty of Neuilly was signed with Bulgaria in November of 1919, a smaller scale version of the treatment given to Austria. Finally, Turkey was dealt with in the Treaty of Sèvres, and this, signed in August of 1920, was the harshest of all. It completely destroyed the old Ottoman Empire, both giving all the victors a bit of spoils and involving them in Middle Eastern difficulties practically until the present day. It also provided for the virtual occupation of the Turkish heart of the empire and eventually had to be replaced by the Treaty of Lausanne in 1923, negotiated with a new nationalist government led by the hero of Gallipoli, Mustafa Kemal.

How good, or bad, any or all of these treaties was, is a matter of debate still. Give the conditions under which they were created, the ongoing trauma stemming from the war, the enormous dislocation of the moment, they were probably not as bad as they were subsequently painted by special pleaders. Those who, from the security of academic studies, consider denigrating the men of Versailles might reflect that the world's leaders have not managed to do significantly better in their treaty-making in the years since. Even nursery-school children know that it is impossible to put Humpty-Dumpty back together again.

# 24. Epilogue

MORE THAN ANY OTHER CONFLICT in human history, World War I illustrates the wastefulness of war as a social process. War certainly does solve problems, but usually not in the way anticipated by those who start it, and there have been wars which have seemed virtually unavoidable, since it does not, after all, take two to start a quarrel. Yet war tends to develop its own ends as it progresses, and the chief difficulty of violence is its uncontrollability. Man has never yet possessed an effective weapons system that he has failed to use *in extremis*, and both the world wars of the twentieth century have demonstrated his willingness to go as far as he physically could on the path to self-destruction. Clausewitz was correct in his observation that there can be no inherent limits to the act of violence. Once man enters the world of force, the world, that is, of the irrational, his ability to impose rational limits on his actions becomes increasingly precarious.

The greater the degree of violence, the more the emotions and passions of the belligerents are engaged, the less predictable the outcome. This is precisely what happened in and during the First World War. In 1928 the American historian Sidney B. Fay produced a classic two-volume study called *The Origins of the World War;* though some of his conclusions have been challenged or revised in the half-century since he wrote, his work remains the starting point for study of this great problem. Fay concluded that the underlying causes of the war were the secret alliance system, militarism, nationalism, economic imperialism, and the newspaper press, which aggravated every little question until it became a crisis. One would think, if these conclusions be accepted, that a major upheaval such as the war would have done at least something to rid society of such cancers. On the contrary, it can be argued that the war removed virtually none of the things that had caused it, though it did indeed hold some of them in abeyance for a while, more a truce of exhaustion than any definitive resolution of society's problems.

Lest one think that these are mere academic matters of interest only to historians, it might well be pointed out that if Fay's underlying causes of World War I were dressed up in modern jargon, every one of them is present and active in our contemporary world. Today we have our alliance systems, our military and industrial establishment, our rabid nationalism, our revived colonialism in one guise or another, and we certainly have our yellow press, though it does not exactly see itself in that light.

None of this is to say that World War I was without tangible results, for it had enormous effects. The problem was that almost none of them were what the people who started the war hoped to achieve by it. But many things were accomplished, both politically and socially.

For example, all three of the great autocratic monarchies that went to war in 1914 did so in the expectation of preserving or enhancing their positions. All three were destroyed by the war. The Russians backed Serbia because they thought it was absolutely essential to their position as protector and mentor of the Balkan States and counterweight to Austria-Hungary. At the end of the war, the Tsar and his family were dead, shot by nervous captors, and the entire Romanov Empire was in chaos, its border territories breaking away, its rulers and aspirants to rule fighting like beasts over the carcass of the empire. Sixty years later, Russia lives under a regime every bit as autocratic as that of the Tsar, its empire indeed reestablished, in such a way that the masters have become prisoners of their own empire and their own ideology and have backed themselves into a corner from which they may not emerge without destroying us all.

Austria-Hungary went to war to destroy the constant threat of the small states that surrounded her and threatened to suborn her own subject peoples. Instead those small states ate her up, and the great empire was thrown on history's junk pile, bringing to an end at last the fabulous story of a dynasty that had occupied the most august throne in Europe for six centuries. The Ottoman Empire went the same way, and it is questionable if any of the governments and states set up in the sacred name of self-determination have been much better than what they replaced.

Finally, the German Empire collapsed. The Second Reich lasted a mere half-century. Far from achieving a "place in the sun" for his people, the Kaiser managed only a retirement estate for himself and a darkness for his subjects from which they would not emerge for another generation.

The collapse of these empires was matched by the engorgement to the saturation point of the victors in the war. Desperate for some positive gain, the peacemakers at Paris fell greedily on the remains of the losers and divided the spoils among them, carrying home scraps of the German and Ottoman empires to display before their voters. To the widows and orphans of his more than a million dead, and the 3 million who nursed their wounds and their sorrows, Clemenceau could say, "Ah, but we have regained Alsace and Lorraine!" and Lloyd George could solace a million dead and 2 million wounded by pointing out that now there was an all-British railway route from the Cape of Good Hope to Cairo, and now Britain controlled Palestine! If anyone had seen the trouble *that* bit of real estate was to cause Britain, Lloyd George would have been turned out of office long before he was.

Versailles saw the imperial syndrome carried to its farthest point, and the great empires became even greater, just at a point when the whole imperial business was coming seriously into question anyway. Even before the peace treaties were signed, British imperial troops were shooting down unarmed Indians at Amritsar, and a little man in a loincloth was asking himself if his country really wanted the benefits of civilization which had demonstrated its presumed superiority by drowning its sons in the mud of Flanders. Though it would take another two generations to work out, the imperial idea died in France and on the dusty ridges of Gallipoli, even before the politicians painted their national colors on more little bits of map.

While it was beginning the process of destroying Europe, the war also began to fulfill prophecy. In the nineteenth century that amazing Frenchman Alexis de Tocqueville, one of the great renaissance men of his day, foresaw a future in which the world would be divided between the United States and Russia. Both would expand east and west until the buffers between them were absorbed or subordinated, and eventually they would meet. Though it would take another conflict of equally immense proportions to complete, that process was surely quickened by the catastrophe of the Great War. Europe was impoverished and exhausted, Asia was already in chaos after the collapse of China. The two men whom Hegel might have considered for the status of "world-historical" figures were a Russian and an American, Lenin and Wilson. It was perhaps more significant that they were the two who held out a vision to the masses of the world than it was that neither of them was able to live up to that vision. The two future superpowers were born in the travail of revolution and war; for another generation Russia would be incapable of assuming that role, the United States unwilling to do so, but World War I was clearly a giant step for both along the road to unprecedented power.

Changes in political status were probably exceeded by those in ideas and attitudes. In an era of mass attacks, mass slaughters, and mass production, the common man at last came into his own. The rulers of states found that in mobilizing all of their peoples they had unlocked Pandora's box. The "revolt of the masses," in the phrase of the Spanish philosopher Ortega y Gasset, went back before World War I, into the social and political developments of the late nineteenth century, but it received a tremendous impetus from the events of the war. If the common man was good enough to die in unprecedented numbers for his country, he was good enough to have a say in running it. The Labour party gained greater power in Britain, postwar governments of the Third Republic in France took more account of the proletariat than their predecessors ever had, and in Germany and Russia, the archetypal common man eventually came to power. With the advent of Hitler and Stalin, Vulgarity was crowned king.

The mystique of the old "classes and masses" was pretty well destroyed. Not only had society's potential leaders died in alarmingly high numbers, those who had survived appeared to have forfeited their right to mastery. How could any group claim precedence when it had led its followers into the morass? In the years after the war, an incredibly fertile war literature grew up, the product of some of Europe's best minds reacting to the horror through which they had lived. Implicit in their revelations of mud, stink, and brutal death was the rejection of the society and the leaders that had allowed, even encouraged, such things to happen.

That view was, indeed, the most profound change to come out of World War I. In 1914, Europeans almost uniformly believed in the superiority of European culture, in their God-given right to dominate the rest of the world, to impose upon it their value systems, their ideas of politics, their economies. They had gone through

the world carrying Manchester cotton and Solingen steel, the Bible
in one hand and a repeating rifle in the other, and they had assumed
that "lesser breeds without the law" would eventually see the wisdom
and superiority of their ways. Europeans thought they had a right
to patrol Chinese rivers and run the Chinese customs service, and
indeed they did it pretty well. An Englishman could face down an
Indian mob simply because he was an Englishman and the mob
were not. That was gone now. Spengler memorialized "the decline
of the West," and the natural dominance of the white race, or of the
European, was no longer evident even to themselves. World War I
showed Europeans in stark clarity that they were human after all.
To be human is not only to err, it is also to doubt, and once it
doubted its ability to do so, this little corner of the earth, this little
appendix of Asia, would no longer be able to dictate to the rest of
the world. What World War I really killed was Europe's sense of
itself. It was not Europeans, in the long run, who caught the torch
thrown by failing hands.

None of this was immediately apparent; few things in human
affairs ever are. In the short run, the most important aspect of
World War I was its indecisiveness. Particularly it failed to resolve
two questions. The first of these was the problem of Germany. The
Germans obviously did not win the war; unfortunately, they did
not lose it so decisively that they were unwilling to try again a
generation later. Germany remained, truncated and burdened with
political misery though she was, potentially the strongest power in
Europe. In spite of the immense bloodletting, she retained her
energies and her industries. To the sense of inferiority that has run
like a bleeding ulcer through modern German history, fruit of her
fragmented political structure and a unification that came three to
five centuries later than it might have, was added the sense of grievance resulting from Versailles. All that Hitler's ranting and raving
boiled down to was this: Why should we be punished for trying to
do what France, Britain, Spain did in their turn before us? None
of the punitive measures of the victors really altered the fundamental European principle, that Germany was the strongest state
around. The French perhaps had the right idea with their dreams of
a separate Rhenish republic. Put the clock back before 1870. The
other Allies thought that was absolutely unacceptable—until they
did it themselves in 1945.

The second unresolved matter was simply the basic problem of
force itself. Even after the death of 12 million of its dearest and

best, there still remained men in the world who were perfectly content, even eager, to resort once again to war to settle their differences. Oscar Wilde wrote that war's fascination lay in its being regarded as wicked, and that as soon as it was seen to be vulgar it would cease to be popular. That was in 1895, and he could not have been more mistaken. After 1918 few could still have thought war anything but vulgar, yet its fascination remained, and, regrettably, does still.

So, someday, it would all have to be done over again. The German troops marching home from France were met by politicians, desperate for the support of the army, who told them it was not they who had failed; the army had never been defeated, but Germany had been "stabbed in the back," by the Communists, the Socialists, the Jews, by anyone but those leaders who so successfully passed the burden of their failure onto other shoulders. In a time of troubles, the military men took this myth to their bosoms and nourished it until a better day should dawn.

Others were less certain who had won and who had lost. At the peace-signing ceremony a young British delegate, Harold Nicolson, sat next to Marie Murat, a member of the old Bonapartist nobility. Near them was Paul Painlevé. When Georges Clemenceau walked slowly through the crowd after the conclusion of the signing, he stopped to shake hands with his fellow politician. Tears in his eyes, he said, "Well, it's a great day for France." Nicholson leaned over and whispered to Marie Murat, "Are you sure of that?" and she replied, "Not at all." The old Premier shambled on down the aisle.

One comment was even more trenchant. When he read the peace treaty, Marshal Foch burst out, "This isn't peace! This is a truce for twenty years!" The Treaty of Versailles was signed on June 28, 1919. Twenty years and sixty-seven days later, Great Britain and France declared war on Hitler's Germany.

# Suggestions for
# Further Reading

WORLD WAR I appeared to those who had lived through it, or grew to maturity in its aftermath, as the greatest event of human history, and as such it inspired an enormous amount of study and investigation. That interest has continued for the past half-century, and if interest in the Great War has been rather preempted by World War II, there still continues to be an ongoing literature on the first conflict. Most of the works produced soon after the war have not stood the test of time; some have become standard historical studies. As military history, in the sense of the study of operations, has tended to be somewhat of a poor relation among professional historians, the reader is likely to find that scholarly studies concentrate more on political and diplomatic matters than on the actual fighting, and that the latter is left, though not without exception, to soldiers and nonacademic writers, who have indeed reached a larger public generally than their university colleagues.

The suggestions which follow are divided, very roughly, into general, political, and diplomatic studies, and then into military studies by theater. The arbitrariness of the division will be readily apparent from the fact that biographies of political figures are listed among the former, and biographies of military and naval figures are listed among the latter, in spite of the obvious point that men such as Lloyd George and Clemenceau had their influence on operations, while men such as Foch and Haig certainly had their influence on politics. There is also the problem that most books, like most people, defy easy classification and could well be put in two or more categories. A final cautionary note is that these suggestions are hardly exhaustive; anyone wishing to delve extensively into World War I can look forward to several years of interesting reading.

*General and background material:*

As the twentieth century nears its end, contemporary histories tend to compress more and more the events of the earlier part of it. Several books have excellent treatments of the period, however. S. Hughes, *Contemporary Europe: A History* (Englewood Cliffs, 1961), is good; the standard treatment in the multi-volume *New Cambridge Modern History* is D. Thomson, *The Era of Violence, 1898–1945* (Cambridge, 1960); the original "Old" *Cambridge Modern History* was produced before World War I. R. Albrecht-Carrie wrote a short survey which has since become a standard work, *The Meaning of the First World War* (Englewood Cliffs, 1965). An excellent, readable coverage of the period is in E. Taylor, *The Fall of the Dynasties: The Collapse of the Old Order, 1905–1922* (New York, 1963). Barbara Tuchman wrote an evocative examination of European society and how it regarded itself before the war, in *The Proud Tower* (New York, 1966). A longer-range view is D. Thomson, *Europe since Napoleon* (New York, 1958), and a much more episodic, less historical and more literary view is Philip Guedalla's *The Hundred Years* (New York, 1937); Guedalla is probably little read today, but he was a supreme essayist and stylist, often summing up in a delightful phrase what would cost other writers a labored chapter. A scholarly, though highly argumentative, treatment of the same span is A. J. P. Taylor, *The Struggle for Mastery in Europe, 1848–1918* (Oxford, 1954).

There are numerous studies of all the belligerent states and of their leaders during the period. The two volumes covering this era in the Oxford History of England are R. C. K. Ensor, *England, 1870–1914* (Oxford, 1960, first published in 1936), and A. J. P. Taylor, *England, 1914–1945* (Oxford, 1965). A. F. Havighurst's *Twentieth Century Britain* (New York, 1962) is a useful survey. The wartime Prime Minister wrote *War Memoirs of David Lloyd George* (London, 4 vols., 1933). There are numerous studies of France and its leaders and problems. A good short survey is A. Sedgwick, *The Third French Republic* (New York, 1968). P. A. Gagnon wrote *France Since 1789* (New York, 1964). Older but still readable are J. B. Wolff, *France, 1814–1919* (New York, 1963, first published in 1940), and D. W. Brogan's *The Development of Modern France* [*1870–1939*] (London, 1967, also first published in 1940). On the great French wartime leader D. R.

Watson wrote *Georges Clemenceau: A Political Biography* (London, 1974).

There is an extensive literature on Russia, most of it centered around the revolution, and that more specific topic will be dealt with later in connection with the Eastern Front. General studies are H. Seton-Watson, *The Decline of Imperial Russia* (London, 1952), and J. D. Clarkson, *A History of Russia* (New York, 2nd ed., 1969). R. K. Massie wrote a generally sympathetic biography in *Nicholas and Alexandra* (New York, 1967). The history of the smaller Balkan States is covered in L. S. Stavrianos, *The Balkans since 1453* (New York, 1958). Writers on Italy have generally concentrated on an attempt to explain the growth of Fascism, as in C. Seton-Watson, *Italy from Liberalism to Fascism, 1870–1925* (London, 1967); somewhat more to the point of World War I is J. A. Thayer's *Italy and the Great War: Politics and Culture, 1870–1915* (Madison, Wis., 1964). Treatment of Belgium is rather skimpy; Theo Aronson, biographer of the Bonapartes, wrote *Defiant Dynasty: The Coburgs of Belgium* (Indianapolis, 1968), with a chapter on King Albert; an older, a more extensive study is E. Cammaerts' *Albert of Belgium: Defender of Right* (London, 1935), which contains substantial material on Belgium's wartime operations.

General studies of the United States in the period are L. M. Hacker and H. S. Zahler, *The United States in the Twentieth Century* (New York, 1952), and A. S. Link's *American Epoch: A History of the United States since the 1890's* (New York, 1955). The latter's multi-volume *Wilson* (Princeton, 1947–65) is the standard biography.

Among the Central Powers, Germany has naturally attracted the greatest amount of attention. General histories are G. Mann, *The History of Germany Since 1789* (New York, English translation, 1968), Agatha Ramm, *Germany, 1789–1919* (London, 1967), and an excellent newer work, G. A. Craig, *Germany, 1866–1945* (New York, 1978). Wilhelm II wrote *The Kaiser's Memoirs* (English edition, New York, 1922), an unsuccessful apologia for his career; the standard biography is Virginia Cowles, *The Kaiser* (London, 1963). There has been an impressive amount of work done on the problem of relations between the German military leaders and their political counterparts. Most exhaustive is G. Ritter, *The Sword and the Scepter: The Problem of Militarism in Germany* (English edition, Coral Gables, Florida, 4 volumes, 1969–73), which covers and is indispensable to the period of the nineteenth century and ending in 1918. Both Walter Goerlitz' *History of the German General Staff, 1657–1945* (English edition, New York, 1953) and G. A. Craig's *The Politics of the Prussian Army, 1640–1945* (New York, 1964) are more especially concerned with the Hitlerian period, though having much useful information on the World War I era. Martin Kitchen wrote a fascinating study of *The German Officer Corps, 1890–1914* (Oxford, 1968).

On Austria-Hungary A. J. P. Taylor wrote *The Habsburg Monarchy, 1809–1918* (London, 1958), which has useful background if not a great deal on World War I itself; E. Crankshaw's *The Fall of the House of Habsburg* (New York, 1963) is excellent, and A. J. May deals more particularly with war and the dynasty in *The Passing of the Habsburg Monarchy, 1914–1918* (Philadelphia, 2 volumes, 1966). Volume 2 of S. J. Shaw and E. K. Shaw, *History of the Ottoman Empire and Modern Turkey* (Cambridge, 1977), covers the period 1808–1975.

The diplomatic history of the war has concentrated on its origins, on the peacemaking efforts, and then on certain more specific problems within the war itself. C. J. H. Hayes, *A Generation of Materialism, 1871–1900* (New York, 1941), and O. J. Hale, *The Great Illusion, 1900–1914* (New York, 1971), volumes 16 and 17 of *The Rise of Modern Europe Series*, give extensive background pictures of Europe and European attitudes and diplomacy before the war. After 1918 virtually all of the belligerents or their successors published series of documents, essentially hoping to prove to the world that the war was someone else's fault. G. P. Gooch and H. Temperley edited *British Documents on the Origins of the War, 1898–1914* (London, 10 volumes, 1927–36), and E. T. S. Dugdale edited *German Diplomatic Documents, 1871–1914* (New York, 4 volumes, 1928–31). There are similar collections for the other states. A useful collection on the immediate crisis that started the war is I. Geiss, *July 1914: Selected Documents* (London, English edition 1967).

The publication of documents did nothing to clear up the argument as to who, if anyone, had caused World War I, and a great many historians have spent their careers proving that Germany was guilty, that she was not guilty, that everyone was, or that no one was. The classic early statement was S. B. Fay, *The Origins of the World War* (New York, 2 vols., 1966, originally published in 1928–30). Probably the most thorough recent study is L. Albertini, *The Origins of the War of 1914* (New York, 3 vols., 1952–57). For the beginning student, the conflicting judgments are excerpted and summarized in D. Lee, ed., *The Outbreak of the First World War: Who Was Responsible* (Boston, 1963), one of the excellent pamphlets in the Heath *Problems in European Civilization* series; it also contains a good bibliography. An exhaustive but narrower study, concentrating on Balkan affairs, is V. Dedijer, *The Road to Serajevo* (London, 1967). About all that can be said for sure on the origins question is that it is likely to go on indefinitely.

Turning to studies of assorted diplomatic problems during the war, there are numerous works grappling with specific questions. Fritz Fischer's classic *Germany's Aims in the First World War* (English translation, New York, 1967), has become absolutely indispensable, though it has provoked bitter opposition in Germany, showing how alive these issues still remain. The involvement of the German General Staff in political questions is thoroughly discussed in M. Kitchen, *The Politics of German High Command under Hindenburg and Ludendorff, 1916–1918* (New York, 1976), and J. W. Wheeler-Bennett's *Hindenburg: The Wooden Titan* (New York, 1967), deals with its subject more in a political than a military context. T. G. Masaryk's *The Making of a State: Memories and Observations, 1914–1918* (English edition, London, 1928) covers his view of the development of Czechoslovakia, as does L. Valiani, *The End of Austria-Hungary* (English edition, New York, 1973). The question of American involvement has been thoroughly studied; good reviews are E. R. May, *The World War and American Isolation* (Cambridge, Mass., 1957), and the newer P. Devlin, *Too Proud to Fight: Woodrow Wilson's Neutrality* (New York, 1975). K. E. Birnbaum covered *Peace Moves and U-Boat Warfare: A Study of Imperial Germany's Policy Towards the United States, April 18, 1916–January 9, 1917* (Hamden, Conn., 1970, originally published in 1958). A very useful overview is B. Collier's *The Lion and the Eagle: British and Anglo-American Strategy, 1900–1950* (New York, 1972). Barbara Tuchman in *The Zimmermann Telegram* (New York, 1958) examined that odd episode. For the Ottoman Empire there is H. Howard, *The Partition of*

*Turkey: A Diplomatic History, 1913–1923* (New York, 1961, originally published in 1931), John Kimche's very readable *The Second Arab Awakening* (New York, 1970), and the excellent B. C. Busch, *Britain, India, and the Arabs* (Berkeley, California, 1971), which puts the military operations in the empire in a political context.

The treaties made around Paris at the end of the war have inspired as much controversy as the start of it. Clemenceau wrote his own view of what happened in the revealingly titled *Grandeur and Misery of Victory* (New York, 1930); a useful discussion of his views, as opposed to his military leader's, is J. C. King, *Foch Versus Clemenceau: France and German Dismemberment, 1918– 1919* (Cambridge, Mass., 1960). Lloyd George presented his side of it in *Memoirs of the Paris Peace Conference* (New Haven, 2 volumes, 1939); Wilson did not live to defend himself from his erstwhile allies, but T. A. Bailey wrote *Wilson and the Peacemakers* (New York, 1947). Among the commentators and revisionists P. Birdsall's *Versailles Twenty Years After* (Hamden, Conn., 1962, originally published in 1941) is still readable, and F. Czernin's *Versailles, 1919* (New York, 1964) is a detailed and thorough examination. A. J. Mayer in *Politics and Diplomacy of Peacemaking: Containment and Counterrevolution at Versailles, 1918–1919* (New York, 1967), saw the treaty in the context of Cold War diplomacy and attitudes fifty years later. Along the line of the Russian question J. M. Thompson wrote *Russia, Bolshevism, and the Versailles Peace* (Princeton, 1966), and J. W. Wheeler-Bennett covered *Brest-Litovsk: The Forgotten Peace, March, 1918* (London, 1966, first edition 1938). I. J. Lederer wrote on *Yugoslavia at the Paris Peace Conference* (New Haven, 1963) and R. Albrecht-Carrie did *Italy at the Paris Peace Conference* (New York, 1938). On war costs there is J. M. Clark, *The Costs of the War to the American People* (New Haven, 1931, sponsored by the Carnegie Endowment for International Peace), and the much more recent R. E. Brunselmeyer, *The Cost of the War, 1914–1919: British Economic War Aims and the Origins of Reparations* (Hamden, Conn., 1975). Harold Nicolson's memoir of *Peacemaking, 1919* (London, 1933) is a fascinating account of the actual process of negotiation, and R. M. Watt in *The Kings Depart: The Tragedy of Germany: Versailles and the German Revolution* (New York, 1968) tied these two great events together.

*Military studies:*

A number of works provides general views of the war. Hanson Baldwin, in *World War I* (New York, 1962), did a short survey. B. H. Liddell Hart wrote *The Real War, 1914–1918* (Boston, 1964, originally published in 1930). A straightforward professional account is J. E. Edmonds, *A Short History of World War I* (Oxford, 1951), and probably the best known account is Cyril Falls, *The Great War* (New York, 1959), which is well written, strongly British-oriented, and generally favorable to Sir Douglas Haig. An encyclopedic treatment is V. J. Esposito, ed., *A Concise History of World War I* (New York, 1964). As most English-language works do concentrate on the British role L. Koeltz, *La Guerre de 1914–1918: Les Operations Militaires* (Paris, 1966), is a useful corrective for those who read French. A larger-scale work is Winston Churchill's *The World Crisis* (New York, 5 vols., 1923–31); this fine study sets the pattern for his equally famous treatment of World War II, though in it there are reminders of one of his friend's comments at the time, "Winston has written a book about himself and called it 'The World Crisis.' " Short biographies of the major commanders are in Sir Michael Carver, ed., *The War Lords: Military Commanders of the Twentieth Century* (Boston, 1976). An engrossing study of four crucial ones, von Moltke, Jellicoe, Pétain, and Ludendorff, is in Corelli Barnett, *The Sword-bearers: Supreme Command in The First World War* (New York, 1964). Certain other biographies as well are useful to more than one area of the war, such as D. J. Goodspeed's *Ludendorff: Genius of World War I* (Boston, 1966); volume 3 of Sir George Arthur's *Life of Lord Kitchener* (New York, 1920) is on World War I, and a far less sympathetic portrait, about the last third of which is also on the war, is P. Magnus, *Kitchener: Portrait of an Imperialist* (London, 1958). C. E. Callwell wrote a two-volume work on *Field Marshal Sir Henry Wilson* (New York, 1927). Also in this vein there is V. Bonham-Carter's *The Strategy of Victory, 1914–1918: The Life and Times of the Master Strategist of World War I: Field Marshal Sir William Robertson* (New York, 1964), the title of which pretty well gives away the author's thesis. Robertson wrote his own memoirs in *Soldiers and Statesmen* (London, 2 vols., 1926).

The French generals tended to be more specifically involved with the Western Front. Joffre wrote *Personal Memoirs of Joffre* (English edition, New York, 2 vols., 1932), and Foch did *Memoirs of Marshal Foch* (English edition, New York, 1931). Sir George Aston, a noted theorist on amphibious warfare in his day, did a eulogistic *Biography of the Late Marshal Foch* (New York, 1929). A more balanced but still favorable study is T. M. Hunter, *Marshal Foch: A Study in Leadership* (Ottawa, 1961). Most of the works on Pétain concentrate more on his later life and its tragic close, especially R. Griffiths, *Pétain* (New York, 1972), but there is the specifically military treatment by G. Pedroncini, *Pétain: General en chef, 1917–1918* (Paris, 1974). For the English counterpart of these French Western Front generals, John Terraine has written *Haig: The Educated Soldier* (London, 1960), an excellent biography which is very favorably disposed toward its subject; in his collection of essays, *The Western Front, 1914–18* (London, 1964) he deals with specific aspects of the war there. An earlier apologia for Haig is G. A. B. Dewar, *Sir Douglas Haig's Command* (Boston, 2 vols., 1923). General treatments of the Americans are in E. M. Coffman, *The War to End all Wars: The American Military Experience in World War I* (New York, 1969), and the very popularly written L. Stallings and M. S. Wyeth, Jr., *The Doughboys: The AEF in World War I* (New York, 1966). The American commander is well covered in F. E. Vandiver, *Black Jack: The Life and Times of John J. Pershing* (College Station, Texas, 2 vols., 1977). Further treatment of the Americans is in H. A. DeWeerd, *President Wilson Fights His War: World War I and the American Intervention* (New York, 1968); and R. F. Weigley's two volumes, *History of the United States Army* (New York, 1967), and *The American Way of War: A History of United States Military Strategy and Policy* (New York, 1973), all three of the foregoing being volumes of the *Macmillan Wars of the United States* series.

Numerous works deal with specific battles, campaigns, or episodes on the Western Front. Taking them in rough chronological order, there is G. Ritter, *The Schlieffen Plan: Critique of a Myth* (London, 1958), and Barbara Tuchman's excellent *The Guns of August* (New York, 1962). John Terraine wrote *Mons: Retreat to Victory* (London, 1960). G. Blond did *The Marne* (English edition, London, 1965), and R. Asprey wrote *The First Battle of the Marne* (Philadelphia, 1962). The whole of the opening campaign and the race to the sea is covered in *The Western Front, 1914*

(Ottawa, Historical Section, General Staff, Army Headquarters, 1957). T. Carew wrote a popular picture of the old B. E. F. in *The Vanished Army* (London, 1964), and A. H. Farrar-Hockley covered First Ypres in *Death of an Army* (New York, 1968). Alan Clarke wrote on the 1915 campaign and particularly the battle of Loos, in *The Donkeys* (London, 1961), and the monstrosity of the Somme is treated in A. H. Farrar-Hockley's *The Somme* (London, 1964), and what has become the classic study, M. Middlebrook's *The First Day on the Somme* (London, 1971). It would be difficult to improve A. Horne's work on *The Price of Glory: Verdun, 1916* (London, 1962), and R. M. Watt followed it up with *Dare Call It Treason* (New York, 1963), an outstanding study of the French mutinies of 1917. An earlier work, E. L. Spears' *Prelude to Victory* (London, 1939), followed the story from Nivelle's disastrous command to the battle of Arras, and Leon Wolff wrote *In Flanders Field* (New York, 1958) on the 1917 campaign and the slaughter at Third Ypres. Vimy Ridge has attracted a good deal of attention, especially, naturally, in Canada, and Alexander McKee's book of that name (Toronto, 1966) is but one of several good studies. The last year is covered in J. Gies, *Crisis, 1918* (New York, 1974), and the fine book by Barrie Pitt, *The Last Act* (London, 1962).

The other fronts have received far less coverage in English than the Western Front, with a couple of notable exceptions. The newest work on the Russian war is N. Stone, *The Eastern Front, 1914–17* (New York, 1975), which both updates and challenges the earlier standard work, N. Golovin, *The Russian Army in the World War* (New Haven, 1932). General Brusilov wrote his memoirs in *A Soldier's Notebook, 1914–1918* (Westport, Conn., 1971, reprint of 1930 edition). Another useful memoir is A. Knox, *With the Russian Army, 1914–1917* (London, 2 vols., 1921). There is also Churchill's volume of his history, issued separately as *The Unknown War: The Eastern Front* (London, 1931). Most of the Russian history of the period concentrates less on the army than on the political affairs of the revolution. A standard life of Lenin is R. Payne, *The Life and Times of Lenin* (New York, 1964). I. Deutscher produced a classic three-volume life of *Trotsky* (London, 1954), under assorted titles. A very readable popular study is A. Moorehead, *The Russian Revolution* (New York, 1958). A. Summers and T. Mangold wrote a fascinating piece of investigative journalism in *The File on the Tsar* (London, 1976), which convincingly contradicts the standard version that all of the Romanovs were killed together at Ekaterinburg. Finally, J. Swettenham wrote the excellent *Allied Intervention in Russia, 1918–1919* (Toronto, 1967) which, while concentrating especially on the Canadian role in that misadventure, goes far to explain Bolshevik distrust of the West.

For the war around the Mediterranean, A. Palmer wrote *The Gardeners of Salonika* (London, 1965). There have been two treatments of the Mesopotamian campaign, aside from the works referred to earlier in connection with the breakup of the Ottoman Empire; R. Braddon wrote *The Siege* and R. Millar did *Kut* (both London, 1969). For Palestine, General Wavell wrote *Allenby: A Study in Greatness* (Toronto, 2 vols., 1944). As one of the few people who managed to emerge from the war a distinct, if difficult, personality, T. E. Lawrence has attracted a great deal of attention. He himself wrote *Revolt in the Desert* (New York, 1926); B. H. Liddell Hart did *'T. E. Lawrence'* (London, 1934), and more recently there is J. E. Mack, *A Prince of Our Disorder: The Life of T. E. Lawrence* (Boston, 1976).

None of these campaigns, however, has attracted the attention that the Dardanelles has; that remains one of the most studied and debated episodes of the war. General Hamilton quite bravely published his diary, warts and all, in *Gallipoli Diary* (New York, 2 vols., 1920). C. E. Callwell, a British expert on combined operations, did *The Dardanelles* (Boston, 1919), Admiral Sir Roger Keyes wrote *The Fight for Gallipoli* (London, 1941), and the German view was covered by Hans Kannengeiser Pasha, *The Campaign in Gallipoli* (English edition, London, 1928). All these people were fairly well up in the command structure; perhaps the last word by a participant was from a man who had been a stretcher-bearer at Suvla Bay, John Hargrave, *The Suvla Bay Landing* (London, 1964). Trumbull Higgins did a more academic study of Churchill's fascination with Europe's "soft underbelly" in *Winston Churchill and the Dardanelles* (London, 1963). Excellent general histories are A. Moorehead, *Gallipoli* (London, 1956) and R. R. James, *Gallipoli* (London, 1965).

On other colonial campaigns there is C. Miller's *Battle for the Bundu: The First World War in East Africa* (New York, 1974), and L. Mosley, *Duel for Kilimanjaro* (London, 1963). C. B. Burdick did *The Japanese Siege of Tsingtau* (Hamden, Conn., 1976).

\* \* \*

Much has been written both on the problem of navalism and the Anglo-German rivalry, and also on naval operations during the war itself. The British official history is Sir J. Corbett and H. Newbolt, *Naval Operations* (London, 5 vols., 1920–31). A. J. Marder produced the classic study of the Fisher era in *Fear God and Dread Nought* (London, 3 vols., 1952–59). E. L. Woodward wrote a thorough study of the prewar rivalry in *Great Britain and the German Navy* (London, 1935), and Admiral von Tirpitz wrote *My Memoirs* (English edition, New York, 2 vols., 1919). General surveys of operations are in G. Bennett, *Naval Battles of the First World War* (London, 1968) and the more popularly written A. A. Hoehling, *The Great War at Sea: A History of Naval Action, 1914–18* (New York, 1965).

Jutland alone, as the greatest dreadnought battle ever, has inspired a substantial literature. Admiral Jellicoe wrote *The Grand Fleet, 1914–16* (London, 1919) and Scheer countered with *Germany's High Seas Fleet in the World War* (English edition, New York, 1934). Most rivalry has centered, however, less around British and German than around British and British, and the great argument has been between those writers who supported the claims of Admiral Beatty's greatness, versus those who favored Jellicoe; though this might seem fairly petty in the aftermath of universal catastrophe, the controversy reached very considerable levels of acrimony in the years after the war, and certain Royal Naval officers had their careers jeopardized by taking the wrong side, whichever that happened to be. The American H. H. Frost wrote what was for long the standard study of *The Battle of Jutland* (Annapolis, Maryland, 1936), and L. Gibson and J. E. T. Harper did *The Riddle of Jutland* (New York, 1934). More recent are D. MacIntyre's *Jutland* (London, 1957), and G. Bennett's *The Battle of Jutland* (London, 1964), and an excellent study is J. J. C. Irving, *The Smoke Screen of Jutland* (London, 1966).

Specific works deal with other battles. The *Goeben* and *Breslau* affair is covered in E. W. R. Lumby, ed., *The Mediterranean, 1912–1914* (Vol. 115 of the publications of the Navy Records Society, London, 1970). Barrie Pitt wrote *Coronel and Falkland* (London, 1960) and G. Bennett did *Coronel and the Falklands* (London, 1962); Admiral Keyes dealt with the naval side of the Dardanelles in *The Naval Memoirs of Admiral of the Fleet Sir Roger Keyes* (London, 2 vols., 1935). Barrie Pitt wrote *Zee-*

*brugge: St. George's Day, 1918* (London, 1958), and D. Horn covered *The German Naval Mutinies of World War I* (New Brunswick, N. J., 1969). On what is probably the most famous single incident of the submarine war there is C. Simpson, *The Lusitania* (Boston, 1972), and there have also been studies of practically all the cruises of the different German surface raiders.

A popular history of the war in the air is Quentin Reynolds, *They Fought for the Sky* (New York, 1957); a similar work is A. Norman, *The Great Air War* (New York, 1968). More specific studies are J. Morris, *The German Air Raids on Great Britain, 1914–1918* (London, 1969), and K. Poolman, *Zeppelins over England* (London, 1960). As was the desert revolt, the air war was one of the places where individuality might be preserved, and several classic memoirs of the air aces have recently been reprinted by Doubleday in New York. These include W. A. Bishop's *Winged Warfare* (1967), D. Grinnell-Milne's *Wind in the Wires* (1968), J. T. B. McCudden, *Flying Fury* (1968), Rene Fonck's *Ace of Aces* (1969), and Eddie Rickenbacker's *Fighting the Flying Circus* (1965). Floyd Gibbons' *The Red Knight of Germany* (New York, 1927) is the first of a substantial literature on Baron von Richthofen alone.

Finally, the cautionary note should be repeated that this list does just skim the surface. Many of these works contain very thorough bibliographies of their own; in addition to them, there are far more massive official histories than the British naval work, which is the only one mentioned by name. Many of the participants beyond the major ones noted here left memoirs; this was not only the most terrible war in history to date, it was also one which drew into it an enormous number of educated, highly literate men, and after the war the survivors produced a war literature, in poetry and fiction, that is unsurpassed in depth or feeling. For the true picture of what the war did to those who fought it, that is the place to start.

# Index